Bennion on Statutory Interpretation

A Code

Cumulative Second Supplement to Fifth Edition
Including Replacement Index

Oliver Jones, LLB (Hons) BA (Int'l Studies) (UTS); BCL (Oxon)

Lawyer
Clayton Utz, Sydney

LexisNexis®

Members of the LexisNexis Group worldwide

United Kingdom	LexisNexis, a Division of Reed Elsevier (UK) Ltd, Halsbury House, 35 Chancery Lane, LONDON, WC2A 1EL, and London House, 20–22 East London Street, EDINBURGH EH7 4BQ
Australia	LexisNexis Butterworths, CHATSWOOD, New South Wales
Austria	LexisNexis Verlag ARD Orac GmbH & Co KG, VIENNA
Benelux	LexisNexis Benelux, AMSTERDAM
Canada	LexisNexis Butterworths, MARKHAM, Ontario
China	LexisNexis China, BEIJING and SHANGHAI
France	LexisNexis SA, PARIS
Germany	LexisNexis GmbH, DUSSELDORF
Hong Kong	LexisNexis Hong Kong, HONG KONG
India	LexisNexis India, NEW DELHI
Italy	Giuffrè Editore, MILAN
Malaysia	Malayan Law Journal Sdn Bhd, KUALA LUMPUR
New Zealand	LexisNexis NZ Ltd, WELLINGTON
Poland	Wydawnictwo Prawnicze LexisNexis Sp, WARSAW
Singapore	LexisNexis Singapore, SINGAPORE
South Africa	LexisNexis Butterworths, DURBAN
USA	LexisNexis, DAYTON, Ohio

First edition of main work 1984; supplement to first edition 1989; second edition of main work 1992; first supplement to second edition 1993; second supplement to second edition (cumulative) 1995; third edition of main work 1997; supplement to third edition 1999; fourth edition of main work 2002; supplement to fourth edition 2005; fifth edition of main work 2008; first supplement to fifth edition 2010.

© Reed Elsevier (UK) Ltd 2012
Published by LexisNexis Butterworths

ISBN 9781405782319

Typeset by Letterpart Ltd, Reigate, England
Printed and bound in Great Britain by Hobbs the Printers Ltd, Totton, Hampshire
Visit LexisNexis Butterworths at www.lexisnexis.co.uk

Bennion on Statutory Interpretation

Prefatory Note

General

In general this Cumulative Second Supplement to the fifth edition of Bennion's Statutory Interpretation, which was published in 2008, aims to present the law as at 1 October 2012.

The Supplement begins with the updating of Parts I to XXX of the Code by means of textual amendments to the affected pages in the main work.

*The Supplement goes on to include updated versions of **Appendix C** (text of Interpretation Act 1978) and **Appendix F** (amended text of the Human Rights Act 1998).*

The Supplement ends with a complete updated and corrected version of the Index to the work.

Page numbering

To avoid confusion with the main work, the page numbers in the Supplement have the prefix S.

This means that in all cases a page reference in the revised Index should be checked with this Supplement. Either (if it has an S prefix) it will refer to a page contained in the Supplement or (if it does not have an S prefix) it will refer to a page in the original volume which may be modified by the Supplement.

Contents

Prefatory Note   **v**

Table of Cases mentioned in Supplement   **ix**

Table of Statutes mentioned in Supplement   **xxxv**

Table of Statutory Instruments mentioned in Supplement   **xxxvii**

Table of European Material mentioned in Supplement   **xxxix**

Table of Foreign Enactments mentioned in Supplement   **xli**

Text of Supplement–

   Introduction   **S1**

   Updating of Parts I to XXX of Code   **S3**

   Replacement Appendix C (updated text of Interpretation Act 1978)   **S115**

   Replacement Appendix F (updated text of Human Rights Act 1998)   **S119**

Replacement Index to main work and Supplement   **S121**

Supplementary Table of Cases

A v B (Investigatory Powers Tribunal:
jurisdiction) [2009] UKSC 12,
[2010] 1 All ER 1149,
[2010] 2 WLR 1, (2009) Times,
11 December, [2009] All ER (D)
78 (Dec), sub nom R (on the
application of A) v Director of
Establishments of the Security
Service [2010] 2 AC 1 . . . . S16, S72

A v H (Registrar General for England
and Wales intervening)
[2009] EWHC 636 (Fam),
[2009] 4 All ER 641,
[2009] 3 FCR 95, [2010] 1 FLR
1, [2009] Fam Law 917, [2009]
All ER (D) 136 (Jun) S100

A v Hoare [2008] UKHL 6,
[2008] 1 AC 844,
[2008] 2 All ER 1,
[2008] 2 WLR 311,
[2008] Fam Law 402, 100 BMLR
1, [2008] NLJR 218, (2008)
Times, 31 January, [2008] All ER
(D) 251 (Jan) S30, S66

A v Securities and Futures
Commission [2008] 1 HKLRD
591 . . . . S51, S55

A Solicitor v Law Society of Hong
Kong [2005] 3 HKLRD 622 . . . . S15

AIC Ltd v Federal Government of
Nigeria [2003] EWHC 1357
(QB), [2003] All ER (D) 190
(Jun) S61

AM (Ethiopia) v Entry Clearance
Officer [2008] EWCA Civ 1082,
[2008] All ER (D) 150 (Oct); sub
nom AM (Somalia) v Entry
Clearance Officer [2009] EWCA
Civ 634, [2009] All ER (D) 09
(Jul); sub nom Mahad (previously
referred to as AM) (Ethiopia) v
Entry Clearance Officer [2009]
UKSC 16, [2010] 2 All ER 535,
[2010] 1 WLR 48, (2009) Times,
21 December, 153 Sol Jo (no 48)
34, [2009] All ER (D) 156
(Dec) S35

AS (Somalia) v Secretary of State for
the Home Department
[2009] UKHL 32,
[2009] 4 All ER 711,
[2009] 1 WLR 1385, (2009)
Times, 22 June, 153 Sol Jo (no
24) 32, [2009] All ER (D) 163
(Jun) S111

AXA General Insurance Ltd v
Lord Advocate (Scotland) [2011]
UKSC 46, [2012] AC 868,
[2011] 3 WLR 871, 122 BMLR
149, (2011) Times, 19 October,
2012 SC (UKSC) 122, 2011 SLT
1061, [2011] All ER (D) 101
(Oct) S81

Aboriginal Development Commission,
Re [1988] FCA 160 . . . . S35

Abou-Rahmah v Abacha
[2006] EWCA Civ 1492, [2007]
1 All ER (Comm) 827, [2007]
Bus LR 220, [2007] 1 Lloyd's
Rep 115, 9 ITELR 401, [2006]
All ER (D) 80 (Nov) S52

Ackland v Yonge-Esplanade
Enterprises Ltd (1992) 10 OR
(3d) 97 . . . . S87

Adorian v Metropolitan Police Comr
[2009] EWCA Civ 18,
[2009] 4 All ER 227,
[2009] 1 WLR 1859, (2009)
Times, 23 February, [2009] All
ER (D) 176 (Jan) S6

Afzal v Secretary of State for the
Home Department [2012] EWHC
1487 (Admin), [2012] All ER (D)
148 (Jun) S102

Ahmed v HM Treasury (No 2) [2010]
UKSC 5, [2010] 2 AC 534,
[2010] 4 All ER 829,
[2010] 2 WLR 378,
[2011] 1 LRC 123, [2010] All
ER (D) 40 (Feb) S80, S81, S82

Ainsworth v IRC. See Revenue and
Customs v Stringer

Al Rawi v Security Service [2011]
UKSC 34, [2012] AC 531,
[2012] 1 All ER 1,
[2011] 3 WLR 388,
[2011] 30 LS Gaz R 23,
[2011] NLJR 1027, (2011)
Times, 15 July, [2012] 1 LRC
585, [2011] All ER (D) 110
(Jul) S19

Alcan (NT) Alumina Pty Ltd v Comr
of Territory Revenue (2009) 239
CLR 27 . . . . S59, S85, S86, S91

Alcan Australia Ltd, Re,
ex p Federation of Industrial
Manufacturing & Engineering
Employees (1994) 181 CLR 96 . . . . . S62

Algama v Minsiter for Immigration
and Mulitcultural Affairs
(2001) 115 FCR 253, 261 .... S30
Application by the Local Government
Auditor, Re [2003] NIQB 21 .... S50,
S51, S74
Aribisala v St James Homes
(Grosvenor Dock) Ltd
[2007] EWHC 1694 (Ch),
[2007] 3 EGLR 39, [2007] All
ER (D) 101 (Jun) S9
Assange v Swedish Prosecution
Authority [2012] UKSC 22,
[2012] 2 WLR 1275,
[2012] 24 LS Gaz R 22,
[2012] NLJR 781, (2012) Times,
19 June, [2012] All ER (D) 232
(May) S14, S84
A-G (Qld) v Australian Industrial
Relations commission (2002) 213
CLR 485 .... S59
A-G's Reference (No 3 of 1999), Re
British Broadcasting Corpn
[2009] UKHL 34, [2010] 1 AC
145, [2010] 1 All ER 235,
[2009] 3 WLR 142, (2009)
Times, 18 June, 153 Sol Jo (no
24) 31, 27 BHRC 522,
[2009] EMLR 421, [2009] All
ER (D) 175 (Jun) S99
A-G's Reference (No 24 of 2008), R v
Sanchez [2008] EWCA Crim
2936, [2009] 3 All ER 839,
[2009] 2 Cr App Rep (S) 289,
[2008] All ER (D) 62 (Dec) S46
Au Wing Lun v Solicitors Disciplinary
Tribunal (CACV 4154/2001)
(9 September 2002, unreported),
HKCA S15
Austereo Ltd v Trade Practices
Commission (1993) 41 FCR 1 ...... S51
Austin v Southwark London Borough
Council [2010] UKSC 28,
[2011] 1 AC 355,
[2010] 4 All ER 16,
[2010] 3 WLR 144,
[2011] 1 P & CR 176, [2010]
PTSR 1311, [2010] HLR 615,
[2010] 3 EGLR 45,
[2010] 26 EG 90 (CS), (2010)
Times, 29 June, 154 Sol Jo (no
25) 42, [2010] All ER (D) 199
(Jun) S30
Australasian Correctional
Management Ltd v Corrections
Association of New Zealand (Inc)
[2002] 3 NZLR 250 .... S97
Australian Education Union v General
Manager of Fair Work Australia
[2012] HCA 19 .... S40, S41
Australian Prudential Regulation
Authority v ACN (00000492)
[2011] FCA 353 .... S37

Australian Securities Commission v
Lucas (1992) 36 FCR 165 .... S75
Autoclenz Ltd v Belcher [2011] UKSC
41, [2011] 4 All ER 745,
[2011] ICR 1157, [2011] IRLR
820, [2011] NLJR 1099, (2011)
Times, 05 August, [2011] All ER
(D) 251 (Jul) S94
Aveng (Africa) Ltd v Government of
the Gabonese Republic
[2012] EWHC 1687 (Comm),
[2012] All ER (D) 150 (Jun) S44
Avowal Administrative Attorneys Ltd v
District Council at North Shore
[2007] NZHC 714 .... S61
Ayrshire Pullman Motor Services and
D M Ritchie v IRC (1929) 14 TC
754, Ct of Sess S94
B (children) (sexual abuse: standard of
proof), Re [2008] UKHL 35,
[2009] AC 11, [2008] 4 All ER 1,
[2008] 3 WLR 1, [2008] 2 FCR
339, [2008] 2 FLR 141,
[2008] Fam Law 837,
[2008] Fam Law 619, (2008)
Times, 12 June, [2008] All ER
(D) 134 (Jun) S45, S46, S99
BCGEU v British Columbia (2007)
283 DLR (4th) 307 .... S76
BH (AP) v Lord Advocate [2012]
UKSC 24, (2012) Times, 03 July,
2012 SLT 799, 2012 SCCR 562,
[2012] All ER (D) 126 (Jun) S39
BUPA Purchasing Ltd v Revenue and
Customs Comrs [2007] EWCA
Civ 542, [2008] STC 101, (2007)
Times, 5 July, [2007] All ER (D)
84 (Jun) S95
Bahamas Hotel Maintenance and
Allied Workers Union v Bahamas
Hotel Catering and Allied
Workers Union [2011] UKPC 4,
[2011] All ER (D) 288 (Feb) S13
Baker v Quantum Clothing Group
[2011] UKSC 17,
[2011] 4 All ER 223,
[2011] 1 WLR 1003, [2011] ICR
523, [2011] 17 LS Gaz R 13,
(2011) Times, 14 April, 155 Sol
Jo (no 15) 38, [2011] All ER (D)
137 (Apr) S49, S87
Baker v R [1975] AC 774,
[1975] 3 All ER 55,
[1975] 3 WLR 113, 119 Sol Jo
491, PC S30
Barnard v Ford (1869) 4 Ch App 247,
38 LJ Ch 671, 17 WR 478, 20 LT
289 .... S88
Begg v IRC [2009] 3 NZLR 353 .... S58
Behzadi v Shaftesbury Hotels Ltd
[1992] Ch 1, [1991] 2 All ER
477, [1991] 2 WLR 1251, 62 P &
CR 163, [1990] NLJR

Behzadi v Shaftesbury Hotels Ltd
[1992] Ch 1, [1991] 2 All ER 477,
[1991] 2 WLR 1251, 62 P & CR 163,
[1990] NLJR – *contd*
1385, CA S104

Belmont Park Investments PTY Ltd v
BNY Corporate Trustee
Services Ltd [2011] UKSC 38,
[2012] AC 383, [2012] 1 All ER
505, [2011] 3 WLR 521, [2011]
Bus LR 1266, [2012] 1 BCLC
163, (2011) Times, 15 August,
[2011] All ER (D) 259 (Jul) S94

Benner v Secretary of State of Canada
[1997] 1 SCR 358, [1997] 2 LRC
469, Can SC S41

Beoku-Betts v Secretary of State for
the Home Department
[2008] UKHL 39, [2009] AC
115, [2008] 4 All ER 1146,
[2008] 3 WLR 166, (2008)
Times, 8 July, 152 Sol Jo (no 26)
31, 25 BHRC 245, [2008] All ER
(D) 335 (Jun) S93

Bezier Acquisitions Ltd, Re
[2011] EWHC 3299 (Ch), [2012]
Bus LR 636, [2012] 2 BCLC
322, (2012) Times, 06 January,
[2011] All ER (D) 119 (Dec) S6

Bhamjee v Forsdick (No 2)
[2003] EWCA Civ 1113,
[2004] 1 WLR 88,
[2003] 36 LS Gaz R 41, (2003)
Times, 31 July, [2003] BPIR
1252, [2003] All ER (D) 429
(Jul) S85

Birmingham City Council v Shafi
[2008] EWCA Civ 1186,
[2009] 3 All ER 127,
[2009] 1 WLR 1961, [2009] LGR
367, [2009] PTSR 503,
[2009] HLR 429, 152 Sol Jo (no
43) 31, [2008] All ER (D) 304
(Oct) S10

Blackpool Council v Howitt
[2008] EWHC 3300 (Admin),
[2009] 4 All ER 154, [2009]
PTSR 1458, 173 JP 101, [2008]
All ER (D) 28 (Dec) S107

Bloomsbury International Ltd v Sea
Fish Industry Authority [2011]
UKSC 25, [2011] 4 All ER 721,
[2011] NLJR 883, (2011) Times,
18 June, [2011] All ER (D) 91
(Jun) S72

Blue Metal Industries Ltd v Dilley
[1970] AC 827, [1969] 3 All ER
437, [1969] 3 WLR 357, 113 Sol
Jo 448, [1969] ALR 595, PC S58

Boardwalk Reit LLP v Edmonton
(2008) 91 Alta LR (4th) 1 .... S91, S102

Bocardo SA v Star Energy UK
Onshore Ltd [2009] EWCA Civ
579, [2010] Ch 100,
[2010] 1 All ER 26,
[2009] 3 WLR 1010,
[2009] 2 P & CR 419,
[2010] RVR 127, [2009] 25 EG
136 (CS), [2009] All ER (D) 132
(Jun); affd [2010] UKSC 35,
[2011] 1 AC 380,
[2010] 3 All ER 975,
[2010] 3 WLR 654,
[2010] 3 EGLR 145,
[2010] NLJR 1114, [2010] RVR
339, [2011] BLR 13,
[2010] 31 EG 63 (CS), (2010)
Times, 29 July, [2010] All ER
(D) 333 (Jul) S43, S46, S47

Boswell v Secretary, Department of
Foreign Affairs and Trade
(1993) 46 FCR 434 .... S104

Bournemouth University Higher
Education Corpn v Buckland
[2009] ICR 1042, [2009] IRLR
606, [2009] All ER (D) 160
(Aug), EAT; revsd sub nom
Buckland v Bournemouth
University Higher Education
Corpn [2010] EWCA Civ 121,
[2011] QB 323, [2010] 4 All ER
186, [2010] 3 WLR 1664,
[2010] ICR 908, [2010] IRLR
445, (2010) Times, 3 May, [2010]
All ER (D) 299 (Feb) S97

Bovale Ltd v Secretary of State for
Communities and Local
Government [2009] EWCA Civ
171, [2009] 3 All ER 340,
[2009] 1 WLR 2274,
[2009] 2 P & CR 103, (2009)
Times, 23 March, [2009] All ER
(D) 115 (Mar) S17

Bowers v Gloucester Corpn
[1963] 1 QB 881,
[1963] 1 All ER 437,
[1963] 2 WLR 386, 61 LGR 209,
127 JP 214, 107 Sol Jo 94, DC S81

Boyle v SCA Packaging Ltd (Equality
and Human Rights Commission
intervening) [2009] UKHL 37,
[2009] NI 317, [2009] 4 All ER
1181, [2009] ICR 1056,
[2009] IRLR 746, 109 BMLR 53,
(2009) Times, 6 July, 153 Sol Jo
(no 26) 27, [2009] All ER (D) 05
(Jul) S70

Braganza v Minister for Immigration
and Multicultural Affairs
(2001) 109 FCR 364 .... S92

Brants v DPP [2011] EWHC 754
(Admin), 175 JP 246, [2011] All
ER (D) 92 (Mar) S44

Bridge Trustees Ltd v Houldsworth
(Secretary of State for Work and
Pensions, intervener) [2011]
UKSC 42, [2012] 1 All ER 659,
[2011] 1 WLR 1912, [2011] ICR
1069, (2011) Times, 09 August,
[2011] All ER (D) 252 (Jul) S4
Briere v Hailstone [1969] Crim LR
36 .... S102
Brighton and Hove City Council v
Collinson [2004] EWCA Civ
678, [2004] 2 P & CR D29,
[2004] 2 EGLR 65,
[2004] 28 EG 178, [2004] 21 EG
150 (CS), 148 Sol Jo LB 630,
[2004] All ER (D) 257 (Jun) S9
British Broadcasting Corpn v
Information Comr [2009] EWHC
2348 (Admin), [2010] EMLR
121, [2009] All ER (D) 10
(Oct) S71
BBC Scotland v Souster 2001 SC 458,
[2001] IRLR 150, Ct of Sess S62
Brown v Innovatorone plc
[2009] EWHC 1376 (Comm),
[2010] 2 All ER (Comm) 80, 153
Sol Jo (no 25) 27, [2009] All ER
(D) 211 (Jun) S74, S75
Buckland v Bournemouth University
Higher Education Corpn. See
Bournemouth University Higher
Education Corpn v Buckland
Byrne v Australian Airlines Ltd (1995)
185 CLR 410 .... S89
Byrne v Transport Accident
Commission [2008] VSC 92 .... S95
C v Director of Immigration (CACV
132/2008) (21July 2011,
unreported), HKCA S82
C v Director of Immigration (CACV
132/2008) (14 December 2011,
unreported), HKCA S82
C & E Pty Ltd v CMC Brisbane
Pty Ltd (Administrators
Appointed) [2004] QCA 60 .... S60
CD, Re (No 2) [2011] NICA 21 .... S41
CGU International Insurance plc v
AstraZeneca Insurance Co Ltd
[2006] EWCA Civ 1340, [2007]
1 All ER (Comm) 501, [2007]
Bus LR 162, [2007] 1 Lloyd's
Rep 142, (2006) Times,
3 November, [2006] All ER (D)
176 (Oct) S25
CM (A Child), Re [2010] ScotSC 24 ..... S75
Caltex Oil (Aust) Pty Ltd v Best
(1990) 170 CLR 516 .... S8
Campbell v Tow Truck Directorate of
Victoria (1995/34314) [2000]
VICCAT 3 .... S6
Carroll v DPP [2009] EWHC 554
(Admin), 173 JP 285, [2009] All
ER (D) 35 (Mar) S46

Cassell & Co Ltd v Broome
[1972] AC 1027, [1972] 1 All ER
801, [1972] 2 WLR 645, 116 Sol
Jo 199, HL S30
Cave v Robinson, Jarvis & Rolf (a
firm) [2001] EWCA Civ 245,
[2002] 1 WLR 581,
[2001] Lloyd's Rep PN 290, 78
ConLR 1, [2001] NPC 36, 17
Const LJ 262, [2001] PNLR 573,
[2001] All ER (D) 232 (Feb);
revsd [2002] UKHL 18,
[2003] 1 AC 384,
[2002] 2 All ER 641,
[2002] 2 WLR 1107, 81 ConLR
25, [2002] 20 LS Gaz R 32,
[2002] NLJR 671,
[2002] 19 EGCS 146, (2002)
Times, 7 May, [2002] All ER (D)
233 (Apr) S30
Chan Ching Kit v Lam Sik Shi [2002]
HKCFI 132 .... S60
Chief Executive, Department of
Natural Resources and Mines v
Kent Street P/L [2009] QCA
399 .... S66
China Field Ltd v Appeal Tribunal
(Buildings) (No 2) [2009] 5
HKLRD 662 .... S77
Christian v R [2006] UKPC 47,
[2007] 2 AC 400, [2007] 2 WLR
120, (2006) Times, 15 November,
150 Sol Jo LB 1464,
[2007] 1 LRC 726, [2006] All
ER (D) 358 (Oct) S34
Clyde & Co LLP v Van Winkelhof
[2011] EWHC 668 (QB),
[2012] ICR 928, [2011] IRLR
467, [2011] NLJR 475, (2011)
Times, 13 June, 155 Sol Jo (no
12) 30, [2011] All ER (D) 270
(Mar) S8
Coke-Wallis v Institute of Chartered
Accountants in England and
Wales [2009] EWCA Civ 730,
[2009] All ER (D) 147 (Jul);
revsd sub nom R (on the
application of Coke-Wallis) v
Institute of Chartered
Accountants in England and
Wales [2011] UKSC 1,
[2011] 2 AC 146,
[2011] 2 All ER 1,
[2011] 2 WLR 103, [2011] ICR
224, [2011] NLJR 138, (2011)
Times, 31 January, [2011] All ER
(D) 120 (Jan) S98
Collector of Customs v Arrowtown
Assets Ltd [2004] 1 HKLRD
77 .... S85, S91, S95
Coogan v News Group
Newspapers Ltd [2012] EWCA
Civ 48, [2012] 2 All ER 74,

Coogan v News Group Newspapers Ltd
[2012] EWCA Civ 48, [2012] 2 All ER
74, – contd
[2012] 2 WLR 848,
[2012] IP & T 363,
[2012] 07 LS Gaz R 17,
[2012] NLJR 295, [2012] NLJR
213, (2012) Times, 06 February,
[2012] All ER (D) 12 (Feb); sub
nom Phillips v Mulcaire [2012]
UKSC 28, [2012] IP & T 681,
[2012] 29 LS Gaz R 29, (2012)
Times, 20 July, [2012] All ER
(D) 28 (Jul), sub nom Phillips v
News Group Newspapers Ltd
[2012] 4 All ER 207,
[2012] 3 WLR 312 . . . . . . S56, S57, S98,
S107
Comr of Inland Revenue v Common
Empire Ltd [2006] 1 HKLRD
942 . . . . S90
Comr of Inland Revenue v Loganathan
[2000] 1 HKLRD 914 . . . . S91
Comr of Inland Revenue v N Evans
[2008] NZHC 1017 . . . . S62
Comr of Police v Privacy Comr for
Personal Data [2012] 3 HKLRD
710 . . . . S83
Comr of Taxation v Citibank Ltd
(1989) 20 FCR 403 . . . . S79
Comr of Taxation v Lamesa
Holdings BV (1997) 77 FCR
597 . . . . S68
Comptroller and Auditor General v
Ireland [1997] 1 IR 248 . . . . S74
Corporate Officer of the House of
Commons v Information Comr
[2008] EWHC 1084 (Admin),
[2009] 3 All ER 403,
[2008] NLJR 751, (2008) Times,
22 May, [2008] All ER (D) 217
(May) S112, S114
Courage Ltd v Crehan [1999] Eu LR
834, [1999] 25 LS Gaz R 29,
[1999] EGCS 85, [1999] All ER
(D) 551, CA; refd: C-453/99
[2002] QB 507, [2001] ECR
I-6297, [2001] All ER (EC) 886,
[2001] 3 WLR 1646,
[2001] 5 CMLR 1058,
[2002] ICR 457, [2001] All ER
(D) 55 (Sep), ECJ S29
Craftrule Ltd v 41–60 Albert Palace
Mansions (Freehold) Ltd
[2010] EWHC 1230 (Ch),
[2010] 3 All ER 952,
[2010] 1 WLR 2046,
[2010] 2 EGLR 45, [2010] NLJR
806, [2010] 31 EG 64, (2010)
Times, 20 July, [2010] All ER
(D) 267 (May); affd sub nom
41–60 Albert Palace Mansions
(Freehold) Ltd v Craftrule Ltd

Craftrule Ltd v 41–60 Albert Palace Mansions
(Freehold) Ltd [2010] EWHC 1230
(Ch), [2010] 3 All ER 952,
[2010] 1 WLR 2046, [2010] 2 EGLR
45, [2010] NLJR 806, [2010] 31 EG 64,
(2010) Times, 20 July, [2010] All ER
(D) 267 (May); affd sub nom 41–60
Albert Palace Mansions (Freehold) Ltd v
Craftrule Ltd – contd
[2011] EWCA Civ 185,
[2011] 2 All ER 925,
[2011] 1 WLR 2425,
[2011] 1 P & CR 394,
[2011] HLR 395, [2011] 2 EGLR
35, [2011] 19 EG 98, [2011] All
ER (D) 262 (Feb) S43
Creaven v Criminal Assets Bureau
[2004] IEHC 26 . . . . S78
Crofts v Cathay Pacific Airways Ltd.
See Lawson v Serco Ltd
Cropp v A Judicial Committee [2008]
3 NZLR 774 . . . . S80, S82
Crown Estate Comrs v Governors of
Peabody Trust [2011] EWHC
1467 (Ch), [2011] NLJR 884,
[2011] 24 EG 109 (CS), [2011]
All ER (D) 63 (Jun) S32
Cusack v Harrow London Borough
Council [2011] EWCA Civ 1514,
[2012] RTR 247, [2012] PTSR
970, [2012] 1 EGLR 43, [2012]
10 Estates Gazette 90,
[2011] 50 EG 59 (CS), (2012)
Times, 10 January, [2011] All ER
(D) 47 (Dec) S44, S105
Dairy Farmers of Britain Ltd, Re
[2009] EWHC 1389 (Ch),
[2010] Ch 63, [2009] 4 All ER
241, [2010] 2 WLR 311, [2009]
Bus LR 1627, [2010] 1 BCLC
637, [2009] All ER (D) 205
(Jun) S57
Dale Farm Dairy Group Ltd v Akram
[1998] ICR 349, CA S50
Dato Tan Leong Min v Insider Dealing
Tribunal [1999] 2 HKC 83 . . . . S15
Davidson v M [2009] CSIH 70,
[2010] IRLR 439, 2010 SC 100,
2009 SLT 1009 . . . . S105
Davidson v Scottish Ministers
[2005] UKHL 74, (2005) Times,
19 December, 2006 SLT 110,
2006 SCLR 249 . . . . S42, S66
Delaney v Judge Coughlan [2012]
IESC 40 . . . . S83
Department of Land Affairs v
Goedgelegen Tropical Fruits
[2007] ZACC 12 . . . . S54
Digital Satellite Warranty Cover Ltd,
Re [2011] EWHC 122 (Ch),
[2011] Bus LR 981, [2011] All
ER (D) 01 (Feb); affd sub nom
Digital Satellite Services, Re

Digital Satellite Warranty Cover Ltd, Re
[2011] EWHC 122 (Ch), [2011] Bus LR
981, [2011] All ER (D) 01 (Feb); affd
sub nom Digital Satellite Services, Re –
contd
Financial Services Authority v
Digital Satellite Warranty
Cover Ltd [2011] EWCA Civ
1413, [2012] 2 All ER (Comm)
38, [2012] Bus LR 990,
[2012] Lloyd's Rep IR 112,
[2011] All ER (D) 78 (Dec) S83
DPP v Wright [2009] EWHC 105
(Admin), [2010] QB 224,
[2009] 3 All ER 726, 169 JP 173,
(2009) Times, 17 February,
[2009] All ER (D) 30 (Feb) S100
DPP of the Virgin Islands v Penn
[2008] UKPC 29, [2009] 2 LRC
90, [2008] All ER (D) 136
(May) S6
Dolphin Quays Developments Ltd v
Mills [2008] EWCA Civ 385,
[2008] 4 All ER 58,
[2008] 1 WLR 1829, [2008] Bus
LR 1520, [2008] 2 BCLC 774,
[2008] All ER (D) 257 (Apr), sub
nom Mills v Birchall [2008] BCC
471, [2008] 4 Costs LR 599,
[2008] BPIR 607 .... S51
Dorset County Council v House. See
R v House
Du Plessis v Fontgary Leisure
Parks Ltd [2012] EWCA Civ
409, [2012] All ER (D) 34
(Apr) S110
Dunhill (by her litigation friend, Paul
Tasker) v Burgin [2011] EWHC
464 (QB), [2011] All ER (D) 70
(Mar); revsd sub nom Dunhill (by
her litigation friend) v Burgin
[2012] EWCA Civ 397, [2012]
All ER (D) 32 (Apr) S18, S19
Dunne v Donohoe [2001] IEHC 126 .... S110
ETI Euro Telecom International NV v
Republic of Bolivia
[2008] EWCA Civ 880, [2009] 2
All ER (Comm) 37,
[2009] 1 WLR 665, [2009] Bus
LR 310, [2008] 2 Lloyd's Rep
421, [2008] All ER (D) 358
(Jul) S74
East Devon District Council v
Electoral Commission (The
Boundary Committee for
England) [2009] EWHC 4
(Admin) S60
Eastman v Comr of Superannuation
(1987) 15 FCR 139 .... S110
Ecuador (Republic of) v Occidental
Exploration and Production Co
[2005] EWCA Civ 1116,
[2006] QB 432, [2006] 2 All ER

Ecuador (Republic of) v Occidental
Exploration and Production Co
[2005] EWCA Civ 1116, [2006] QB
432, [2006] 2 All ER – contd
225, [2005] 2 All ER (Comm)
689, [2006] 2 WLR 70,
[2005] 2 Lloyd's Rep 707, (2005)
Times, 23 September, [2005] All
ER (D) 48 (Sep) S16
Edelsten v Health Insurance
Commission (1990) 27 FCR 56 ..... S52
Egan v Basildon Borough Council
[2011] EWHC 2416 (QB),
[2011] 39 LS Gaz R 19, [2011]
All ER (D) 128 (Sep) S51
Elders New Zealand Ltd v PGG
Wrightson Ltd [2009] 1 NZLR
577 .... S78
Electrical Supply Assoc of
Australia Ltd v ACCC
(2001) 113 FCR 250 .... S50
Elliot v Joicey [1935] AC 209, 104 LJ
Ch 111, [1935] All ER Rep 578,
79 Sol Jo 144, 152 LT 398, 51
TLR 261, 1935 SC (HL)
57, HL S42
Enfield v R (2008) 51 MVR 200 .... S47
Equuscorp Pty Ltd v Belperio [2006]
VSC 14 .... S95
Equuscorp Pty Ltd v Haxton [2012]
HCA 7, [2012] 3 LRC 716, Aus
HC S48, S49
Esso Australia Resources Ltd v Comr
of Taxation (1999) 2 ITLR 429,
201 CLR 49, Aus HC S79
FA (Iraq) v Secretary of State for the
Home Department [2010] EWCA
Civ 696, [2010] 1 WLR 2545,
[2010] All ER (D) 161 (Jun) S68
FP (Iran) and MB (Libya) v Secretary
of State for the Home
Department [2007] EWCA Civ
13, (2007) Times, 26 January,
[2007] All ER (D) 155 (Jan) S36
Fairfax v Ireton [2009] 1 NZLR 540 .... S107
Far Service, The. See Farstad Supply
A/S v Enviroco Ltd The Far
Service
Farah Constructions Pty Ltd v Say-Dee
Pty Ltd [2007] HCA 22, 230
CLR 89, 10 ITELR 136,
[2007] 3 LRC 374, Aus HC S29
Farnell Electronic Components Pty Ltd
v Collector of Customs
(1996) 72 FCR 125 .... S102
Farquharson v R [1973] AC 786 .... S63
Farstad Supply A/S v Enviroco Ltd,
The Far Service [2011] UKSC
16, [2011] 3 All ER 451, [2011]
2 All ER (Comm) 269,
[2011] 1 WLR 921, [2011] Bus
LR 1108, [2011] 2 Lloyd's Rep
72, [2011] 2 BCLC 165,

Farstad Supply A/S v Enviroco Ltd, The Far
    Service [2011] UKSC 16,
    [2011] 3 All ER 451, [2011] 2 All ER
    (Comm) 269, [2011] 1 WLR 921, [2011]
    Bus LR 1108, [2011] 2 Lloyd's Rep 72,
    [2011] 2 BCLC 165, – contd
    [2011] 16 LS Gaz R 18,
    [2011] NLJR 552, (2011) Times,
    12 April, [2011] All ER (D) 55
    (Apr) S87
Financial Services Compensation
    Scheme Ltd v Abbey National
    Treasury Services plc
    [2008] EWHC 1897 (Ch), [2009]
    Bus LR 465, [2008] All ER (D)
    36 (Aug) S52
Fingleton v R (2005) 216 ALR 474 ...... S19
Fletcher (Executrix of the estate of
    Carl Fletcher (dec'd)) v A Train
    & Sons Ltd [2008] EWCA Civ
    413, [2008] 4 All ER 699, [2008]
    All ER (D) 333 (Apr) S20
Floor v Davis (Inspector of Taxes)
    [1980] AC 695, [1979] 2 All ER
    677, [1979] 2 WLR 830,
    [1979] STC 379, 52 TC 609,
    [1979] TR 163, 123 Sol Jo 374,
    L(TC) 2726, HL S58
Fong Yau Hei v Gammon
    Construction Ltd [2008] 3
    HKLRD 604 .... S87
41–60 Albert Palace Mansions
    (Freehold) Ltd v Craftrule Ltd.
    See Craftrule Ltd v 41–60 Albert
    Palace Mansions (Freehold) Ltd
Freeman v Higher Park Farm
    [2008] EWCA Civ 1185,
    [2009] PIQR P103, 152 Sol Jo
    (no 43) 32, [2008] All ER (D)
    310 (Oct) S104
Frucor Beverages Ltd v Rio
    Beverages Ltd [2001] 2 NZLR
    604 .... S50, S91
Fun World Co Ltd v Municipal
    Council of Quatre Bornes
    [2009] UKPC 8, [2009] 5 LRC
    224, [2009] All ER (D) 43
    (Apr) S105
Futures Commission v Stock Exchange
    of Hong Kong Ltd [1992] 1
    HKLR 135 .... S53, S58
Generics (UK) Ltd v H Lundbeck A/S
    [2008] EWCA Civ 311,
    [2008] RPC 437, 101 BMLR 52,
    [2008] All ER (D) 152 (Apr);
    affd [2009] UKHL 12,
    [2009] 2 All ER 955, [2009] Bus
    LR 828, [2009] RPC 407,
    [2009] IP & T 496, 107 BMLR
    121, 153 Sol Jo (no 8) 30, [2009]
    All ER (D) 258 (Feb) S68

George Wimpey UK Ltd v Tewkesbury
    Borough Council (MA
    Holdings Ltd intervening)
    [2008] EWCA Civ 12,
    [2008] 3 All ER 859,
    [2008] 1 WLR 1649, 127 ConLR
    17, (2008) Times, 25 February,
    [2008] All ER (D) 177 (Jan) S86
Gesner Investments Ltd v
    Bombardier Inc [2011] EWCA
    Civ 1118, [2011] All ER (D) 90
    (Oct) S106
Gibson v Government of United States
    of America [2007] UKPC 52,
    [2007] 1 WLR 2367, (2007)
    Times, 3 August, 70 WIR 34,
    [2008] 3 LRC 30, [2007] All ER
    (D) 358 (Jul) S86, S88
Giles v Rhind [2009] Ch 191,
    [2008] 3 All ER 697,
    [2008] 3 WLR 1233, [2008] Bus
    LR 1103, [2008] 2 BCLC 1,
    [2008] EWCA Civ 118, [2008]
    BPIR 342, [2008] All ER (D)
    410 (Feb), CA S49, S77
Glasgow City Council v AD [2005]
    Scot SC 35 .... S7
Goldie v Minister for Immigration and
    Multicultural Affairs
    (2002) 121 FCR 383 .... S61
Goshawk Dedicated (No 2) Ltd v
    Governor and Co of Bank of
    Scotland [2005] EWHC 2906
    (Ch), [2006] 2 All ER 610,
    [2005] All ER (D) 205 (Dec) S6
Government of Canada v Aronson
    [1990] 1 AC 579,
    [1989] 2 All ER 1025,
    [1989] 3 WLR 436, 90 Cr App
    Rep 199, HL S34
Gow (FC) v Grant [2012] UKSC 29,
    [2012] 3 FCR 73,
    [2012] 29 LS Gaz R 29, (2012)
    Times, 31 August, [2012] All ER
    (D) 32 (Jul) S64, S65, S66, S69
Grays Timber Products Ltd v Revenue
    and Customs Comrs [2010]
    UKSC 4, [2010] 2 All ER 1,
    [2010] 1 WLR 497, [2010] STC
    782, 80 TC 96, (2010) Times,
    4 February, 2010 SC (UKSC) 1,
    2011 SLT 63, 2010 SCLR 239,
    154 Sol Jo (no 5) 30, [2010] All
    ER (D) 31 (Feb) S4, S31, S70
Grealis v DPP [2001] IESC 50 .... S77
Gregory v Turner [2003] EWCA Civ
    183, [2003] 2 All ER 1114,
    [2003] 1 WLR 1149,
    [2003] 3 EGLR 129, (2003)
    Times, 21 February, [2003] All
    ER (D) 267 (Feb) S18

Guelph (City) v Wyndham Street
    Investments Inc (2003) 63 OR
    (2d) 481 .... S105
Guidance for McKenzie Friends (Civil
    and Family Courts) [2010] Lexis
    Citation 39, [2010] All ER (D)
    169 (Jul) S17
Gumbs v A-G of Anguilla
    [2009] UKPC 27, [2010] 2 LRC
    221, [2009] All ER (D) 92
    (Nov) S91
H (minors) (abduction: acquiescence),
    Re [1998] AC 72,
    [1997] 2 All ER 225,
    [1997] 2 WLR 563,
    [1997] 2 FCR 257, [1997] 1 FLR
    872, [1997] Fam Law 468, HL S69
HKSAR v Cheung Kwun Yin
    (November 2008, unreported) S67
HKSAR v Cheung Kwun Yin [2009]
    12 HKCFAR 568 .... S65
HKSAR v Hung Chan Wa [2006] 3
    HKLRD 841 .... S29
HKSAR v Lam Kwong Wai [2006] 3
    HKLRD 808 .... S112
HKSAR v Tang Hoi On [2003] 3 HKC
    123 .... S83
HKSAR v Tin's Label Factory Ltd
    (2008) 11 HKCFAR 637 .... S18, S97
Ha v State of New South Wales (1997)
    189 CLR 465 .... S29
Hampstead Heath Winter Swimming
    Club v Corpn of London
    [2005] EWHC 713 (Admin),
    [2005] LGR 481, [2005] NLJ
    827, (2005) Times, 19 May,
    [2005] All ER (D) 353 (Apr), sub
    nom R (on the application of
    Hampstead Heath Winter
    Swimming Club) v Corpn of
    London [2005] 1 WLR 2930 .... S78
Hamzy v Tricon International
    (2001) 115 FCR 78 .... S23
Hanchett-Stamford v A-G
    [2008] EWHC 330 (Ch),
    [2009] Ch 173, [2008] 4 All ER
    323, [2009] 2 WLR 405,
    [2008] 2 P & CR 102, [2009]
    PTSR 1, [2008] NLJR 371,
    [2008] All ER (D) 391 (Feb) S22,
                                       S114
Hanna v Migration Agents Registration
    Authority (1999) 94 FCR 358,
    363 .... S35
Harbour Radio Pty td v Australian
    Communications and Media
    Authority [2012] FCA 614 .... S37
Hatzl v XL Insurance Co Ltd
    [2009] EWCA Civ 223,
    [2009] 3 All ER 617, [2009] 2
    All ER (Comm) 699,
    [2010] 1 WLR 470, [2010] Bus
    LR 50, [2009] RTR 326,

Hatzl v XL Insurance Co Ltd [2009] EWCA
    Civ 223, [2009] 3 All ER 617, [2009] 2
    All ER (Comm) 699, [2010] 1 WLR
    470, [2010] Bus LR 50, [2009] RTR
    326, – contd
    [2009] 1 Lloyd's Rep 555, (2009)
    Times, 16 April, [2009] All ER
    (D) 212 (Mar) S68
Hawke's Bay Raw Milk Producers
    Co-operative Co Ltd v New
    Zealand Milk Board [1961]
    NZLR 218 .... S37
Health Service Comrs for Valuation
    [2008] IEHC 178 .... S57
Henry Boot Construction (UK) Ltd v
    Malmaison Hotel
    (Manchester) Ltd [2001] QB 388,
    [2001] 1 All ER 257, [2000] 2
    All ER (Comm) 960,
    [2000] 3 WLR 1824,
    [2000] 2 Lloyd's Rep 625, 72
    ConLR 1, [2000] NLJR 867,
    [2000] BLR 509, CA S105
HM Advocate v Cadder [2010] UKSC
    43, [2010] 1 WLR 2601, (2010)
    Times, 28 October, 2011 SC
    (UKSC) 13, 2010 SCCR 951,
    154 Sol Jo (no 41) 30, 30 BHRC
    257, [2011] 3 LRC 100, [2010]
    All ER (D) 251 (Oct) S18, S29
Hertfordshire County Council v Veolia
    Water Central Ltd (formerly
    Three Valleys Water plc)
    [2010] EWHC 278 (QB), [2010]
    PTSR 871, [2010] All ER (D)
    273 (Feb); revsd sub nom
    Hertfordshire County Council v
    Veolia Water Central Ltd
    [2010] EWCA Civ 887, [2011]
    PTSR 261, (2010) Times,
    4 October, [2010] All ER (D) 282
    (Jul) S36
Hilali, Re [2008] UKHL 3,
    [2008] 1 AC 805,
    [2008] 2 All ER 207,
    [2008] 2 WLR 299, (2008)
    Times, 1 February, [2008] All ER
    (D) 245 (Jan) S84
Hillingdon London Borough Council v
    ARC Ltd [1999] Ch 139,
    [1998] 3 WLR 754, [1999] LGR
    282, 75 P & CR 346,
    [1998] 15 LS Gaz R 34,
    [1998] 20 LS Gaz R 34,
    [1998] RVR 242, [1998] 39 EG
    202, 142 Sol Jo LB 149, CA S45
Hin Lin Yee v HKSAR [2010] 2
    HKLRD 826 .... S98
Hollins v Russell [2003] EWCA Civ
    718, [2003] 28 LS Gaz R 30,
    [2003] 4 All ER 590,
    [2003] 1 WLR 2487,
    [2003] NLJR 920, (2003) Times,

Hollins v Russell [2003] EWCA Civ 718,
[2003] 28 LS Gaz R 30,
[2003] 4 All ER 590, [2003] 1 WLR
2487, [2003] NLJR 920, (2003) Times, –
contd
10 June, 147 Sol Jo LB 662,
[2003] All ER (D) 311 (May) S5
Home Office v Tariq [2011] UKSC 35,
[2012] AC 452, [2012] 1 All ER
58, [2011] 3 WLR 322,
[2012] 1 CMLR 14, [2011] ICR
938, [2011] IRLR 843,
[2011] NLJR 1027, (2011)
Times, 18 July, [2011] All ER
(D) 108 (Jul) S82
Horton v Sadler [2006] UKHL 27,
[2007] 1 AC 307,
[2006] 3 All ER 1177,
[2006] 2 WLR 1346, [2006] RTR
330, 91 BMLR 60, [2006] NLJR
1024, (2006) Times, 19 June, 150
Sol Jo LB 808, [2007] 3 LRC
146, [2006] All ER (D) 130
(Jun) S30
Housden v Conservators of Wimbledon
and Putney Commons
[2008] EWCA Civ 200,
[2008] 3 All ER 1038,
[2008] 1 WLR 1172,
[2008] 2 EGLR 107,
[2008] 12 EG 97 (CS), [2008]
All ER (D) 266 (Mar) S29
Hrushka v Canada (Minister of
Foreign Affairs) [2009] FCA
69 .... S56
Hua Tian Long (No 3) [2010] 3 HKC
557 .... S32
Hulme v Secretary of State for
Communities and Local
Government [2011] EWCA Civ
638, [2011] All ER (D) 262
(May) S36
Hungary (Szombathely City Court) v
Fenyvesi [2009] EWHC 231
(Admin), [2009] 4 All ER 324,
[2009] All ER (D) 202 (Feb) S25
Hyde Park Residence Ltd v Secretary
of State for the Environment,
Transport and the Regions
(2000) 80 P & CR 419, [2000] 1
PLR 85, [2000] NPC 7,
[2000] EGCS 14, [2000] JPL
936, [2000] All ER (D) 64, CA S47
Iarnroid Eireann v Social Welfare
Tribunal [2007] IEHC 406 .... S99
Ignatious v Minister for Immigration
& Multicultural & Indigenous
Affairs (2004) 139 FCR 254,
268 .... S35
Imperial Tobacco Ltd, petitioner
[2012] CSIH 9, 2012 SCLR
251 .... S3, S46, S47, S61, S66, S67,
S74, S89, S90, S106

Independent Committee for the
Supervision of Standards of
Telephone Information Services v
Hornan [2007] EWHC 2307
(Admin), [2007] All ER (D) 114
(Sep) S84
Inglis v Loh Lai Kuen Eda [2005] 3
HKC 115, 127 .... S30
IRC v McGuckian [1997] NI 157,
[1997] 3 All ER 817,
[1997] 1 WLR 991, [1997] STC
908, 69 TC 1, 1 OFLR(ITLR)
120, [1997] 94 LS Gaz R 23, 141
Sol Jo LB 153, HL S85, S91, S95
IRC v Scottish Provident Institution
[2004] UKHL 52,
[2005] 1 All ER 325,
[2004] 1 WLR 3172, [2005] STC
15, 76 TC 538, 7 ITLR 403,
(2004) Times, 26 November,
[2004] All ER (D) 403 (Nov) S85,
S91, S95
Insight Vacations Pty Ltd v Young
(2011) 243 CLR 149 .... S100
Insurance and Superannuation Comr v
Hiscock (1995) 59 FCR 1 .... S78
Interchase Corp Ltd (in liq) (No 2), Re
(1993) 47 FCR 253 .... S57
Irish Life and Permanent Group
Holdings plc v Credit Institutions
Stabilisation Act 2010 [2012]
IEHC 89 .... S55
Isle of Anglesey County Council v
Welsh Ministers [2009] EWCA
Civ 94, [2010] QB 163,
[2009] 3 All ER 1110,
[2009] 3 WLR 813, 153 Sol Jo
(no 8) 27, [2009] All ER (D) 237
(Feb) S63
JF v Minister for Health and Children
[2008] IESC 16 .... S73
JT (Cameroon) v Secretary of State for
the Home Department
[2008] EWCA Civ 878,
[2009] 2 All ER 1213,
[2009] 1 WLR 1411, [2008] All
ER (D) 348 (Jul) S53, S82
Jade City International Ltd v Director
of Lands [2002] 3 HKLRD 33 ...... S79
James, Re [2005] NIQB 38 .... S105
Jayasinghe v Minister for Immigration
& Ethnic Affairs (1997) 76 FCR
301 .... S50
Jeffrey v Sawyer (1993) 16 OR (3d)
75, 78 .... S86
Joseph's Estate, Re (1993) 14 OR (3d)
628 .... S79
Jude v HM Advocate [2011] UKSC
55, [2011] 47 LS Gaz R 21, 2012
SC (UKSC) 222, 2012 SLT 75,
2012 SCCR 88, [2011] All ER

Jude v HM Advocate [2011] UKSC 55,
[2011] 47 LS Gaz R 21, 2012 SC
(UKSC) 222, 2012 SLT 75, 2012 SCCR
88, [2011] All ER – *contd*
(D) 173 (Nov) S90

K/S Victoria Street v House of Fraser
(Stores Management) Ltd
[2011] EWCA Civ 904,
[2012] 2 WLR 470,
[2011] 2 P & CR 239,
[2011] 2 EGLR 11,
[2011] 31 EG 52 (CS), (2011)
Times, 30 August, [2011] All ER
(D) 262 (Jul) S98

KJM Superbikes Ltd v Hinton
[2008] EWCA Civ 1280,
[2009] 3 All ER 76,
[2009] 1 WLR 2406,
[2008] NLJR 1683, [2008] All
ER (D) 200 (Nov) S14

Kalway v Secretary, Department of
Social Security (1992) 38 FCR
295 .... S72

Kao Lee & Yip (a firm) v Lau Wang
(2008) 11 HKCFAR 576 ..... S73, S104

Kartinyeri v Commonwealth (1998)
195 CLR 337 .... S37

Kaupthing Singer and Friedlander Ltd
(in admin), Re [2011] UKSC 48,
[2012] AC 804, [2012] 1 All ER
883, [2011] 3 WLR 939, [2011]
Bus LR 1644, [2012] 1 BCLC
227, [2011] 42 LS Gaz R 21,
[2011] NLJR 1485, (2011)
Times, 14 November, [2011]
BPIR 1706, [2011] All ER (D)
158 (Oct) S25

Kay v Metropolitan Police Comr
[2008] UKHL 69,
[2009] 2 All ER 935,
[2008] 1 WLR 2723, [2009] RTR
176, (2008) Times, 27 November,
152 Sol Jo (no 46) 31, [2008] All
ER (D) 255 (Nov) S46, S110

Kaye v Lawrence [2010] EWHC 2678
(TCC), [2011] 1 All ER 1088,
[2011] 1 WLR 1948,
[2011] 1 EGLR 47, [2010] NLJR
1532, [2011] BLR 77, (2011)
Times, 25 March, [2010] All ER
(D) 264 (Oct) S55

Kennedy v Information Comr
[2011] EWCA Civ 367 .... S37

Kennet District Council v Young
[1999] RTR 235, 163 JP 622, 163
JP 854 .... S44

King v Director of Serious Fraud
Office [2009] UKHL 17,
[2009] 2 All ER 223,
[2009] 1 WLR 718, [2009] 2 Cr
App Rep 43, (2009) Times,
19 March, 153 Sol Jo (no 11) 27,
[2009] All ER (D) 189 (Mar) S43

King's Application for Judicial
Review, Re [2002] NICA 48,
[2003] NI 43, NI CA S95, S96

Kirk v Walton [2008] EWHC 1780
(QB), [2009] 1 All ER 257,
[2008] All ER (D) 323 (Jul) S14

Knowsley Housing Trust v White
[2008] UKHL 70, [2009] AC
636, [2009] 2 All ER 829,
[2009] 2 WLR 78,
[2009] 1 P & CR 519, [2009]
PTSR 281, [2009] 1 EGLR 131,
[2008] 50 EG 73 (CS), (2008)
Times, 15 December, 153 Sol Jo
(no 1) 32, [2008] All ER (D) 115
(Dec) S86

Kok Cheng Weng v Wiener
(2007) 2 SLR 709 .... S47

Kuehne & Nagel Drinks Logistics Ltd
v Revenue and Customs Comrs
[2012] EWCA Civ 34,
[2012] STC 840, [2012] All ER
(D) 05 (Feb) S52

La Generale des Carrieres et des
Mines v FG Hemisphere
Associates LLC (Jersey)
[2012] UKPC 27,
[2012] 2 Lloyd's Rep 443, [2012]
All ER (D) 218 (Jul) S43

Ladele v Islington London Borough
Council [2009] EWCA Civ 1357,
[2010] 1 WLR 955, [2010] LGR
690, [2010] ICR 532,
[2010] IRLR 211, [2010] PTSR
982, (2010) Times, 1 January,
[2009] All ER (D) 148 (Dec) S113

Lai v Chamberlains [2007] 2 NZLR
7 .... S77

Lamichhane v Secretary of State for
the Home Department
[2012] EWCA Civ 260,
[2012] NLJR 426, (2012) Times,
30 May, [2012] All ER (D) 88
(Mar) S13

Landlord's Association for Northern
Ireland, Re [2005] NIQB 22 .... S85

Law Society v Sephton & Co
[2006] UKHL 22, [2006] 2 AC
543, [2006] 3 All ER 401,
[2006] 2 WLR 1091,
[2006] NLJR 844, (2006) Times,
11 May, 150 Sol Jo LB 669,
[2006] All ER (D) 123 (May) S45

Law Society of Upper Canada v
Ontario (A-G) (1995) 21 OR (3d)
666 .... S36

Lawrence v Kent County Council
[2012] EWCA Civ 493, [2012]
All ER (D) 142 (Apr) S24

Lawson v Serco Ltd [2004] EWCA
Civ 12, [2004] 2 All ER 200,
[2004] ICR 204, [2004] IRLR
206, (2004) Times, 30 January,

Lawson v Serco Ltd [2004] EWCA Civ 12,
[2004] 2 All ER 200, [2004] ICR 204,
[2004] IRLR 206, (2004) Times,
30 January, – contd
148 Sol Jo LB 148, [2004] All
ER (D) 217 (Jan); sub nom
Crofts v Cathay Pacific
Airways Ltd [2005] EWCA Civ
599, [2005] ICR 1436,
[2005] IRLR 624, (2005) Times,
31 May, [2005] All ER (D) 305
(May); sub nom Lawson v
Serco Ltd [2006] UKHL 3,
[2006] 1 All ER 823,
[2006] IRLR 289,
[2006] 06 LS Gaz R 36,
[2006] NLJR 184, 150 Sol Jo LB
131, [2006] All ER (D) 184
(Jan) S43
Lee Chez Kee v Public Prosecutor
[2008] SGCA 20 .... S78
Lee Yiu Kee v Chinese University of
Hong Kong [2010] HKCA 218 ..... S60,
S61
Leeds Group plc v Leeds City Council
[2011] EWCA Civ 1447,
[2012] 1 WLR 1561, [2012] LGR
561, [2011] All ER (D) 19
(Dec) S41
Legal Services Commission v Loomba
[2012] EWHC 29 (QB),
[2012] 2 All ER 977,
[2012] 1 WLR 2461,
[2012] NLJR 138, [2012] All ER
(D) 58 (Jan) S41, S72
Legal Services Commission v Rasool
[2008] EWCA Civ 154,
[2008] 3 All ER 381,
[2008] 1 WLR 2711,
[2008] NLJR 414, (2008) Times,
21 April, [2008] 4 Costs LR 529,
[2008] All ER (D) 43 (Mar) S45
Leontjava v DPP [2004] IESC 37,
[2004] 1 IR 591, Ir SC S76
Letang v Cooper [1965] 1 QB 232,
[1964] 2 All ER 929,
[1964] 3 WLR 573,
[1964] 2 Lloyd's Rep 339, 108
Sol Jo 519, CA S66
Leung v Secretary for Justice [2006] 4
HKLRD 211 .... S23
Leung Kwok Hung v President of the
Legislative Council of Hong
Kong [2012] 3 HKLRD 470 .... S28
Lewisham London Borough Council v
Malcolm [2007] EWCA Civ 763,
[2008] Ch 129, [2008] 2 WLR
369, [2008] LGR 189,
[2008] HLR 198, [2007] 32 EG
88 (CS), (2007) Times,
28 August, [2007] All ER (D)
401 (Jul); revsd [2008] UKHL
43, [2008] 1 AC 1399,

Lewisham London Borough Council v
Malcolm [2007] EWCA Civ 763,
[2008] Ch 129, [2008] 2 WLR 369,
[2008] LGR 189, [2008] HLR 198,
[2007] 32 EG 88 (CS), (2007) Times,
28 August, [2007] All ER (D) 401 (Jul);
revsd [2008] UKHL 43, [2008] 1 AC
1399, – contd
[2008] 4 All ER 525,
[2008] 3 WLR 194, [2008] LGR
549, [2008] 2 P & CR 358,
[2008] IRLR 700, 102 BMLR
170, (2008) Times, 26 June, 152
Sol Jo (no 26) 29, [2008] All ER
(D) 342 (Jun) S66, S100
Li Wang Pong v Medical Council of
Hong Kong [2009] HKCFI 2 .... S77
Liu Pik Han v Hong Kong Federation
of Insurers Appeals Tribunal
[2005] 3 HKC 242 .... S50
Lucasfilm Ltd v Ainsworth [2011]
UKSC 39, [2012] AC 208,
[2011] 4 All ER 817, [2012] 1
All ER (Comm) 1011,
[2011] 3 WLR 487, [2011] Bus
LR 1211, [2011] FSR 945,
[2011] IP & T 733, [2011] NLJR
1098, (2011) Times, 03 August,
[2012] EMLR 59, [2011] All ER
(D) 257 (Jul) S44
Luckins, ex p Columbia Pictures
Industries Inc, Re (1996) 67 FCR
549 .... S44
M (by his litigation friend TM) v
Hackney London Borough
Council [2011] EWCA Civ 4,
[2011] 3 All ER 529,
[2011] 1 WLR 2873, [2011]
PTSR 1419, (2011) Times,
17 February, [2011] All ER (D)
76 (Jan) S6
M v Watson [2009] HJC 3 .... S112
MH (Syria) v Secretary of State for the
Home Department [2009] EWCA
Civ 226, [2009] 3 All ER 564,
[2009] All ER (D) 234 (Mar) S68
McCombie v Cadotte (2001) 53 OR
(3d) 704 .... S10
Macmillan & Co v Dent
[1907] 1 Ch 107, 76 LJ Ch 136,
51 Sol Jo 46, 95 LT 730, 23 TLR
45, CA S38
McNally v Secretary of State for
Education [2001] EWCA Civ
332, [2002] LGR 584,
[2002] ICR 15, [2001] 2 FCR 11,
[2001] ELR 773,
[2001] 19 LS Gaz R 36, [2001]
All ER (D) 119 (Mar) S96
Maguire v Director of Public
Prosecutions [2004] 3 IR 241 .... S86

Mahad (previously referred to as AM)
(Ethiopia) v Entry Clearance
Officer. See AM (Ethiopia) v
Entry Clearance Officer
Majeau Carrying Co Pty Ltd v Coastal
Rutile Ltd (1973) 129 CLR 48, 1
ALR 1, Aus HC S40
Majorstake Ltd v Curtis [2008] UKHL
10, [2008] 1 AC 787,
[2008] 2 All ER 303,
[2008] 2 WLR 338,
[2008] 1 P & CR D65,
[2008] 2 P & CR 20,
[2008] 1 EGLR 44, [2008] NLJR
262, [2008] 06 EG 131 (CS),
[2008] 14 EG 102, (2008) Times,
12 February, [2008] All ER (D)
70 (Feb) S106
Manly Council v Malouf
(2004) 61 NSWLR 394 .... S56
Manor Electronics Ltd v Dickson
(1990) Times, 8 February S30
Marks & Spencer plc v Revenue and
Customs Comrs [2009] UKHL 8,
[2009] 1 All ER 939, [2009] STC
452, [2009] All ER (D) 39
(Feb) S111
Maroussem v Director General,
Mauritius Revenue Authority
[2011] UKPC 30, [2011] STC
1908, [2011] All ER (D) 45
(Sep) S42
Masciantonio v R (1995) 183 CLR
58 .... S96
Mason v Boscawen [2008] EWHC
3100 (Ch), [2009] 1 All ER 1006,
[2009] 1 WLR 2139,
[2009] 1 P & CR 499,
[2009] STC 624, [2009] 02 EG
80 (CS), [2008] All ER (D) 228
(Dec) S89, S92, S93
Masri v Consolidated Contractors
International Co SAL
[2009] UKHL 43, [2010] 1 AC
90, [2009] 4 All ER 847, [2010]
1 All ER (Comm) 220,
[2009] 3 WLR 385, [2009] Bus
LR 1269, [2009] 2 Lloyd's Rep
473, [2009] 2 BCLC 382,
[2009] NLJR 1250, (2009)
Times, 13 August, [2009] All ER
(D) 340 (Jul) S43
Mastercigars Direct Ltd v Withers LLP
[2007] EWHC 2733 (Ch),
[2008] 3 All ER 417,
[2009] 1 WLR 881,
[2008] IP & T 946, [2007] NLJR
1731, [2008] 1 Costs LR 72,
[2007] All ER (D) 385 (Nov) S44
Meagher v Luke J Healy
Pharmacy Ltd [2010] IESC 40 ...... S79

Medcalf v Mardell [2002] UKHL 27,
[2003] 1 AC 120,
[2002] 3 All ER 721,
[2002] 3 WLR 172,
[2002] 31 LS Gaz R 34,
[2002] NLJR 1032, (2002)
Times, 28 June, [2002] All ER
(D) 228 (Jun) S37
Medical Council of Hong Kong v
Chow Siu Shek (2000) 3
HKCFAR 144, [2000] 2 HKLRD
674 .... S54, S79
Metronet Rail BCV Ltd (in PPP
administration), Re
[2007] EWHC 2697 (Ch),
[2008] 2 All ER 75, [2008] Bus
LR 823, [2008] 1 BCLC 760,
[2007] All ER (D) 370 (Nov) S23
Midland Bank Trust Co Ltd v Hett,
Stubbs & Kemp (a firm)
[1979] Ch 384, [1978] 3 All ER
571, [1978] 3 WLR 167, 121 Sol
Jo 830 .... S30
Midlands Co-operative Society Ltd v
Revenue and Customs Comrs
[2008] EWCA Civ 305, [2008]
Bus LR 1187, [2008] STC 1803,
(2008) Times, 22 April, [2008]
All ER (D) 121 (Apr) S103
Miliangos v George Frank
(Textiles) Ltd [1976] AC 443,
[1975] 3 All ER 801,
[1975] 3 WLR 758,
[1975] 2 CMLR 585,
[1976] 1 Lloyd's Rep 201, 9
LDAB 408, 119 Sol Jo
774, HL S30
Mills v Birchall. See Dolphin Quays
Developments Ltd v Mills
Minister for Immigration and
Citizenship v SZMDS (2010) 240
CLR 611 .... S86
Minister for Immigration and
Multicultural Affairs v B (2004)
219 CLR 365 .... S96
Minister for Immigration and
Multicultural Affairs v Hu
(1997) 79 FCR 309 .... S56
Minister for Immigration and
Multicultural Affairs v Savvin
(2000) 98 FCR 168 .... S75
Minister for Immigration and
Multicultural and Indigenous
Affairs v QAAH of 2004 (2003)
231 CLR 1 .... S69
Morris v London Iron and
Steel Co Ltd [1988] QB 493,
[1987] 2 All ER 496,
[1987] 3 WLR 836, [1987] ICR
855, [1987] IRLR 182, 131 Sol
Jo 1040,
[1987] LS Gaz R 2274, CA S3

Morrison Sports Ltd v Scottish Power
(Scotland) [2010] UKSC 37,
[2010] 1 WLR 1934, (2010)
Times, 31 August, 2011 SC
(UKSC) 1, 2010 SLT 1027,
[2010] All ER (D) 302 (Jul) ... S10, S11

Mount Lawley Pty Ltd v Western
Australi Planning Commission
[2004] WASCA 149, (2004) 136
LGERA 16 .... S83

Moweno Pty Ltd v Stratis Promotions
Pty Ltd [2003] NSWCA 376 .... S58

Mucelli v Government of Albania
[2009] UKHL 2, [2009] 3 All ER
1035, [2009] 1 WLR 276, (2009)
Times, 27 January, 153 Sol Jo
(no 4) 28, [2009] All ER (D) 135
(Jan) S56

Mullins v Harnett [1997] IEHC 18,
[1998] 4 IR 426 ..... S40, S41, S53, S55

Munn v Agus (1997) 6 NTLR 84 .... S56

N (a child) (McKenzie friends: rights
of audience), Re [2008] EWHC
2042 (Fam), [2008] 1 WLR 2743,
[2008] 3 FCR 642, [2008] 2 FLR
1899, [2008] Fam Law 1093,
[2008] All ER (D) 116 (Aug) S17,
                                    S18, S19, S20

NML Capital Ltd v Republic of
Argentina [2011] UKSC 31,
[2011] 2 AC 495,
[2011] 4 All ER 1191, [2012] 1
All ER (Comm) 1081,
[2011] 3 WLR 273,
[2011] 2 Lloyd's Rep 628,
[2011] NLJR 990, (2011) Times,
8 July, [2012] 1 LRC 180, [2011]
All ER (D) 44 (Jul) S43, S49, S87

Nangles Nurseries v Comrs of
Valuation [2008] IEHC 73 .... S54

Neilson v Overseas Projects Corpn of
Australia (2005) 223 CLR 331 .... S100

New Cap Reinsurance Corpn Ltd (in
liq), Re [2011] EWCA Civ 971,
[2012] 1 All ER 755, [2012] 1
All ER (Comm) 1207,
[2012] 2 WLR 1095, [2012] Bus
LR 772, [2011] All ER (D) 55
(Aug); sub nom New Cap
Reinsurance Corp (in liq) v Grant
[2012] UKSC 46, [2012] All ER
(D) 258 (Oct) S61

New South Wales Crime Commission
v Yu [2009] NSWCA 349 .... S20

New Zealand Customs Service v Wang
[2010] NZAR 322 .... S56

Ng Ka Ling v Director of Immigration
(1999) 2 HKCFAR 4 .... S54

Nguyen v Minister for Health &
Ageing [2002] FCA 1241 .... S51

Niagara-on-the-Lake (Town) v Gross
Estate (1993) 12 OR (3d) 1 .... S94

Nolan v Wright [2009] EWHC 305
(Ch), [2009] 3 All ER 823,
[2009] 2 All ER (Comm) 503,
[2009] NLJR 395, [2009] BPIR
854, [2009] All ER (D) 45
(Mar) S5

Norman v Cheshire Fire and Rescue
Service [2011] EWHC 3305
(QB), [2011] All ER (D) 110
(Dec) S36, S62

North Somerset District Council v
Honda Motor Europe Ltd
[2010] EWHC 1505 (QB),
[2010] RA 285, [2010] All ER
(D) 13 (Jul) S6

OTC International AG v Perfect
Recovery Ltd [2009] 3 HKLRD
13 .... S86

Oakley Inc v Animal Ltd (Secretary of
State for Trade and Industry
intervening) [2005] EWCA Civ
1191, [2006] Ch 337,
[2006] 2 WLR 294, [2006] RPC
301, [2006] IP & T 251, (2005)
Times, 7 November, [2005] All
ER (D) 222 (Oct) S35

Oceania Manufacturing Co Ltd v Pang
Kwong-Hon [1979] HKLR 445 ..... S40

Odelola v Secretary of State for the
Home Department [2009] UKHL
25, [2009] 3 All ER 1061,
[2009] 1 WLR 1230, (2009)
Times, 22 May, [2009] All ER
(D) 180 (May) S33, S41, S96

Official Bay Heritage Protection
Society Incoporated v Auckland
City Council [2007] NZCA
511 .... S75

Ofulue v Bossert [2009] UKHL 16,
[2009] AC 990, [2009] 3 All ER
93, [2009] 2 WLR 749,
[2010] 1 FLR 475,
[2009] Fam Law 1042,
[2009] 11 EG 119 (CS), (2009)
Times, 13 March, 153 Sol Jo (no
11) 29, [2009] All ER (D) 119
(Mar) S100

Omagh District Council, Re, Judicial
Review [2007] NIQB 61 .... S105

O'Reilly v Mackman [1983] 2 AC
237, [1982] 3 All ER 1124,
[1982] 3 WLR 1096, 126 Sol Jo
820, HL S27

Osbourne v Chief Executive of
Ministry of Social Development
[2010] 1 NZLR 559 .... S87

Ostrowski v Palmer (2004) 218 CLR
493 .... S5

Oyarce v Cheshire County Council
[2008] EWCA Civ 434,
[2008] 4 All ER 907, [2008] ICR
1179, [2008] IRLR 653, [2008]

Oyarce v Cheshire County Council
[2008] EWCA Civ 434, [2008] 4 All ER
907, [2008] ICR 1179, [2008] IRLR
653, [2008] – *contd*
All ER (D) 24 (May) S35
P, Re [2009] EWHC 163 (Ch),
[2010] Ch 33, [2009] 2 All ER
1198, [2009] All ER (D) 160
(Feb) S79
PNPF Trust Co Ltd v Taylor
[2010] EWHC 1573 (Ch), [2010]
All ER (D) 251 (Jun) S36
Palm Developments Ltd v Secretary of
State for Communities and Local
Government [2009] EWHC 220
(Admin), [2009] 2 P & CR 262,
[2009] NLJR 308, [2009] All ER
(D) 132 (Feb) S107
Pang Yiu Hung v Comr of Police
[2003] 2 HKLRD 125 .... S92
Paulin v Paulin [2009] EWCA Civ
221, [2009] 3 All ER 88n,
[2010] 1 WLR 1057,
[2009] 2 FCR 477, [2009] 2 FLR
354, [2009] Fam Law 567,
[2009] NLJR 475, [2009] BPIR
572, [2009] All ER (D) 187
(Mar) S18
Penny's Bay Investment Co Ltd v
Director of Lands [2010] HKCFA
12 .... S57
Pepper v A-G (No 2) [2008] QCA
207 .... S109
Pepper (Inspector of Taxes) v Hart
[1990] 1 WLR 204, [1990] STC
6, 65 TC 421; affd
[1991] Ch 203, [1991] 2 All ER
824, [1991] 2 WLR 483,
[1990] STC 786, 65 TC 421,
[1991] ICR 681, [1991] IRLR
125, 134 Sol Jo 1479, CA; revsd
[1993] AC 593, [1993] 1 All ER
42, [1992] 3 WLR 1032,
[1992] STC 898, 65 TC 421,
[1993] ICR 291, [1993] IRLR 33,
[1993] NLJR 17, [1993] RVR
127, HL S64, S65, S66, S69
Perpetual Trusteee Company Ltd v
Albert and Rose Khoshaba
[2006] NSWCA 41 .... S20
Perrin v Northampton Borough
Council [2007] EWCA Civ 1353,
[2008] 4 All ER 673,
[2008] 1 WLR 1307, [2008] LGR
379, [2008] 1 P & CR 454,
[2008] 1 EGLR 93, [2008] BLR
137, [2008] 02 EG 146 (CS),
(2008) Times, 21 January, 152
Sol Jo (no 2) 34, [2007] All ER
(D) 286 (Dec) S53
Perry v Serious Organised Crime
Agenc. See Serious Organised
Crime Agency v Perry

Perry v Serious Organised Crime Agenc. See
Serious Organised Crime Agency v
Perry – *contd*
(proceedings under the Proceeds
of Crime Act 2002)
Phillips v Mulcaire. See Coogan v
News Group Newspapers Ltd
Pilling v Reynolds [2008] EWHC 316
(QB), [2009] 1 All ER 163,
[2008] All ER (D) 54 (Mar) S107
Poets Chase Freehold Co Ltd v
Sinclair Gardens Investments
(Kensington) Ltd. See Sinclair
Gardens Investments
(Kensington) Ltd v Poets Chase
Freehold Co Ltd
Prem Singh v Director of Immigration
[2003] 1 HKLRD 550 .... S102
Premier Foods (Holdings) Ltd v
Revenue and Customs Comrs
[2007] EWHC 3134 (Ch),
[2008] STC 176, [2007] All ER
(D) 363 (Oct) S57
Presidential Insurance Co Ltd v
Resha St Hill [2012] UKPC 33 .... S64,
S69, S90
Preston v Comr for fair Trading [2011]
NSWCA 40 .... S67
Project Blue Sky v Australian
Broadcasting Authority (1998)
194 CLR 355, 384 .... S4, S46
Purba v Ryan (2006) 61 Alta LR (4th)
112 .... S48
QBE Worker's Compensation
(Vic) Ltd v Freisleben
[1999] 3 VR 401 .... S91
Qema (Besnik) v News Group
Newspapers Ltd [2012] EWHC
1146 (QB), [2012] All ER (D) 37
(May) S15
Quinlivan v Governer of Portlaoise
Prison [1997] IEHC 181, [1998]
2 IR 113 .... S40, S41, S55
R v A [2008] EWCA Crim 2908,
[2009] 2 All ER 898, [2009] 1 Cr
App Rep 347, [2009] Crim LR
739, [2008] All ER (D) 03 (Dec),
sub nom R v Andrews
[2009] 1 WLR 1947 .... S99, S101
R v Ahmed [2011] EWCA Crim 184,
[2011] Crim LR 734, 175 CL&J
141, [2011] All ER (D) 277
(Feb) S21
R (W) v Alberta (2006) 62 Alta LR
(4th) 6 .... S93
R (on the application of Ahmed) v
Asylum Support Adjudicator
[2008] EWHC 2282 (Admin),
[2008] All ER (D) 12 (Oct) S74
R v Athwal [2009] EWCA Crim 789,
[2009] 1 WLR 2430, [2009] 2 Cr
App Rep 204, [2009] Crim LR
726, (2009) Times, 14 July,

R v Athwal [2009] EWCA Crim 789,
    [2009] 1 WLR 2430, [2009] 2 Cr
    App Rep 204, [2009] Crim LR 726,
    (2009) Times, 14 July, – contd
    [2009] All ER (D) 61 (May) S99
R (on the application of Jackson) v
    A-G [2005] UKHL 56,
    [2006] 1 AC 262,
    [2005] 4 All ER 1253,
    [2005] 3 WLR 733, [2005] NLJR
    1600, (2005) Times, 14 October,
    [2006] 2 LRC 499, [2005] All
    ER (D) 136 (Oct) S16
R v Australian Broadcasting Tribunal,
    ex p Hardiman (1980) 144 CLR
    13 . . . . S23
R v B [2000] EWCA Crim 42 . . . . S5, S7
R v B [2012] EWCA Crim 770,
    [2012] 3 All ER 1093,
    [2012] 2 Cr App Rep 164, 176 JP
    312, 176 CL&J 273, (2012)
    Times, 30 July, [2012] All ER
    (D) 146 (Apr) S89
R v Barker [2010] EWCA Crim 4,
    (2010) Times, 5 February, [2010]
    All ER (D) 126 (Jan) S20, S99
R (on the application of Boyejo) v
    Barnet London Borough Council
    [2009] EWHC 3261 (Admin),
    (2010) Times, 22 January, [2009]
    All ER (D) 169 (Dec) S35
R (on the application of Newcastle
    City Council) v
    Berwick-upon-Tweed Borough
    Council [2008] EWHC 2369
    (Admin), [2009] LGR 195,
    [2009] RTR 413, [2008] All ER
    (D) 33 (Nov) S12
R (on the application of Aweys) v
    Birmingham City
    Council[2009] UKHL 36,
    [2009] 4 All ER 161,
    [2009] 1 WLR 1506, [2009] LGR
    749, [2009] PTSR 1270, 153 Sol
    Jo (no 26) 29, [2009] All ER (D)
    19 (Jul) S106
R (on the application of C) v
    Birmingham City Council
    [2008] EWHC 3036 (Admin),
    [2009] 1 All ER 1039,
    [2009] 1 FCR 657, [2009] 1 FLR
    838, [2009] Fam Law 200,
    [2008] All ER (D) 171 (Nov);
    affd on other grounds sub nom R
    (on the application Clue) v
    Birmingham City Council
    [2010] EWCA Civ 460,
    [2010] 4 All ER 423,
    [2011] 1 WLR 99, [2010] LGR
    485, [2010] PTSR 2051,
    [2010] 3 FCR 475, [2010] 2 FLR
    1011, [2010] Fam Law 802,
    (2010) Times, 7 May, 154 Sol Jo

R (on the application of C) v Birmingham
    City Council [2008] EWHC 3036
    (Admin), [2009] 1 All ER 1039,
    [2009] 1 FCR 657, [2009] 1 FLR 838,
    [2009] Fam Law 200, [2008] All ER (D)
    171 (Nov); affd on other grounds sub
    nom R (on the application Clue) v
    Birmingham City Council
    [2010] EWCA Civ 460, [2010] 4 All ER
    423, [2011] 1 WLR 99, [2010]
    485, [2010] PTSR 2051, [2010] 3 FCR
    475, [2010] 2 FLR 1011,
    [2010] Fam Law 802, (2010) Times,
    7 May, 154 Sol Jo – contd
    (no 18) 29, [2010] All ER (D) 27
    (May) S21
R (on the application of Okandeji) v
    Bow Street Magistrates Court
    [2005] EWHC 2925 (Admin),
    [2006] 1 WLR 674, [2005] All
    ER (D) 166 (Nov) S17
R v Braintree District Council,
    ex p Halls (2000) 80 P & CR
    266, 32 HLR 770,
    [2000] 3 EGLR 19,
    [2000] 36 EG 164, [2000] EGCS
    32, [2000] All ER (D) 511, CA S12
R (on the application of Risk
    Management Partners Ltd) v
    Brent London Borough Council
    [2008] EWHC 692 (Admin),
    [2008] LGR 331, [2008] All ER
    (D) 302 (Apr); affd sub nom Risk
    Management Partners Ltd v Brent
    London Borough Council
    [2008] EWHC 1094 (Admin),
    [2008] LGR 429, [2008] All ER
    (D) 226 (May); affd
    [2009] EWCA Civ 490,
    [2010] LGR 99, [2010] PTSR
    349, [2009] All ER (D) 109
    (Jun); revsd [2011] UKSC 7,
    [2011] 2 AC 34, [2011] 2 All ER
    209, [2011] 2 WLR 166,
    [2011] 2 CMLR 627,
    [2011] LGR 169, [2011] PTSR
    481, [2011] NLJR 256, (2011)
    Times, 10 February, 155 Sol Jo
    (no 6) 31, [2011] All ER (D) 103
    (Feb) S51, S70, S71
R (on the application of Kadhim) v
    Brent London Borough Council
    Housing Benefit Review Board
    [2001] QB 955, [2001] 2 WLR
    1674, [2000] All ER (D)
    2408, CA S29
R v Bristol [2007] EWCA Crim 3214,
    172 JP 161, 172 JPN 421, [2007]
    All ER (D) 47 (Dec) S7
R v C [2007] EWCA Crim 2581,
    [2008] 1 WLR 966, [2008] 1 Cr
    App Rep 311, 175 CL&J 677,
    [2007] All ER (D) 102 (Nov),

R v C [2007] EWCA Crim 2581,
[2008] 1 WLR 966, [2008] 1 Cr
App Rep 311, 175 CL&J 677, [2007]
All ER (D) 102 (Nov), – contd
sub nom R v Cartwright (2007)
Times, 6 December S40

R (on the application of KM) (by his
mother and litigation friend) v
Cambridgeshire County Council
[2012] UKSC 23,
[2012] 3 All ER 1218, [2012]
PTSR 1189, 126 BMLR 186,
[2012] 24 LS Gaz R 23,
[2012] NLJR 780, [2012] All ER
(D) 254 (May) S71

R v Chaytor [2010] UKSC 52,
[2011] 1 AC 684,
[2011] 1 All ER 805,
[2010] 3 WLR 1707, [2011] 1 Cr
App Rep 274, [2010] NLJR
1718, 174 CL&J 782, (2010)
Times, 6 December,
[2011] 3 LRC 1, [2010] All ER
(D) 19 (Dec) S28

R (on the application of G) v Chief
Constable of West Yorkshire
Police [2008] EWCA Civ 28,
[2008] 4 All ER 594,
[2008] 1 WLR 550, [2008] 2 Cr
App Rep 53, [2008] Crim LR
558, (2008) Times, 21 February,
[2008] All ER (D) 46 (Feb) S84

R (on the application of Hilali) v City
of Westminster Magistrates'
Court [2008] EWHC 2892
(Admin), [2009] 1 All ER 834,
[2010] 1 WLR 241, [2008] All
ER (D) 241 (Nov) S33

R v Clark (application under s 58 of
the Criminal Justice Act 2003)
[2007] EWCA Crim 2532, (2007)
Times, 29 October, [2007] All
ER (D) 120 (Oct), sub nom R v
Clarke (application under s 58 of
the Criminal Justice Act 2003)
[2008] 1 Cr App Rep 403 .... S20

R v Cockburn [2008] EWCA Crim
316, [2008] QB 882,
[2008] 2 All ER 1153,
[2008] 2 WLR 1274, [2008] 2 Cr
App Rep 47, [2008] Crim LR
802, [2008] All ER (D) 401
(Feb) S88

R (on the application of Hampstead
Heath Winter Swimming Club) v
Corpn of London. See
Hampstead Heath Winter
Swimming Club v Corpn of
London

R (on the application of Morris) v
Criminal Cases Review
Commission [2011] EWHC 117
(Admin), [2011] All ER (D) 80

R (on the application of Morris) v Criminal
Cases Review Commission
[2011] EWHC 117 (Admin), [2011] All
ER (D) 80 – contd
(Feb) S25

R (on the application of Gujra) v
Crown Prosecution Service
[2011] EWHC 472 (Admin),
[2012] 1 WLR 254, [2011] 2 Cr
App Rep 130, 175 JP 161, [2011]
All ER (D) 99 (Mar) S15

R (on the application of A) v Croydon
London Borough Council [2009]
UKSC 8, [2010] 1 All ER 469,
[2009] 1 WLR 2557, [2010] LGR
183, [2010] PTSR 106,
[2009] 3 FCR 607, [2010] 1 FLR
959, [2010] Fam Law 137,
[2009] NLJR 1701, (2009)
Times, 30 November, 153 Sol Jo
(no 46) 34, [2009] All ER (D)
288 (Nov) S113

R v Demers [2004] 2 SCR 489, 2004
SCC 46, 19 BHRC 247,
[2005] 1 LRC 263, Can SC S29

R (on the application of A) v Director
of Establishments of the Security
Service. See A v B (Investigatory
Powers Tribunal: jurisdiction)

R (on the application of Guest) v DPP
[2009] EWHC 594 (Admin),
[2009] 2 Cr App Rep 426, 173 JP
511, [2009] Crim LR 730, [2009]
All ER (D) 53 (Mar) S14

R (on the application of Corner House
Research) v Director of the
Serious Fraud Office (BAE
Systems plc, interested party)
[2008] UKHL 60, [2009] AC
756, [2008] 4 All ER 927,
[2009] Crim LR 47, [2008] NLJR
1149, (2008) Times, 31 July, 152
Sol Jo (no 32) 29, [2009] 1 LRC
343, [2008] All ER (D) 399
(Jul) S14

R v Dowds [2012] EWCA Crim 281,
[2012] 3 All ER 154,
[2012] 1 WLR 2576, [2012] 1 Cr
App Rep 455, (2012) Times,
25 April, [2012] All ER (D) 149
(Feb) S53, S83

R (on the application of Breckland) v
Electoral Commission Boundary
Committee for England [2009]
PTSR 1611 .... S60

R (on the application of European
Metal Recycling Ltd) v
Environment Agency
[2012] EWHC 2361 (Admin),
[2012] All ER (D) 06 (Sep) S28

R (on the application of Thomas) v
Greenwich Magistrates' Court
[2009] EWHC 1180 (Admin),

R (on the application of Thomas) v
Greenwich Magistrates' Court
[2009] EWHC 1180 (Admin), – contd
173 JP 345, [2009] Crim LR 800,
[2009] All ER (D) 85 (May) S103
R v H [2004] UKHL 03, [2004] 2 AC
134, [2004] 1 All ER 1269,
[2004] 2 WLR 335, [2004] 2 Cr
App Rep 179, [2004] Crim LR
861, [2004] 08 LS Gaz R 29,
(2004) Times, 6 February, 148
Sol Jo LB 183, [2004] 5 LRC
293, 16 BHRC 332, [2004] All
ER (D) 71 (Feb) S14
R (on the application of Morge) v
Hampshire County Council
[2011] UKSC 2, [2011] 1 All ER
744, [2011] 1 WLR 268,
[2011] LGR 271, [2011] PTSR
337, [2011] NLJR 138, (2011)
Times, 26 January, [2011] All ER
(D) 114 (Jan) S101
R (on the application of Warden and
Fellows of Winchester College) v
Hampshire County Council
[2008] EWCA Civ 431,
[2008] 3 All ER 717,
[2009] 1 WLR 138, [2008] RTR
301, [2008] 18 EG 127 (CS),
(2008) Times, 8 May, [2008] All
ER (D) 396 (Apr) S102
R v Hape [2007] 2 SCR 292 .... S80
R (on the application of Attwood) v
Health Service Comr
[2008] EWHC 2315 (Admin),
[2009] 1 All ER 415, [2009]
PTSR 1330, [2008] All ER (D)
40 (Oct) S11
R v Henry [2005] 3 SCR 609 .... S29
R (on the application of Kaupthing
Bank HF) v HM Treasury
[2009] EWHC 2542 (Admin),
[2009] All ER (D) 220 (Oct) S111
R v Horncastle [2009] UKSC 14,
[2010] 2 AC 373,
[2010] 2 All ER 359,
[2010] 2 WLR 47, [2010] 1 Cr
App Rep 194, [2010] Crim LR
496, (2009) Times, 10 December,
153 Sol Jo (no 48) 32,
[2010] 4 LRC 125, [2009] All
ER (D) 88 (Dec) S99, S112
R v House [2010] EWCA Crim 2270,
[2010] All ER (D) 121 (Oct), sub
nom Dorset County Council v
House (2010) Times,
9 November S83
R v Hughes (2000) 202 CLR 535 .... S49
R v Ikram [2008] EWCA Crim 586,
[2008] 4 All ER 253,
[2009] 1 WLR 1419, [2008] 2 Cr
App Rep 347, [2008] 2 Cr App
Rep (S) 648, [2008] Crim LR

R v Ikram [2008] EWCA Crim 586,
[2008] 4 All ER 253, [2009] 1 WLR
1419, [2008] 2 Cr App Rep 347, [2008]
2 Cr App Rep (S) 648, [2008] Crim LR
– contd
912, [2008] All ER (D) 305
(Mar) S45
R (on the application of the Secretary
of State for the Home
Department) v Immigration
Appeal Tribunal [2001] EWHC
Admin 261, [2001] QB 1224,
[2001] 4 All ER 430,
[2001] 3 WLR 164, [2001] All
ER (D) 85 (Apr) S109
R (on the application of Coke-Wallis)
v Institute of Chartered
Accountants in England and
Wales. See Coke-Wallis v
Institute of Chartered
Accountants in England and
Wales
R v Kelly [2008] EWCA Crim 137,
[2008] 2 All ER 840,
[2009] 1 WLR 701, [2008] 2 Cr
App Rep 133, 172 JP 231, 172
JPN 474, [2008] All ER (D) 122
(Feb) S101
R (on the application of SA) v Kent
County Council [2011] EWCA
Civ 1303, [2012] PTSR 912,
[2012] 1 FCR 355, [2012] 1 FLR
628, (2011) Times, 06 December,
[2011] All ER (D) 79 (Nov) S29
R v L [2009] 1 Cr App R 16 .... S59
R (on the application of TG) v
Lambeth London Borough
Council [2011] EWCA Civ 526,
[2011] 4 All ER 453,
[2011] LGR 889, [2012] PTSR
364, [2011] 2 FCR 443,
[2011] 2 FLR 1007,
[2011] Fam Law 808, (2011)
Times, 3 June, [2011] All ER (D)
39 (May) S108
R (on the application of Gilboy) v
Liverpool City Council
[2008] EWCA Civ 751,
[2009] QB 699, [2008] 4 All ER
127, [2009] 3 WLR 300,
[2008] LGR 521,
[2008] 2 P & CR 544, [2009]
PTSR 987, (2008) Times,
20 August, 152 Sol Jo (no 27)
30, [2008] All ER (D) 13 (Jul) S23
R v Malcolm [2011] EWCA Crim
2069, [2012] Crim LR 238,
[2011] All ER (D) 04 (Sep) S22,
S103
R (on the application of GC) v
Metropolitan Police Comr [2011]
UKSC 21, [2011] 3 All ER 859,
[2011] 2 Cr App Rep 206,

R (on the application of GC) v Metropolitan
Police Comr [2011] UKSC 21,
[2011] 3 All ER 859, [2011] 2 Cr
App Rep 206, – *contd*
[2011] Crim LR 964,
[2011] 22 LS Gaz R 18,
[2011] NLJR 744, 175 CL&J
326, (2011) Times, 19 May,
[2011] All ER (D) 167 (May) S25

R (on the application of L) v
Metropolitan Police Comr [2009]
UKSC 3, [2010] 1 AC 410,
[2010] 1 All ER 113,
[2009] 3 WLR 1056, [2010]
PTSR 245, [2010] 2 FCR 25,
[2010] 1 FLR 643,
[2010] Fam Law 21,
[2009] NLJR 1549, 153 Sol Jo
(no 42) 30, 28 BHRC 391,
[2009] All ER (D) 296 (Oct) S113

R (on the application of Public and
Commercial Services Union) v
Minister for the Civil Service
[2010] EWHC 1027 (Admin),
[2011] 3 All ER 54, [2010] ICR
1198, (2010) Times, 24 May,
[2010] All ER (D) 70 (May) S66,
S73

R v North and East Devon Health
Authority, ex p Coughlan
(Secretary of State for Health and
another intervening) [2001] QB
213, [2000] 3 All ER 850,
[2000] 2 WLR 622, 97 LGR 703,
[1999] Lloyd's Rep Med 306, 51
BMLR 1,
[1999] 31 LS Gaz R 39, 2 CCL
Rep 285, 143 Sol Jo LB 213,
[1999] All ER (D) 801, CA S35

R v Omarjee (1995) 79 A Crim
R 355 .... S38

R (on the application of Roberts) v
Parole Board. See Roberts v
Parole Board

R (on the application of Langley) v
Preston Crown Court
[2008] EWHC 2623 (Admin),
[2009] 3 All ER 1026,
[2009] 1 WLR 1612, 172 JP 605,
172 JPN 845, [2008] All ER (D)
300 (Oct) S14, S113

R (on the application of Gentle) v
Prime Minister [2006] EWCA
Civ 1689, [2007] QB 689,
[2007] 2 WLR 195, (2007)
Times, 1 January, [2006] All ER
(D) 147 (Dec); affd
[2008] UKHL 20, [2008] 1 AC
1356, [2008] 3 All ER 1, (2008)
Times, 10 April, 27 BHRC 1,
[2008] All ER (D) 111 (Apr) S34

R v R [2003] EWCA Crim 2199,
[2003] 4 All ER 882,
[2004] 1 WLR 490, [2004] 1 Cr
App Rep (S) 346,
[2003] Crim LR 898, (2003)
Times, 4 August, [2003] All ER
(D) 437 (Jul) S29

R v Rahman [2008] EWCA Crim
1465, [2008] 4 All ER 661,
[2009] 1 Cr App Rep (S) 402,
[2008] Crim LR 906, (2008)
Times, 15 July, 152 Sol Jo (no
29) 32, [2008] All ER (D) 104
(Jul) S5

R v Raza [2009] EWCA Crim 1413,
[2009] Crim LR 820 .... S52

R (on the application of Heffernan) v
Rent Service [2008] UKHL 58,
[2009] 1 All ER 173,
[2008] 1 WLR 1702, [2009] LGR
87, [2008] HLR 738, (2008)
Times, 20 August, [2008] All ER
(D) 404 (Jul) S56

R v Reynhoudt (1962) 107 CLR 381 ..... S62

R (on the application of McDonald) v
Royal Borough of Kensington
and Chelsea [2011] UKSC 33,
[2011] 4 All ER 881,
[2012] LGR 107, [2011] PTSR
1266, 121 BMLR 164,
[2011] 29 LS Gaz R 17,
[2011] NLJR 1026, (2011)
Times, 7 July, [2011] All ER (D)
47 (Jul) S19, S45

R v S [2009] EWCA Crim 85,
[2009] 2 Cr App Rep 171,
[2009] Crim LR 723, [2009] All
ER (D) 84 (Feb) S103

R v St Lawrence Cement Inc (2002)
60 OR (3d) 712 .... S76

R (on the application of CALA Homes
(South) Ltd) v Secretary of State
for Communities and Local
Government [2011] EWCA Civ
639, [2011] 34 EG 68,
[2011] 2 EGLR 75,
[2011] 22 EG 103 (CS), [2011]
All ER (D) 279 (May) S12

R (on the application of Shrewsbury
and Atcham Borough Council) v
Secretary of State for
Communities and Local
Government [2008] EWCA Civ
148, [2008] 3 All ER 548, (2008)
Times, 12 March, [2008] All ER
(D) 25 (Mar) S32, S33, S63

R (on the application of Animal
Defenders International) v
Secretary of State for Culture,
Media and Sport [2008] UKHL
15, [2008] 1 AC 1312,
[2008] 3 All ER 193,
[2008] 2 WLR 781,

R (on the application of Animal Defenders
    International) v Secretary of State for
    Culture, Media and Sport [2008] UKHL
    15, [2008] 1 AC 1312, [2008] 3 All ER
    193, [2008] 2 WLR 781, – contd
    [2008] IP & T 902, 24 BHRC
    217, [2008] EMLR 299,
    [2008] 5 LRC 687, [2008] All
    ER (D) 155 (Mar) S113
R (on the application of Luton
    Borough Council) v Secretary of
    State for Education
    [2011] EWHC 217 (Admin),
    [2011] LGR 553, [2011] NLJR
    256, [2011] All ER (D) 133
    (Feb) S12
R (on the application of Friends of the
    Earth) v Secretary of State for
    Energy and Climate Change
    [2009] EWCA Civ 810,
    [2010] HLR 313, (2009) Times,
    13 October, [2009] All ER (D)
    331 (Jul) S63
R (on the application of Friends of the
    Earth Ltd) v Secretary of State
    for Energy and Climate Change
    [2012] EWCA Civ 28, 156 Sol Jo
    (no 4) 31, [2012] All ER (D) 139
    (Jan) S41, S42
R (on the application of Bancoult) v
    Secretary of State for Foreign
    and Commonwealth Affairs
    [2008] UKHL 61, [2009] AC
    453, [2008] 4 All ER 1055,
    [2008] 3 WLR 955, [2008] NLJR
    1530, (2008) Times, 23 October,
    152 Sol Jo (no 41) 29,
    [2008] 5 LRC 769, [2008] All
    ER (D) 219 (Oct) S33, S43, S96,
                                        S114
R (on the application of Youssef) v
    Secretary of State for Foreign
    and Commonwealth Affairs
    [2012] EWHC 2091 (Admin),
    [2012] All ER (D) 257 (Jul) S82
R (on the application of Wright) v
    Secretary of State for Health
    [2009] UKHL 3, [2009] AC 739,
    [2009] 2 All ER 129,
    [2009] 2 WLR 267, [2009] PTSR
    401, 106 BMLR 71, (2009)
    Times, 23 January, 153 Sol Jo
    (no 4) 30, 26 BHRC 269, [2009]
    All ER (D) 150 (Jan) S112
R v Secretary of State for Health,
    ex p Hammersmith and Fulham
    London Borough Council
    (1997) 96 LGR 277, 30 HLR
    525; affd [1998] EWCA Civ
    1300, (1998) 31 HLR 475, 49
    BMLR 201, CA S89

R (on the application of Black) v
    Secretary of State for Justice
    [2009] UKHL 1, [2009] AC 949,
    [2009] 4 All ER 1,
    [2009] 2 WLR 282, (2009)
    Times, 30 January, 153 Sol Jo
    (no 4) 27, 26 BHRC 664, [2009]
    All ER (D) 138 (Jan) S113
R (on the application of Bromley) v
    Secretary of State for Justice
    [2010] EWHC 112 (Admin),
    [2010] All ER (D) 23 (Feb) S6
R (on the application of Garland) v
    Secretary of State for Justice
    [2011] EWCA Civ 1335,
    [2012] 1 WLR 1879, [2011] All
    ER (D) 130 (Nov) S6
R (on the application of Shields) v
    Secretary of State for Justice
    [2008] EWHC 3102 (Admin),
    [2010] QB 150, [2009] 3 All ER
    265, [2009] 3 WLR 765, (2009)
    Times, 14 January, [2008] All ER
    (D) 182 (Dec) S33
R v Secretary of State for Social
    Services, ex p Camden London
    Borough Council
    [1987] 2 All ER 560,
    [1987] 1 WLR 819, 131 Sol Jo
    539,
    [1987] LS Gaz R 1242, CA S76
R v Secretary of State for Social
    Security, ex p Sarwar
    [1997] 3 CMLR 648 .... S35
R v Secretary of State for the
    Environment, Transport and the
    Regions, ex p O'Byrne
    [2001] EWCA Civ 499,
    [2002] HLR 567,
    [2001] 16 LS Gaz R 36,
    [2001] EGCS 52, [2001] All ER
    (D) 47 (Apr); affd [2002] UKHL
    45, [2003] 1 All ER 15,
    [2002] 1 WLR 3250, [2003] LGR
    1, [2003] HLR 398,
    [2002] 46 LS Gaz R 35,
    [2002] 48 EGCS 138, (2002)
    Times, 18 November, 146 Sol Jo
    LB 262, [2002] All ER (D) 197
    (Nov) S39
R v Secretary of State for the
    Environment, Transport and the
    Regions, ex p Spath Holme Ltd
    [2001] 2 AC 349,
    [2001] 1 All ER 195,
    [2001] 2 WLR 15, 33 HLR 301,
    [2000] NLJR 1855, 150 NLJ
    1855, 145 Sol Jo LB 39, HL S38
R (on the application of Alvi) v
    Secretary of State for the Home
    Department [2012] UKSC 33,
    [2012] 1 WLR 2208, (2012)
    Times, 08 August, [2012] All ER

R (on the application of Alvi) v Secretary of
State for the Home Department [2012]
UKSC 33, [2012] 1 WLR 2208, (2012)
Times, 08 August, [2012] All ER –
contd
(D) 173 (Jul) S34, S35, S76, S101

R (on the application of BA (Nigeria))
v Secretary of State for the Home
Department [2009] UKSC 7,
[2010] 1 AC 444,
[2010] 2 All ER 95,
[2009] 3 WLR 1253, (2009)
Times, 1 December, 153 Sol Jo
(no 46) 33, [2009] All ER (D)
285 (Nov) S60

R (on the application of BAPIO
Action Ltd) v Secretary of State
for the Home Department
[2008] UKHL 27, [2008] 1 AC
1003, [2009] 1 All ER 93,
[2008] 2 WLR 1073, [2008] ICR
659, (2008) Times, 1 May, [2008]
All ER (D) 410 (Apr) S11, S32, S70

R (on the application of Baiai) v
Secretary of State for the Home
Department [2008] UKHL 53,
[2009] AC 287, [2008] 3 All ER
1094, [2008] 1 FCR 1,
[2008] 2 FLR 1462,
[2008] Fam Law 994,
[2008] Fam Law 955,
[2008] NLJR 1225, (2008)
Times, 13 August, 152 Sol Jo (no
31) 29, 26 BHRC 429, [2008] All
ER (D) 411 (Jul) S53

R (on the application of Daly) v
Secretary of State for the Home
Department [2001] UKHL 26,
[2001] 2 AC 532,
[2001] 3 All ER 433,
[2001] 2 WLR 1622,
[2001] 26 LS Gaz R 43, 145 Sol
Jo LB 156, [2001] 4 LRC 345,
[2001] All ER (D) 280 (May) S61

R (on the application of HRH Sultan
of Pahang) v Secretary of State
for the Home Department
[2011] EWCA Civ 616,
[2011] NLJR 781, (2011) Times,
13 June, [2011] All ER (D) 243
(May) S33

R (on the application of Lumba) v
Secretary of State for the Home
Department [2011] UKSC 12,
[2012] AC 245, [2011] 4 All ER
1, [2011] 2 WLR 671,
[2011] 14 LS Gaz R 20, (2011)
Times, 24 March, 155 Sol Jo (no
12) 30, [2011] All ER (D) 262
(Mar) S13, S17

R (on the application of MM (Ghana))
v Secretary of State for the Home
Department [2012] EWCA Civ

R (on the application of MM (Ghana)) v
Secretary of State for the Home
Department [2012] EWCA Civ – contd
827 .... S16

R (on the application of Mirza) v
Secretary of State for the Home
Department [2011] EWCA Civ
159, (2011) Times, 02 March,
[2011] All ER (D) 245 (Feb) S13

R (on the application of Niazi) v
Secretary of State for the Home
Department [2008] EWCA Civ
755, (2008) Times, 21 July, 152
Sol Jo (no 29) 29, [2008] All ER
(D) 127 (Jul) S96

R (on the application of ST (Eritrea)) v
Secretary of State for the Home
Department [2012] UKSC 12,
[2012] 3 All ER 1037,
[2012] 2 WLR 735,
[2012] 14 LS Gaz R 22, (2012)
Times, 03 April, [2012] All ER
(D) 149 (Mar) S68

R (on the application of Staff Side of
the Police Negotiating Board) v
Secretary of State for the Home
Department [2008] EWHC 1173
(Admin), [2008] All ER (D) 101
(Jun) S63

R (on the application of Stellato) v
Secretary of State for the Home
Department [2007] UKHL 5,
[2007] 2 AC 70, [2007] 2 All ER
737, [2007] 2 WLR 531, (2007)
Times, 16 March, 151 Sol Jo LB
395, [2007] All ER (D) 251
(Mar) S34

R v Secretary of State for the Home
Department, ex p Adan
[2001] 2 AC 477,
[2001] 1 All ER 593,
[2001] 2 WLR 143, (2000)
Times, 20 December, 145 Sol Jo
LB 15, [2000] All ER (D)
2357, HL S69

R v Secretary of State for the Home
Department, ex p Stafford
[1999] 2 AC 38, [1998] 4 All ER
7, [1998] 3 WLR 372,
[1998] 34 LS Gaz R 31,
[1998] NLJR 1142, 142 Sol Jo
LB 244, [1998] All ER (D)
368, HL S81

R (on the application of Irving) v
Secretary of State for Transport
[2008] EWHC 1200 (Admin),
172 JP 425, 172 JPN 594, [2008]
All ER (D) 124 (May) S111

R (on the application of Bradley) v
Secretary of State for Work and
Pensions [2008] EWCA Civ 36,
[2009] QB 114, [2008] 3 All ER
1116, [2008] 3 WLR 1059,

R (on the application of Bradley) v Secretary
of State for Work and Pensions
[2008] EWCA Civ 36, [2009] QB 114,
[2008] 3 All ER 1116, [2008] 3 WLR
1059, – contd
(2008) Times, 25 February,
[2008] All ER (D) 98 (Feb) S15

R (on the application of Payne
(Eunice) & Cooper (Gail)) v
Secretary of State for Work and
Pensions [2010] EWHC 2162
(Admin), [2010] BPIR 1389 . . . . S63

R (on the application of RD) v
Secretary of State for Work and
Pensions [2010] EWCA Civ 18,
[2010] 1 WLR 1782, 112 BMLR
140, (2010) Times, 1 February,
[2010] All ER (D) 172 (Jan) S55

R v Sekhon [2002] EWCA Crim 2954,
[2003] 3 All ER 508,
[2003] 1 WLR 1655, [2003] 1 Cr
App Rep 575, [2003] 2 Cr App
Rep (S) 207, [2003] Crim LR
642, [2003] 08 LS Gaz R 29,
(2002) Times, 27 December, 147
Sol Jo LB 148, [2002] All ER
(D) 233 (Dec); affd
[2005] UKHL 50, [2006] 1 AC
368, [2005] 4 All ER 347,
[2005] 3 WLR 330, [2006] 1 Cr
App Rep (S) 460,
[2006] Crim LR 171,
[2005] NLJR 1316, (2005)
Times, 27 July, [2005] All ER
(D) 307 (Jul) S7

R (on the application of M) v Slough
Borough Council [2008] UKHL
52, [2008] 4 All ER 831,
[2008] 1 WLR 1808, [2008] LGR
871, [2008] HLR 763, (2008)
Times, 5 September, 152 Sol Jo
(no 32) 30, [2008] All ER (D)
412 (Jul) S106

R v Smith [2003] NSWCCA 381 . . . . S20

R v South Ribble Borough Council
Housing Benefit Review Board,
ex p Hamilton [2000] EWCA Civ
518, 32 HLR 261 . . . . S103

R (on the application of Morgan
Grenfell & Co Ltd) v Special
Comr of Income Tax
[2002] UKHL 21, [2003] 1 AC
563, [2002] 3 All ER 1,
[2002] 2 WLR 1299, [2002] STC
786, 74 TC 511, 4 ITLR 809,
[2002] 25 LS Gaz R 35, (2002)
Times, 20 May, 146 Sol Jo LB
126, [2002] All ER (D) 239
(May) S81

R (on the application of Green &
Green Scaffolding Co) v Staines
Magistrates' Court [2008] EWHC
1443 (Admin), 172 JP 353,

R (on the application of Green & Green
Scaffolding Co) v Staines Magistrates'
Court [2008] EWHC 1443 (Admin), 172
JP 353, – contd
[2008] All ER (D) 211 (May),
sub nom R (on the application of
Green) 172 JPN 525 . . . . S99

R v T [2009] 1 Ac 1310 . . . . S98

R v T [2010] 1 WLR 630 . . . . S85

R (on the application of Woolas) v The
Parliamentary Election Court
[2010] EWHC 3169 (Admin),
[2012] QB 1, [2010] NLJR 1756,
[2010] All ER (D) 60 (Dec) . . . S62, S73

R v Tran Viet Tran [1992] 2 HKLR
184 . . . . S42

R (on the application of Cart) v Upper
Tribunal [2009] EWHC 3052
(Admin), [2011] QB 120,
[2010] 1 All ER 908,
[2010] 2 WLR 1012, [2010] STC
493, [2010] PTSR 824,
[2010] 2 FCR 309, [2009] All ER
(D) 22 (Dec); affd on other
grounds sub nom R (on the
application of Cart) v Upper
Tribunal (Secretary of State for
Justice, interested party) (Public
Law Project intervening)
[2010] EWCA Civ 859,
[2011] QB 120, [2010] 4 All ER
714, [2011] 2 WLR 36,
[2010] STC 2556, [2011] PTSR
42, [2010] NLJR 1115, (2010)
Times, 4 October, [2010] All ER
(D) 246 (Jul); affd on other
grounds sub nom R (on the
application of Cart) v Upper
Tribunal [2011] UKSC 28,
[2012] AC 663, [2011] 4 All ER
127, [2011] STC 1659, [2011]
PTSR 1053, [2012] 1 FLR 997,
[2012] Fam Law 398,
[2011] NLJR 916, (2011) Times,
23 June, [2011] All ER (D) 149
(Jun) S16

R (on the application of
Sivasubramaniam) v Wandsworth
County Court [2002] EWCA Civ
1738, [2003] 2 All ER 160,
[2003] 1 WLR 475,
[2003] 03 LS Gaz R 34, (2002)
Times, 30 November, [2002] All
ER (D) 431 (Nov) S16

R (on the application of Governors of
Brynmawr Foundation School) v
Welsh Ministers [2011] EWHC
519 (Admin), [2011] All ER (D)
110 (Mar) S39

R (on the application of Sainsbury's
Supermarkets Ltd) v
Wolverhampton City Council
[2010] UKSC 20, [2011] 1 AC

R (on the application of Sainsbury's
Supermarkets Ltd) v Wolverhampton
City Council [2010] UKSC 20,
[2011] 1 AC – *contd*
437, [2010] 4 All ER 931,
[2010] 2 WLR 1173, [2010] LGR
727, [2011] 1 P & CR 1, [2010]
PTSR 1103, [2010] 2 EGLR 103,
[2010] NLJR 731, [2010] RVR
237, (2010) Times, 13 May, 154
Sol Jo (no 20) 36, [2010] All ER
(D) 98 (May) S83

R v Wonderland Gifts Ltd (1996) 140
Nfld & PEIR 219 .... S3

R v Zafar [2008] EWCA Crim 184,
[2008] QB 810, [2008] 4 All ER
46, [2008] 2 WLR 1013,
[2008] 2 Cr App Rep 84,
[2008] NLJR 298, (2008) Times,
15 February, [2008] All ER (D)
189 (Feb) S67

R & R Fazzolari Pty Ltd v Parramatta
City Council [2009] HCA 12 .... S83

Radin v Vekic [1997] NCWSC 234 .... S40

Ramdass (Herman) v Bahaw-Nanan
(Marilyn) [2009] UKPC 51 .... S65

Ravat v Halliburton Manufacturing and
Services Ltd [2012] UKSC 1,
[2012] 2 All ER 905, [2012] ICR
389, [2012] IRLR 315, 156 Sol
Jo (no 6) 31,
[2012] 08 LS Gaz R 19,
[2012] NLJR 262, (2012) Times,
15 February, 2012 SLT 406,
[2012] All ER (D) 49 (Feb) S44

Registrar of Liquor Licences v Iliadis
(1988) 19 FCR 311 .... S84

Repatriation Commission v Morris
(1997) 79 FCR 455 .... S94

Revenue and Customs Comrs v
Dunwood Travel Ltd
[2008] EWCA Civ 174,
[2008] STC 959, [2008] All ER
(D) 104 (Mar) S35

Revenue and Customs Comrs v
Halcyon Films LLP
[2010] EWCA Civ 261,
[2010] STC 1125, 80 TC 475,
[2010] All ER (D) 197 (Mar) S72

Revenue and Customs Comrs v
Stringer (sub nom Ainsworth v
IRC) [2009] UKHL 31,
[2009] 4 All ER 1205,
[2009] ICR 985, [2009] IRLR
677, (2009) Times, 15 June,
[2009] All ER (D) 168 (Jun) S38

Risk Management Partners Ltd v Brent
London Borough Council. See R
(on the application of Risk
Management Partners Ltd) v
Brent London Borough Council

Roberts v Parole Board [2005] UKHL
45, [2006] 1 All ER 39,
[2005] 3 WLR 152, [2005] NLJR
1096, (2005) Times, 8 July,
[2005] All ER (D) 82 (Jul), sub
nom R (on the application of
Roberts) v Parole Board
[2005] 2 AC 738 .... S17

Roberts v Secretary of State for Social
Security [2001] EWCA Civ
910 .... S102

Robinson v Sunday Newspapers Ltd
[2011] NICA 13 .... S21

Russell (Superintendent of the Royal
Ulster Constabulary) v Devine
[2003] UKHL 24, [2003] NI 224,
[2003] 1 WLR 1187, [2003] 2 Cr
App Rep 421, [2003] Crim LR
808, (2003) Times, 9 May, 147
Sol Jo LB 597, [2003] All ER
(D) 76 (May) S54

Ruttle Plant Ltd v Secretary of State
for the Environment, Food and
Rural Affairs [2008] EWHC 238
(TCC), [2009] 1 All ER 448,
[2008] BPIR 1395, [2008] All ER
(D) 270 (Jun) S77

S (L) v P (E) (1999) 67 BCLR (3d)
254 .... S41

Saeed v Minister for Immigration and
Citizenship (2010) 241 CLR
252 .... S81

Salisbury Independent Living Ltd v
Wirral Metropolitan Borough
Council [2012] EWCA Civ 84,
[2012] PTSR 1221, [2012] HLR
385, [2012] All ER (D) 69
(Feb) S110

Sandvik Australia Pty Ltd v
Commonwealth of Australia
[1990] FCA 386 103

Schanka v Employment National
(Administration) Ltd
(2000) 97 FCR 186 .... S108

Schanka v Employment National
(Administration) Ltd [2001] FCA
1623 .... S66

Scottish & Newcastle plc v Raguz
[2008] UKHL 65,
[2009] 1 All ER 763, [2009] 2
All ER (Comm) 447,
[2008] 1 WLR 2994, [2009] Bus
LR 72, [2009] 1 P & CR 127,
[2008] 3 EGLR 115,
[2008] NLJR 1567, [2008] 44 EG
114 (CS), (2008) Times,
3 November, 152 Sol Jo (no 42)
30, [2008] All ER (D) 283
(Oct) S71, S92

Seafairers' Retirement Fund Pty Ltd v
Oppenhuis (1999) 94 FCR 594 ..... S31

Secretary of State for Justice v Lau
Suk Han [1998] 2 HKLRD 14 ..... S105

Secretary of State for Justice v Tang
Ben [1999] 3 HKC 647 .... S105
Secretary of State for the Home
Department v AY [2012] EWHC
2054 (Admin) S53, S55, S70
Secretary of State for Work and
Pensions v Deane [2010] EWCA
Civ 699, [2011] PTSR 289,
[2010] ELR 662, [2010] All ER
(D) 201 (Jun) S35
Sellers v Maritime Safety Inspector
[1999] 2 NZLR 44 .... S79, S80
Seray-Wurie v Hackney London
Borough Council (No 2)
[2002] EWCA Civ 909,
[2002] 3 All ER 448,
[2003] 1 WLR 257,
[2002] 33 LS Gaz R 21, (2002)
Times, 4 July, [2002] All ER (D)
199 (Jun) S18
Serco Ltd t/a Serco Docklands v
National Union of Rail, Maritime
and Transport Workers
[2011] EWCA Civ 226,
[2011] 3 All ER 913, [2011] ICR
848, [2011] IRLR 399,
[2011] NLJR 405, [2011] All ER
(D) 65 (Mar) S102
Serious Fraud Office v Lexi
Holdings plc [2008] EWCA Crim
1443, [2009] QB 376,
[2009] 1 All ER 586,
[2009] 2 WLR 905, [2009] Bus
LR 647, [2009] 1 Cr App Rep
295, (2008) Times, 18 August,
[2008] BPIR 1598, [2008] All ER
(D) 149 (Jul) S97
Serious Organised Crime Agency v
Perry (proceedings under the
Proceeds of Crime Act 2002)
[2009] EWHC 1960 (Admin),
[2010] 1 WLR 910, [2009] All
ER (D) 337 (Jul); affd sub nom
Serious Organised Crime Agency
v Perry [2010] EWHC 1711
(Admin), [2010] 1 WLR 2761,
(2010) Times, 22 July, [2010] All
ER (D) 101 (Jul); affd
[2010] EWCA Civ 907,
[2011] 1 WLR 542, (2010)
Times, 13 October, [2010] All
ER (D) 317 (Jul); sub nom Perry
v Serious Organised Crime
Agency [2011] EWCA Civ 578,
[2011] 4 All ER 470,
[2011] 1 WLR 2817, 175 CL&J
327, (2011) Times, 10 June,
[2011] All ER (D) 176 (May);
sub nom Perry v Serious
Organised Crime Agency [2012]
UKSC 35, [2012] 3 WLR 379,
[2012] NLJR 1028, (2012)
Times, 17 August, [2012] All ER

Serious Organised Crime Agency v Perry
(proceedings under the Proceeds of
Crime Act 2002) [2009] EWHC 1960
(Admin), [2010] 1 WLR 910, [2009] All
ER (D) 337 (Jul); affd sub nom Serious
Organised Crime Agency v Perry
[2010] EWHC 1711 (Admin),
[2010] 1 WLR 2761, (2010) Times,
22 July, [2010] All ER (D) 101 (Jul);
affd [2010] EWCA Civ 907,
[2011] 1 WLR 542, (2010) Times,
13 October, [2010] All ER (D) 317 (Jul);
sub nom Perry v Serious Organised
Crime Agency [2011] EWCA Civ 578,
[2011] 4 All ER 470, [2011] 1 WLR
2817, 175 CL&J 327, (2011) Times,
10 June, [2011] All ER (D) 176 (May);
sub nom Perry v Serious Organised
Crime Agency [2012] UKSC 35,
[2012] 3 WLR 379, [2012] NLJR 1028,
(2012) Times, 17 August, [2012] All ER
– contd
(D) 252 (Jul) S42
SerVaas Incorporated v Rafidain Bank
[2012] UKSC 40, [2012] 3 WLR
545, [2012] 33 LS Gaz R 16,
[2012] All ER (D) 117 (Aug) S43
Sharratt v London Central Bus Co Ltd
[2002] EWHC 9006 (Costs) S70
Shields v Chief Comr of Police [2008]
VSC 2 .... S37
Sienkiewicz v Greif (UK) Ltd [2011]
UKSC 10, [2011] 2 AC 229,
[2011] 2 All ER 857,
[2011] 2 WLR 523, [2011] ICR
391, 119 BMLR 54, (2011)
Times, 10 March, 155 Sol Jo (no
10) 30, [2011] All ER (D) 107
(Mar) S101
Sinclair Gardens Investments
(Kensington) Ltd v Poets Chase
Freehold Co Ltd [2007] EWHC
1776 (Ch), [2008] 2 All ER 187,
[2007] 49 EG 104, [2007] NLJR
1427, [2007] 32 EG 89 (CS),
[2007] All ER (D) 425 (Jul), sub
nom Poets Chase
Freehold Co Ltd v Sinclair
Gardens Investments
(Kensington) Ltd [2008] 1 WLR
768 .... S86, S97
Sinclair Investments (UK) Ltd v
Versailles Trade Finance Ltd (in
admin) [2011] EWCA Civ 347,
[2011] 4 All ER 335, [2011] Bus
LR 1126, [2011] 2 BCLC 501,
[2011] 2 P & CR D14, [2011] All
ER (D) 321 (Mar) S52
Sloane v Minister of Immigration,
Local Government and Ethnic
Affairs (1992) 37 FCR 429 .... S49

Smith v Northamptonshire County
    Council [2009] UKHL 27,
    [2009] 4 All ER 557, [2009] ICR
    734, 110 BMLR 15, [2009] PIQR
    P292, (2009) Times, 21 May, 153
    Sol Jo (no 20) 39, [2009] All ER
    (D) 170 (May) S49
Society Promoting Environmental
    Conservation v Canada (A-G)
    (2002) FTR 236 .... S84
Solicitor 24/07 v Law Society of Hong
    Kong [2008] 2 HKLRD 576 .... S30,
                                        S100
Sonea v Mehedinti District Court,
    Romania [2009] EWHC 89
    (Admin), [2009] 2 All ER 821,
    [2009] All ER (D) 167 (Jan) S87
Southern Pacific Personal Loans Ltd v
    Walker [2009] EWCA Civ 1218,
    [2010] 1 All ER (Comm) 854,
    [2010] Bus LR 418, [2009] All
    ER (D) 139 (Nov); affd [2010]
    UKSC 32, [2010] 4 All ER 277,
    [2011] 1 All ER (Comm) 164,
    [2010] 1 WLR 1819, [2010] Bus
    LR 1396, [2010] NLJR 1011,
    (2010) Times, 12 July, [2010] All
    ER (D) 66 (Jul) S57
Specialiser Tech Inc v Specialalloy
    Indsuctries Ltd [1999] 12 WWR
    139 .... S105
Spencer v Secretary of Work and
    Pensions [2008] EWCA Civ 750,
    [2009] QB 358, [2009] 1 All ER
    314, [2009] 2 WLR 593,
    [2008] 3 CMLR 429, [2009] RTR
    39, [2008] ICR 1359,
    [2008] IRLR 911, [2008] PIQR
    P374, (2008) Times, 24 July, 152
    Sol Jo (no 27) 31, [2008] All ER
    (D) 20 (Jul) S111
Spencer-Franks v Kellogg Brown and
    Root Ltd [2008] UKHL 46,
    [2009] 1 All ER 269, [2008] ICR
    863, [2008] NLJR 1004,
    [2008] PIQR P389, (2008)
    Times, 3 July, 2008 SLT 675,
    2008 SCLR 484, 152 Sol Jo (no
    27) 30, [2008] All ER (D) 26
    (Jul) S111
Spirerose Ltd (in admin) v Transport
    for London (formerly London
    Underground Ltd) [2009] UKHL
    44, [2009] 4 All ER 810,
    [2009] 1 WLR 1797, [2009]
    PTSR 1371, [2009] 3 EGLR 103,
    [2009] RVR 225, (2009) Times,
    17 August, [2009] All ER (D)
    324 (Jul) S46
Spread Trustee Co Ltd v Hutcheson
    [2011] UKPC 13,
    [2012] 1 All ER 251,
    [2012] 2 WLR 1360, 14 ITELR

Spread Trustee Co Ltd v Hutcheson
    [2011] UKPC 13, [2012] 1 All ER 251,
    [2012] 2 WLR 1360, 14 ITELR – contd
    37, [2012] 1 LRC 102, [2011] All
    ER (D) 51 (Jul) S40
Standard Chartered Bank v Ceylon
    Petroleum Corpn [2012] EWCA
    Civ 1049, [2012] All ER (D) 317
    (Jul) S51
Steele Ford & Newton v Crown
    Prosecution Service (No 2)
    [1994] 1 AC 22, [1993] 2 All ER
    769, [1993] 2 WLR 934,
    [1993] 27 LS Gaz R 34,
    [1993] NLJR 847, 137 Sol Jo LB
    152, HL S65
Stubbings v Webb [1993] AC 498,
    [1993] 1 All ER 322,
    [1993] 2 WLR 120,
    [1993] 2 FCR 699, [1993] 1 FLR
    714, [1993] Fam Law 342, 11
    BMLR 1, [1993] 6 LS Gaz R 41,
    137 Sol Jo LB 32, HL S66
Sugar v British Broadcasting CorpN
    [2012] UKSC 4, [2012] 2 All ER
    509, [2012] 1 WLR 439,
    [2012] NLJR 294, (2012) Times,
    28 February, 156 Sol Jo (no 11)
    31, [2012] All ER (D) 108
    (Feb) S111
Syed v DPP [2010] EWHC 81
    (Admin), [2010] 1 Cr App Rep
    480, 174 JP 97,
    [2010] 04 LS Gaz R 14, (2010)
    Times, 26 January, [2010] All ER
    (D) 48 (Jan) S108
T (children), Re [2012] UKSC 36,
    [2012] 1 WLR 2281,
    [2012] 3 FCR 137, [2012] NLJR
    1028, (2012) Times, 14 August,
    [2012] All ER (D) 254 (Jul) S21
Taylor v Centennial Newstan Pty Ltd
    [2009] NSWCA 276 .... S86
Taylor v Lawrence [2002] EWCA Civ
    90, [2002] QB 528,
    [2002] 2 All ER 353,
    [2002] 3 WLR 640,
    [2002] 12 LS Gaz R 35,
    [2002] NLJR 221, (2002) Times,
    8 February, 146 Sol Jo LB 50,
    [2002] All ER (D) 28 (Feb) S18
Taylor Woodrow Property Co Ltd v
    Lonrho Textiles Ltd
    (1986) 52 P & CR 28,
    [1985] 2 EGLR 120, 275 Estates
    Gazette 632 .... S30
Transpower New Zealand Ltd v Taupo
    District Council [2007] NZHC
    999 .... S61
Trendtex Trading Corpn v Central
    Bank of Nigeria [1977] QB 529,
    [1977] 1 All ER 881,
    [1977] 2 WLR 356,

Trendtex Trading Corpn v Central Bank of
    Nigeria [1977] QB 529, [1977] 1 All ER
    881, [1977] 2 WLR 356, – *contd*
    [1977] 2 CMLR 465,
    [1977] 1 Lloyd's Rep 581, 10
    LDAB 8, 121 Sol Jo 85, CA S21,
                                          S82
Trent Taverns Ltd v Sykes
    (1999) Eu LR 492, (1999) Times,
    5 March, CA S29
Trim v North Dorset District Council
    of Nordon [2010] EWCA Civ
    1446, [2011] 1 WLR 1901,
    [2011] 2 P & CR 115, [2011]
    PTSR 1110, [2011] 1 EGLR 61,
    (2011) Times, 18 January, [2010]
    All ER (D) 227 (Dec) S27
Tse Mui Chun v HKSAR (2003) 6
    HKCFAR 601 .... S99
Uganda Co (Holdings) v Government
    of Uganda [1979] 1 Lloyd's Rep
    481, 123 Sol Jo 48 .... S30
UK Waste Management, Re [1999]
    NICA 2 .... S50
United States Securities and Exchange
    Commission v Manterfield
    [2009] EWCA Civ 27,
    [2009] 2 All ER 1009, [2009] 2
    All ER (Comm) 941,
    [2009] 1 Lloyd's Rep 399, (2009)
    Times, 18 March, [2009] All ER
    (D) 225 (Jan) S34
Vector Ltd v Transpower New
    Zealand Ltd [1999] 3 NZLR
    646 .... S31
Victims Compensation Fund Corpn v
    Brown (2003) 201 ALR 260 .... S20,
                                         S107
Victor Chandler (International) Ltd v
    Zhou Chu Jian He (CACV 373 of
    2007) (22 May 2008,
    unreported), HKCA S98
Virdi v Law Society (Solicitors
    Disciplinary Tribunal intervening)
    [2010] EWCA Civ 100,
    [2010] 3 All ER 653,
    [2010] 1 WLR 2840,
    [2010] 09 LS Gaz R 14, [2010]
    All ER (D) 172 (Feb) S15, S52
WD, Re [2007] Scot CS CSOH 139 ...... S93
Waitakere CC v Bennett [2008] NZCA
    428 .... S41
Walker v Baird [1892] AC 491, 61
    LJPC 92, 67 LT 513, PC S79
Walker v New South Wales (1994) 182
    CLR 45, 49 .... S43
Wang v Minster for Immigration &
    Multicultural Affairs
    (1997) 71 FCR 386 .... S50, S95
Wang v SWCA 321 .... S23
Ward v Chief Adjudication Officer
    [1998] EWCA Civ 1552 ...... S62, S63,
                                          S72

Ward-Price v Mariners Haven Inc
    (2001) 57 OR (3d) 410 .... S95
Warren v Random House Group Ltd
    [2008] EWCA Civ 834,
    [2009] QB 600, [2009] 2 All ER
    245, [2009] 2 WLR 314,
    [2009] EMLR 1, [2008] All ER
    (D) 224 (Jul) S97
Wealthcare Financial Planning Pty Ltd
    v Financial Industry Complaints
    Service Ltd (2009) 69 ACSR
    418 .... S56
Webster, Re, Webster v Norfolk
    County Council [2009] EWCA
    Civ 59, [2009] 2 All ER 1156,
    [2009] 1 FCR 673, [2009] 1 FLR
    1378, [2009] Fam Law 381, 153
    Sol Jo (no 7) 31, [2009] All ER
    (D) 106 (Feb) S78
Welwyn Hatfield Borough Council v
    Secretary of State for
    Communities and Local
    Government [2010] EWCA Civ
    26, [2010] 2 P & CR 157, [2010]
    PTSR 1296, [2010] 1 EGLR 98,
    [2010] 07 LS Gaz R 19,
    [2010] 13 EG 84, 154 Sol Jo (no
    5) 28, [2010] All ER (D) 199
    (Jan); revsd [2011] UKSC 15,
    [2011] 2 AC 304,
    [2011] 4 All ER 851,
    [2011] 2 WLR 905, [2011] LGR
    459, [2011] 2 P & CR 160,
    [2011] PTSR 825,
    [2011] 2 EGLR 151,
    [2011] 16 LS Gaz R 16,
    [2011] NLJR 550, (2011) Times,
    8 April, 155 Sol Jo (no 14) 30,
    [2011] All ER (D) 44 (Apr) ... S77, S94,
                                         S103
Westbrook Dolphin Square Ltd v
    Friends Life Ltd [2012] EWCA
    Civ 666, [2012] 4 All ER 148,
    [2012] 1 WLR 2752,
    [2012] 2 P & CR 150,
    [2012] HLR 604, [2012] NLJR
    751, [2012] 32 Estates Gazette
    42, 156 Sol Jo (no 21) 31, [2012]
    All ER (D) 156 (May) S79
Wicken (Litigation Guardian of) v
    Harssar (2004) 73 OR (3d) 600 .... S91,
                                    S92, S93
Wilson v First County Trust Ltd
    [2003] UKHL 40, [2004] 1 AC
    816, [2003] 4 All ER 97, [2003]
    2 All ER (Comm) 491,
    [2003] 3 WLR 568,
    [2003] 35 LS Gaz R 39, (2003)
    Times, 11 July, 147 Sol Jo LB
    872, [2004] 2 LRC 618, [2003]
    All ER (D) 187 (Jul) S41

Woodward v Abbey National plc
   [2005] 4 All ER 1346,
   [2005] ICR 1702, [2005] IRLR
   782, [2005] All ER (D) 64
   (Aug), EAT; revsd [2006] EWCA
   Civ 822, [2006] 4 All ER 1209,
   [2006] ICR 1436, [2006] IRLR
   677, (2006) Times, 11 July, 150
   Sol Jo LB 857, [2006] All ER
   (D) 253 (Jun) S5
X (minors) v Bedfordshire County
   Council [1995] 2 AC 633,
   [1995] 3 All ER 353,
   [1995] 3 WLR 152, 160 LG
   Rev 103, [1995] 3 FCR 337,
   [1995] 2 FLR 276,
   [1995] Fam Law 537,
   [1995] ELR 404, 26 BMLR 15,
   [1995] NLJR 993, HL S10
Yarl's Wood Immigration Ltd v
   Bedfordshire Police Authority
   [2009] EWCA Civ 1110,
   [2010] QB 698, [2010] 2 All ER
   221, [2010] 2 WLR 1322, [2009]
   All ER (D) 246 (Oct) S66
Yearworth v North Bristol NHS Trust
   [2009] EWCA Civ 37,
   [2010] QB 1, [2009] 2 All ER
   986, [2009] 3 WLR 118, 107
   BMLR 47, (2009) Times,

Yearworth v North Bristol NHS Trust
   [2009] EWCA Civ 37, [2010] QB 1,
   [2009] 2 All ER 986, [2009] 3 WLR
   118, 107 BMLR 47, (2009) Times, –
   contd
   10 February, 153 Sol Jo (no 5)
   27, [2009] All ER (D) 33 (Feb) S59
Yemshaw v Hounslow London
   Borough Council [2009] EWCA
   Civ 1543 .... S70
Yemshaw v Hounslow London
   Borough Council [2011] UKSC
   3, [2011] 1 All ER 912,
   [2011] 1 WLR 433, [2011] PTSR
   462, [2011] 1 FCR 576,
   [2011] 1 FLR 1614,
   [2011] Fam Law 349,
   [2011] HLR 251,
   [2011] 06 LS Gaz R 20,
   [2011] NLJR 174, (2011) Times,
   28 January, 155 Sol Jo (no 5) 30,
   [2011] 4 LRC 191, [2011] All
   ER (D) 187 (Jan) S48, S49, S87
Yukos Capital Sarl v OJSC Rosneft
   Oil Co [2012] EWCA Civ 855,
   [2012] 2 Lloyd's Rep 208, 143
   ConLR 1, [2012] All ER (D) 188
   (Jun) S33
Zaoui v A-G (No 2) [2006] 1 NZLR
   289 .... S80

Supplementary Table of Statutes

Administration of Justice Act 1960
  s 1(1)(a) S26
  (2) S26
Animals Act 1971
  s 5(2) S104
Anti-terrorism, Crime and Security
  Act 2001
s 109 .... S44
  Arbitration Act 1996
s1 .... S15
Care Standards Act 2000
  s 82(4)(b) S112
Children Act 1989 .... S108
Companies Act 1985
  s 36C(1) S4
Constitutional Reform Act 2005
  Pt III S26
  s 23 .... S15
  s 40(2) S26
  (3) S25, S76
  (4)(b) S27
  (6) S26
  s 41(3)(a) S30
  Sch 9 .... S27
Consumer Credit Act 1974 .... S56
Courts and Legal Services Act 1990 ...... S17
  s 27(2)(c) S20
Criminal Appeal Act 1968
  Pt II S26
  s 33(2) S26
Criminal Justice Act 1967
  s 91(1) S45
Criminal Justice Act 2003
  s 44(6) S74
  s 78 .... S99
  s 166(3)(b) S52
  s 269, 270 .... S46
Criminal Justice and Court Services
  Act 2000
  Sch 2
    para 16 .... S32
Criminal Justice and Immigration
  Act 2008
  s 79 .... S31
  s 149 .... S31
  s 153(2) S31
  Sch 28 .... S31
Criminal Law Act 1967
  s 14 .... S77
Defamation Act 1996
  s 2–4 .... S97
Electricity Act 1989
  s 29(3) S9
Employment Rights Act 1996
  s 203(1)(b) S8

Equality Act 2010
  s 144(1) S8
Extradition Act 2003
  s 34 .... S84
Female Genital Mutilation Act 2003
  s 6(1) S57
Firearms Act 1968
  s 5(1A) S39
Gaming Act 1968
  s 52(1) S101
Government of Wales Act 2006
  s 78 .... S4
Healthcare Identifiers Act 2010
  s 15 .... S104
Housing Act 1996 .... S108
Human Rights Act 1998 .... S33
  s 3(1) S81, S112
Hunting Act 2004
  s 1 .... S100
Immigration Act 1971
  s 22(2)(a) S108, S109
Immigration, Asylum and Nationality
  Act 2006
  s 54 .... S68
Immigration (Treatment of Claimants,
  Etc) Act 2004
  s 19(3)(b) S53
Income Tax (Earnings and Pensions)
  Act 2003 .... S31
  Pt 7 .... S4
Interpretation Act 1901 .... S3
  s 13(3) S104
Interpretation Act 1978
  s 6(c) S60
  s 16 .... S39
Interpretation Act 2005 .... S58, S59
Landlord and Tenant Act 1954
  Pt II S8
  s 38(1) S8
  (4) S8
Limitation Act 1980
  s 2 .... S111
Local Government and Public
  Involvement in Health Act 2007
  s 5(3)(c) S59
  s 7(1)(b) S59
Localism Act 2011
  s 28(4) S6
National Assistance Act 1948
  s 21(1)(a) S106
Patents Act 1977 .... S67
  s 130(7) S68
Perjury Act 1911 .... S104

Police and Criminal Evidence
  Act 1984
  s 17(1)(e) S108
Proceeds of Crime Act 2002
  s 14(11) S7
Public Order Act 1986
  s 11 .... S110
Restrictive Trade Practices Act 1976 ..... S50
Senior Courts Act 1981 ... S7, S13, S17, S18,
                     S22, S23, S24, S27,
                     S28, S29, S39, S42,

Senior Courts Act 1981 – *contd*
                     S44, S52, S76, S78,
                     S87, S96, S97, S106,
                     S109, S111
  s 72(5) S107
Sexual Offences Act 2003
  s 72 .... S44
Terrorism Act 2000
  s 1 .... S68
Tribunals and Inquiries Act 1992
  s 11(1) S24

Supplementary Table of Statutory Instruments

Civil Procedure Rules 1998,
   SI 1998/3132 .... S74, S75
Pt 32
   r 32.14 .... S14

Conditional Fee Agreements
   Regulations 2000, SI 2000/692 .... S4

Supplementary Table of European Material

European Convention on the Grant of
European Patents of 5 October
1973 (European Patent
Convention) (EPC) S68
European Convention on Human
Rights (Rome, 4 November 1950)
art 5(4) S113

European Convention on Human Rights
(Rome, 4 November 1950) – *contd*
art 6 .... S100, S113
art 9 .... S113

Supplementary Table of Foreign Enactments

AUSTRALIA
Australian Capital Territories:
Legislative Instruments Act 2003 .... S37
    s 14 .... S76
Magistrates Act 1991 (Queensland) S19

New South Wales:
Crimes Act 1900
    s 312 .... S47
    s 319 .... S47

COMMONWEALTH
Acts Interpretation Act 1901 .... S3

TRININDAD AND TOBAGO
Motor Vehicles Insurance (Third-Party
    Risks)
    s 4(7) S90

NEW ZEALAND
Interpretation Act 1999
    s 5(1) S3

Introduction

This is the Second, and Cumulative, Supplement to the Fifth Edition of *Bennion on Statutory Interpretation*. The Sixth Edition is underway and will be published in 2014. Due to the scale of the task of preparing the Sixth Edition, and the many developments since the publication of the First Supplement to the Fifth Edition, the Second Supplement has been released. This has occurred at a time of change in the life of the author, having returned from Hong Kong to his native Australia and from academia to legal practice. I am grateful to my colleagues at Clayton Utz for their ideas and support. My work there has enhanced the perspective I seek to bring to *Bennion*. I anticipate the same will occur when I enter practice as a barrister at Seven Wentworth Chambers in September 2013. I trust the Second Supplement will be useful for readers and look forward to introducing the Sixth Edition in 2014.

Oliver Jones

Parts I to XXX

Updates

(p 6)

Intro

In footnote 3 delete second sentence and insert–

See generally Devolution: Its Effect on the Practice of Legislation at Westminster HK Paper 192, 18 November 2004, including the paper by C Himsworth at App 1. See also, by the same author, 'Devolution and its Jurisdictional Assymetries', (2007) 70 MLR 31–58.

(p 23)

s 1

In footnote 5 at end insert–

Compare the remark by the Hon Murray Gleeson, when Chief Justice of Australia, 'I shall use the words 'interpretation' and 'construction' interchangeably, as they are in the Acts Interpretation Act 1901 (Cth) in 'The meaning of legislation: context, purpose and respect for fundamental rights' (2009) 20 Public Law Review 26, at 27 n 2.

(p 24)

s 2

After sideheading Subsection (1), insert–

This subsection of the Code has been judicially approved.[8A]

(p 24)

Insert new footnote 8A–

See the opinion of Lord Brodie in *Imperial Tobacco Ltd v Lord Advocate* [2012] CSIH 9 at [175].

(p 25)

s 3

After sideheading Subsection (2) insert–

This subsection of the Code has been judicially approved.[5A]

(p 25)

Insert new footnote 5A–

See the decision of the Newfoundland Supreme Court, Appeal Division in *R v Wonderland Gifts Ltd* (1996) 140 Nfld & PEIR 219, [20]. See also the opinion of Lord Brodie in *Imperial Tobacco Ltd v Lord Advocate* [2012] CSIH 9 at [175].

(p 25)

In footnote 6 delete citation and insert–

[1988] QB 493.

(p 25)

In footnote 7 at end insert–

See also paper dated April 1997 by Legal Department of Hong Kong available at www.legco.gov.hk/yr96–97/english/panels/ajls/papers/zzz2604z.htm.

(p 25)   **In foonote 7, delete 'Government of Wales Act 1998 s 47' and insert:**

Government of Wales Act 2006 s 78.

(p 25)   **In footnote 10 at end insert–**

s 3   See also the endorsement of the term 'legal meaning' by the High Court of Australia in *Project Blue Sky v Australian Broadcasting Authority* (1998) 194 CLR 355, 384.

(p 25)   **After heading 'Comment on Code s 3', at end of first sentence, insert footnote indicator 10A, with following text in footnote–**

Use of the term 'real doubt' was effectively endorsed by the UK Supreme Court in *Grays Timber Products Ltd v Revenue and Customs Commissioners* [2010] 1 WLR 497, 509 where Lord Walker JSC said: 'I am left in real doubt as to whether Parliament has, in Part 7 of ITEPA 2003, enacted [a certain scheme].'

(p 27)   **After reference to 'Companies Act 1985 s 36C(1)' insert–**

s 4   (repealed)

(p 27)   **In footnote 4 delete citations and insert–**

[2002] Ch 273.

(p 31)   **In footnote 4 at end insert–**

s 6   See further A Braun, 'Bury the Living? The Citation of Legal Writings in English Courts' (2010) 58 *American Journal of Comparative Law* 27.

(p 32)   **In footnote 3 replace 'Charleson' with–**

Charlson

(p 32)   **Also in footnote 3, add to citation–**

[2007] 3 All ER 163

(p 35)   **In 'Comment on Code s 7' after sentence beginning, 'The notion that labour legislation', at end insert footnote indicator 4A.**

(p 35)   **In newly created footnote 4A, insert–**

Houldsworth & Anor v Bridge Trustees Ltd & Anor [2011] UKSC 42 at [57].

(p 36)   **In Example 7.3 after 'Conditional Fee Agreements Regulations 2000' insert–**

(repealed)

(p 36)   **In footnote 4 at end insert–**

See also *Hollins v Russell* [2003] EWCA Civ 718, [2003] 4 All ER 590.

(p 38)   **In footnote 6 at end insert–**

s 8   See also *Woodward v Abbey National Plc (No 2)* [2005] 4 All ER 1346.

(p 39)   **In footnote 7 at end insert–**

; *Nolan v Wright* [2009] 3 All ER 823.

(p 41)   **At end of fifth paragraph, immediately before subheading 'Mistake as a defence', insert–**

s 9   In 2008, the Court of Appeal stated that 'Ignorance of the law is no defence, but it can sometimes amount to mitigation': *R v Rahman (Abdul)* [2008] 4 All ER 661, [43]. The Court proceeded to allow in mitigation the fact that the appellant was aware of the general nature of recently enacted anti-terrorism legislation, but unaware that his conduct had, as a result, become an offence. The Court indicated, though, that such mitigation would be unlikely for that offence in the future, due to anticipated knowledge of the 'successful prosecutions that have now taken place': *Ibid.*

(p 41)   **In footnote 8 at end insert–**

See also the judgment of the High Court of Australia in *Ostrowski v Palmer* (2004) 218 CLR 493.

(p 41)   **In footnote 10 delete citations and insert–**

[2007] 1 AC 558.

(p 42)   **In footnote 3 at end insert–**

See also the judgment of the High Court of Australia in *Ostrowski v Palmer* (2004) 218 CLR 493.

(p 45)   **After heading 'Comment on Code s 10', at end of first sentence, before footnote indicator 1 insert–**

s 10   and in a 2000 case.

(p 45)   **In footnote 1 at end, insert–**

; *R v B* [2000] EWCA Crim 42.

(p 45)   **In second sentence, delete 'in a 2000 case' and insert–**

in another 2000 case.

(p 45)

In footnote 7, at end insert–

Compare Localism Act 2011 s 28(4) (a decision 'is not invalidated just because something that occurred in the process of making the decision involved a failure to comply with the code').

(p 45)

In footnote 8, at end insert–

Note, though, that Lord Steyn remarked that the distinction and 'its many artificial requirements' had 'outlived their usefulness'. Instead, 'the emphasis ought to be on the consequences of non-compliance, and posing the question whether Parliament can fairly be taken to have intended total invalidity': *ibid*, [23]. Lords Cullen and Brown agreed: *ibid*, [52], [70]. See also *DPP (Virgin Islands) v Penn* [2008] UKPC 29 at [18] and *North Somerset District Council v Honda Motor Europe Ltd* [2010] EWHC 1505 at [43] and *Re Bezier Acquisitions Ltd* [2011] EWHC 3299 (Ch). The courts remain bound by judgments that pre-date *Soneji*, and apply the mandatory-directory terminology, where it can be established that those judgments *'addressed the question of Parliamentary intention'*: *R (Garland) v Secretary of State for Justice* [2011] EWCA Civ 1335 at [22]. The question of Parliamentary intention is not to be equated with the *'judge's view of the seriousness of the non-compliance on the particular facts'*: *TTM v London Borough of Hackney* [2011] EWCA Civ 4 at [94].

(p 46)

In footnote 5 at end insert–

See also the decision of the Divisional Court in *R (Bromley) v Secretary of State for Justice* [2010] EWHC 112 (Admin), [43].

(p 46)

In footnote 7 at end insert–

; *Adorian v Commissioner of Police* [2009] 4 All ER 227, [42].

(p 47)

In footnote 3 at end insert–

In the context of civil procedure, the disobedience may be reflected in costs: *Adorian v Commissioner of Police* [2009] 4 All ER 227.

(p 48)

In the final paragraph, at the end of the second sentence, immediately before Example 10.4, insert footnote indicator 7A and, in the footnote, insert–

This passage was considered in *Goshawk Dedicated (No 2) Ltd v Bank of Scotland* [2006] 2 All ER 610, [108].

(p 49)

At end of sentence beginning 'A duty to do a thing in a certain way', insert footnote indicator 4A and, in the footnote, insert–

This passage was applied by an Australian tribunal in *Campbell v Tow Truck Directorate of Victoria* (1995/34314) [2000] VICCAT 3.

(p 52)   **At the end of the first sentence, insert footnote indicator 1 and, in the footnote, insert–**

This sentence was applied in *R v B* [2000] EWCA Crim 42.

(p 52)   **Replace footnote indicators 1 to 10 with footnote indicators 2 to 11 respectively.**

(p 52)   **In Example 10.9 after 'Homicide Act 1957', insert–**

(repealed).

(p 52)   **In footnote 7 at end, insert–**

See now Senior Courts Act 1981.

(p 52)   **Before subheading 'Interference with property', insert–**

Similarly, procedures required of the police in the context of a search of a person may, if not observed, lead to a conviction arising out of the search being quashed.[7A]

(p 52)   **In the new footnote indicator 7A, insert–**

R v Bristol [2007] EWCA Crim 3214.

(p 54)   **In Example 10.19, after 'Sch 12 para 39(2)', insert–**

(repealed).

(p 54)   **In footnote 6 at end insert–**

(repealed).

(p 55)   **In Example 10.22, after '12(2)(f)', insert–**

(repealed).

(p 56)   **In Example 10.25, after 'Companies Act 1985 s 356' insert–**

(repealed).

(p 56)   **In footnote 2, at end of second sentence, insert–**

This passage was approved in *Glasgow City Council v AD* [2005] Scot SC 35, [22].

(p 56)   **In footnote 2, at end insert–**

Note that Parliament sometimes states expressly that purely technical contraventions are not to vitiate an act: see eg Proceeds of Crime Act 2002 s 14(11) and *Sekhon & Ors v R* [2002] EWCA Crim 2954 at [28].

(p 56)   **In footnote 6 at end, insert–**

(repealed).

(p 60)   **In Example 11.2 after 'Companies Act 1985 s 319(6)' insert–**

s 11   (repealed)

(p 61)   **After Example 12.2, insert–**

s 12   *Example 12.2A* Section 203(1)(b) of the Employment Rights Act 1996 rendered void a provision in an agreement that prevented a person from bringing any proceedings before an employment tribunal under the Act. Section 144(1) of the Equality Act 2010 rendered a term of a contract unenforceable 'in so far as it purports to exclude or limit a provision of or made under this Act'. A person entered into agreement as a partner of a law firm. The agreement provided for dispute resolution, including arbitration. The person brought proceedings in an employment tribunal. The firm sought a stay of proceedings pending dispute resolution under the agreement. Slade J held that the agreement was void or unenforceable under the above provisions. The words 'bringing any proceedings' in s 203(1)(b) of the Employment Rights Act extended to 'continuing any proceedings' already instituted. A 'provision' of the Equality Act referred to in s 144(1) was not restricted to substantive protections against discrimination and extended to provision for the continuation of proceedings in an employment tribunal.[4A]

(p 61)   **In newly created footnote 4A, insert–**

Clyde & Co LLP v Bates Van Winkelhof [2011] EWHC 668 (QB).

(p 61)   **After Example 12.4, before the sideheading 'Severable agreements', insert–**

Parliament may create a procedure under which contracting out is typically prohibited, but may be allowed upon application to a court.

Example 12.4A Part II of the Landlord and Tenant Act 1954 (repealed) provided for the continuation and renewal of tenancies, including by application to a court. Section 38(1) of the Act rendered void a tenancy agreement seeking to exclude these protections. However, s 38(4) of the Act enabled a court, upon a joint application by a landlord and tenant, to exclude the protections in relation to a particular tenancy agreement.

(p 61)   **In footnote 7, at end insert–**

For an interesting discussion of the construction of a similar provision by the High Court of Australia, see *Caltex Oil (Aust) Pty Ltd v Best* (1990) 170 CLR 516, 522. Compare Example 12.2A, above.

(p 61)   **At the end of Example 12.4A, insert footnote indicator 7A.**

(p 61)   **In newly created footnote 7A, insert–**

See further *Brighton and Hove City Council v Collinson* [2004] EWCA
Civ 678.

(p 62)   **After paragraph beginning 'The law has taken the view', insert–**

Jurisdiction of courts Similarly, it has been held that, where a statutory
provision confers a jurisdiction on the courts, and the jurisdiction
necessarily involves interference with contractual rights agreed between
the parties, it would be inconsistent 'for the legislature at the same time
to allow for the parties to contract out of that interference'.[8A]

(p 62)   **In the newly created footnote indicator 8A, insert–**

Aribisala v St James Homes (Grosvenor Dock) Ltd [2007] EWHC 1694
(Ch), [36].

(p 70)   **Before sideheading 'Subsection 2 Subject to any contrary
               legislative intention, the breach may give rise in civil law to a
               general public law remedy, or a general private law remedy, or
                                both', insert–**

In recent times, the courts have been reluctant to construe statutory
provisions concerning liability for breach of the statute as impliedly
giving rise to the breach tort.

> *Example 14.1A* Section 29 of the Electricity Act enabled the
> Secretary of State to make regulations. Section 29(3) enabled the
> regulations to provide that contravenes the regulations 'shall be
> liable on summary conviction to a fine not exceeding level 5 on the
> standard scale'. Section 29(3) went on to state that 'nothing in this
> subsection shall affect any liability of any such person to pay
> compensation in respect of any damage or injury which may have
> been caused by the contravention'. A lower court understood the
> 'plain meaning' of this reservation to be that a person was 'entitled
> to raise an action for damages against the person who contravened
> the regulations, founding the action upon that breach of statutory
> duty'.
>
> The Supreme Court rejected this approach as 'untenable'. It stated:
>
> 'There is no basis whatever for thinking that the drafter of the
> provision intended to introduce a civil right of action but –
> somehow – botched that comparatively straightforward task and
> came up with the words in the subsection which are so singularly
> ill-suited to the supposed purpose. On the contrary, the main thrust
> of the subsection is to provide that, where the regulations so
> stipulate, a person who contravenes a provision is to be guilty of a
> criminal offence ... [the remainder of] the subsection merely
> confirms that liability to the criminal penalty is not to affect 'any

s 14

liability' of the offender to pay compensation. By 'any liability' Parliament means the offender's liability, 'if any', to pay compensation.'[4A]

(p 70)   **In newly created footnote 4A, insert:**

Morrison Sports Ltd v Scottish Power [2010] UKSC 37 at [12], [16].

(p 74)   **In footnote 9, at end insert–**

As to the use of this provision in place of a relator action see Example 87.3 and *Birmingham City Council v Shafi and another* [2009] 1 WLR 1961, [2009] 3 All ER 127.

(p 74)   **In footnote 10 at end insert–**

See also the decision of the Ontario Court of Appeal in *McCombie v Cadotte* (2001) 53 OR (3d) 704, [30].

(p 75)   **In footnote 2 at end insert–**

The passage to which this footnote relates was approved by the Ontario Court of Appeal in *McCombie v Cadotte* (2001) 53 OR (3d) 704, [30].

(p 75)   **Before paragraph beginning 'A statutory duty', insert–**

The strength of the general rule was recently affirmed by the Supreme Court. Their Lordships, referring to a well-known speech in the House of Lords, stated 'if a statute provides some means, other than a private law action for damages, of enforcing any duty which it imposes, that will normally indicate that the statutory right was intended to be enforceable by those means and not by private right of action'.[5A]

(p 75)   **In newly created footnote 5A, insert–**

Morrison Sports Ltd v Scottish Power [2010] UKSC 37 at [29], referring to *X (Minors) v Bedfordshire County Council* [1995] 2 AC 633.

(p 76)   **In footnote 2, at end of quotation, insert–**

See also *Morrison Sports Ltd v Scottish Power* [2010] UKSC 37. The Supreme Court held at [32] that '*individuals raising private actions*' would be '*basically inconsistent*' with the '*scheme for enforcement*' for which the statute expressly provided. The Court also stated at [37] '*the scheme of the legislation, with its carefully worked-out provisions for various forms of enforcement on behalf of the public, points against individuals having a private right of action for damages*'.

(p 76)   **After sideheading Expressio unius principle, at end of sentence, insert–**

Likewise, where the enactment provides for damages or compensation in specific circumstances, it may follow that there is no wider liability for the same under private law. As the Supreme Court recently stated, 'the natural inference is that [Parliament] does not intend there to be a right to damages or compensation for loss or injury caused by other breaches of the statute or of subordinate legislation for which no such specific provision is made'.[2A]

(p 76)   **In newly created footnote 2A, insert–**

Morrison Sports Ltd v Scottish Power [2010] UKSC 37 at [13].

(p 77)   **In footnote 1, at end insert–**

It may be added that, if it is difficult to identify any limited class of persons who would benefit from the breach tort, this may be a further indication that the tort does not arise: *Morrison Sports Ltd v Scottish Power* [2010] UKSC 37 at [38].

(p 78)   **After sideheading 'Physical injury', at end of sentence, insert–**

However, the Supreme Court recently stated 'the fact that legislation is designed to reduce the risk of personal injury or damage to property is by no means an infallible indication that Parliament intended to give individuals a private right of action for breach of its provisions. It is simply one factor to be taken into account'.[6A]

(p 78)   **In newly created footnote 6A, insert–**

Morrison Sports Ltd v Scottish Power [2010] UKSC 37 at [41].

(p 80)   **In footnote 6, at end insert–**

Note that the ombudsman, in exercising the supervisory duties, may be operating under enabling legislation which has not drawn the clear line necessary between standards of conduct justifying a finding of negligence and those justifying an adverse finding by an Ombudsman: *R (Attwood) v Health Service Commissioner* [2009] 1 All ER 415 at [29]–[30], [35].

(p 83)   **In Example 14.20, after s 320, insert–**

(repealed)

(p 86)   **In footnote 2, at end insert–**

s 15   In *R (Bapio Action Ltd) v Secretary of State for the Home Department* [2008] 1 AC 1003 at 1018, Lord Rodger of Earlsferry said that the Interpretation Act 'expresses a principle of constitutional law of considerable practical importance: all Secretaries of State carry on Her Majesty's government and can, when required, exercise any of the powers conferred by statute on the Secretary of State.'

(p 87)   **In Example 15.2, after Fair Trading Act 1973, insert–**

(repealed).

(p 88)   **At top of page, in first quotation, after 'Companies Act 1985' insert–**

(repealed)

(p 90)   **In footnote 1, after 'R v Crown Court at Stafford, ex p Shipley [1998] 2 All ER 465 insert–**

; *R (Newcastle City Council) v Berwick-upon-Tweed BC* [2008] EWHC 2369 (Admin) at [29],

(p 90)   **After quotation of Laws LJ, insert–**

The test for the *Padfield* approach has been described by the Court of Appeal as follows:

> 'The rule is not that the exercise of the power is only to be condemned if it is incapable of promoting the Act's policy, rather the question always is: what was the decision-maker's purpose in the instant case and was it calculated to promote the policy of the Act?'[2A]

(p 90)   **In newly created footnote 2A, insert–**

R v Braintree District Council; Ex parte Halls (2000) 32 HLR 770 at 779.

(p 90)   **At top of page, after quotation, before sentencing beginning 'There may be …', insert–**

The *Padfield* approach does not prevent a decision-maker from having regard to proposed changes in the law, where having such regard is compatible with the policy and objects of the enactment and, preferably, where the decision-maker gives very clear and cogent reasons for doing so. However, the stage the proposal has reached in the legislative process may affect the weight it is to be accorded, with the latter judicially reviewable for irrationality.[2B]

(p 90)   **In newly created footnote 2B, insert–**

R (Cala Homes (South) Ltd) v Secretary of State for Communities and Local Government [2011] EWCA 639 at [20], [22], [25], [30], [33].

(p 90)   **In footnote 7 at end, insert–**

See *R (Luton Borough Council) v Secretary of State for Education* [2011] EWHC 217 at [61], where Holman J found discretion to be fettered where 'rules were indeed applied, and continued to be applied, in a hard edged way, with no residual individual discretion'. See also *Lumba (Congo) v Secretary of State for Home Department* [2011] UKSC 12.

(p 91)   **In paragraph beginning 'Recently judges have developed', at end insert–**

However, rules of good public administration will not support the conclusion that a statutory power cast in discretionary or elective terms is required to be exercised in certain circumstances.[6A] Even so, the same rules will influence the exercise by judges of the discretion to grant or refuse relief by way of judicial review.[6B]

(p 91)   **In newly created footnote 6A, insert–**

R (Mirza) v Secretary of State for Home Department [2011] EWCA Civ 159 at [25], as considered in *Lamichhane v Secretary of State for Home Department* [2012] EWCA Civ 260 at [30].

(p 91)   **In newly created footnote 6B, insert–**

Bahamas Hotel Maintenance & Allied Workers Union v Bahamas Hotel Catering & Allied Workers Union [2011] UKPC 4 at [40].

(p 92)   **In footnote 6, after 'Betting, Gaming and Lotteries Act 1963 s 3', delete 'as amended' and insert–**

s 16   repealed.

(p 93)   **Delete quotation beginning 'I AB do solemnly and sincerely declare' and insert–**

'I AB do solemnly and sincerely declare and affirm that I will well and truly serve the Queen in the office of constable, with fairness, integrity, diligence and impartiality, upholding fundamental human rights and according equal respect to all people; and that I will, to the best of my power, cause the peace to be kept and preserved and prevent all offences against people and property; and that while I continue to hold the said office I will, to the best of my skill and knowledge, discharge all the duties thereof faithfully according to law.'

(p 93)   **In footnote 1 after 'Sch 4', insert–**

(as amended).

(p 94)   **At top of page, in second line, delete 'Supreme Court Act 1981' and insert–**

s 17   Senior Courts Act 1981

(p 94)   **In footnote 3, at end insert–**

As to hybridity and appeals see *R (Langley) v Preston Crown Court*
[2009] 1 WLR 1612, 1618–1619.

(p 96)   **In footnote 4 at end, insert–**

s 18   The Attorney General's role as guardian of the public interest extends to
other matters. See, for example, *R v H* [2004] 2 AC 134 at [46].

(p 99)   **In footnote 7, delete (5ᵗʰ edn, 2004) and insert–**

(2010),   available   at   http://www.cps.gov.uk/publications/docs/
code2010english.pdf.

(p 99)   **In footnote 7 at end, insert–**

In addition to the Code, there may be a prosecution policy for a
particular class of cases. See, for example, Policy for Prosecutors in
Respect of Cases of Encouraging or Assisting Suicide (2010), available
at   http://www.cps.gov.uk/publications/prosecution/assisted_suicide_
policy.html. As to that policy, see further FAR Bennion, 'Ultra Vires and
the Rule of Law: the Scandalous Case of Assisted Suicide in England',
Commonwealth   Lawyer,   April   2012,   p   27,   available   at
http://www.francisbennion.com/pdfs/fb/2012/2012–015-com-l- assisted-
suicide.pdf.

(p 100)   **In footnote 1, at end insert–**

As to judicial review in relation to cautions see *R (Guest) v DPP* [2009]
EWHC 594; [2009] Crim LR 730. See further on judicial review *R (on
the application of Corner House and another) v Director of Serious
Fraud Office (BAE Systems plc, interested party)* [2009] 1 AC 756. It has
also been suggested that a prosecution policy as to a particular class of
cases, rather than a decision on whether or not to prosecute in one case
or another, may be subject to judicial review: F A R Bennion, 'The DPP
and Assisted Suicide: a Conspectus', Criminal Law and Justice Weekly,
27   March   2010,   available   at
http://www.francisbennion.com/pdfs/fb/2010/2010–010-assisted-suicide-
policy-unlawful.pdf.

(p 100)   **In footnote 7 at end insert–**

As to the Council Framework Decision on the European Arrest Warrant
and the Surrender Procedures between Member States, see *Assange v
Swedish Prosecution Authority* [2012] UKSC 22.

(p 100)   **In footnote 8, at end insert–**

Akin to the right of private prosecution is the right to bring proceedings
for contempt of court under CPR r. 32.14: see *KJM Superbikes Limited v
Hinton* [2008] EWCA Civ 1280. These are public law civil proceedings
with a criminal standard of proof: *Kirk v Walton* [2008] EWHC 1780
(QB), [2009] 1 All ER 257, at [25]–[27].

(p 101)   **After second quotation, before paragraph beginning 'A prosecution is commenced', insert–**

A private prosecutor is subject to an action in tort for malicious prosecution.[4A]

(p 101)   **In newly created footnote 4A, insert–**

See the authorities collected in *Besnik Qema v News Group Newspapers Ltd* [2012] EWHC 1146 (QB).

(p 101)   **In footnote 2, at end insert–**

As to the legality of the Crown Prosecution Service taking over a private prosecution for the purpose of discontinuing it, see *R (Gujra) v Crown Prosecution Service* [2012] 1 WLR 254. This case is currently on appeal to the Supreme Court of the United Kingdom.

(p 103)   **In footnote 6 at end insert–**

s 19   In any event, the successor to the Appellate Committee, the Supreme Court of the United Kingdom, is undoubtedly a court: Constitutional Reform Act 2005 s 23.

(p 104)   **In footnote 4 at end insert–**

There is, also, a 'separation, in national government, between the powers of the executive and the powers of Parliament': *R (on the application of Bradley and Others) v Secretary of State for Work and Pensions* [2009] QB 114, 167, 169.

(p 105)   **In footnote 10 at end, insert–**

Arbitration is also different: see Arbitration Act 1996 s 1.

(p 107)   **In paragraph beginning 'A court cannot delegate its responsibility', after second sentence, insert–**

This prohibition on delegation operates to preclude a tribunal from excessive reliance on counsel or members of its staff in the making of its decisions. A breach of this prohibition may cause the decision of the tribunal to be quashed for want of procedural fairness.[5A]

(p 107)   **In newly created footnote 5A, insert–**

Dato Tan Leong Min v Insider Dealing Tribunal [1999] 2 HKC 83; *Au Wing Lun v Solicitors Disciplinary Tribunal* (unreported, Hong Kong Court of Appeal, CACV 4154/2001, 9 September 2002) and *A Solicitor v Law Society of Hong Kong* [2005] 3 HKLRD 622. The last two authorities were considered by the Court of Appeal in *Virdi v Law Society of England and Wales* [2010] 3 All ER 653 at [39] but distinguished as in that case '[t]he findings of the Tribunal are clearly their findings'.

(p 107)   **In paragraph beginning 'Municipal courts do not have', at
end insert–**

A court may also interpret a treaty where such interpretation is required
in order to determine rights or duties under domestic law.

(p 107)   **In newly created footnote 10, insert–**

Republic of Ecuador v Occidental Petroleum and Production Co [2006]
2 All ER 225.

(p 108)   **In footnote 4 at end insert–**

See also *R (Sivasubramaniam) v Wandsworth* [2003] 2 All ER 160, [44].
Note the criticism of this approach, and alternative appeal to constitutional law, in *R (C) v Upper Tribunal* [2009] EWHC 3092, [33]. See
further p 109 footnote 8. As to ouster of jurisdiction by contract see
Code s 12, including the authority cited at p 62 footnote 9.

(p 109)   **In footnote 8, at end insert–**

Note that Lord Steyn has suggested that the ouster clause would be
ineffective, not due to the scope of its terms, but possibly as a matter of
constitutional law, representing a limit on the doctrine of parliamentary
sovereignty: *R (Jackson) v Attorney-General* [2006] 1 AC 262, 302–303.
Compare the view that the retention of judicial involvement despite
ouster clauses is referable to the rule of law and, in truth, an affirmation
of parliamentary sovereignty: *R (C) v Upper Tribunal* [2010] 1 All ER
908, [38]–[39]. See further *Cart v the Upper Tribunal* [2011] UKSC 28
at [73].

(p 109)   **In footnote 12, at end insert–**

See further *R(A) v B* [2010] UKSC 12 at [23]–[24]; *R (MM (Ghana)) v
Secretary of State for Home Department* [2012] EWCA 827 at [40].

(p 110)   **At end of first complete quotation, insert new paragraph–**

An *Anisminic* clause has also been contrasted by the Supreme Court of
the United Kingdom with a clause that, instead of purporting to remove
any judicial supervision of a determination by an inferior as to its own
jurisdiction, allocates scrutiny of a certain subject matter to a court or
other judicial body of like standing and authority to that of the High
Court, even if it operates with special procedures apt for the subject
matter and without a right of appeal.[2A] Indeed, it has been said that a
provision restricting appeals does not warrant 'any special rule of
construction'.[2B]

(p 110)   **In newly created footnote 2A, insert–**

A v B [2010] 2 WLR 1, 9–10.

(p 110)   **In newly created footnote 2B, insert–**

Okandeji v Bow Street Magistrates Court [2006] 1 WLR 674, 678–679.

(p 110)   **In paragraph beginning 'The ouster clause', delete 'Supreme Court Act 1981' and insert–**

Senior Courts Act 1981

(p 111)   **After Example 19.10, before subheading 'Inherent jurisdiction', insert–**

Different considerations may arise with respect to an ouster clause and its application in the field of private law.[5A]

(p 111)   **In newly created footnote 5A, insert–**

Lumba (Congo) v Secretary of State for Home Department [2011] UKSC 12.

(p 111)   **After subheading 'Inherent jurisdiction', in the first quotation, replace 'only the Supreme Court' with–**

only the Supreme Court [of England and Wales].

(p 112)   **In footnote 2, delete second sentence and insert–**

As to practice directions, rules of court and similar matters see Example 45.2 and *Bovale Ltd v Secretary of State for Communities and Local Government* [2009] 3 All ER 340.

(p 112)   **In footnote 4 at end insert–**

As to the contribution of an SAA to procedural justice, see *R (Roberts) v Parole Board* [2005] 2 AC 738.

(p 112)   **In footnote 5 at end insert–**

This is subject to additional step of the *McKenzie* friend being granted rights of audience under the Courts and Legal Services Act 1990, as discussed at the end of this page.

(p 112)   **In footnote 6 at end insert–**

For a full update regarding the use of a *McKenzie* friend see *Re: N (A Child)* [2008] 1 WLR 2743.

(p 112)   **In footnote 8 at end insert–**

Court of Appeal, Guidance for McKenzie Friends (Civil and Family Courts) [2010] All ER (D) 169 (July).

(p 112)   **Delete the penultimate paragraph beginning 'The Courts and Legal Services Act' and insert–**

The courts are slow to allow lay representation but do so on a case by case basis.

(p 112)   **In footnote indicator 11, delete text and insert–**

Re: N (A Child) [2008] 1 WLR 2743; *McKenzie* Friends Guidance, 12 July 2010, http://www.judiciary.gov.uk/publications-and-reports/ guidance/index/mckenzie-friends.

(p 113)   **At end of sentence beginning 'A court has an inherent power', insert–**

Further, a court has power to recall and vary an order before it is perfected[3A] and, in the case of an appellate court, even after perfection.[3B] It has been suggested that power extends to limiting the retrospective effect of an order in an appropriate case.[c]

(p 113)   **In newly created footnote 3A, insert–**

Paulin v Paulin [2009] 3 All ER 88. See also, in Hong Kong, *HKSAR v Tin's Label Factory Ltd* (unreported, Court of Final Appeal, Li CJ, Bokhary Chan and Ribeiro PJJ and Lord Woolf of Barnes NPJ, FACC 5/2008, 5 December 2008) and the slip rule discussed on p 110 above.

(p 113)   **In newly created footnote 3B, insert–**

Taylor v Lawrence [2003] QB 528. See also *Seray-Wurie v Hackney LBC* [2002] 3 All ER 448; *Gregory v Turner* [2003] 2 All ER 1114.

(p 113)   **In newly created footnote 3C, insert–**

Cadder v Her Majesty's Advocate [2010] UKSC 43 at [58]. But see *infra* p 172 n 10.

(p 114)   **In footnote 1 at end delete–**

As to a court's power to reopen a judgment.

(p 115)   **In Example 19.18, delete 'Supreme Court Act 1981' and insert–**

Senior Courts Act 1981

(p 116)   **After sideheading 'Consent orders' at end of second sentence, insert–**

Nonetheless, a party must have capacity to enter into the agreement leading to the consent order and such an order may be set aside in the event that capacity was absent.

(p 116) **In newly created footnote 7, insert–**

Dunhill v Burgin [2011] EWHC 464.

(p 118) **In footnote 3 at end insert–**

See further *Al Rawi v Security Service* [2011] UKSC 34.

(p 118) **After heading 'Open court principle', at end of first paragraph, insert–**

The principle has recently been described as ' "transparency' in the current jargon'.³ᴬ

(p 118) **In newly created footnote indicator 3A, insert–**

Re: N (A Child) [2008] 1 WLR 2743, 2748.

(p 121) **After sideheading 'Courts Service', delete 'Her Majesty's Courts Services' and insert–**

Her Majesty's Courts and Tribunal's Service.

(p 122) **After Example 20.1, insert–**

s 20 *Example 20.1A* The Chief Magistrate in Queensland, Australia, was tried and convicted by the Queensland Supreme Court of an offence of unlawful retaliation against a witness. An appeal to the Queensland Court of Appeal was dismissed. On appeal to the High Court of Australia, the Chief Magistrate was allowed to argue, for the first time, that she enjoyed an immunity from prosecution conferred by s 21A of the Queensland Magistrates Act 1991. The provision was held to be a complete answer to the case against the Chief Magistrate and her conviction was quashed.

(p 122) **In newly created footnote 4, insert–**

See *Fingleton v R* (2005) 216 ALR 474.

(p 127) **In paragraph beginning 'Although 'may'', after 's 416(6)', insert–**

(repealed)

(p 127) **In Example 20.9, after 's 55(1)', insert–**

(repealed)

(p 127) **In footnote 2 after www.francisbennion.com/1998/012.htm, insert–**

and *R (McDonald) v Royal Borough of Kensington and Chelsea* [2011] UKSC 33 at [8], [70]–[75].

(p 128)   **In footnote 7 at end insert–**

This article, and the distinction between judgment and discretion, has been approved by the NSW Court of Appeal: *New South Wales Crime Commission v Yu* [2009] NSWCA 349, [7].

(p 128)   **At end of penultimate paragraph insert–**

Similarly, the Court of Appeal, including Lord Judge LCJ, recently said:

> '[A]lthough the distinction is a fine one, whenever the competency question is addressed, what is required is not the exercise of a discretion but the making of a judgment, that is whether the witness fulfils the statutory criteria. In short, it is not open to the judge to create or impose some additional but non-statutory criteria ... '[8A]

(p 128)   **In newly created footnote 8A, insert–**

R v Barker [2010] EWCA Crim 4, [39]. See also *R v Clarke* [2007] EWCA Crim 2532, [29] and, in Australia, see, eg, *R v Smith* [2003] NSWCCA 381, [95] and *Perpetual Trustee Company Limited v Albert and Rose Khoshaba* [2006] NSWCA 41, [34].

(p 129)   **In Example 20.12, after 's 92(2)(a)', insert–**

(repealed).

(p 129)   **In footnote 6 after 's 71', insert–**

(repealed)

(p 130)   **In footnote 2 at end insert–**

This may be affected by the extent to which the relevant pronouncement is considered binding, a matter which will depend upon whether the court intended to articulate a mere rule of practice, subject to subsequent variation, or to lay down a rule of law, leaving no room for doubt: *A Train & Sons Ltd v Fletcher* [2008] 4 All ER 699, at [11], [24]. See also p 168 n 5.

(p 130)   **In footnote 3 at end insert–**

Re: N (A Child) [2008] 1 WLR 2743, 2753 (discretion conferred by Courts and Legal Services Act 1990 s 27(2)(c) to grant rights of audience to a layperson, including a *McKenzie* friend).

(p 131)   **In footnote 3 at end insert–**

See also the remark by Heydon J of the High Court of Australia in *Victims Compensation Fund Corporation v Brown* (2003) 201 ALR 260, at [10]: 'It is, of course, common for seemingly small points of construction to generate such sharp and evenly held differences of opinion ...'.

(p 133)   **Before Section 21, at end of paragraph beginning 'We now have a multicultural society', insert footnote indicator 4 –**

Nonetheless, the English Court of Appeal has indicated '[w]e sit as secular judges serving a multi-cultural community of many faiths' and, echoing Chief Justice Hale, described the 'aphorism that 'Christianity is part of the common law of England'' as 'mere rhetoric'. See *R (Johns) v Derby City Council* [2011] EWHC 375 (Admin) at [39]. See further Code s 275.

(p 136)   **At end of first paragraph, insert–**

s 21   Where applicable, courts take judicial notice of public international law.[3A]

(p 136)   **In newly created footnote 3A, insert–**

Trendtex Trading Corp v Central Bank of Nigeria [1977] QB 529 at 569. See Code s 270.

(p 137)   **In footnote 11 at end, insert–**

On the other hand, the time has not yet been reached where judicial notice may be taken of 'generally accepted facts about Al Qaeda': *Ahmed v R* [2011] EWCA Crim 184 at [58].

(p 137)   **In footnote 12 at end insert–**

A similar statement has been made in relation local authorities and illegal immigrants: *R (Clue) v Birmingham City Council* [2008] EWHC 3036 (Admin), [2]. Indeed, the Supreme Court of the United Kingdom has taken judicial notice of the fact that local authorities are 'financially hard pressed' more generally: *Re: T (Children)* [2012] 1 WLR 2281 at [34].

(p 137)   **In middle of page, after quotation from Elias J, insert–**

A Northern Irish court took judicial notice of the fact that 'social networking sites, Twitter and the internet generally now provides an alternative means of publication to traditional daily or Sunday newspapers'.[12A]

(p 137)   **In newly created footnote 12A, insert–**

Robinson v Sunday Newspapers Ltd [2011] NICA 13 at [24].

(p 137)   **In paragraph beginning 'Judicial notice is also taken of the facts of nature', insert after second sentence–**

However, this does not necessarily extend to the perception of nature. Thus, in response to a submission as to a shift in the public perception of animals and their welfare, Lewison J did not consider 'an alleged social transformation of that kind is one of which the court can take judicial notice'.[14A]

(p 137)   **In newly created footnote 14A, insert–**

Hanchett-Stamford v Attorney General [2009] Ch 173, 182.

(p 138)   **After sideheading 'High Court of Justice', delete 'Supreme Court Act 1981' and insert–**

s 22   Senior Courts Act 1981.

(p 138)   **After sideheading 'High Court of Justice', delete 'Supreme Court of England and Wales' and insert–**

Senior Courts of England and Wales.

(p 138)   **After sideheading 'High Court of Justice', delete footnote marker 9**

(p 139)   **In first paragraph, delete Supreme Court and insert–**

Senior Courts.

(p 139)   **Delete second paragraph beginning, 'The Supreme Court' and delete footnote 2**

(p 139)   **In third paragraph, delete 'Supreme Court Act 1981' and insert–**

Senior Courts Act 1981.

(p 140)   **At of end first sentence, insert–**

A court cannot impose a penalty for contempt of court in respect of an offence for which a statutory punishment is imposed.[1A]

(p 140)   **In newly created footnote 1A, insert–**

Malcolm v R [2011] EWCA Crim 2069 at [71].

(p 140)   **In second paragraph, delete 'the Lord Chancellor',.**

(p 140)   **In second paragraph, delete 'ninety-eight' and insert–**

'108'

(p 140)   **In second paragraph delete ', though the Lord Chancellor is the nominal President'.**

(p 140)   **In third paragraph, after sideheading 'Crown Court' and in footnotes 2, 4, 5, 8 and 9, delete 'Supreme Court Act 1981' and insert–**

Senior Courts Act 1981.

(p 140)   **In footnote 4, delete 's 5.' and insert–**

s 6.

(p 141)   **In footnotes 1 and 6, delete 'Supreme Court Act 1981' and insert–**

Senior Courts Act 1981.

(p 141)   **After sideheading 'County courts', after 'Courts Act 1971', insert–**

(repealed)

(p 142)   **In first paragraph, delete 'Lands Tribunal and the Immigration
Appeal Tribunal'. Also delete the text of footnotes 2 and 3**

(p 142)   **In footnote 5, at end insert–**

See also, generally, the judgment of the High Court of Australia in *R v
Australian Broadcasting Tribunal, ex p Hardiman* (1980) 144 CLR 13 at
35.

(p 142)   **In footnote 7 at end, insert–**

Compare the judgment of the Federal Court of Australia in *Hamzy v
Tricon International* (2001) 115 FCR 78 at [20]–[23].

(p 143)   **In footnote 2 at end insert–**

s 23   See also the judgment of the New South Wales Court of Appeal in *Wang
v NSW* [2011] NSWCA 321 at [23].

(p 143)   **In footnote 8 at end insert–**

An additional reason has been propounded by Patten J, namely that
construing statutory provisions in the absence of relevant factual information 'risks giving the words used an over-wide or unrealistic explanation …': *Re Metronet Rail BCV Ltd (In PPP Administration)* [2008]
2 All ER 75, at [21], [22].

(p 144)   **In footnote 3 at end insert–**

For a case similar to Example 23.1 see *R (Gilboy) v Liverpool City
Council* [2009] QB 699, 704. See also the judgment of the Hong Kong
Court of Appeal in *Leung v Secretary for Justice* [2006] 4 HKLRD 211
at [28].

(p 144)   **Before sideheading 'Appeal by successful party', insert–**

A similar, but distinct, approach is applied to appeals from findings of
fact.[7A]

(p 144)   **In newly created footnote 7A, insert–**

Lawrence v Kent County Council [2012] EWCA Civ 493 at [19]–[21].

(p 146)   **In paragraph beginning 'The Supreme Court Act 1981', delete those words and insert–**

The Senior Courts Act 1981

(p 146)   **In footnotes 7 and 9, delete 'Supreme Court Act 1981' and insert:**

Senior Courts Act 1981

(p 147)   **After sideheading 'High Court', delete 'Betting, Gaming and Lotteries Act 1963, the Licensing Act 1964, the Gaming Act 1968 or' and ', by any provision of those Acts,'.**

(p 147)   **In paragraph beginning 'Various other enactments', delete 'Agriculture (Miscellaneous Provisions) Act 1954 s 6 (appeal from Agricultural Land Tribunals);'**

(p 147)   **In footnotes 1 and 7, delete 'Supreme Court Act 1981' and insert–**

Senior Courts Act 1981

(p 147)   **In footnote 8, delete 'Tribunals and Inquiries Act 1971 s 13(1)' and insert–**

Tribunals and Inquiries Act 1992 s 11(1)

(p 148)   **After sideheading 'Court of Appeal', in second sentence, delete 'Supreme Court Act 1981' and insert–**

Senior Courts Act 1981

(p 148)   **In footnotes 4, 7, 9 and 11 delete 'Supreme Court Act 1981' and insert–**

Senior Courts Act 1981

(p 149)   **In second complete sentence, delete 'Supreme Court Act 1981' and insert–**

Senior Courts Act 1981

(p 149)   **In second complete sentence, after s 18(1)(f), insert–**

(repealed)

(p 149)   **In footnote 4 after Cetelem SA v Roust Holdings Ltd [2005]**
             EWCA Civ 618, [2005] 4 All ER 52 at [23], [28], insert–

CGU International Insurance Plc v AstraZeneca Insurance Co Ltd
[2006] EWCA Civ 1340 at [40]–[47],

(p 150)   **In footnote 7 at end insert–**

As to the circumstances in which fresh evidence will be admitted on
appeal: see *Hungary v Fenyvesi* [2009] 4 All ER 324 at [2].

(p 150)   **In footnote 9, at end, insert–**

As to the role of the Commission and judicial review of its decisions, see
R (Morris) v Criminal Cases Review Commission [2011] EWHC 117
(Admin).

(p 151)   **After sideheading '"Leapfrogging' appeals', in following**
             paragraphs, delete House of Lords and insert–

Supreme Court of the United Kingdom.

(p 151)   **In footnote 4 at end insert–**

See also *GC v Commissioner of Police of the Metropolis* [2011] UKSC
21 and *Re Kaupthing Singer and Friedlander Ltd* [2011] UKSC 48.

(p 151)   **Delete sideheading 'House of Lords' and insert–**

Supreme Court

(p 151)   **After sideheading House of Lords, delete all paragraphs and**
             footnotes and insert–

An appeal lies to the Supreme Court from any decision of the Court of
Appeal. Section 40(3) of the Constitutional Reform Act 2005 also
provides, by a piece of archival drafting, for an appeal to lie to the
Supreme Court from an order or judgment 'of a court in Scotland if an
appeal lay from that court to the House of Lords at or immediately
before the commencement of this section'.

An appeal also lies to the Supreme Court from a decision of the High
Court where it is: (1) a decision of the High Court in a criminal cause or
matter[8] or (2) a 'leapfrogging' appeal. The Supreme Court also has
certain other appellate jurisdiction, for example from courts in Northern
Ireland.

The leave of the court below or the Supreme Court is required for
appeals to that Court. In the case of criminal appeals, leave must not be
given unless the court below certifies that a point of law of general
importance is involved and it appears to the court below or to the
Supreme Court that the point is one that ought to be considered by the
Supreme Court.

(p 151)   **In footnote 7, insert–**

Constitutional Reform Act 2005 s 40(2); Criminal Appeal Act 1968 Pt II.

(p 151)   **In footnote 8, insert–**

Administration of Justice Act 1960 s 1(1)(a).

(p 151)   **In footnote 9, insert–**

As to these see above.

(p 151)   **In footnote 10, insert–**

Administration of Justice Act 1960 s 1(2); Constitutional Reform Act 2005 s 40(6); Criminal Appeal Act 1968 s 33(2).

(p 151)   **In footnote 11, insert–**

Administration of Justice Act 1960 s 1(2).

(p 152)   **Delete paragraphs before sideheading 'Constitutional Reform Act' and insert–**

The members of the Supreme Court comprise at least 12 permanent justices and, in addition, acting justices. Acting justices are either senior territorial judges or persons with membership of a body called the Supplementary Panel. In a given case, the Court must be constituted by at least three members, more than half of whom must be permanent justices. The Court is typically constituted by three justices for decisions on leave to appeal and five or more justices for the appeals themselves. The number of justices for a given case is determined in light of published criteria.

(p 152)   **In footnote 1, insert–**

Constitutional Reform Act 2005 Part 3. See further http://www.supremecourt.gov.uk.

(p 152)   **Delete footnotes 2 to 7.**

(p 152)   **Delete sideheading 'Constitutional Reform Act' and paragraph beginning 'A revolution in the top appellate structure' and insert–**

(p 153)   **Delete first paragraph beginning, 'This will replace the House of Lords' and footnote 1.**

(p 153)   **After quotations from second quotation from Lord Lloyd, insert–**

Another public critic of the creation of the Supreme Court was Lord Neuberger who, instead of becoming one of the first members of the Court, sat in the Court of Appeal as Master of the Rolls. However, his

Lordship has since been appointed President of the Supreme Court. At the time of his appointment, he stated that the Supreme Court 'like its predecessor, the Appellate Committee of the House of Lords, is rightly respected throughout the world'.

(p 153)   **Renumber footnotes 2 to 4 as footnotes 1 to 3.**

(p 153)   **In newly created footnote 4, insert–**

See the radio broadcast of Lord Neuberger reported at http://news.bbc.co.uk/2/hi/uk_news/8237855.stm and the remarks made at the time of his appointment as President of the Supreme Court described at http://www.supremecourt.gov.uk/news/new-president-of-the-supreme-court.html.

(p 153)   **Delete sentence beginning 'As this revolutionary system for our highest courts'.**

(p 153)   **Delete 'Before that however it is apposite to mention' and insert–**

It is apposite to mention

(p 154)   **After sideheading 'Judicial Committee of the Privy Council', delete 'consists mostly of law lords' and insert–**

'usually consists of permanent justices of the Supreme Court'

(p 154)   **At end of second paragraph insert–**

The devolution jurisdiction of the Judicial Committee of the Privy Council has been transferred to the Supreme Court of the United Kingdom.[6A]

(p 154)   **In newly created footnote 6A, insert–**

Constitutional Reform Act 2005 s 40(4)(b), Sch 9.

(p 154)   **In Comment on Code s 24, delete 'Supreme Court Act 1981' and insert–**

s 24   Senior Courts Act 1981

(p 154)   **In footnote 7 at end, insert–**

Note, however, that cases in which *O'Reilly v Mackman* is squarely applicable still arise: see, eg, *North Dorset District Council v Trim* [2010] EWCA Civ 1446 at [20]–[30].

(p 157)   **In footnote 4 at end, insert–**

See further, in relation to criminal proceedings, *R v Chaytor* [2010] UKSC 52. As to the position under a written constitution, see *Leung Kwok Hung v President of the Legislative Council of Hong Kong* [2012] 3 HKLRD 470 at [29]–[37].

(p 159)   **In footnote 8 at end insert–**

Note that the sufficiency of the alternative remedy includes it being 'equally effective and convenient': *R (European Metal Recycling Ltd) v Environment Agency* [2012] EWHC 2361 (Admin) at [33].

(p 159)   **Before Example 24.2, after 'Charities Act 1993 s 33(1)' insert–**

(repealed)

(p 161)   **In paragraph beginning 'Section 7(1) repealed' delete 'Supreme Court Act 1981' and insert–**

Senior Courts Act 1981

(p 163)   **After sideheading 'Declaration, injunction or damages' delete 'Supreme Court Act 1981' and insert–**

Senior Courts Act 1981

(p 164)   **In footnote 7 delete 'Supreme Court Act 1981' and insert–**

Senior Courts Act 1981

(p 166)   **At top of page delete 'Supreme Court Act 1981' and insert–**

Senior Courts Act 1981

(p 166)   **In footnote 1, after 'Local Government Act 1972 s 101' insert–**

(repealed)

(p 168)   **In the second paragraph, at the end of the third sentence insert–**

The *ratio decidendi* is binding. This can, albeit to a diminished extent, be contrasted with *obiter dictum*. The term derives from the Latin for a saying uttered 'by the way', originally two words ob iter. The OED (2nd edn 1992) cites, from the title page of Augustine Birrell's book *Obiter Dicta* (1884): 'An obiter dictum, in the language of the law, is a gratuitous opinion, an individual impertinence [that is something strictly not pertinent] which, whether it be wise or foolish, right or wrong, bindeth none – not even the lips that utter it.'

s 26   In 2008 Mummery LJ said: 'There is no point in cluttering up the law reports with *obiter dicta*, which could, in some cases, embarrass a court having to decide the issue later on'. [3A] Nevertheless they are so cluttered up. Indeed, appellate courts in England and the Commonwealth have gone so far as to create a category of *obiter dicta* that are authoritative, ie pronouncements so fully considered by the court as to bind lower courts in the same way as the *ratio decidendi*.[3B]

(p 168)   **In newly created footnote 3A insert–**

Housden v Conservators of Wimbledon and Putney Commons [2008] 3 All ER 1038, [31]

(p 168)   **In newly created footnote 3B insert–**

Trent Taverns Ltd v Sykes [1999] Eu LR 492, 497–498; *Crehan v Courage Ltd* [1999] EU LR 834, 895; *R v Henry* [2005] 3 SCR 609, [57]; *Farah Constructions Pty Ltd v Say Dee Pty Ltd* (2007) 230 CLR 89, [134], [158].

(p 171)   **In footnote 6 delete 'Supreme Court Act 1981' and insert–**

Senior Courts Act 1981

(p 172)   **In Example 26.3 delete 'Supreme Court Act 1981' and insert–**

Senior Courts Act 1981

(p 172)   **In footnote 10, at end insert–**

See also *Cadder v Her Majesty's Advocate* [2010] UKSC 43 at [58]. Compare *Ha v State of New South Wales* (1997) 189 CLR 465 at 503–504 and 515; *R v Demers* [2004] 2 SCR 489 at [56]–[65]; *HKSAR v Hung Chan Wa* [2006] 3 HKLRD 841 at [28]–[33].

(p 173)   **In footnote 6 at end, insert–**

Compare *R (SA) v Kent County Council* [2011] EWCA Civ 1303 at [38]. See also *R (Kadhim) v Brent London Borough Council Housing Benefit Review Board* [2001] QB 955 at [33].

(p 174)   **In footnote 5, after 'followed by the Court of Appeal in' insert–**

R v BR [2003] 4 All ER 882 and

(p 174)   **In footnote 5, delete sentence beginning 'This passage of the Code' and insert at the end of footnote 4.**

(p 174)   **Delete sentence beginning 'The doctrine of course' and the sentence beginning 'It also applies'. Insert–**

The doctrine applies in the Court of Appeal in relation to previous decisions of that court. However, there is high authority that the rule is not generally available to a court in relation to a decision of a court placed above it in the judicial hierarchy.

(p 174)   **In footnote 5, at beginning insert–**

Broome v Cassell & Co Ltd [1972] AC 1027, 1054, 1113, 1131, 1132;
Baker v R [1975] AC 774, 788, 795; *Miliangos v George Frank
(Textiles) Ltd* [1976] AC 443, 477–480; *Algama v Minister for Immigration and Multicultural Affairs* (2001) 115 FCR 253, 261; *Inglis v Loh Lai
Kuen Eda* [2005] 3 HKC 115, 127. The exception, if it be one, is where
a lower court judge is faced with irreconcilable decisions by the same
higher court, where the later decision has not expressly considered the
earlier: *Broome v Cassell & Co Ltd* [1972] AC 1027, 1107; *Uganda Co
(Holdings) Ltd v Government of Uganda* [1979] 1 Lloyds Rep 481, 484;
Midland Bank Trust Co Ltd v Hett, Stubbs and Kemp [1979] Ch 384,
405; *Taylor Woodrow Property Co Ltd v Lonrho Textiles Ltd* (1986) 52
P&CR 28, 39–40; *Manor Electronics Ltd v Dickson* (The Times,
8 February 1990).

(p 174)   **In footnote 5 at end, insert–**

See also O Jones, 'When is the Federal Magistrates Court Bound by the
Federal Court?' (2012) 86 ALJ 478, 484–488.

(p 174)   **In footnote 7 at end insert–**

Compare *Solicitor 24/07 v Law Society of Hong Kong* [2008] 2 HKLRD
576.

(p 174)   **In footnote 8 after 'See further' insert–**

Cave v Robinson Jarvis & Rolf (a firm) [2002] 1 WLR 581 and

(p 175)   **In footnote 1 delete '[2006] UKHL 27, [2006] 3 All ER 1777'
                                  and insert–**

[2007] 1 AC 307; *A v Hoare* [2008] 1 AC 844.

(p 175)   **At top of page, at end of sentence beginning 'The change of
                                  practice', insert–**

The Supreme Court of the United Kingdom has not found it necessary to
make a statement as to the binding effect of decisions of the House of
Lords or its own decisions. This is because the statement of 1966 'has as
much effect in this court as it did before'.[2A]

(p 175)   **In newly created footnote 2A, insert–**

Austin v Southwark London Borough Council [2010] UKSC 28 at [25].
See also the Constitutional Reform Act 2005 s 41(3)(a).

(p 177)   **In footnote 7, before sentence beginning 'See further', insert–**

See p 172 note 10.

(p 188)   **In footnote 6, at beginning insert–**

s 28   This passage was applied by the Federal Court of Australia in *Seafarers'*
            Retirement Fund Pty Ltd v Oppenhuis (1999) 94 FCR 594, 597–598.

(p 191)   **In second sentence under sideheading 'Tax law rewrite project',**
            after 'Income Tax (Earnings and Pensions) Act 2003', insert–

            (repealed) (ITEPA 2003)

(p 191)   **In footnote 5, at end insert–**

            Note that, on occasions, the fruits of the project have been undermined.
            In *Grays Timber Products Ltd v Revenue and Customs (Scotland)* [2010]
            1 WLR 497, Lord Walker JSC said, on behalf of the United Kingdom
            Supreme Court, (at 501): 'It is regrettable that ITEPA 2003, which came
            into force on 6 April 2003 and was intended to rewrite income tax law
            (as affecting employment and pensions) in plain English, was almost at
            once overtaken by massive amendments which are in anything but plain
            English'. Lord Hope JPSC spoke, also with the agreement of the Court,
            to similar effect: *Ibid*, 515.

(p 198)   **Under sideheading 'Rug analogy', at sentence ending 'the Act is**
            repealed', create footnote indicator 3A.

(p 198)   **In newly created footnote 3A insert–**

            The foregoing sentences of the rug analogy were described by a majority
            of the New Zealand Court of Appeal as 'graphically put': *Vector Ltd v*
            Transpower New Zealand Ltd [1999] 3 NZLR 646, [53]. Their Honours
            added: 'To complete the metaphor, the rug and the floor must run the
            same way. The Bennion explanation is subject to the obvious qualifica-
            tion that the statute serves similar goals to the common law rule': *Ibid*.

(p 199)   **After example 32.9, insert–**

            Example 32.9A The common law offences of blasphemy and blas-
            phemous libel were abolished by the Criminal Justice and Immi-
            gration Act 2008 ss 79, 149 and 153(2) and Sch 28. See further
            Francis Bennion, '*Farewell to the Blasphemy Laws*' (2008) 172
            JPN 448.

(p 200)   **Toward bottom of page, after 'Companies Act 1985**
            s 36C(1)' insert–

            (repealed)

(p 205)   **At the end of text, insert–**

s 33   Further, a Secretary of State may take some preparatory steps for the
            promotion of new legislation in advance of its enactment. However, the
            source and scope of this power, including a qualification of consistency
            with existing legislation, is controversial.[9A]

(p 205)   **In newly created footnote 9A, insert–**

R (Shrewsbury) v Secretary of State for Communities and Local Government [2008] 3 All ER 548. See also, generally, B V Harris, *'The "Third Source" of Authority for Government Action Revisited'* (2007) 123 LQR 225.

(p 206)   **In Comment on Code s 34, before 'Lord Templeman said', insert–**

s 34   This section of the Code has been judicially approved.[1A]

(p 206)   **In newly created footnote 1A, insert–**

Crown Estate Commissioners v Governors of the Peabody Trust [2011] EWHC 1467 (Ch) at [77].

(p 207)   **In footnote 9, at end insert–**

Compare Criminal Justice and Court Services Act 2000 Sch 2 para 16.

(p 208)   **In the second paragraph, at end of first sentence, insert footnote indicator 2A.**

(p 208)   **In newly created footnote indicator 2A, insert–**

This would explain why, according to some judges, a legitimate expectation created by one Secretary of State, as an emanation of the Crown, may not be disappointed by another such Secretary: *R (Bapio Action Ltd) v Secretary of State for the Home Department* [2008] 1 AC 1003, 1017–1018 (Lord Rodger), 1026 (Lord Mance). Compare 1016 (Lord Scott). As to this doctrine of legitimate expectation, see pp 1056–1057, 1060.

(p 211)   **Before sideheading 'Taking of benefit by Crown', insert–**

Conversely, where an Act states some of its provisions bind the Crown, but is silent as to others, it may be appropriate to infer that the latter were not intended to bind the Crown.[1A]

(p 211)   **In newly created footnote 1A, insert–**

Crown Estate Commissioners v Governors of the Peabody Trust [2011] EWHC 1467 (Ch) at [77]–[78].

(p 212)   **In footnote 2, at end insert–**

For an interesting example of the doctrine in relation to the People's Republic of China, see *Re Hua Tian Long (No 3)* [2010] 3 HKC 557. See also O Jones, *In Defence of Crown Liability*, Hong Kong Lawyer, January 2011, pp 41–47.

(p 238)   **In footnote 2, at end of first sentence, insert–**

s 48   See, generally, *R (Shields) v Secretary of State for Justice* [2010] QB
            150.

(p 238)   **At the end of the second full paragraph, insert a new paragraph–**

While an exercise of prerogative legislative power is primary rather than
subordinate, legislative power, it is, unlike a statute enjoying the principle of Parliamentary sovereignty, reviewable on ordinary principles of
legality, rationality and procedural impropriety.[9A] Further, even where it
has the effect of creating legal rights, a prerogative instrument may not
be legislative in nature. In particular, it may comprise administrative
policy as the future exercise of a prerogative power. A prerogative
instrument, at least of this kind, may be made by a minister on his own
authority.[9B] Controversy exists over whether there is a 'third power'
which, apart from legislation and the prerogative, authorises state
action.[9C]

(p 238)   **In newly created footnote 9A, insert–**

R (Bancoult) v Secretary of State for Foreign and Commonwealth Affairs
[2009] 1 AC 453. As to the status of prerogative legislative power under
the Human Rights Act 1998, see p 1374.

(p 238)   **In newly created footnote 9B, insert–**

Odelola v Secretary of State for the Home Department [2009] 1 WLR
1230.

(p 238)   **In newly created footnote 9C, insert–**

*R (Shrewsbury) v Secretary of State for Communities and Local Govern-
ment* [2008] 3 All ER 548. See also, generally, B V Harris, '*The "Third
Source" of Authority for Government Action Revisited*' (2007) 123 LQR
225.

(p 238)   **In footnote 11 at end insert–**

See also *R (Sultan of Pahang) v Secretary of State for Home Department*
[2011] EWCA Civ 616 and *Yukos Capital SARL v OJSC Rosneft Oil Co*
[2012] EWCA Civ 855.

(p 238)   **Under sideheading 'Acts of State', at end of second sentence,
                                 insert–**

Such jurisdiction as the courts have over the former is exceptional.[11A]

(p 238)   **In newly created footnote 11A, insert–**

See, in relation to acts of a foreign sovereign state, *R (on the application
of Hilali) v City of Westminster Magistrates' Court* [2010] 1 WLR 241,
256. For the rule that municipal courts lack jurisdiction to entertain an
action which is founded on an act of state, or which seeks to enforce the

penal, fiscal or other public law of a foreign state, see *United States Securities and Exchange Commission v Manterfield* [2009] EWCA Civ 27, [2009] 2 All ER 1009. Compare, in relation to the conduct by the Crown of overseas affairs, *R (Gentle) v Prime Minister* [2006] QB 689, 713, affd: *R (Gentle) v Prime Minister* [2008] 1 AC 1356, 1367.

(p 238)   **Under sideheading 'Acts of State', at beginning of third sentence, delete 'The courts retain jurisdiction' and insert–**

However, the courts undoubtedly possess

(p 238)   **In footnote 12, at end insert–**

Compare *Christian v R* [2007] 2 AC 400, 409, 415, 419.

(p 242)   **In footnote 8 at end insert–**

s 49   See also *Government of Canada v Aronson* [1990] 1 AC 579, 610 where the House of Lords felt 'it may be permissible to derive some slight assistance' from the same.

(p 245)   **In final paragraph, after 'Deregulation and Contracting Out Act 1994 s 1', insert–**

s 50   (repealed)

(p 247)   **In footnote 8, at end, insert–**

s 51   See, generally, *R (Stellato) v Secretary of State for Home Department* [2007] 2 AC 70.

(p 248)   **In footnote 4 at end, insert–**

See also *R (Alvi) v Secretary of State for Home Department* [2012] UKSC 33.

(p 249)   **In footnote 1, at end, insert–**

In *R (Alvi) v Secretary of State for Home Department* [2012] UKSC 33 at [37], Lord Hope noted that it is 'very rare for a motion against an instrument under the negative resolution procedure to be carried'.

(p 249)   **In footnote 2, at end insert–**

See, generally, *R (Alvi) v Secretary of State for Home Department* [2012] UKSC 33.

(p 256)   **In footnote 8, at end insert–**

s 58   Similarly, where there is no duty to consult, but the delegate or other decision-maker chooses to do so, 'the consultation must be carried out properly. It must be undertaken at a time when the proposals are still at a formative stage. Sufficient reasons [for the proposals] must be given to allow those consulted to give intelligent consideration and an intelligent response. There must also be adequate time for such a response': *R (Boyejo) v Barnet LBC* [2009] EWHC 3261 (Admin), [67]. Again, the product of the consultation must receive 'conscientious consideration': *R v North and East Devon Health Authority; Ex parte Coughlan* [2001] QB 213, 258.

(p 260) **In footnote 2, delete text and insert–**

[2006] Ch 337. See also the discussion in *Oyarce v Cheshire County Council* [2008] 4 All ER 90, [17], [59] regarding whether it would be ultra vires for delegated legislation implementing a Community obligation go any wider than was required by that obligation.

(p 263) **At beginning of Comment on Code s 59, insert–**

s 59 This section of the Code has twice been approved by the Court of Appeal.

(p 263) **In newly created footnote 1, insert–**

See *R v Secretary of State for Social Security; Ex parte Sarwar* [1997] 3 CMLR 648, 651–652; *Secretary of State for Work and Pensions v Deane* [2010] EWCA Civ 699, [37]. It was also recognised, but not applied to the facts, in *HM Revenue & Customs v Dunwood Travel Ltd* [2008] EWCA Civ 174 at [14], [15], [23].

(p 263) **Replace footnote indicators 1 to 9 with footnote indicators 2 to 10.**

(p 263) **In renumbered footnote 10 at end, insert–**

This passage was applied by the Federal Court of Australia in *Re Aboriginal Development Commission* [1988] FCA 160, [37].

(p 264) **In footnote 1 at end insert–**

s 60 Indeed, there are instances where the courts have applied provisions of the Code to delegated legislation. See, for example, the decisions of the Federal Court of Australia in *Hanna v Migration Agents Registration Authority* (1999) 94 FCR 358, 363 (Code s 271) and *Ignatious v Minister for Immigration & Multicultural & Indigenous Affairs* (2004) 139 FCR 254, 268.

(p 264) **In footnote 8 at end insert–**

See also *AM (Ethiopia) v Entry Clearance Officer* [2008] EWCA Civ 1082 at [54]–[57] and *R (Alvi) v Secretary of State for Home Department* [2012] UKSC 33.

(p 265)   **In footnote 10 at end insert–**

This passage was considered in *Hertfordshire CC v Veolia Water Central Ltd* [2010] EWHC 278 (QB), [37]. The court should also have considered other passages, including Code ss 157–160, 195 and 287.

(p 266)   **In footnote 1 at end insert–**

See also the discussion of Code s 60, and note of caution sounded, in *PNPF Trust Co Ltd v Taylor* [2010] EWHC 1573 (Ch) at [479].

(p 266)   **In footnote 2 at end, insert–**

This sentence has been judicially approved: *Norman v Cheshire Fire & Rescue Service* [2011] EWHC 3305 (QB) at [53].

(p 267)   **In Example 61.1, after 'Supply of Machinery (Safety) Regulations 1992', insert–**

s 61   (revoked)

(p 267)   **In footnote 3 at end insert–**

See also preamble to the Supply of Machinery (Safety) Regulations 2008.

(p 268)   **In Comment on Code s 64, insert at beginning of section–**

s 64   This section of the Code has been judicially approved.[5A]

(p 268)   **In newly created footnote 5A insert–**

Law Society of Upper Canada v Ontario (Attorney-General) (1995) 21 OR (3d) 666, [19].

(p 269)   **In footnote 3, after 'Water Resources Act 1991 s 210', insert–**

s 65   (repealed)

(p 270)   **In footnote 1 at end, insert–**

See also *FP (Iran) v Secretary of State for Home Department* [2007] EWCA Civ 13.

(p 270)   **In footnote 10 at end insert–**

See also *Hulme v Secretary of State for Communities and Local Government* [2011] EWCA Civ 638 at [13].

(p 272)   **In footnote 3 at end insert–**

s 66   See also Legislative Instruments Act 2003 (Australia) and *Harbour Radio Pty Ltd and Australian Communications and Media Authority* [2012] FCA 614 at [127]–[140].

(p 272)   **In footnote 6 after '575', insert–**

s 67   and *Hawke's Bay Raw Milk Producers Co-operative Co Ltd v New Zealand Milk Board* [1961] NZLR 218.

(p 290)   **At end of paragraph beginning 'However it is submitted' insert footnote indicator 4A.**

(p 290)   **In newly created footnote 4A, insert–**

This sentence was applied by the Supreme Court of Victoria in *Shields v Chief Commissioner of Police* [2008] VSC 2 at [102]–[104].

(p 291)   **In footnote 3, delete '[2002] UKHL 27, [2002] 3 All ER 721 at [20]' and insert–**

[2003] 1 AC 120, 133–134. Compare *Craftrule Ltd v 41–60 Albert Palace Mansions (Freehold) Ltd* [2010] EWHC 1230 (Ch), [28] where the above passage was considered inapplicable so long as 'the point of so doing is not to modify or contradict the meaning of [the relevant provision] as originally enacted, but merely to provide confirmation [through the fact] that Parliament [later] intended [the provision] to bear the same meaning as it always had'. This is difficult to reconcile with the authorities just mentioned, especially *Brown*, which rejected the use of the amending Act for assistance in any form, obviously including confirmation, subject only to Code s 234.

(p 293)   **In footnote 2 at end insert–**

s 79   See also the judgment of the High Court of Australia in *Kartinyeri v Commonwealth* (1998) 195 CLR 337 and *Kennedy v Information Commissioner* [2011] EWCA Civ 367.

(p 293)   **After 'Comment on Code s 80', insert–**

s 80   This section of the code has been judicially approved.[3A]

(p 293)   **In newly created footnote 3A, insert–**

See the judgment of the Federal Court of Australia in *Australian Prudential Regulation Authority v ACN 000 007 492* [2011] FCA 353 at [15].

(p 294)   **In footnote 4, at end of second sentence, insert–**

s 81   It has been justified by reference to the 'primary law making role of Parliament', while also restricted as 'only appropriate where there is a genuine doubt about the effect of the statutory provision in question': *R (Spath Holme Ltd) v Secretary of State for the Environment, Transport and Regions* [2001] 2 AC 349, 383.

(p 295)   **In sentence beginning 'An example of', after 's 101(4)', insert–**

(repealed)

(p 297)   **In footnote 1, at end insert–**

s 82   and *Revenue and Customs Commissioners v Stringer* [2009] 4 All ER 1205, [28].

(p 301)   **At beginning of Comment on Code s 85, insert–**

s 85   This section of the code was approved by an Australian court in a 1995 case.

(p 301)   **In newly created footnote 1, insert–**

See the decision of the Full Court of the Supreme Court of Victoria in *R v Omarjee* (1995) 79 A Crim R 355, [46].

(p 301)   **Replace footnote indicators 1 to 9 with footnote indicators 2 to 10.**

(p 301)   **At end of fourth full paragraph, before sideheading 'Types of repeal', insert–**

Thus, while it is possible for repealing legislation that contains successor provisions to those repealed to divide its work into repealing provisions and enacting provisions,[4A] the same can be achieved by a single set of new provisions expressed to be in substitution of the existing provisions.[4B]

(p 301)   **In newly created footnote 4A, insert–**

Macmillan & Co v Dent [1907] 1 Ch 107, 123–124.

(p 301)   **In newly created footnote 4B, insert–**

Such substitution was considered 'clearly an express repeal' by the Full Court of the Supreme Court of Victoria in *R v Omarjee* (1995) 79 A Crim R 355.

(p 304)   **In Comment on Code s 87, at end of second paragraph, before Example 87.1, insert footnote indicator 3A.**

(p 304)   **In newly created footnote indicator 3A, insert–**

In previous editions of this work, the foregoing paragraph ended with the sentence: 'Other interpretative criteria may indicate implied repeal, for example the commonsense construction rule or the presumption that

Parliament wishes to avoid an anomalous result'. The sentence was criticised by Buxton LJ (dissenting) in *O'Byrne v Secretary of State for Environment, Transport & Regions* [1996] EWCA Civ 499, [26]. In essence, his Lordship saw the sentence as contrary to the notion that the 'court will not lightly find a case of implied repeal, and the test for it is a high one': *Ibid*, [22]. Accordingly, the sentence has been removed.

(p 305)   **In paragraph beginning 'The presumption against implied repeal', at end of sentence beginning 'It is also stronger', insert footnote indicator 6A.**

(p 305)   **In newly created footnote 6A, insert–**

The preceding two sentences have been judicially approved: *BH v Lord Advocate* [2012] UKSC 24 at [30].

(p 305)   **In footnote 7, after '(Metric Martyrs)', insert–**

; *BH v Lord Advocate* [2012] UKSC 24 at [30] and *R (Governors of Brynmawr Foundation School) v Welsh Ministers* [2011] EWHC 519 (Admin) at [72].

(p 305)   **Delete the third paragraph and replace it with the following, while leaving the contents of footnotes 8 to 9 unchanged–**

In an unreported 1998 case, Popplewell J adopted Code s 87(1). He held that the Firearms Act 1968 s 5(1A) (prohibition of ownership etc without permission of a gun etc) impliedly 'gave the citizen the right to hold arms'. In the latter respect, he was mistaken. The wording of the provision in question, not included in the judgment, is:

> 'That the Subjects which are Protestants may have Arms for their Defence suitable to their Conditions *and as allowed by Law*'.

(p 306)   **In footnote 6 at end, insert–**

s 88   See also *R (Governors of Brynmawr Foundation School) v Welsh Ministers* [2011] EWHC 519 (Admin) at [85].

(p 307)   **In Example 88.3, delete 'Supreme Court Act 1981' and insert–**

Senior Courts Act 1981

(p 307)   **In Example 88.4, delete 's 25(1)(a)' and insert–**

s 25(2)(a)

(p 308)   **In footnote 3 at end, insert–**

Compare the approach of the High Court of Australia, under which the common law presumption against retrospectivity means that a repeal at common law is similar to a provision such as s 16 of the Interpretation

Act 1978: *Australian Education Union v General Manager of Fair Work Australia* [2012] HCA 19 at [24] *et seq.*

(p 309)   **In footnote 4, at end insert–**

s 89   See also *Majeau Carrying Co Pty Ltd v Coastal Rutile Ltd* (1973) 129 CLR 48, 51–52; *Oceania Manufacturing Co Ltd v Pang Kwong-Hon* [1979] HKLR 445, 448–449, 452.

(p 309)   **In footnote 6 at end insert–**

See also the use to which the above discussion was put in *Radin v Vekic* [1997] NSWSC 234.

(p 311)   **In Example 91.1, after 'Companies Act 1985 ss 736 and 736A' insert–**

s 91   (repealed)

(p 314)   **At end of Code s 96, insert footnote indicator 2A.**

(p 314)   **In newly created footnote 2A, insert–**

Code s 96 was approved in *Quinlivan v Governor of Portlaoise Prison* [1998] 2 IR 113. See also *Mullins v Harnett* [1998] 4 IR 426.

(p 314)   **After sideheading 'Subsection (1)', in second sentence, after 'comes into force on a', insert–**

specified date

(p 314)   **In footnote 3, at end insert–**

The above discussion was approved in *Quinlivan v Governor of Portlaoise Prison* [1997] IEHC 181, [1998] 2 IR 113.

(p 315)   **In footnote 1, at end insert–**

See also *R v Cartwright* [2007] EWCA Crim 2581, [27]–[30].

(p 315)   **After heading 'Comment on Code s 97' and words in the first sentence 'in a 1999 case', insert–**

s 97   and the Privy Council in a 2011 appeal.

(p 315)   **In newly created footnote 7, insert–**

Spread Trustee Company Ltd v Hutcheson & Ors (Guernsey) [2011] UKPC 13 at [65].

(p 316)   **In footnote 7 at end, insert–**

See, for example, *Legal Services Commission v Loomba* [2012] EWHC
29 at [63].

(p 317)   **In footnote 3 at end insert–**

and by the British Columbia Court of Appeal in *S (L) v P (E)* (1999) 67
BCLR (3d) 254, [51].

(p 317)   **At the end of the second paragraph, after Example 97.2, insert a
new paragraph–**

Furthermore, some judges have suggested that the presumption does not
apply in relation to an executive statement of policy as to the future
exercise of statutory or prerogative powers.[4A]

(p 317)   **In newly created footnote 4A, insert–**

Odelola v Secretary of State for the Home Department [2009] 1 WLR
1230, 1240–1241, cf 1233, 1243.

(p 317)   **In passage beginning 'It is important to grasp' at end insert
footnote indicator 5A.**

(p 317)   **In newly created footnote 5A insert–**

This passage has been approved by the New Zealand Court of Appeal:
Waitakere CC v Bennett [2008] NZCA 428, [52].

(p 317)   **In footnote 6 after 'at [26]', insert–**

Wilson v First County Trust Ltd (No 2) [2004] 1 AC 816 at 873; *Benner
v Canada (Secretary of State)* [1997] 1 SCR 358 at [39]; *Re: CD (No 2)*
[2011] NICA 21 at [18]; *Australian Education Union v General Manager of Fair Work Australia* [2012] HCA 19 at [26]–[27]. Nonetheless,
some enactments 'do not neatly fall into either category': *Secretary of
State for Energy and Climate Change v Friends of the Earth* [2012]
EWCA Civ 28 at [45]. See also *Leeds Group Plc v Leeds City Council*
[2011] EWCA Civ 1447 at [18]–[19].

(p 319)   **At end of second complete paragraph, before Example 97.5, insert
footnote indicator 4A.**

(p 319)   **In newly created footnote 4A, insert–**

This passage was approved in *Quinlivan v Governor of Portlaoise Prison*
[1997] IEHC 181, [1998] 2 IR 113 and *Mullins v Harnett* [1998] 4 IR
426.

(p 320)   **In footnote 6 at end insert–**

s 98   ; and *R v Tran Viet Tran* [1992] 2 HKLR 184, 188–189. See also the judgment of the Privy Council in *Maroussem v Mauritius Revenue Authority* [2011] UKPC 30 at [20].

(p 324)   **At end of paragraph beginning 'Since the principles regarding retrospectivity', insert–**

s 100   The courts are even more reluctant to accord delegated legislation a retrospective operation and will require a 'clear provision' in the enabling Act conferring power to that effect.[2A]

(p 324)   **In newly created footnote 2A, insert–**

Secretary of State for Energy and Climate Change v Friends of the Earth [2012] EWCA Civ 28 at [43].

(p 325)   **In Example 101.2, after 'Serious Organised Crime and Police Act 2005 ss 132 to 138', insert–**

s 101   (repealed)

(p 329)   **In Comment on Code s 103 at beginning insert–**

s 103   This section of the Code has been judicially approved.[3A]

(p 329)   **In newly created footnote 3A insert–**

See *Serious Organized Crime Agency v Perry* [2009] EWHC 1960 (Admin), [50], where Foskett J rightly recognised that a statement of the extent of an Act in terms of the territories of the United Kingdom to which the Act applied did not decide whether or not it had any application outside of those territories. See further Code ss 130–132.

(p 330)   **In Example 103.5, delete 'Supreme Court Act 1981' and insert–**

Senior Courts Act 1981

(p 331)   **In footnote 8 at end insert–**

s 104   For an affirmation of this approach by the House of Lords, see *Davidson v Scottish Ministers* [2005] UKHL 74.

(p 333)   **In footnote 4 at end, insert–**

See also *Elliot v Joicey* [1935] AC 209, 236. Note that these decisions use the term '*commune forum*' to suggest that proof of the law of any country subject to the jurisdiction of the House of Lords is not required. In other words, that law is not foreign law to be treated as a question of fact. However, the term '*commune forum*' is a useful a description of a court with jurisdiction over more than one country or legal system. See further footnote 8.

(p 333) **In footnote 8 at end, insert–**

See also O Jones, 'When is the Federal Magistrates Court Bound by the Federal Court?' (2012) 86 ALJ 478, 481.

(p 335) **In footnote 2, at end insert–**

s 105 Note, though, the criticism in *Bocardo SA v Star Energy UK Onshore Ltd* [2010] Ch 100, 122.

(p 335) **In footnote 3, at end insert–**

As to the substrata beneath the surface of the land, see *Bocardo SA v Star Energy UK Onshore Ltd* [2010] Ch 100.

(p 336) **In footnote 1, at end insert–**

s 106 See also the reference by the House of Lords to the 'well-established canon of construction that requires clear language if an Act is to be given extra-territorial effect': *King v Serious Fraud Office* [2009] 1 WLR 718, 725.

(p 360) **In footnote 2, at beginning insert–**

s 128 *Walker v New South Wales* (1994) 182 CLR 45, 49; *Lawson v Serco Ltd* [2004] 2 All ER 200, [16].

(p 360) **In footnote 2, at end insert–**

See also *Masri v Consolidated Contractors International Co SAL* [2010] 1 AC 90, 133, where Lord Mance, speaking for the House of Lords, approved of Code s 128, adding '[it] may not apply, at any rate with the same force, to English subjects ...but that is presently irrelevant'. The position of such subjects is in fact dealt with by Code s 131.

(p 362) **In footnote 1, at end insert–**

See further *R (Bancoult) v Secretary of State For Foreign and Common-wealth Affairs* [2009] 1 AC 453, 488, 506–507, 512.

(p 363) **In Example 128.5, after 'ss 555–558', insert–**

(repealed)

(p 366) **In footnote 5, at end insert–**

s 129 See also *Walker v New South Wales* (1994) 182 CLR 45, 49–50.

(p 368) **In footnote 6 at end, insert–**

NML Capital Ltd v Argentina [2011] UKSC 31; *La Generale des Carrieres et des Mines v Hemisphere Associates LLC* [2012] UKPC 27 and *SerVaas Inc v Rafidian Bank* [2012] UKSC 40.

(p 371)   **In footnote 1, at end insert–**

See, eg, *Aveng (Africa) Ltd v Gabonese Republic* [2012] EWHC 1687.

(p 376)   **In Example 130.11, delete 'Supreme Court Act 1981' and insert–**

s 130   'Senior Courts Act 1981'

(p 380)   **At end of first paragraph, delete '(repealed) and Anti-terrorism,
               Crime and Security Act 2001 s 109' and insert–**

s 131   (repealed); Anti-terrorism, Crime and Security Act 2001 s 109 and
             Sexual Offences Act 2003 s 72 (sex tourism).

(p 381)   **In footnote 2, at end, insert–**

See *Lucasfilm Ltd & Ors v Ainsworth & Anor* [2011] UKSC 39.

(p 383)   **In footnote 4 at end, insert–**

See also *Ravat v Halliburton Manufacturing and Services Ltd* [2012]
UKSC 1.

(p 387)   **In 'Comment on Code s 133', at end of second sentence insert–**

s 133   This sentence and Code s 133 were considered by the Divisional Court
             in *Kennet District Council v Young & Ors* [1999] RTR 235, 242–243 and
             by the Federal Court of Australia in *Re: Luckins; Ex parte Columbia
             Pictures Industries Inc* (1996) 67 FCR 549, 556–557.

(p 388)   **In footnote 3, at end insert–**

In reaching this conclusion, Sedley J considered Code s 134: *Ibid*,
242–243.

(p 389)   **In footnote 2 at end, insert–**

s 134   *Brants v DPP* [2011] EWHC 754 at [36]–[37] (deeming for purpose of
             conferring jurisdiction on a court).

(p 393)   **In footnote 5 at end, insert–**

s 136   See also *Cusack v London Borough of Harrow* [2011] EWCA Civ 1514
             (highway barriers authorised to be erected under either s 66 or s 80 of the
             Highways Act 1980).

(p 394)   **In footnote 4 at end, insert–**

As to a limit on that function, see also *Mastercigars Direct Ltd v Withers
LLP* [2009] 1 WLR 881, 919 where Morgan J revealed that his assessors
did not agree with parts of his decision.

(p 394)   **In footnote 6 at end insert–**

and *Re: B (Children)* [2009] 1 AC 11, 38.

(p 403)   **At bottom of page, at the end of the sentence beginning 'For another example', insert–**

s 139   As to the use, in essence, of selective comminution by a trial judge when directing a jury and approval of his doing so on appeal, see *R v Ikram* [2009] 1 WLR 1419, 1432–1433.

(p 413)   **After Example 141.9, insert–**

s 141   *Example 141.10* Lord Dyson has said: 'In construing assessments and care plan reviews, it should not be overlooked that these are documents that are usually drafted by social workers. They are not drafted by lawyers, nor should they be. They should be construed in a practical way against the factual background in which they are written and with the aim of seeking to discover the substance of their true meaning.'[5A]

(p 413)   **In newly created footnote 5A, insert–**

R (McDonald) v Royal Borough of Kensington and Chelsea [2011] UKSC 33 at [53].

(p 422)   **In footnote 6, delete text and insert–**
s 144   [2006] 2 AC 543.

(p 422)   **In footnote 7, delete text and insert–**

Ibid, 556, 569. Note that the accrual of a cause of action for a sum recoverable by virtue of an enactment is a question of a construction of that enactment. In general, though, accrual occurs notwithstanding that the sum remains to be quantified: *Hillingdon LBC v ARC Ltd (No 1)* [1999] Ch 139, 147, 153–154, 157; *Legal Services Commission v Rasool* [2008] 1 WLR 2711, 2722.

(p 426)   **At end of first sentence, before sideheading 'Law and fact', insert–**

Relevance may fall to be determined by implication.

s 145   *Example 145.6* Section 91(1) of the Criminal Justice Act 1967 says: 'any person who in any public place is guilty while drunk of disorderly behaviour, shall be liable on summary conviction to a fine not exceeding level 3 on the standard scale'. Under the ordinary and natural meaning of the relevant terms, this means that the defendant must be drunk by the voluntary consumption of alcohol and also that the disorderly behaviour must not be accidental. Accordingly, it is not relevant to ask whether the defendant had specific drunken intent or was reckless.[1A]

(p 426)   **In newly created footnote 1A, insert–**

Carroll v Director of Public Prosecutions [2009] EWHC 554 (Admin).

(p 427)   **In Comment on Code s 146, at end of second sentence insert footnote indicator 2A.**

(p 427)   **In newly created footnote 2A, insert–**

Re: B (Children) [2009] 1 AC 11, 17, 25.

(p 427)   **In footnote 3, after 'at 704', insert–**

Re: B (Children) [2009] 1 AC 11, 17, 25.

(p 434)   **In footnote 8 at end insert–**

s 149   Compare *Kay v Commissioner of Police of Metropolis* [2008] 1 WLR 2723, 2742.

(p 435)   **In footnote 3 at end insert–**

For an extraordinary failure by prosecuting counsel to assist the court properly see *Attorney General's Reference (No 24 of 2008)* [2008] EWCA Crim 2936, [2009] 3 All ER 839, [30], [37]–[39] (failure to mention Criminal Justice Act 2003 ss 269, 270). Of course, all of the foregoing remarks as to assistance cannot apply to litigants in person or other lay person exercising a right of audience unless they happen to be legal experts. See further p 112.

(p 441)   **After heading Comment on Code s 150, insert–**

s 150   This section of the Code has been judicially approved.

(p 441)   **In the new footnote indicator 1, insert–**

See the opinion of Lord Brodie in *Imperial Tobacco Ltd v Lord Advocate* [2012] CSIH 9 at [175]–[176].

(p 442)   **In footnote 2 at end insert–**

The above passage was adopted by the High Court of Australia in *Project Blue Sky v Australian Broadcasting Authority* (1998) 194 CLR 355, 384.

(p 442)   **In footnote 6 after '384' insert–**

; *Spirerose Ltd v Transport for London* [2009] 1 WLR 1797; *Bocardo SA v Star Energy UK Onshore Ltd* [2010] Ch 100.

(p 442) **At bottom of page, at end of sentence beginning 'This rule may operate', insert footnote 7.**

(p 442) **In newly created footnote 7, insert–**

See *Star Energy Weald Basin Ltd & Anor v Bocardo SA* [2011] AC 380, [146] ('clear' that the *Pointe Gourde* rule 'is a principle of statutory construction' and 'applies …as a matter of construction'.

(p 444) **After sideheading subsection (1), insert–**

s 152 This subsection of the Code has been judicially approved.[1A]

(p 444) **In the newly created footnote 1A, insert–**

See the opinion of Lord Brodie in *Imperial Tobacco Ltd v Lord Advocate* [2012] CSIH 9 at [175].

(p 458) **In Comment on Code s 158 at beginning insert–**

s 158 This Section of the Code has been applied in England and overseas.[4A]

(p 458) **In newly created footnote 4A insert–**

For s 158(a), see *Hyde Park Residence Ltd v Secretary for Environment, Transport & Regions* (2000) 80 P&CR 419, 425. As to s 158 in its entirety, see *Kok Cheng Weng v Wiener* (2007) 2 SLR 709, 731–732.

(p 461) **At end of Example 158.4 insert–**

Example 158.4A In New South Wales, the Crimes Act 1900 s 319 created an offence of perverting the course of justice. Section 312 defined such perverting as 'obstructing, preventing, perverting or defeating the course of justice or the administration of the law'. The Court of Criminal Appeal declined to give the words 'administration of the law' their literal meaning, especially as doing so would criminalise 'a very wide range of conduct, including conduct that was not previously unlawful'. Rather, their Honours understood those words as 'the administration of the civil and criminal law by courts and tribunals', even though this understanding 'differ[ed] little, if at all, from the expression 'the course of justice".'[2A]

(p 461) **In newly created footnote indicator 2A, insert–**

Einfeld v R (2008) 51 MVR 200, [97], [99].

(p 463) **In Comment on Code s 159 at beginning insert–**

s 159 This section of the Code and the Comment thereon has been judicially considered.[2A]

(p 463)   **In newly created footnote 2A insert–**

See the decision of the Alberta Court of Appeal in *Purba v Ryan* (2006) 61 Alta LR (4th) 112, [56].

(p 465)   **At the end of the paragraph beginning 'Some of the grounds',**
insert–

Justice James Edelman of the Supreme Court of Western Australia questions the present work for discounting the former equitable construction in favour of the current strained construction. This is on the ground that equitable construction is based on a meaning the language cannot bear.[A]

Unfortunately, this criticism misfires. Firstly, strained construction within the meaning of the present work is about departure from literal meaning. See further Code s 157. Second, Mr Justice Edelman provides, as examples of equitable construction wrongly maligned by this work, construction that can be taken as effected under other sections of the Code. The judge discusses a construction of the Statute of Frauds that permits proof of a contract by oral evidence so that the Statute is not used as an instrument of fraud or unconscionably relied upon.

This can be classified as a strained construction under Code s 158(b), ie where the consequences of a literal construction are 'so undesirable that Parliament cannot have intended them'. So too can the judge's description of a grant of specific performance notwithstanding the Statute of Frauds. It would also be connected with the presumption that rules of equity apply under Code s 330 and, perhaps, the maxim against profiting from wrong in Code s 349. The presumption in Code s 330, and the principle that the common law should not be subject to casual change under Code s 269, also underpin the decision of the High Court in *Equuscorp Pty Ltd v Haxton*[2B]. That decision was not, as his Honour suggests, an instance of equitable construction. Such construction 'must not be confused' with equity in the proper sense – see Code s 330, pp 1065–1066.

Mr Justice Edelman then refers to a decision of the Supreme Court of the United Kingdom, *Yemshaw v London Borough of Hounslow*[2C] However, as his Honour expressly states, this case involved 'judicial updating of a statute'. This is dealt with as 'updating construction' in Code s 288. That section of the Code has been cited with approval by the Supreme Court, where it has been described by Lord Kerr as the 'more principled way of addressing the question'[2D] and by Lord Clarke as 'entirely consistent' with *Yemshaw*[E].

s 160   In short, equitable construction should not be revived. It goes back to a time when judicial authority was of a breadth that has long been considered outdated (see Code s 330, p 1065–1066). Where equitable construction reflects contemporary concerns, it is adequately dealt with by other sections of the Code. The great danger of equitable construction is that it suggests that judges can depart from the literal meaning of legislation wherever their conscience demands. By discarding equitable construction in favour of strained construction under Code s 157 a more methodical, and measured, treatment of departure from literal meaning arises.

(p 465)   **In newly created footnote 2A, insert–**

Mr Justice Edelman, 'Uncommon Statutory Interpretation', http://www.
supremecourt.wa.gov.au/_files/Uncommon_Statutory_Interpretation_
May_2012.pdf.

                           In newly created footnote 2B, insert–

[2012] HCA 7.

                           In newly created footnote 2C, insert–

[2011] UKSC 3 (*Yemshaw*).

                           In newly created footnote 2D, insert–

Baker v Quantum Clothing Group Ltd [2011] UKSC 17 at [173].

                           In newly created footnote 2E, insert–

NML Capital Ltd v Argentina [2011] UKSC 31 at [142]–[143].

(p 467)   **In Example 162.2, after 'Taxes Management Act 1970 s 20C',**
                                    insert–

s 162   (repealed)

(p 470)   **In footnote 2, delete 'another reference' and replace with–**

s 163   other references

(p 470)   **In footnote 2, after 'at [11]' insert–**

Giles v Rhind [2009] Ch 191, 200. See also p 1091 n 3.

(p 474)   **In footnote 2 at end insert–**

s 165   Note, though, that Gleeson CJ's successor as Chief Justice of Australia
          once described legislative intention as a 'convenient phantom': *Sloane v
          the Minister of Immigration, Local Government and Ethnic Affairs*
          (1992) 37 FCR 429, 443 (French J). See also *R v Hughes* (2000) 202
          CLR 535, 563 (Kirby J). Fortunately, Gleeson CJ's successor as Chief
          Justice of New South Wales shares his belief in legislative intention:
          Spigelman CJ, 'The Principle of Legality and the Clear Statement
          Principle' (2005) 79 ALJ 769. See further R Ekins, 'The Intention of
          Parliament', *Public Law,* October 2010, pp 709–72 and R Ekins, *The
          Nature of Legislative Intent*, OUP, 2012.

(p 479)   **At end of final paragraph, insert footnote indicator 5A.**

(p 479)   **In newly created footnote 5A, insert–**

For effective judicial recognition of dynamic processing, see *Smith v
Northamptonshire CC* [2009] 4 All ER 557, [77]–[78].

(p 484)   **In footnote 3, at end insert–**

s 171   In this respect, see the comment by the Court of Appeal that the
          Restrictive Trade Practices Act 1976 'clearly represents a compromise
          between a variety of commercial and political considerations': *Dale
          Farm Dairy Group Ltd (t/a Northern Dairies) v Akram & Ors* [1998]
          ICR 349, 356.

(p 489)   **In footnote 2, at end insert–**

s 172   For a refusal to draw an implication from a provision on the basis of an
          ellipsis, due to inconsistency with another provision, see *Re: UK Waste
          Management* [1999] NICA 2, [24].

(p 489)   **In paragraph beginning 'In such cases', at end of first sentence
            insert footnote indicator 4A.**

(p 489)   **In newly created footnote 4A, insert–**

          For a discussion of implication in this context, see *Electricity Supply
          Assoc of Australia Ltd v ACCC* (2001) 113 FCR 230, 258.

(p 491)   **In Comment on Code s 173, at beginning insert–**

s 173   This section of the Code has been judicially approved in several
          jurisdictions.

(p 491)   **In newly created footnote 1, insert–**

          Wang v Minister for Immigration & Multicultural Affairs (1997) 71 FCR
          386, 396.

(p 491)   **Replace footnote indicators 1 to 5 with footnote indicators 2 to 6.**

(p 494)   **In Comment on Code s 174, at beginning, before sideheading
            'Guides to legislative intention', insert–**

s 174   This section of the Code has been judicially approved.[2A]

(p 494)   **In newly created footnote 2A, insert–**

          Frucor Beverages Ltd v Rio Beverages Ltd [2001] 2 NZLR 604, [36];
          Re: Application by the Local Government Auditor [2003] NIQB 21, [11].

(p 494)   **In footnote 6, at end of second sentence insert–**

          Further, in *Jayasinghe v Minister for Immigration & Ethnic Affairs*
          (1997) 76 FCR 301, 315, the Federal Court of Australia remarked '[t]he
          threshold of 'necessity' has been rejected in favour of the formulation
          that the implication be 'proper''. See also *Liu Pik Han v Hong Kong
          Federation of Insurers Appeals Tribunal* [2005] 3 HKC 242, [23].

(p 495)   **In footnote 6 delete text and insert–**

This paragraph has been adopted by the Full Federal Court of Australia: *Austereo Ltd v Trade Practices Commission* (1993) 41 FCR 1, 37.

(p 497)   **In footnote 4 at end insert–**

See also *Nguyen v Minister for Health & Ageing* [2002] FCA 1241 (express power to revoke an approval granted to two people carried implicit power of partial revocation affecting only one of those people) and *A v Securities and Futures Commission* [2008] 1 HKLRD 591, [23] (power to conduct interview impliedly enabled audio recording of interview).

(p 497)   **In footnote 8, at end of first sentence insert–**

Brent London Borough Council v Risk Management Partners Ltd [2010] PTSR 349.

(p 497)   **In footnote 8, after '[1996] 4 All ER 129', insert–**

Egan v Basildon Borough Council [2011] EWHC 2416 at [27] (s 111(1) 'reflects the long established rule' in *A-G v Great Eastern Rly Co*).

(p 498)   **In footnote 2, at end of second sentence insert–**

See also *Dolphin Quays Development Ltd v Mills* [2008] 1 WLR 1829. This sentence was adopted in *Re: Application by the Local Government Auditor* [2003] NIQB 21, [12].

(p 498)   **After Example 174.4, insert–**

Example 174.5 The Court of Appeal held that where a statute created a 'commercial entity for the purpose of engaging in international and domestic trade', Parliament intended the entity 'have the capacity to enter into the whole range of transactions that a commercial organisation acting in that field of business would ordinarily undertake and that the Act should be interpreted as giving it capacity to enter into any transaction that could fairly be said to be incidental or conducive to its statutory objects'.[2A]

(p 498)   **In newly created footnote 2A, insert–**

Standard Chartered Bank v Ceylon Petroleum Corporation [2012] EWCA Civ 1049 at [31].

(p 498)   **After sentence beginning 'Implied ancillary powers do not include', insert–**

Further, the 'implied conferment of powers is subject to any express or implied statutory restriction'.[3A] In particular, the powers 'cannot expand the functions of a statutory body'.[3B]

(p 498)   **In newly created footnote 3A, insert–**

Virdi v The Law Society of England and Wales & Anor [2010] EWCA
Civ 100 at [30].

(p 498)   **In newly created footnote 3B, insert–**

*Financial Services Compensation Scheme Ltd v Abbey National Treasury
Services Plc* [2008] EWHC 1897 at [30]. As to the distinction between
functions and powers, see the judgment of the Federal Court of Australia
in *Edelsten v Health Insurance Commission* (1990) 27 FCR 56 at 62–63.

(p 498)   **In final paragraph, delete 'Supreme Court Act 1981' and insert–**

Senior Courts Act 1981

(p 499)   **In first paragraph, delete 'Supreme Court Act 1981' and insert–**

Senior Courts Act 1981

(p 502)   **In footnote 4 at end insert–**

s 176   The common law referred to in the Criminal Justice Act 2003
          s 166(3)(b), being the totality principle relevant to consecutive sen-
          tences, exemplifies the need for further processing referred to by
          Donaldson J. As to the principle, see *R v Raza* [2009] EWCA Crim
          1413; [2009] Crim LR 820.

(p 503)   **In footnote 1 at end, insert–**

See also *Kuehne v Revenue and Customs* [2012] EWCA Civ 34 at [14],
[42].

(p 504)   **In footnote 5 at end, insert–**

See also *Abou-Rahmah v Abacha* [2007] 1 Lloyd's Rep 115 and *Sinclair
Investments (UK) Ltd v Versailles Trade Finance Ltd* [2011] EWCA Civ
347. In the latter case, it was suggested at [74]–[75] that, before the
Privy Council would be followed in preference to the Supreme Court, it
must be a 'foregone conclusion' that, in the event of an appeal, the
Supreme Court would do so. See further O Jones, 'When is the Federal
Magistrates Court Bound by the Federal Court?' (2012) 86 ALJ 478,
480–483.

(p 504)   **At end of final paragraph, insert, as a new paragraph–**

s 177   It should be noted that an interstitial articulation is not concerned with
          improving the drafting of the enactment in question. It keeps to the
          official wording except so far as is needed to express clearly the rival
          legal meanings. Defects in that wording, such as unnecessary repetition,
          should therefore be ignored. An interstitial articulation is directed solely
          to bringing out a possible operative legal meaning of the enactment.

(p 508)   **After Example 179.9, insert–**

s 179   *Example 179.9A* The House of Lords held that a requirement in the Asylum and Immigration (Treatment of Claimants, Etc.) Act 2004 s 19(3)(b) for the written permission of the Secretary of State to marry in the United Kingdom was to be read as if there were appended to it 'such permission not to be withheld in the case of a qualified applicant seeking to enter into a marriage which is not one of convenience and the application for, and grant of, such permission not to be subject to conditions which unreasonably inhibit exercise of the applicant's right under article 12 of the European Convention'.[10A]

(p 508)   **In newly created footnote 10A, insert–**

R (Baiai) v Secretary of State for the Home Department [2009] 1 AC 287, 306.

(p 508)   **In footnote 11, at end of first sentence insert–**

Perrin v Northampton BC [2008] 1 WLR 1307, 1329–1330; *JT (Cameroon) v Secretary of State for the Home Department* [2009] 1 WLR 1411, 1418.

(p 513)   **In footnote 6 at end insert–**

s 180   This statement and the above commentary were adopted in *Securities and Futures Commission v Stock Exchange of Hong Kong Ltd* [1992] 1 HKLR 135, 144.

(p 517)   **In footnote 8 at end, insert–**

s 182   Cf *Dowds v R* [2012] EWCA Crim 281 at [37]–[38].

(p 517)   **In final paragraph, at end of third sentence, insert footnote indicator 9.**

(p 517)   **In newly created footnote 9 insert–**

This passage was adopted in *Mullins v Harnett* [1998] 4 IR 426.

(p 518)   **In footnote 1 at end, insert–**

See also *Dowds v R* [2012] EWCA Crim 281 at [37]–[38] and *Secretary of State for the Home Department* v AY [2012] EWHC 2054 at [148].

(p 519)   **In footnote 7 at end, insert–**

The New Zealand provision was interpreted by New Zealand courts as merely mandating purposive construction. It has since been replaced with a provision more clearly mandating such construction. See *Interpretation Act 1999* (NZ) s 5(1) and J Burrows and R Carter, *Statute Law in New Zealand* (4th edn, Wellington, Lexis Nexis, 2009), pp 203–207.

There is a similar provision in Hong Kong, Interpretation and General Clauses Ordinance (Cap 1) (HK) s 19, which has been described by the Hong Kong Court of Final Appeal as 'dealing with what is to be done rather than how to do it': *Medical Council of Hong Kong v Chow Siu Shek* [2000] 2 HKLRD 674, 683. The Court found the 'how' in Code s 193. As to the Canadian provision, see R Sullivan, *Sullivan and Driedger's Construction of Statutes* (4th edn, Markham, Butterworths, 2002), pp 199–200.

(p 521)   **In Comment on Code s 185, at beginning insert–**

s 185   This section of the Code has been judicially approved.[5A]

(p 521)   **In newly created footnote 5A, insert–**

Nangles Nurseries v Commissioners of Valuation [2008] IEHC 73, 41.

(p 526)   **In Example 186.9, after 's 14(1)(b)', insert–**

s 186   (repealed)

(p 531)   **In footnote 1 at end, insert–**

See further *Russell v Devine* [2003] WLR 1187.

(p 544)   **In Comment on Code s 193, at beginning, insert–**

s 193   This section of the Code has been judicially approved.[6A]

(p 544)   **In newly created footnote 6A, insert–**

Medical Council of Hong Kong v Chow Siu Shek [2000] 2 HKLRD 674, 683.

(p 546)   **After sideheading 'The basic rule', at end of first sentence, insert footnote indicator 7.**

(p 546)   **In newly created footnote 7, insert–**

Note that different rules, including a rule of generous construction, may apply in jurisdictions with a written constitution. See, for example, *Ng Ka Ling & Others v. Director of Immigration* (1999) 2 HKCFAR 4; *Department of Land Affairs v Goedgelegen Tropical Fruits* [2007] ZACC 12, [53], [55].

(p 548)   **After heading 'Comment on Code s 195', insert–**

s 195   This section of the Code has been judicially approved.

(p 548) **In newly created footnote 3, insert–**

Kaye v Lawrence [2010] EWHC 2678 (TCC) at [43]; *Secretary of State for Home Department v AY* [2012] EWHC 2054 at [148]; *Irish Life and Permanent Group Holdings PLC v Credit Institutions Stabilisation Act 2010* [2012] IEHC 89 at [21].

(p 549) **In footnote 3 at end insert–**

This statement has been judicially approved: *R (RD) v Secretary of State for Work and Pensions* [2010] EWCA Civ 18, [47].

(p 551) **After Section 196, insert heading 'Comment on Code s 196'.**

(p 551) **After newly created heading 'Comment on Code s 196', insert–**

This section of the Code has been judicially approved.

(p 551) **In newly created footnote indicator 6, insert–**

Kaye v Lawrence [2010] EWHC 2678 (TCC) at [43].

(p 552) **In Comment on Code s 197, at beginning insert–**

s 197 This section of the Code has been judicially approved.

(p 552) **In newly created footnote 1, insert–**

Quinlivan v Governor of Portlaoise Prison [1998] 2 IR 113; *Mullins v Harnett* [1998] 4 IR 426.

(p 552) **After sentence 'This section of the Code has been judicially approved' insert–**

Indeed the High Court has said that, 'in construing the statute', s 197 is one of 'the basic principles of construction to be followed'.

(p 552) **In newly created footnote indicator 2, insert–**

Kaye v Lawrence [2010] EWHC 2678 (TCC) at [43]–[44].

(p 552) **Replace footnote indicators 1 to 9 with footnote indicators 3 to 11.**

(p 554) **In paragraph beginning 'Drafters are often silent', at end of second sentence insert footnote indicator 2A.**

(p 554) **In newly created footnote 2A insert–**

This paragraph has been judicially approved: *A v Securities and Futures Commission* [2008] 1 HKLRD 591, [20].

(p 554)   **In footnote 5 at end insert–**

Note, though, that where a period ends in Sunday or other *dies non* it is common sense to treat it as extended to include the next *dies utilis* or working day: see *Mucelli v Government of Albania* [2009] 1 WLR 276, 298.

(p 555)   **In footnote 7 at end insert–**

For judicial approval of this passage, see *New Zealand Customs Service v Wang* [2010] NZAR 322, [32].

(p 562)   **In footnote 7 at end insert–**

s 199   The sentence to which this footnote relates has been judicially approved: *Wealthcare Financial Planning Pty Ltd v Financial Industry Complaints Service Ltd* (2009) 69 ACSR 418, [37].

(p 562)   **In footnote 8 at end insert–**

See also the approval of the Full Federal Court of Australia in *Minister for Immigration and Multicultural Affairs v Hu* (1997) 79 FCR 309, 324 ('usual occupation') and the NSW Court of Appeal in *Manly Council v Malouf* (2004) 61 NSWLR 394, [8] ('shop'). See also *Phillips v Mulcaire* [2012] UKSC 28 at [21], where the Court considered this passage and said '[h]ere there is no particular potency about the expression ... because there is a general consensus as to its core content ... but no general consensus as to its limits'. However, the Court also said '[s]uch limited potency as there is in the expression ... may be of assistance in determining the meaning'.

(p 562)   **In footnote 9 at end insert–**

; *R (Heffernan) v Rent Service* [2008] 1 WLR 1702, 1720–1721 ('locality').

(p 565)   **In third paragraph, at end of third sentence, before Example 199.14, insert footnote indicator 6A.**

(p 565)   **In newly created footnote 6A, insert–**

This passage was approved by an Australian intermediate appellate court in *Munn v Agus* (1997) 6 NTLR 84 and by the Federal Court of Canada in *Hrushka v Canada (Minister of Foreign Affairs)* [2009] FC 69, [16].

(p 565)   **After Example 199.14, insert–**

Example 199.14A Mummary LJ said: 'If it was the legislative intention to prohibit interest on charges for credit, the prohibition would not have been by way of a side wind in a definition section: it is the kind of measure that would have been expressly and clearly spelt out somewhere else in [the Consumer Credit Act 1974] and it is not.'[7A]

(p 565)   **In newly created footnote 7A, insert–**

Southern Pacific Personal Loans Ltd v Walker [2009] EWCA Civ 1218 at [34].

(p 569)   **In footnote 6 at end insert–**

See also *Re: Dairy Farmers of Britain Ltd* [2010] Ch 63.

(p 569)   **In footnote 7 at end insert–**

See also the decision of the Federal Court of Australia in *Re: Interchase Corp Ltd (in liq) (No 2)* (1993) 47 FCR 253, 260–261.

(p 570)   **In footnote 5 at end insert–**

This dictum was applied in *Health Service Executives v Commissioners for Valuation* [2008] IEHC 178, [9].

(p 570)   **In footnote 7 at end, insert–**

This example was considered by the Supreme Court in *Phillips v Mulcaire* [2012] UKSC 28 at [20].

(p 571)   **In Example 199.28, after 'the Judicature Act 1925', insert–**

(definition repealed)

(p 573)   **In footnote 8 at end insert–**

It is submitted that Lord Hoffmann NPJ, speaking for the Hong Kong Court of Final Appeal, effectively recognised enlarging definitions in *Penny's Bay Investment Co Ltd v Director of Lands* [2010] HKCFA 12, [38].

(p 573)   **In third complete paragraph, at end insert–**

In particular, the presence of X does not, apart from the operation of its ordinary meaning, normally affect the width of the ordinary meaning of T.[8A] Despite the typical form, it is possible for an enlarging definition to appear alongside a definition of the term subject to the enlarging definition. Instead of comprising 'T includes X', the enactment will state 'T means X and includes Y', with Y being the enlarging definition.[8B]

(p 573)   **In newly created footnote 8A, insert–**

Revenue & Customs v Premier Foods Ltd [2007] EWHC 3134 (Ch), [17]. Note that the opposite may be true, in the sense that T may affect the width of the ordinary meaning of X under the potency of the term defined: see pp 562–564. For an example of an enlarging definition arguably attracting the latter, see Female Genital Mutilation Act s 6(1) ('girl includes woman').

(p 573)   **In newly created footnote 8B insert–**

Begg v Commissioner of Inland Revenue [2009] 3 NZLR 353, [18]–[19];
Moweno Pty Ltd v Stratis Promotions Pty Ltd [2003] NSWCA 376,
[61].

(p 576)   **In first complete paragraph, at end of first sentence, before
                  Example 200.1, insert footnote indicator 3A.**

(p 576)   **In newly created footnote 3A, insert–**

It has been said of this sentence 'That holds weight in respect of
Interpretation Acts where the purpose is to collect generally applicable
definitions and terms. Provisions of the [Irish] Interpretation Act 2005,
however, go much further than this 'traditional' function of Interpretation Acts': D Dodd Statutory Interpretation in Ireland (Tottel, 2008) p.
254.

(p 576)   **After Example 200.1, insert–**

In other words, the Interpretation Act 'supplements and does not override' other legislation and 'has to give way' where the legislation
'provides otherwise'.[4A] The effect of the reasoning of the Judicial
Committee in Example 200.1, which has been applied by the House of
Lords,[4B] is as follows. In ascertaining whether a provision of the
Interpretation Act has been displaced, it is first necessary to consider the
provision 'in its setting in the legislation' and also 'the substance and
tenor of the legislation as a whole'. It is then necessary to ask whether:

- the legislature, had it been offered an amendment to the relevant
Bill corresponding to the provision, would have rejected it; or
- whether the application of that provision would 'change the
character' of the legislation or 'presuppose a different legislative
policy'.[4C]

The High Court of Australia has suggested a different test. A provision
of interpretation legislation will not apply where it is 'clearly inconsistent' with the substantive enactment.[4D]

(p 576)   **In newly created footnote 4A, insert–**

Securities and Futures Commission v Stock Exchange of Hong Kong Ltd
[1992] 1 HKLR 135, 143.

(p 576)   **In newly created footnote 4B, insert–**

Floor v Davis [1980] AC 695.

(p 576)   **In newly created footnote 4C, insert–**

Blue Metal Industries Ltd v Dilley [1970] AC 827 at 846–848. The above
summary of the jurisprudence of the Board is taken from O Jones,
'Noxious Antiquity? Life in Hong Kong without the Application of
English Law Ordinance' (2009) 39 HKLJ 793 at 803.

(p 576)   **In newly created footnote 4D, insert–**

Attorney-General (Qld) v Australian Industrial Relations Commission (2002) 213 CLR 485 at [52]. See also *Alcan (NT) Alumina Pty Ltd v Commissioner of Territory Revenue* (2009) 239 CLR 27 at [39].

(p 576)   **At bottom of page, insert new paragraph–**

However, the effect of the Interpretation Act is that an unincorporated association may be criminally liable, at least for offences involving strict liability. The Crown may, at its discretion, in light of relevant considerations and subject to oppression involving abuse of process, bring a prosecution against either the association its own name or its members.[9A]

(p 576)   **In newly created footnote 9A, insert–**

R v L [2009] 1 Cr App R 16.

(p 578)   **In Example 200.7, after 'Homicide Act 1957 s 3', insert–**

(repealed)

(p 579)   **At end of second sentence, insert–**

Further, damage to a substance from or part of the body of a person, where the substance or part has previously been separated from the body without unlawful injury to the person, cannot give rise to such injury.[3A]

(p 579)   **In newly created footnote 3A, insert–**

Yearworth v North Bristol NHS Trust [2010] QB 1, 11–12. See, generally, R Hardcastle, Law and the Human Body: Property Rights, Ownership and Control (Oxford, Hart Publishing, 2007).

(p 579)   **In footnote 4, at end insert –**

As to contrary intention see Example 200.10A below.

(p 580)   **At top of page, at end of quotation, before paragraph beginning 'As so often happens', insert new paragraph–**

Care must be taken to ensure that recourse to the rule is necessary. A challenge to conduct by reference to the rule could fail because the conduct is lawful regardless of whether a particular term is pluralised.

> *Example 200.10A* Section 6(4) of the Local Government and Public Involvement in Health Act 2007 says that the Boundary Committee must, before making an alternative proposal as to the structure of local government for an area to the Secretary of State under s 5(3)(c) of the Act, publish and facilitate representations as to a draft of the alternative proposal. The Secretary of State had a discretion to implement the alternative proposal under s 7(1)(b) of the Act. The Committee acted on the basis that it could only

consult in respect of and transmit to the Secretary of State one draft alternative proposal. The trial judge upheld a challenge to this course, ruling that s 6(c) of the Interpretation Act 1978 applied, emphasising that 'any contrary intention must be garnered not simply from one statutory provision but from a consideration of the legislation as a whole and the purposes behind it'. The Court of Appeal endorsed this analysis. However, the Court suggested that the assistance of s 6(c) was unnecessary. The Committee could consult on various draft alternative proposals. Further, the Secretary of State could received and consider all of those, but could only implement one. The Court seems to be saying that, even if the relevant terms were read in the singular, the powers to which they relate could be exercised more than once. If so, functus officio should have been discussed. In short, though, the Committee and the Secretary could act *intra vires* even without pluralisation.[1A]

(p 580)   **In newly created footnote 1A insert–**

East Devon District Council v Electoral Commission (The Boundary Committee for England) [2009] EWHC 4 (Admin) [37]–[38], reversed on other grounds; *R (Breckland District Council) v Electoral Commission Boundary Committee for England* [2009] PTSR 1611, [78]–[80]. See also F A R Bennion, ' *"Never On The Cards": Fighting For Two-Tier Local Government'*, 173 CL&J (31 Jan 2009) pp 72–75, www.francisbennion.com/2009/005.htm, [15]–[23]. For a more restrictive approach to the ascertainment of contrary intention in this context, see *C & E Pty Ltd v CMC Brisbane Pty Ltd (Administrators Appointed)* [2004] QCA 60, [20].

(p 585)   **At beginning of Comment on Code s 201, after Subsection (1) insert–**

s 201   This section of the Code was recently considered by the Supreme Court of the United Kingdom.

(p 585)   **In newly created footnote 1 insert–**

R (BA (Nigeria)) v Secretary of State for the Home Department [2010] 1 AC 444, 458. Regrettably, the Court reduced s 201 and Part XIV of the Code to the *Barras* principle, as to which see Code s 210(3). The Court then said one should look beyond Code s 201 and Part XIV to the 'elementary principle … that the words of the statute should be construed in the context of the scheme of the statute as a whole'. This is something plainly embraced by Code ss 201(2) and 202. Thus, it was necessary for the Court to look not beyond but further within the informed interpretation rule. For broader recognition of Code s 201, see *Chan Ching Kit v Lam Sik Shi* [2002] HKCFI 132, [18]–[19] and *Lee Yiu Kee v Chinese University of Hong Kong* [2010] HKCA 218, [73].

(p 588)   **In Comment on Code s 202 at beginning insert–**

s 202   This section of the Code has been judicially approved.[1A]

(p 588)   **In newly created footnote 1A insert–**

Lee Yiu Kee v Chinese University of Hong Kong [2010] HKCA 218, [73].
See also the opinion of Lord Brodie in *Imperial Tobacco Ltd v
Lord Advocate* [2012] CSIH 9 at [176].

(p 589)   **In second complete paragraph, at end of sentence 'The words are
not deployed in a vacuum', insert–**

Rather, as Lord Steyn has said, 'in law, context is everything'.[3A]

(p 589)   **In newly created footnote 3A, insert–**

R (Daly) v Secretary of State for Home Department [2001] 2 AC 532,
548.

(p 591)   **In sentence beginning 'In any proceedings', at end insert footnote
indicator 7.**

(p 591)   **In newly created footnote 7, insert–**

Note that Code s 203(b) is directed to the need to avoid prolonging
proceedings in which an issue of interpretation arises. It does not permit
a court in such proceedings to prefer one construction over another on
the ground that it will consequently avoid prolongation of some kind.
See O Jones, 'Neglectful statutory interpretation? A commentary on
Goldie v Minister for Immigration and Multicultural Affairs' (2005) 45
AIAL Forum 48 at 53, discussing the reasons of Carr J of the Federal
Court of Australia in *Goldie v Minister for Immigration and Multicultural Affairs* (2002) 121 FCR 383 at 398.

(p 593)   **In footnote 3 at end insert–**

s 205   The above passage was approved in *Transpower New Zealand Limited v
Taupo District Council* [2007] NZHC 999, [13] and *Avowal Administrative Attorneys Ltd v District Court at North Shore* [2007] NZHC 714,
[7].

(p 594)   **In Comment on Code s 206, after 'David Pannick QC', insert–**

s 206   (as his Lordship then was)

(p 600)   **In footnote 1 at end, insert–**

s 210   Compare *Aic Ltd v Nigeria* [2003] EWHC 1357 at [34] where, in the
context of state immunity, it was said the Greer Report 'casts no light on
this point'. See also *New Cap Reinsurance Corporation Ltd v Grant*
[2012] 1 All ER 755 at [34] where the Court of Appeal found the Greer
Report '*at worst equivocal and unclear*' in relation to the application of
the Act to judgments in insolvency proceedings.

(p 600)   **In footnote 6 at end, insert–**

For other judicial consideration of Code s 210(3), see *Ward v Chief Adjudication Officer* [1998] EWCA Civ 1552; *BBC Scotland v Souster* 2001 SC 458, [28].

(p 600)   **After sideheading 'Subsection (3)', at end of sentence beginning 'What follows', insert footnote indicator 6A.**

(p 600)   **In newly created footnote 6A, insert–**

Subsection (3) of this section of the Code was effectively applied by the High Court, constituted by three justices, in *R (Woolas) v Speaker of the House of Commons* [2010] EWHC 3169 at [86].

(p 601)   **In footnote 1 after 'construed in the same way' insert–**

Commissioner of Inland Revenue v N Evans [2008] NZHC 1017, [34] (repeated appearance of concept of aiding and abetting in criminal legislation).

(p 601)   **In footnote 10 at end, insert–**

See also *Norman v Cheshire Fire & Rescue Service* [2011] EWHC 3305 (QB) at [52] where it was stated that Code s 210(3) 'applies to secondary as well as primary legislation, and it is not confined to statements of the law made by way of binding precedent'.

(p 601)   **After paragraph beginning 'The Barras principle', insert–**

The *Barras* principle has been criticised by Sir Owen Dixon of the High Court of Australia as 'quite artificial' and 'the mechanics of law-making no longer provide it with the foundation in probability which the doctrine was supposed once to have possessed'.[A] That court has since noted criticisms such as Sir Owen's, but nonetheless applied the *Barras* principle where it was 'considerably strengthened' by legislative history.[B] It is submitted that, in light of Code s 193, the approach of the High Court should be understood as giving varying weight to the *Barras* principle from case to case, without denying its application for all time. This reflects the way the *Barras* principle operates in England. For example, the High Court recently stated that it 'does not offer a solution in this case'.[C]

(p 601)   **In newly created footnote 10A, insert–**

R v Reynhoudt (1962) 107 CLR 381 at 388.

(p 601)   **In newly created footnote 10B, insert–**

Re: Alcan Australia Ltd; Ex parte Federation of Industrial Manufacturing & Engineering Employees (1994) 181 CLR 96 at 106–107.

(p 601)   **In newly created footnote 10C, insert–**

R (Payne) v Secretary of State for Work and Pensions [2010] EWHC 2162 (Admin) at [44].

(p 603)   **At bottom of page, in the last line, after 'was intended', insert footnote indicator 10A.**

(p 603)   **In newly created footnote 10A, insert–**

These words were considered by the Court of Appeal in *Ward v Chief Adjudication Officer* [1998] EWCA Civ 1552 and by the Irish High Court in *Action Aid Ltd v Revenue Commissioners* [1997] IEHC 196.

(p 604)   **In footnote 7 at end insert–**

See also *R (Friends of the Earth) v Secretary of State for Business, Enterprise and Regulatory Reform* [2009] EWCA Civ 810, [25].

(p 606)   **In second paragraph, at end of fourth sentence, insert footnote indicator 5A**

(p 606)   **In newly created footnote 5A, insert–**

This passage was approved by the Divisional Court in *Staff Side of the Police Negotiating Board & Anor v Secretary of State for the Home Department* [2008] EWHC 1173 (Admin), [44].

(p 607)   **In footnote 1 at end insert–**

For a case where a consolidation with amendments was effected and was considered in support of an interpretation of the legislation as it stood before the consolidation, see *Isle of Anglesey CC v Welsh Ministers* [2010] QB 163, 177–180. In that case, the Court of Appeal also considered the history of consolidations with amendments.

(p 608)   **In footnote 4, after 'at 144', insert–**

s 212   Lord Herschell's rule was cited with approval by the Privy Council in *Farquharson v R* [1973] AC 786.

(p 610)   **In footnote 2 at end insert–**

s 213   This could extend to preparatory steps taken by the Executive for the promotion of new legislation in advance of its enactment, to the extent that they shed light on its meaning. As to such steps, see *R (Shrewsbury) v Secretary of State for Communities and Local Government* [2008] 3 All ER 548. See also p 205 n 10.

(p 617)   **Before sideheading 'Nature of parliamentary materials', insert
               sideheading 'Aim of rule'**

The Supreme Court recently observed that the 'purpose of the exercise is
to determine the intention of the legislator'.[2A] A month later, the Judicial
Committee of the Privy Council remarked:

> 'The textual changes do not therefore make clear the purpose of
> the amendments to s.4(7). The respondent submits that assistance
> can, however, be obtained as to the general background and as to
> the mischief which the legislation was addressing by looking at the
> reports of the proceedings in Parliament ... But Lord Steyn was
> careful to distinguish this principle from the more radical separate
> principle recognised in *Pepper v Hart* ... He said of the former
> principle that "the use of Hansard material to identify the mischief
> at which legislation was directed and its objective setting" was
> permissible, but that "trying to discover the intentions of the
> Government from Ministerial statements in Parliament is constitu-
> tionally unacceptable'.
>
> The separate principle in *Pepper v Hart* ... only allows a court to
> have regard to go further in looking at statements in Parliament
> where (a) legislation is ambiguous or obscure or leads to absurdity,
> (b) the Parliamentary material relied upon consists of one or more
> statements by a minister or other promoter of a bill together with
> such other statements and material as are necessary to understand
> such statements and (c) the statements relied upon are clear ... It is
> therefore permissible as a first step to look at Hansard to try to
> identify the mischief at which the [provision] was aimed and its
> objective setting.'[2B]

It appears, therefore, that the Judicial Committee would allow regard to
Parliamentary material wherever to do so would throw light on the
mischief, irrespective of ambiguity in the legislation. This approach has
previously been taken by the Judicial Committee and the Hong Kong
Court of Final Appeal.[2C] At first blush, it would appear to contradict the
Supreme Court, which identifies the aim of the rule in *Pepper v Hart*,
including its prerequisite of ambiguity, as ascertaining the intention of
the legislator.

s 217   Whatever may be said of the general propriety of regard to parliamentary material, it is submitted that the Supreme Court was not intending to
adopt an approach inconsistent with that of the Judicial Committee. It
was simply suggesting that, when regard is had to parliamentary material, the purpose is to shed light on the meaning intended by Parliament
with the words used in the legislation.

(p 617)   **In newly created footnote 2A, insert–**

Gow v Grant [2012] UKSC 29 at [29].

(p 617)   **In newly created footnote 2B, insert–**

Presidential Insurance Co Ltd v Resha St. Hill [2012] UKPC 33
at [23]–[24].

(p 617)   **In newly created footnote 2C, insert–**

Ramdass v Bahaw-Nanan [2009] UKPC 51 at [16] (materials form the legislature 'cast no light at all on the main issue of statutory construction raised in this appeal (and so cannot possibly qualify under the rule in *Pepper v Hart* ... but they do help to explain the social background and general purpose of the Bill'); *HKSAR v Cheung Kwun Yin* (2009) 12 HKCFAR 568 at [15]–[17] (materials from the legislature 'may be used to identify the purpose of the statutory provision [but] employing [those materials] in order to ascertain the meaning of the statutory words stands in a fundamentally different position'). Compare discussion of *Steele Ford v Newtown v Crown Prosecution Service (No 2)* [1994] 1 AC 22 at p 621.

(p 617)   **After sideheading 'Nature of parliamentary materials', at end of paragraph, insert–**

Nonetheless, in recent times, the courts have not been restrictive as to the nature of the parliamentary materials attracting the rule in *Pepper v Hart*.[8A]

(p 617)   **In newly created footnote 8A, insert–**

Gow v Grant [2012] UKSC 29 at [29] (rule applying to letter setting out the government's views in response to issues raised by parliamentary committee).

(p 617)   **After sideheading 'Cases where rule applies', at end of quotation from Lord Browne-Wilkinson, insert–**

However, the Supreme Court recently observed that the 'rather strict rules that were laid down in [*Pepper v Hart*] have become gradually more relaxed'.[9A]

(p 617)   **In newly created footnote 9A insert–**

Gow v Grant [2012] UKSC 29 at [29].

(p 618)   **At end of paragraph beginning 'The rule in Pepper v Hart', insert–**

Nonetheless, despite observing that the rule in *Pepper v Hart* had become 'gradually more relaxed', the Supreme Court has still insisted that legislation be 'ambiguous' before the rule can apply.

(p 618)   **In newly created footnote 11, at end insert–**

Gow v Grant [2012] UKSC 29 at [29].

(p 621)   **At end of first passage, before paragraph beginning 'It has been suggested', insert–**

Lord Neuberger has also recently exhibited a similar lack of enthusiasm for the use of Hansard, albeit without reference to the *Pepper v Hart* conditions.[3A]

(p 621)   **In newly created footnote 3A, insert–**

See *Malcolm v Lewisham LBC* [2008] 1 AC 1399, where Lord Neuberger was 'in insufficient doubt as to the correct answer to justify
looking at the parliamentary material' and thought doing so was only in
'rare cases …appropriate' (at 1446) and an 'exceptional course' (at
1447). On the other hand, Baroness Hale considered the *Pepper v Hart*
conditions to be met (at 1427) and referred to parliamentary material
'[f]or what it may additionally be worth' and to 'confirm the [relevant]
construction' (at 1428). See also *Yarl's Wood Immigration Ltd v Bedfordshire Police Authority* [2010] 2 WLR 1322, 1347.

(p 623)   **Before sideheading 'Comment Part Six: Duty of Advocates', insert–**

In any event, the Supreme Court recently observed that the 'rather strict
rules that were laid down in [*Pepper v Hart*] have become gradually
more relaxed'.[8A]

(p 623)   **In newly created footnote 8A, insert–**

Gow v Grant [2012] UKSC 29 at [29].

(p 627)   **In footnote 8 at end, insert–**

Stubbings v Webb was overruled and *Letang v Cooper* restored in *A v
Hoare* [2008] 1 AC 844.

(p 640)   **In footnote 2, after sentence beginning 'As to subsequent
changes' insert–**

s 218   See also *Schanka v Employment National (Administration) Pty Ltd*
[2001] FCA 1623 at [35]–[36]; *Chief Executive, Department of Natural
Resources and Mines v Kent Street P/L* [2009] QCA 399 at [101].

(p 642)   **In footnote 1 at end insert–**

s 219   See also *Davidson v Scottish Ministers (No 1)* [2005] UKHL 74, [50].
Note, however, the more recent disapproval of their use in *R (Public and
Commercial Services Union) v Minister for Civil Service* [2010] EWHC
1027 (Admin), [55] where Sales J said 'it is fundamental that all
materials which are relevant to the proper interpretation of such an
instrument should be available to any person who wishes to inform
himself about the meaning of that law. That is not the position in relation
to notes on clauses and for that reason I do not consider they are a
legitimate aid to construction of an Act of Parliament'. For an instance
where notes on clauses may have been, after enactment, reissued as an
explanatory note, see *Imperial Tobacco Ltd v Lord Advocate* [2012]
CSIH 9 at [88], [186].

(p 643)   **At end of quotation appearing at top of page, insert footnote indicator 1A.**

(p 643)   **In new footnote 1A, insert–**

Compare, in relation to an explanatory note after enactment, *Imperial Tobacco Ltd v Lord Advocate* [2012] CSIH 9 at [13], [88], [184]–[188].

(p 643)   **Before sideheading 'Textual memoranda', at end of paragraph, insert–**

The previous sentence has been judicially approved.[2A]

(p 643)   **In new footnote 2A, insert–**

See the opinion of Lord Brodie in *Imperial Tobacco Ltd v Lord Advocate* [2012] CSIH 9 at [187].

(p 662)   **In paragraph beginning 'In another 1976 case', after 'Prevention of Corruption Act 1916', insert–**

s 220   (repealed)

(p 673)   **In footnote 7 at end, insert–**

As to its meaning, see further p 591.

(p 676)   **In footnote 2 at end, insert–**

See also *Preston v Commissioner for Fair Trading* [2011] NSWCA 40.

(p 679)   **In footnote 3, at end insert–**

As to a more general relaxation of the exclusionary rule in Canada, see R Sullivan, *Sullivan and Driedger's Construction of Statutes* (4th edn, Markham, Butterworths, 2002), 481–500.

(p 680)   **In footnote 1, at end insert–**

New Zealand courts have now relaxed the exclusionary rule. See J Burrows and R Carter, *Statute Law in New Zealand* (4th edn, Wellington, Lexis Nexis, 2009), pp 263–266.

(p 682)   **In footnote 2 at end, insert–**

See also *R v Zafar (Aitzaz)* [2008] QB 810, 822. A similar approach prevails in Hong Kong: *HKSAR v Cheung Kwun Yin* (unreported, Hong Kong Court of Final Appeal, FACC 11/2008), [14]–[17].

(p 683)   **After Example 221.3, insert–**

s 221   *Example 221.3A* The current statute governing the validity of patents is, of course, the Patents Act 1977, which must be read together with the European Patent Convention ('the EPC'). Indeed, all the provisions of the 1977 Act of central relevance for present purposes have been specifically framed 'as nearly as practicable' to have 'the same effects in the United Kingdom as the corresponding provisions of the [EPC] have in the territories to which [it applies]': see section 130(7) of the 1977 Act.[10A]

(p 683)   **In newly created footnote 10A, insert–**

Generics (UK) Ltd and others v H Lundbeck A/S [2009] RPC 13, [68].

(p 684)   **In footnote 4, delete text and insert–**

See the Australian case *Commissioner of Taxation v Lamesa Holdings BV* (1997) 77 FCR 597, 603–605 and authority discussed there.

(p 684)   **In footnote 6, at end insert–**

See also *FA (Iraq) v Secretary of State for Home Department* [2010] EWCA Civ 696 (Refugee Convention and Qualification Directive (2004/83/EC).

(p 685)   **In footnote 4 at end insert–**

See also *Hatzl v XL Insurance Company Ltd* [2010] 1 WLR 470, 478–479.

(p 685)   **At end of first full paragraph, before sideheading 'Subsection (2)' insert–**

Another such limitation may be imposed in the course of indirect enactment or by any other enactment.

> *Example 221.5A* Section 54 of the Immigration, Asylum and Nationality Act 2006 says that in the 'construction and application' of Art 1(F)(c) of the Refugee Convention the 'reference to acts contrary to the purposes and principles of the United Nations shall be taken as including' certain conduct related to terrorism, with the last term being defined by the Terrorism Act 2000 s 1. An English court would be obliged to approach the Refugee Convention in this way, regardless of whether it would do the same by independent interpretation.[5A]

(p 685)   **In newly created footnote 5A, insert–**

See further *MH (Syria) v Secretary of State for the Home Department* [2009] EWCA Civ 226, [29].

(p 688)   **In footnote 6 at end, insert–**

See also *R (ST Eritrea) v Secretary of State for Home Department* [2012] UKSC 12 at [30].

(p 691)   **In footnote 2, at end insert–**

s 222   See also *Re: H* [1998] AC 72 at 87. Compare *R v Secretary of State for
the Home Department ex parte Adan* [2001] 2 AC 477 at 518 and
*Minister for Immigration, Multicultural and Indigenous Affairs v QAAH
of 2004* (2006) 231 CLR 1 at [34].

(p 697)   **After paragraph beginning 'As indicated', insert sideheading
'Hansard' and text as follows–**

The Supreme Court recently stated:

> 'Reference to Parliamentary material has, of course, become
> commonplace since the previous rule that excluded this was
> relaxed by *Pepper v Hart* [1983] AC 593, and the rather strict rules
> that were laid down in that case have become gradually more
> relaxed. It remains the case that this approach should be used only
> where the legislation is ambiguous, and then only with circum-
> spection. When it is used, however, the purpose of the exercise is
> to determine the intention of the legislator'[4A]

A month later, the Judicial Committee of the Privy Council remarked:

> 'The textual changes do not therefore make clear the purpose of
> the amendments to s 4(7). The respondent submits that assistance
> can, however, be obtained as to the general background and as to
> the mischief which the legislation was addressing by looking at the
> reports of the proceedings in Parliament ... But Lord Steyn was
> careful to distinguish this principle from the more radical separate
> principle recognised in Pepper v Hart ... He said of the former
> principle that "the use of Hansard material to identify the mischief
> at which legislation was directed and its objective setting" was
> permissible, but that "trying to discover the intentions of the
> Government from Ministerial statements in Parliament is constitu-
> tionally unacceptable'.

> The separate principle in *Pepper v Hart* ... only allows a court to
> have regard to go further in looking at statements in Parliament
> where (a) legislation is ambiguous or obscure or leads to absurdity,
> (b) the Parliamentary material relied upon consists of one or more
> statements by a minister or other promoter of a bill together with
> such other statements and material as are necessary to understand
> such statements and (c) the statements relied upon are clear ... It is
> therefore permissible as a first step to look at Hansard to try to
> identify the mischief at which the [provision] was aimed and its
> objective setting.'[4B]

s 227   This is further discussed in the Comment on Code s 217.

(p 697)   **In newly created footnote 4A, insert–**

Gow v Grant [2012] UKSC 29 at [29]. See further p 617 above.

(p 697)   **In newly created footnote 4B, insert–**

Presidential Insurance Company Ltd v Resha St. Hill [2012] UKPC 33
at [23]–[24].

(p 701)   **In footnote 2 at end, insert–**

s 229   See also *Secretary of State for the Home Department v AY* [2012] EWHC 2054 at [151], [158].

(p 703)   **At end of first passage, before paragraph beginning 'The administration of every Act', insert sentence–**

s 232   Nonetheless, the Court of Appeal has recently emphasised the limits of Code s 232. In particular, 'the judiciary, not the executive, decide the meaning and effect of legislation.' An official statement 'may be of assistance for some purposes, for example, if it throws light on the background to the legislation and thereby enables the court to understand better its general purpose.' Further, 'insofar as the views expressed in such a document are inherently persuasive they may be taken into account.' However, 'that is as far as it goes'.[2A]

(p 703)   **In newly created footnote 2A, insert–**

R (Risk Management Partners Ltd) v Brent LBC [2010] PTSR 349, [227]. See also *Yemshaw v Hounslow LBC* [2009] EWCA Civ 1543, [28]. The Supreme Court has expressed similar sentiments: *Grays Timber Products Ltd v Revenue and Customs* [2010] UKSC 4 at [54]–[55].

(p 703)   **Toward end of page, at end of sentence beginning 'Its significance was a matter of weight', insert footnote indicator 9A.**

(p 703)   **In newly created footnote 9A, insert–**

For other instances of confusion of these concepts, see *Sharratt v London Central Bus Co* [2002] EWHC 9006 (Costs), [46]–[49]; *Grays Timber Products Ltd v Revenue and Customs (Scotland)* [2010] 1 WLR 497, 514–515.

(p 704)   **In Example 232.4, after 'Criminal Justice Act 2003 s 167', insert–**

(repealed)

(p 704)   **In Example 232.4, after 'Section 172 of the Act', insert–**

(repealed)

(p 704)   **In footnote 8 at end insert–**

; *Boyle v SCA Packaging Ltd* [2009] UKHL 37, [2009] 4 All ER 1181, [67]; *R (Risk Management Partners Ltd) v Brent LBC* [2010] PTSR 349, [110]–[111], [227]. Compare *R (Bapio Action Ltd) v Secretary of State for the Home Department* [2008] 1 AC 1003.

(p 705)   **In footnote 7 at end insert–**

and *BBC v Information Commissioner* [2009] EWHC 2348 (Admin), [75].

(p 706)   **After sideheading 'Statutory guidelines', at end of paragraph insert–**

On the other hand, the Supreme Court has indicated that '[a]ny statutory guidance given by the Secretary of State which ran counter to the legislative provision in relation to which it was given would be of no effect'.[5A] It is submitted that such guidance would also be subject to the *Padfield* principle.[5B]

(p 706)   **In newly created footnote 5A, insert–**

R (KM) v Cambridgeshire County Council [2012] UKSC 23 at [19].

(p 706)   **In newly created footnote 5B, insert–**

See further p 90.

(p 706)   **At end of second complete paragraph, before paragraph beginning 'On statutory and judicial guidelines', insert new paragraph–**

The Court of Appeal recently indicated that, while such guidelines would attract Code s 232, be taken into account by and even be of assistance to the judiciary when interpreting the legislation to which the guidelines relate, they 'need not be authority, or even persuasive authority, but what [they] purport[] to be, that is, guidance'.[7A]

(p 706)   **In newly created footnote 7A insert–**

R (Risk Management Partners Ltd) v Brent LBC [2010] PTSR 349, [111].

(p 707)   **In paragraph beginning 'Viscount Dilhorne rejected', after 'Cinematograph (Safety) Regulations 1955', insert-**

s 233   (lapsed).

(p 707)   **In footnote 8, at end insert–**

See also *Scottish & Newcastle plc v Raguz* [2008] 1 WLR 2494, 2504, cf 2497. As to forms prescribes under an enactment, see p 242 n 8.

(p 707)   **In paragraph beginning 'Lord Browne-Wilkinson said', delete 'The latter qualification seems doubtful' and insert–**

While the latter qualification seems doubtful, it has since been endorsed by a Lord Hope SPJ. In relation to regulations made two months after the enabling Act, his Lordship said '[t]he interval was so short that, taken together, they can be regarded as all part of same legislative exercise'.[8A]

(p 707)   **In newly created footnote 8A, insert–**

R (A) v B [2009] UKSC 12 at [41].

(p 707)   **In footnote 9 at end, insert–**

See also *Legal Services Commission v Loomba* [2012] EWHC 29 at [52].

(p 708)   **After heading 'Comment on Code s 234', insert–**

s 234   This section of the Code has been judicially approved.[2A]

(p 708)   **In newly created footnote 2A, insert–**

Bloomsbury International Ltd v Sea Fish Industry Authority and Department for Environment, Food and Rural Affairs [2011] UKSC 25 at [10].

(p 708)   **In footnote 4, delete text and insert–**

This sentence was judicially considered in *Ward v Chief Adjudication Officer* [1998] EWCA Civ 1552.

(p 709)   **In footnote 3 at end insert–**

Revenue and Customs Commissioners v Halcyon Films LLP [2010] EWCA Civ 261, [27].

(p 709)   **In footnote 9 at end insert–**

The sentence to which this footnote relates was applied by the Full Federal Court of Australia in *Kalway v Secretary, Department of Social Security* (1992) 38 FCR 295, 299.

(p 710)   **In Example 234.2, after 'Trading Representations (Disabled Persons) Act 1958', insert–**

(repealed)

(p 710)   **After Example 234.3, insert sideheading and new paragraph as follows–**

Redundant enactments The Court of Appeal recently declined to apply s 234 in relation to an enactment that was never brought into force and, shortly after its passage, was repealed and replaced by another enactment.[4A]

(p 710)   **In newly created footnote 4A, insert–**

Revenue and Customs Commissioners v Halcyon Films LLP [2010] EWCA Civ 261, [27].

(p 710)   **In Comment on Code s 235, at beginning before sideheading
Sub-rules insert new paragraph with text as follows–**

s 235   This section of the Code has been judicially approved.[6A]

(p 710)   **In newly created footnote 6A, insert–**

JF v Minister for Health and Children [2008] IESC 16.

(p 711)   **After sideheading 'Tacit legislation', at end of second sentence,
insert–**

The preceding two sentences have been judicially approved.[1A]

(p 711)   **In newly created footnote 1A, insert–**

R (Woolas) v Speaker of the House of Commons [2010] EWHC 3169
at [86].

(p 711)   **After Example 235.3 insert text as follows–**

However, the implication may not be drawn where the context otherwise
requires. This has arisen where a legislature altered an enactment in light
of a judicial decision in a very specific way, without any suggestion that
it considered any other aspects of the operation of the enactment.

> *Example 235.3A* In Hong Kong, the *ratio* of a decision of an
> intermediate appellate court had been that, under the Employment
> Ordinance (Cap 57), the remedy for unlawful dismissal was
> unliquidated damages subject to a duty to mitigate. The Legisla-
> tive Council inserted a new provision into the Ordinance, s 8A,
> with the intention, as stated in the Second Reading, of reversing
> the decision. The decision had also contained *obiter*, of a majority
> and minority, as to the meaning of Ordinance s 7. In a subsequent
> case before the Court of Final Appeal, including Lord Scott of
> Foscote NPJ, it was argued that the Legislative Council had
> implicitly approved the majority *obiter*. Ribeiro PJ said, for the
> Court, that there was 'no basis for taking the legislature to have
> considered in any shape or form the divided views … on the *obiter*
> question'. It was 'therefore impossible to suggest that the legisla-
> ture's intent was tacitly to confer legislative force on [those
> views].'[7A]

(p 711)   **In newly created footnote 7A insert–**

Kao Lee & Yip (a firm) v Lau Wing (2008) 11 HKCFAR 576, [36].

(p 712)   **In Comment on Code s 236 at beginning insert–**

s 236   This section of the Code has been judicially approved.

(p 712)   **In newly created footnote 1 insert–**

R (Public and Commercial Services Union) v Minister for Civil Service
[2010] EWHC 1027 (Admin), [38]. The court added: 'That is especially

the case where, as here, an Act is being introduced specifically to regulate relations between certain persons and it is those persons who have the understanding in question'.

(p 722)	**After sideheading Headings, at end of first sentence insert–**
s 241	This sentence has been judicially approved.[2A]

(p 722)	**In the new footnote indicator 2A, insert–**

See the opinion of Lord Brodie in *Imperial Tobacco Ltd v Lord Advocate* [2012] CSIH 9 at [195].

(p 725)	**In Comment on Code s 243, at end of third sentence after 'shall ... ', insert–**
s 243	This passage, and Code s 243, has been judicially approved: *Comptroller and Auditor General v Ireland* [1997] 1 IR 248.

(p 734)	**In Example 247.1, after 'Courts and Legal Services Act 1990 s 17', insert–**
s 247	(repealed)

(p 739)	**In footnote 4, after '565–566.', insert–**
s 250	This passage has been described as 'settled law': *R (Ahmed) v Asylum Support Adjudicator* [2008] EWHC 2282 (Admin) at [32].

(p 740)	**Toward end of page, at end of sentence beginning 'Examples were given in' insert–**

and s 44(6) of the Criminal Justice Act 2003.

(p 746)	**In footnote 1 at end of first sentence insert–**
s 255	; *ETI Euro Telecom International NV v Republic of Bolivia* [2009] 1 WLR 665, 682 (citing Code s 255 et seq).

(p 746)	**At end of first full sentence insert footnote indicator 1A.**

(p 746)	**In newly created footnote 1A insert–**

This sentence has been applied by a Northern Irish court: See also *Re Application by the Local Government Auditor* [2003] NIQB 21, [16].

(p 746)	**In footnote 6 at end insert–**

In any event, the same cannot be said of delegated legislation such as the Civil Procedure Rules: *Brown v Innovatorone Plc* [2009] EWHC 1376 (Comm), [17].

(p 748)   **In footnote 9 at end insert–**

s 256   In any event, the same cannot be said of delegated legislation such as the
Civil Procedure Rules: *Brown v Innovatorone Plc* [2009] EWHC 1376
(Comm), [17].

(p 749)   **In Comment on Code s 257 at beginning insert–**

s 257   This section of the Code has been judicially approved.[2A]

(p 749)   **In newly created footnote 2A, insert–**

Australian Securities Commission v Lucas (1992) 36 FCR 165, 170–171.

(p 749)   **In paragraph beginning 'The format or layout', at end of third
sentence, insert–**

The preceding three sentences have been judicially approved.[3A]

(p 749)   **In newly created footnote 3A, insert–**

Re CM (A Child) [2010] Scot SC 24 at [11].

(p 750)   **In Example 257.2, after 'Taxes Management Act 1970 s 20', insert–**

(repealed)

(p 751)   **In Comment on Code s 258, at end of first sentence, insert footnote
indicator 1.**

(p 751)   **In newly created footnote 1 insert–**

This sentence has been judicially approved: *Official Bay Heritage
Protection Society Incorporated v Auckland City Council and another*
[2007] NZCA 511, [33].

(p 754)   **Before sideheading 'Drafting error', insert–**

The Federal Court of Australia has remarked on the significance of the
semi-colon in interpretation.[4A]

(p 754)   **In newly created footnote 4A, insert–**

Minister for Immigration and Multicultural Affairs v Savvin (2000)
98 FCR 168.

(p 754)   **In Example 258.3, after 's 38(4)(b)', insert–**

(repealed)

(p 758)   **In footnote 3 at end insert–**

s 259   This sentence has been approved by the Ontario Court of Appeal:
               R v St Lawrence Cement Inc (2002) 60 OR (3d) 712, [18]. See also
               BCGEU v British Columbia (2007) 283 DLR (4th) 307, [34]–[36].

(p 759)   **In footnote 5, at end, insert–**

s 259   In particular, the courts are mindful that incorporation by reference in
               delegated legislation cannot lead to sub-delegation or circumvention of
               Parliamentary control. It may be suggested that, subject to a contrary
               intention in the enabling Act, incorporation by reference in delegated
               legislation must be of a pre-existing external document, not of such a
               document as it exists from time to time: *R v Secretary of State for Social
               Services, ex p Camden LBC* [1987] 2 All ER 560. See further *R (Alvi) v
               Secretary of State for Home Department* [2012] UKSC 33 and *Legisla-
               tive Instruments Act 2003* (Australia) s 14. In other words, the incorpo-
               ration by reference in delegated legislation may need to be static, rather
               than ambulatory: see, generally, J M Keyes, 'Incorporation by reference
               in legislation' (2004) 25 *Statute Law Review* 180. A statute is not so
               restricted: see, eg, *DPP v Leontjava* [2004] 1 IR 591.

(p 760)   **After Comment on Code s 260, insert–**

s 260   Subsection (1) of this section of the Code has been judicially considered
               and archival drafting described as 'another form of incorporation by
               reference'.[1A]

(p 760)   **In newly created footnote 1A, insert–**

               DPP v Leontjava [2004] 1 IR 591.

(p 761)   **In second and third full paragraph, delete 'Supreme Court
                              Act 1981' and insert–**

               Senior Courts Act 1981

(p 761)   **Before paragraph beginning 'Archival drafting may import',
                                     insert–**

               Archival drafting has also been used to confer jurisdiction on the
               Supreme Court.[6A]

(p 761)   **In newly created footnote 6A, insert–**

               Constitutional Reform Act 2005 s 40(3). See further p 151.

(p 761)   **At end of page insert new paragraph–**

               The contrary intention referred to in Code s 260(2) has been found to be
               present where a constitutional statute of an overseas common law
               jurisdiction imports English common law into the jurisdiction on a
               specific date. Doing so does not preclude the subsequent development of

that law by the courts of the jurisdiction, including by the application of decisions of English courts after the relevant date.[7A]

(p 761)   **In newly created footnote 7A, insert–**

s 263   *Lai v Chamberlains* [2007] 2 NZLR 7, [86]. See also *China Field Ltd v Appeal Tribunal (Buildings) (No 2)* [2009] 5 HKLRD 662, 668–670, 688–690.

(p 773)   **In footnote 9 at end insert–**

For a perspective extending beyond the United Kingdom, see M Kirby, *Judicial Activism: Authority, Principle and Policy in the Judicial Method* (55th Hamlyn Lectures, Sweet & Maxwell, 2004), Ch 2.

(p 778)   **In footnote 3 at end insert–**

Note that maintenance and champerty were abolished as crimes and torts by Criminal Law Act 1967 s 14, but had their relevance to the law of contract, including public policy, preserved. For a recent example, see *Ruttle Plant Ltd v Secretary of State for Environment, Food and Rural Affairs (No 2)* [2008] EWHC 238 (TCC), [2009] 1 All ER 448.

(p 786)   **After heading 'Comment on Code s 264', insert–**

s 264   This section of the Code has been judicially approved.[2A]

(p 786)   **In newly created footnote 2A, insert–**

Grealis v DPP [2001] IESC 50; *Secretary of State for Communities and Local Government and another v Welwyn Hatfield Borough Council* [2011] UKSC 1 at [46].

(p 790)   **Near top of page, at end of sideheading Conflicting interests insert footnote indicator 1A.**

(p 790)   **In newly created footnote 1A insert–**

This discussion has been judicially approved: *Li Wang Pong v Medical Council of Hong Kong* [2009] HKCFI 2, [59].

(p 793)   **In footnote 9 at end insert–**

As to the meaning of fraud, see generally *Giles v Rhind* [2009] Ch 191, 207.

(p 795)   **In Comment on Code s 265 at beginning insert–**

s 265   This section of the Code has been judicially approved.[3A]

(p 795)   **In newly created footnote 3A insert–**

R (Hampstead Heath Winter Swimming Club) v Corporation of London [2005] 1 WLR 2930, [33].

(p 797)   **In footnote 4 at end insert–**

Similarly, public policy may require that an injustice be tolerated, as where the need for the maintenance of an order for the adoption of children outweighed the need to redress injustice in the making of the order: *Webster v Norfolk CC* [2009] 1 FLR 1378.

(p 805)   **In footnote 1 at end insert–**

See, generally, F A R Bennion, 'Is Law Still A Learned Profession?', www.francisbennion.com/2008/016.htm and "Writing Like a Lawyer" (2010) 19 Commonwealth Lawyer 24–27, available at http://www.francisbennion.com/pdfs/fb/2010/2010–017-coml-writing-like-a-lawyer.pdf.

(p 807)   **In Comment on Code s 267 at beginning insert–**

s 267   This section of the Code has been judicially approved.[4A]

(p 807)   **In newly created footnote 4A insert–**

See the decision of Kiefel J (as she then was) of the Federal Court of Australia *Insurance and Superannuation Commissioner v Hiscock* (1995) 59 FCR 1, 3.

(p 808)   **In Comment on Code s 268 at beginning insert–**

s 268   This section of the Code has been judicially approved.[1A]

(p 808)   **In newly created footnote 1A insert–**

See the decision of New Zealand Supreme Court in *Elders New Zealand Ltd v PGG Wrightson Ltd* [2009] 1 NZLR 577, [30] and the majority of the Singapore Court of Appeal in *Lee Chez Kee v Public Prosecutor* [2008] SGCA 20 at [93]–[94]. As to the reasoning in the latter case, see also Example 355.9. See also *Creaven v Criminal Assets Bureau* [2004] IEHC 26.

(p 810)   **In Example 268.4, after 's 3(4)', insert–**

(repealed)

(p 811)   **In Example 268.10, delete "Supreme Court Act 1981" and insert–**

Senior Courts Act 1981

(p 811)   **In Example 268.11, after 'School Standards and Framework
Act 1998 s 64', insert–**

(repealed)

(p 812)   **In Comment on Code s 269 at beginning insert–**

s 269   This section of the Code has been judicially approved.[3A]

(p 812)   **In newly created footnote 3A insert–**

Re: Joseph's Estate (1993) 14 OR (3d) 628, [10]; *Jade City Inter-
national Ltd v Director of Lands* [2002] 3 HKLRD 33, 47. See also
Medical Council of Hong Kong v Chow Siu Shek [2000] 2 HKLRD 674.
See also *Meagher v Luke J. Healy Pharmacy Ltd* [2010] IESC 40.

(p 814)   **In footnote 2 at end insert–**

See also *Re: P* [2010] Ch 33; *Westbrook Dolphin Square Ltd v Friends
Life Ltd* [2012] EWCA Civ 666 at [36]–[38].

(p 816)   **In footnote 3 at end insert–**

See further the reasons of French J (as he then was) in the Full Federal
Court of Australia in *Commissioner of Taxation v Citibank Ltd* (1989)
20 FCR 403, 432–433.

(p 816)   **After Example 269.12, insert–**

Example 269.12A In some jurisdictions of Australia, legislation as
to the law of evidence had altered the common law of legal
professional privilege, so that the test for whether a particular
document attracted privilege had regard to its dominant purpose,
rather than its sole purpose. In light of the legislation, the High
Court of Australia developed the common law, particularly as it
applied in the remaining jurisdictions of Australia, so that it also
applied a dominant purpose test.[4A]

(p 816)   **In newly created footnote 4A, insert–**

Esso Australia Resources v Commissioner of Taxation (1999) 201 CLR
49.

(p 818)   **In footnote 3, at end insert–**

As to the exceptions to *Walker v Baird*, under which effect is accorded to
certain treaties by the common law, see O Jones, 'Federal Treaty
Jurisdiction: a Belated Reply to Mark Leeming SC' (2007) 18 *Public
Law Review* [Australia] 94 at 99–102.

(p 819)   **In footnote 3 at end insert–**

s 270   For a broader approach see *Sellers v Maritime Safety Inspector* [1999] 2
NZLR 44, 61, 62 discussed in P Sales and J Clement, '*International Law*

in Domestic Courts: the Developing Framework' (2008) 124 LQR 388, 393. See also *Zaoui v Attorney-General (No 2)* [2006] 1 NZLR 289, [90]. Compare *R v Hape* [2007] 2 SCR 292, [53]–[56].

(p 819)   **Delete sideheading 'Crimes at international law' together with following sentence, and insert–**

Customary international law It is often said that, unlike treaties, customary international law is part of the common law. However, the precise meaning of this proposition is unclear. It is settled that customary international law can no longer create crimes at common law. One detailed study in England suggests that there is little else customary international law might do, except in the field of immunities.[4A] Canadian commentary, questioning English authority that holds otherwise, argues that customary international law can generate Crown tort liability.[4B]

(p 819)   **In newly created footnote 4A, insert–**

R O'Keefe, 'The Doctrine of Incorporation Revisited' (2008) 79 Brit YB Int'l L 1.

(p 819)   **In newly created footnote 4B, insert–**

O Jones, 'The Doctrine of Adoption of Customary International Law: a Future in Conflicting Domestic Law and Crown Tort Liability' (2012) 89 *Can Bar Rev* 401.

(p 821)   **After Example 270.3, insert––**

An alternative approach has emerged in New Zealand, where the courts have held that 'national law is to be read, if at all possible, consistently with the related international law' even if this appears 'difficult to reconcile with the seemingly generally applicable wording' of executive powers.[3A] However, an English judge has argued that the New Zealand jurisprudence is not applicable in his jurisdiction.[3B]

(p 821)   **In newly created footnote 3A, insert–**

Sellers v Maritime Safety Inspector [1999] 2 NZLR 44 at 62; *Zaoui v Attorney-General (No 2)* [2006] 1 NZLR 289 at 321.

(p 821)   **In newly created footnote 3B, insert–**

P Sales and J Clement, 'International Law in Domestic Courts: the Developing Framework' (2008) 124 LQR 388 at 393, 402.

(p 823)   **At end of first complete sentence, insert footnote indicator 1A.**

(p 823)   **In newly created footnote 1A insert–**

This remark has been noticed by Lord Phillips of Worth Matravers PSC and apparently applied by the Supreme Court of New Zealand: *Ahmed v HM Treasury* [2010] 2 WLR 378, 423; *Cropp v A Judicial Committee* [2008] 3 NZLR 774, [27].

(p 823)   **In footnote 5 at end insert–**

So much has been acknowledged by the House of Lords: *R (Morgan Grenfell & Co Ltd) v Special Cmr of Income Tax* [2003] 1 AC 563, 607.

(p 823)   **In third complete paragraph, at end of sentence beginning 'This so-called principle of legality' insert–**

The previous sentence has been questioned by Lord Phillips of Worth Matravers PSC on the ground that the majority found ambiguity to be present. He did 'not consider that the principle of legality permits a court to disregard an unambiguous expression of Parliament's intention'.[A] It is suggested that the requisite ambiguity should, in general terms, be explained. It seems to go beyond ambiguity under Code s 151(3), which excludes general words. Quite how it embraces the view of the above majority of the House should be clarified.[B]

(p 823)   **In newly created footnote 7A insert–**

Ahmed v HM Treasury [2010] 2 WLR 378, 423. Lord Phillips saw this as a point of departure from interpretation under the Human Rights Act 1998 s 3(1). See further Code s 421, including p 1324 n 3. See also *Saeed v Minister for Immigration and Citizenship* (2010) 241 CLR 252, 259.

(p 823)   **In newly created footnote 7B insert–**

See generally Code s 153 and *Bowers v Gloucester Corporation* [1963] 1 QB 881, 886–887.

(p 823)   **Before sideheading 'Judicial notice', insert–**

A Justice of the Supreme Court recently remarked that the principle of legality 'means not only that Parliament cannot itself override fundamental rights or the rule of law by general or ambiguous words, but also that it cannot confer on another body, by general or ambiguous words, the power to do so'.[A]

It must be emphasised that, strictly speaking, the principle of legality does not concern international law. The principle is only applicable in relation to rights already present in domestic law through 'the necessary contextual backcloth of a relevant basic common law principle'.[B] For this reason, it has been held in Hong Kong not to extend to rights recognised by international law.[C] The same approach can be discerned, and should be upheld, in England.[D]

(p 823)   **In newly created footnote 8A, insert–**

AXA General Insurance Ltd v Lord Advocate [2012] 1 AC 868 at [152].

(p 823)   **In newly created footnote 8B, insert–**

R v Secretary of State for Home Department, Ex p Stafford [1999] 2 AC 38 at 49.

(p 823)   **In newly created footnote 8C, insert–**

C v Director of Immigration (unreported, Hong Kong Court of Appeal, CACV 132/2008, 21 July 2011) at [83]–[85]. Leave to appeal to the Hong Kong Court of Final Appeal granted: *C v Director of Immigration* (unreported, Hong Kong Court of Appeal, CACV 132/2008, 14 December 2011).

(p 823)   **In newly created footnote 8D, insert–**

R (Youssef) v Secretary of State for Foreign & Commonwealth Affairs [2012] EWHC 2091 (Admin) at [54]. Compare *Home Office v Tariq* [2012] 1 AC 452 at [109]. See further O Jones, 'The Doctrine of Adoption of Customary International Law: a Future in Conflicting Domestic Law and Crown Tort Liability' (2012) 89 *Can Bar Rev* 401 at 405–406.

(p 823)   **In footnote 9, at end insert–**

See also *Trendtex Trading Corp v Central Bank of Nigeria* [1977] QB 529 at 569.

(p 823)   **Replace 'Yet in 2006' with**

In this respect, some progress has already been made. In 2006

(p 823)   **In paragraph beginning 'This so-called principle of legality' at end insert–**

In 2008, the Supreme Court of the United Kingdom reaffirmed that the principle can displace general or ambiguous words and, on this basis, held delegated legislation to be in excess of its enabling power.[11A] That year, the Court of Appeal applied the principle in the context of statutory regulation of judicial fact-finding, refusing to convert 'shall take account' into may do so, but reading 'damaging the claimant's credibility' as potentially damaging the same.[11B]

(p 823)   **In newly created footnote 11A insert–**

Ahmed v HM Treasury [2010] 2 WLR 378, 406–407, 438–439, 462. This reflects the recognition by the Supreme Court of New Zealand that the principle of legality naturally applies to words which authorise subordinate legislation': *Cropp v A Judicial Committee* [2008] 3 NZLR 774, [27].

(p 823)   **In newly created footnote 11B insert–**

JT (Cameroon) v Secretary of State for the Home Department [2008] Civ 878, [2009] 2 All ER 1213. See also Code s 281.

(p 825)   **In Comment on Code s 271 at beginning insert–**

s 271   This section of the Code has been judicially approved.[1A]

(p 825) **In newly created footnote 1A insert–**

HKSAR v Tang Hoi On [2003] 3 HKC 123, [32]. See also *Commissioner of Police v Privacy Commissioner for Personal Data* [2012] 3 HKLRD 710 at [18], [37] and *Delaney v Judge John Coughlan* [2012] IESC 40 at [46] ('in interpreting a statute a court must take the greatest care to lean against the possibility of doubtful penalisation').

(p 828) **Before sideheading 'Narrow construction', after sentence 'As Morritt LJ put it', insert–**

The Court of Appeal recently stated that the principle against doubtful penalisation, notwithstanding counsel's reliance on authority describing it as one of 'last resort', was 'alive and well even if it may often give way to other canons of construction'.[8A]

(p 828) **In newly created footnote 8A, insert–**

Dowds v R [2012] EWCA Crim 281 at [37]–[38]. Compare *Dorset County Council v House* [2010] EWCA Crim 2270 at [44].

(p 828) **After preceding insertion, add–**

The reasoning in this passage has been judicially approved.[8B]

(p 828) **In footnote 8B, insert–**

Re Digital Satellite Warranty Cover Ltd [2011] EWHC 122 at [61].

(p 828) **At bottom of page, at end of sentence 'A denial of this must be clearly stated' insert footnote indicator 10.**

(p 828) **In newly created footnote 10 insert–**

See, for example, *Mount Lawley Pty Ltd v Western Australian Planning Commission* [2004] WASCA 149; (2004) 136 LGERA 16, [296].

(p 829) **In footnote 6 at end, insert–**

In *R (Sainsbury's Supermarkets Ltd) v Wolverhampton City Council* [2011] 1 AC 437 at [9], the Supreme Court remarked that the courts are 'astute to impose a strict construction on statutes expropriating private property, and to ensure that rights of compulsory acquisition granted for a specified purpose may not be used for a different or collateral purpose'. Their Lordships also approved a dictum from a judgment of Chief Justice of Australia in *R & R Fazzolari Pty Ltd v Parramatta City Council* [2009] HCA 12 at [43] that, 'As a practical matter [the principle] means that, where a statute is capable of more than one construction, that construction will be chosen which interferes least with private property rights'.

(p 837)   **In footnote 6 at end insert–**

s 273   *R (G) v Chief Constable of West Yorkshire Police* [2008] 1 WLR 550,
          559.

(p 837)   **After Example 273.1, after 'Street Offences Act 1959', insert–**

(repealed)

(p 838)   **In footnote 11, at end insert–**

See also *Assange v Swedish Prosecution Authority* [2012] UKSC 22
at [33].

(p 839)   **At end of first paragraph, before sideheading
                          'Technicalities' insert–**

Further, the House of Lords recently held that, where an appeals process
under the Extradition Act 2003 was available, habeas corpus would be
excluded. This was due to the 'clear and unequivocal wording' of the Act
s 34, which provided for the exclusivity of the process, as well as the
European law implemented by the Act, which had the purpose of
promoting recognition of extradition requests by member states and
removing complexity and delay from extradition procedures.[4A]

(p 839)   **In newly created footnote 4A insert–**

Hilali v Governor of Whitemoore Prison [2008] 1 AC 805, 840–841.

(p 846)   **In footnote 5 at beginning insert–**

s 278   This sentence has, together with Code s 278, been judicially approved:
          *Independent Committee for the Supervision of Standards of Telephone
          Information Services v Andronikou & Ors* [2007] EWHC 2307 (Admin),
          [25].

(p 846)   **In footnote 6 at end of first sentence, before sentence beginning
                          'See also Examples' insert–**

Registrar of Liquor Licences v Iliadis (1988) 19 FCR 311, 315–316
(statutory licence for sale of liquor not to amenable to cancellation).

(p 846)   **At bottom of page, at end of last complete sentence, before
                 Example 278.1 insert footnote indicator 7.**

(p 846)   **In newly created footnote 7 insert–**

This sentence was approved by the Federal Court of Canada in *Society
Promoting Environmental Conservation v Canada (Attorney-General)*
(2002) FTR 236, [31].

(p 848)   **At bottom of page, at end of final sentence insert footnote indicator
9.**

(p 848)   **In newly created footnote 9 insert–**

This sentence has been judicially approved: *Re: Landlord's Association
for Northern Ireland* [2005] NIQB 22, [41].

(p 850)   **In footnote 4, at end, insert–**

The High Court of Australia has said that '[while] tax statutes do not
form a class of their own to which different rules of construction
apply ... the fact that a statute is a taxing Act, or contains penal
provisions, is part of the context and is therefore relevant to the task of
construing the Act in accordance with those settled principles': *Alcan
(NT) Alumina Pty Ltd v Commissioner of Territory Revenue* (2009) 239
CLR 27 at [57].

(p 850)   **In footnote 5, at end insert–**

Further, Australian courts will apply the clear words of a taxing Act, in
preference to a strained construction that simply maximises revenue. See
Alcan (NT) Alumina Pty Ltd v Commissioner of Territory Revenue
(2009) 239 CLR 27 at [5], [50]–[53]. The clear words approach does not
prevent a court, in interpreting revenue legislation, from looking to
matters of context or substance: see, eg, the consideration of the
'*Ramsay* principle' in *Inland Revenue Commissioners v McGuckian*
[1997] 3 All ER 817; *Inland Revenue v Scottish Provident Institution*
[2005] 1 All ER 325 at [19] and *Collector of Customs v Arrowtown
Assets Ltd* [2004] 1 HKLRD 77.

(p 854)   **After sideheading 'Trial by jury', at end of quotation insert–**

s 281   Further, where an Act of Parliament unequivocally restricted the right of
trial by jury in certain circumstances, it was held the right was 'so deeply
entrenched in our constitution' that the presence of the circumstances
had to be established to the 'highest possible forensic standard of proof
[being] the criminal standard'.[5A]

(p 854)   **In newly created footnote 5A insert–**

R v T [2010] 1 WLR 630, 637–638.

(p 854)   **After sideheading 'Right of litigious control', at end of sentence
beginning 'A litigant's right to conduct proceedings', insert–**

Nonetheless, the courts have power to restrain vexatious litigations.[7A]

(p 854)   **In newly created footnote 7A, insert–**

Bhamjee v Forsdick (No 2) [2003] EWCA Civ 1113.

(p 858)   **At end of first paragraph, insert–**

s 282   Nonetheless, a person not a party to first instance proceedings may, in
               appropriate cases, appeal from a decision in the proceedings, especially
               where the person has a real interest in the matter.[4A]

(p 858)   **In newly created footnote 4A insert–**

George Wimpey UK Ltd v Tewkesbury BC [2008] 1 WLR 1649.

(p 864)   **In Comment on Code s 285 at beginning insert–**

s 285   This section has been judicially approved.[3A]

(p 864)   **In newly created footnote 3A insert–**

Jeffrey v Sawyer (1993) 16 OR (3d) 75, 78; *Maguire v Director of Public
Prosecutions* [2004] 3 IR 241, [45]. See also *Alcan (NT) Alumina
Pty Ltd v Commissioner of Territory Revenue* (2009) 239 CLR 27
at [47]. Compare J Spigelman 'The intolerable wrestle: Developments in
statutory interpretation' (2010) 84 ALJ 822.

(p 868)   **In Example 285.5 at end, insert footnote indicator 5A.**

(p 868)   **In newly created footnote 5A, insert–**

Minister for Immigration and Citizenship v SZMDS (2010) 240 CLR
611.

(p 868)   **At bottom of page at end of last sentence insert footnote indicator
                                        7.**

(p 868)   **In newly created footnote 7 insert–**

This can, of course, produce differences of judicial opinion: see, for
example, *Knowsley Housing Trust v White* [2009] 1 AC 636, 651, 675.

(p 871)   **In footnote 8 at end insert–**

s 286   *Sinclair Gardens Investments (Kensington) Ltd v Poets Chase Freehold Co Ltd* [2008] 1 WLR 768.

(p 876)   **In footnote 1 at end insert–**

s 287   This case has recently been applied in England and overseas: *Gibson v
Secretary of State for Justice* [2009] QB 204; *OTC International AG v
Perfect Recovery Ltd* [2009] 3 HKLRD 13. The latter expressly approved
of this Code's description of the process as 'rectifying construction':
at [48]. See also *Taylor v Centennial Newstan Pty Ltd* [2009] NSWCA
276 and *Minister for Immigration and Citizenship v SZJGV* (2009) 239
CLR 462 at [9]. Note that the Supreme Court has distinguished *Inco
Europe*, in a case where the court could not be 'abundantly sure' that

there was an error the court could correct. The construction sought in that case would have been 'an impermissible form of judicial legislation'. See *Farstad Supply AS v Enviroco Ltd* [2011] UKSC 16 at [49].

(p 890) **In Comment on Code s 288 at beginning insert–**

s 288 This section of the Code has been judicially considered.

(p 890) **In newly created footnote 1 insert–**

Ackland v Yonge-Esplanade Enterprises Ltd (1992) 10 OR (3d) 97, [25]; *Fong Yau Hei v Gammon Construction Ltd* [2008] 3 HKLRD 604, 613. See also the description of Code s 288 by Lord Kerr as the 'more principled way of addressing the question' in *Baker v Quantum Clothing Group Ltd* [2011] UKSC 17 at [173] and its endorsement by Lord Clarke in *NML Capital Ltd v Argentina* [2011] UKSC 31 at [142]–[143]. Lord Clarke regarded Code s 288 as 'entirely consistent' with the updating construction performed in *Yemshaw v London Borough of Hounslow* [2011] UKSC 3.

(p 890) **In footnote 4 at end insert–**

For overseas approval of Code s 288(2), see *Osborne v Chief Executive of Ministry of Social Development* [2010] 1 NZLR 559, [64].

(p 892) **In Example 288.2, after 'Betting and Gaming Duties Act 1981 s 9(1)(b)', insert–**

(repealed)

(p 894) **In Example 288.6, delete 'Supreme Court Act 1981' and insert–**

Senior Courts Act 1981

(p 899) **In footnote 2 at end insert–**

Compare *Sonea v Mehedinti District Court, Romania* [2009] EWHC 89 (Admin), [2009] 2 All ER 821.

(p 908) **In first complete paragraph at beginning replace 'The decision' with–**

The decision ('*Munks*')

(p 908) **In first complete paragraph, at end of sentence beginning 'However, the italicised passages'–**

In any event, the Court of Appeal has recently retreated from this conclusion.

> *Example 288.37A*[5A] The accused had attached a sharp metal object to the roof frame of a shed. In the event that a person opened the door to the shed, the object would, through the combination of a wire attached to the door and the force of gravity,

descend and strike the person. When this occurred, the accused was charged with the same offence as that in *Munks*. He submitted that there had been no mechanical contrivance, as that case required. *Held*: *Munks* had no such effect. It had not replaced 'other engine' with 'other mechanical contrivance'. In any event, the latter words should not be applied restrictively. In each case, it was necessary that 'the object itself as well as the manner, if any, in which it may be activated … be examined pragmatically to see whether, looked at overall, it falls within the statutory language'. The object in the present case, which was a mechanical contrivance, did so unquestionably.[5B]

Thus, while purporting not to depart from *Munks*,[5C] the Court gave the decision a flexible operation. As to 'engine', the Court added that:

'Something of the breadth of its meaning at the time when the 1827 Act came into force is identified in the [OED] where, among other references, we find a pair of scissors described as a 'little engine' in the Rape of the Lock (1712–1714) and a description of 'engines of restraint and pain' at the victim's feet in Death Slavery (1866). Indeed at much the same time, in *Barnard v Ford* [1869] LR 4Ch. App. 247, the court rejected a proposition which would turn it 'into an engine of fraud'. None of these references dilutes or could dilute the authority of *Munks*, although they suggest that the Crown's argument in that case was more constrained than it perhaps should have been.'[5D]

This is even more disappointing than *Munks*. The Court built upon that decision by considering the historic meaning of engine but then failed to interpret the enactment under the box principle accordingly.

(p 908)   **In newly created footnote 5A insert–**

R v Cockburn [2008] QB 882.

(p 908)   **In newly created footnote 5B insert–**

At 885–887.

(p 908)   **In newly created footnote 5C insert–**

At 886. The Court, being in its Criminal Division, would have been able to do so: see, for example, *Gibson v United States* [2007] 1 WLR 2367, 2375.

(p 908)   **In newly created footnote 5D insert–**

At 886.

(p 909)   **In first sentence after 'police', insert–**

rent,[7A]

(p 909) **In newly created footnote 7A insert–**

Rent has come to mean not only periodic monetary consideration for the tenant's right to possession of land but such consideration inclusive of VAT: *Mason v Boscawen* [2009] 1 WLR 2139, 2155–2156.

(p 909) **In footnote 1 at end insert–**

The passage to which this footnote relates has been approved by two judges of the High Court of Australia: *Byrne v Australian Airlines Ltd* (1995) 185 CLR 410, 459–460.

(p 914) **In footnote 6 at end insert–**

See also the cautionary words as to Code s 288 in *R (Hammersmith & Fulham LBC) v Secretary Of State For Health* [1998] EWCA Civ 1300.

(p 915) **After heading Introduction to Part XIX, insert–**

s 289 This part has been judicially approved.[1A]

(p 915) **In the new footnote 1A, insert–**

See the opinion of Lord Brodie in *Imperial Tobacco Ltd v Lord Advocate* [2012] CSIH 9 at [177].

(p 922) **After 'Comment on Code s 292', insert–**

s 292 The term 'social mischief' has been judicially utilised.[1A]

(p 922) **In newly created footnote 1A, insert–**

R v B [2012] EWCA Crim 770 at [63].

(p 922) **After 'Comment on Code s 292', after 'Police Act 1964', insert–**

(repealed)

(p 925) **In Example 293.7, after 'Water Act 1973', insert–**

s 293 (repealed)

(p 929) **In footnote 1 at end insert–**

s 294 See generally F A R Bennion, '*Law Churning and the Sociologists*' (2008) 172 JPN 228, available at http://www.francisbennion.com/2008/010.htm.

(p 929) **After heading Comment on Code s 295, insert–**

s 295 This section of the Code has been judicially approved.[1A]

(p 929)   **In the new footnote indicator 1A, insert–**

Jude v Her Majesty's Advocate (Scotland) [2011] UKSC 55 at [19].

(p 938)   **At end of second paragraph, before sideheading Where the**
mischief favours the wider construction, insert–

s 301   The preceding paragraph has been judicially approved.[3A]

(p 938)   **In the new footnote 3A, insert–**

Jude v Her Majesty's Advocate (Scotland) [2011] UKSC 55 at [39].

(p 942)   **After sideheading purposive construction, at end of first sentence**
insert footnote indicator 8A.

(p 942)   **In the new footnote 8A, insert–**

For judicial approval of this description, see the opinion of Lord Brodie
in *Imperial Tobacco Ltd v Lord Advocate* [2012] CSIH 9 at [177].

(p 943)   **After heading Comment on Code s 303, insert–**

s 303   This section has been judicially approved.[1A]

(p 943)   **In the new footnote 1A, insert–**

See the opinion of Lord Brodie in *Imperial Tobacco Ltd v Lord Advocate*
[2012] CSIH 9 at [177].

(p 963)   **In Comment on Code s 308 at beginning insert–**

s 308   This section of the Code has been judicially approved.[2A]

(p 963)   **In newly created footnote 2A insert–**

Commissioner of Inland Revenue v Common Empire Ltd [2006] 1
HKLRD 942, [17].

(p 963)   **At end of 'Comment on Code s 308', insert–**

Example 308.1 The Judicial Committee of the Privy Council, on
appeal from Trinidad and Tobago, was considering s 4(7) of the
Motor Vehicle Insurance (Third Party Risks) Act. The provision
had been amended. However, the Board found there was a 'lack of
any obvious explanation' for the amendment. Further, there was
'no real assistance' to be derived from Hansard and the work of the
Law Commission. The Board held the natural meaning was 'clear'
and 'must prevail'.

(p 963)   **In newly created footnote 4, insert–**

Presidential Insurance Company Ltd v Resha St. Hill [2012] UKPC 33.

(p 965)   **In Comment on Code s 310 at beginning insert–**

s 310   This section of the Code has been judicially approved.[4A]

(p 965)   **In newly created footnote 4A insert–**

Commissioner of Inland Revenue v Loganathan [2000] 1 HKLRD 914, 917.

(p 966)   **Before sentence beginning 'In a 1963 case', insert–**

As the High Court of Australia recently stated, 'tax statutes do not form a class of their own to which different rules of construction apply'.[1A]

(p 966)   **In newly created footnote 1A, insert–**

Alcan (NT) Alumina Pty Ltd v Commissioner of Territory Revenue (2009) 239 CLR 27 at [57].

(p 966)   **In footnote 3, at end insert–**

See also *Inland Revenue Commissioners v McGuckian* [1997] 3 All ER 817; *Inland Revenue v Scottish Provident Institution* [2005] 1 All ER 325 at [19]; *Collector of Customs v Arrowtown Assets Ltd* [2004] 1 HKLRD 77 and *Alcan (NT) Alumina Pty Ltd v Commissioner of Territory Revenue* (2009) 239 CLR 27 at [5], [50]–[53].

(p 969)   **At end of first paragraph, insert–**

Part XXI as a whole has been judicially described as 'most instructive'.

(p 969)   **In newly created footnote 1 insert–**

QBE Worker's Compensation (Vic) Ltd v Freisleben [1999] 3 VR 401, [19].

(p 969)   **In footnote 2 at end insert–**

See also the concurring opinion of Lord Scott of Foscote in *Gumbs v Attorney-General (Anguilla)* [2009] UKPC 27, [44].

(p 969)   **In Comment on Code s 312 at beginning insert–**

s 312   Section 312(1) has been judicially approved.[1A]

(p 969)   **In newly created footnote 1A insert–**

Frucor Beverages Ltd v Rio Beverages Ltd [2001] 2 NZLR 604, [28]; *Wicken (Litigation Guardian of) v Harssar* (2004) 73 OR (3d) 600, [28]; *Boardwalk Reit LLP v Edmonton* (2008) 91 Alta LR (4th) 1, [78].

(p 971)   **In Comment on Code s 313 at beginning insert–**

s 313   This section of the Code has been judicially approved.[1A]

(p 971)   **In newly created footnote 1A insert–**

Braganza v Minister for Immigration and Multicultural Affairs (2001) 109 FCR 364, 376.

(p 971)   **In footnote 2 at end insert–**

See also *Scottish & Newcastle Plc v Raguz* [2008] 1 WLR 2494, 2498 where the House of Lords rejected an interpretation adopted by the courts below on the ground that it produced 'some remarkably silly consequences'.

(p 974)   **In footnote 7 at end insert–**

See also *Pang Yiu Hung v Commissioner of Police* [2003] 2 HKLRD 125, 161 (mere difficulty does not suffice).

(p 976)   **In Example 313.11, after 'Defence (General) Regulations 1939', insert–**

s 313   (revoked)

(p 978)   **In Example 313.18, after the 'Section 43(1) of the Race Relations Act 1976', insert–**

(repealed).

(p 978)   **In Example 313.18, after the 'Sex Discrimination Act 1975 s 53(1)', insert–**

(repealed).

(p 979)   **In footnote 4 at end insert–**

s 314   Lord Shaw's dictum was applied by a Canadian appellate court, in light of the Code, in *Wicken (Litigation Guardian of) v Harssar* (2004) 73 OR (3d) 600, [29].

(p 980)   **In Example 314.2, after 'Section 16(2) of the Betting, Gaming and Lotteries Act 1963', insert–**

(repealed)

(p 982)   **In footnote 3 at end insert–**

Compare *Mason v Boscawen* [2009] 1 WLR 2139, 2156–2157.

(p 983)   **In footnote 3 at end insert–**

As to the courts' general desire to avoid fragmentation of legal and other proceedings, see *Beoku-Betts v Secretary of State for Home Department* [2009] 1 AC 115, 128.

(p 986)   **In footnote 4 at end insert–**

This dictum and preceding sentence in the Comment on Code s 315 were approved in *Wicken (Litigation Guardian of) v Harssar* (2004) 73 OR (3d) 600, [30].

(p 990)   **In Example 315.11, after 'Section 42(1) of the National Assistance Act 1948', insert–**

s 315   (repealed)

(p 998)   **In footnote 1 at end insert–**

In such situations, the courts may overcome anomaly by other means, for example by staying proceedings as oppressive: *R v Morgan* [2008] EWCA Crim 1323, [2008] 4 All ER 890.

(p 999)   **In footnote 6 at end insert–**

Similarly, the courts may consider the invocation of anomaly by counsel as inapt: *Re: WD* [2007] Scot CS CSOH 139.

(p 1000)   **In Example 316.2, after 'Section 16(3) of the Gaming Act 1968', insert–**

s 316   (repealed)

(p 1001)   **In footnote 4 at end insert–**

This extends to beyond court-based proceedings to arbitration: *Mason v Boscawen* [2009] 1 WLR 2139, 2152–2153.

(p 1006)   **In Comment on Code s 318 at beginning insert–**

s 318   This section of the Code has been judicially approved.[1A]

(p 1006)   **In newly created footnote 1A insert–**

See the decision of the Alberta Court of Appeal in *R(W) v Alberta* (2006) 62 Alta LR (4th) 6, [44].

(p 1009)   **In Comment on Code s 319, after sideheading 'Subsection (1)' insert–**

s 319   This subsection of the Code has been judicially approved.

(p 1009)   **In newly created footnote 1 insert–**

Niagara-on-the-Lake (Town) v Gross Estate (1993) 12 OR (3d) 1, [73].

(p 1013)   **In footnote 1 at end insert–**

For a case where counsel failed to raise fraud on an Act and the court
declined to apply a strained construction, saying Parliament should deal
with the problem, see *Welwyn Hatfield Council v Secretary of State for
Communities and Local Government & Anor* [2010] EWCA Civ 26
at [35], [36], [44]–[47].

(p 1013)   **In footnote 8 at end insert–**

As to evasion by a tribunal, see *Repatriation Commission v Morris*
(1997) 79 FCR 455, 461.

(p 1015)   **In footnote 5, at end, insert–**

s 320   See also *Autoclenz Ltd v Belcher & Ors* [2011] UKSC 41.

(p 1017)   **After Example 320.11, insert–**

Anti-avoidance provisions It is common to include anti-avoidance provisions in legislation.

> *Example 320.12* As to such provisions in insolvency or bank-
> ruptcy enactments see *Belmont Park Investments PTY Ltd v BNY
> Corporate Trustee Services Ltd & Anor* [2011] UKSC 38 at [16]
> and [17]. For anti-avoidance provisions in tax legislation see Code
> s 321.

(p 1018)   **Before sentence beginning 'A similar point was made by
                        Lord Greene MR', insert–**

Lord President Clyde said in 1929:

> 'No man in this country is under the smallest obligation, moral or
> other, so to arrange his legal relations to his business or property as
> to enable the Inland Revenue to put the largest possible shovel into
> his stores. The Inland Revenue is not slow – and quite rightly, to
> take every advantage which is open to it under the taxing statutes
> for the purpose of depleting the taxpayer's pocket. And the
> taxpayer is, in like manner, entitled to be astute to prevent, so far
> as he honestly can, the depletion of his means by the Revenue'.[3A]

(p 1018)   **In newly created footnote 3A, insert–**

*Ayrshire Pullman Motor Services & Ritchie v Commissioners of Inland
Revenue* (1929) 14 TC 754.

(p 1020)   **In footnote 3, at end, insert–**

See also *Inland Revenue Commissioners v McGuckian* [1997] 3 All ER 817; *Inland Revenue v Scottish Provident Institution* [2005] 1 All ER 325 at [19] and *Collector of Customs v Arrowtown Assets Ltd* [2004] 1 HKLRD 77.

(p 1025)   **In Comment on Code s 324 at beginning insert–**

s 324   This section of the Code has been judicially approved.[1A]

(p 1025)   **In newly created footnote 1A insert–**

Equuscorp Pty Ltd v Belperio [2006] VSC 14 at [248]–[251].

(p 1025)   **In passage following Example 325.4, after 'Companies Act 1985 s 726(1)' insert–**

s 326   (repealed)

(p 1030)   **In paragraph beginning 'A construction will not be allowed' at end of first sentence insert footnote indicator 1A.**

(p 1030)   **In newly created footnote 1A insert–**

This sentence has been judicially approved: *Wang v Minister for Immigration and Multicultural Affairs* (1997) 71 FCR 386, 394; *Byrne v Transport Accident Commission* [2008] VSC 92, [52].

(p 1033)   **In Comment on Code s 327 at beginning insert–**

s 327   This section of the Code has been judicially approved.

(p 1033)   **In newly created footnote 1 insert–**

Re: King's Application for Judicial Review [2003] NI 43, [58].

(p 1033)   **In footnote 4 at end insert–**

For judicial discussion as to why Parliament does so, see, for example, *Revenue & Customs v BUPA Purchasing Ltd & Ors* [2007] EWCA Civ 542 at [46].

(p 1035)   **In footnote 6 at end insert–**

See also the decision of the Ontario Court of Appeal, citing Code s 327, in *Ward-Price v Mariners Haven Inc* (2001) 57 OR (3d) 410, [24] (statutory trust subject to equitable remedies for breach of trust).

(p 1041)   **In Example 327.22, after 'Sexual Offences Act 1956 s 1 as amended by the Sexual Offences (Amendment) Act 1976 s 1', insert–**

(repealed)

(p 1042)   **In footnote 4, at end, insert-**

Compare the remark of a Justice of the High Court of Australia regarding the objective test for provocation of the accused at common law. It was 'too deeply entrenched … to be excised by judicial decision': *Masciantonio v R* (1995) 183 CLR 58.

(p 1044)   **In footnote 8, at end insert–**

s 328   The High Court of Australia has held that the *parens patriae* jurisdiction conferred by statute on the Family Court of Australia was restricted by the *Migration Act 1958* (Cth): *Minister for Immigration and Multicultural Affairs v B* (2004) 219 CLR 365.

(p 1048)   **In Example 328.7, delete 'Supreme Court Act 1981' and insert–**

Senior Courts Act 1981

(p 1050)   **In Comment on Code s 329 at beginning insert–**

s 329   This section of the Code has been judicially approved.[3A]

(p 1050)   **In newly created footnote 3A insert–**

Re: King's Application for Judicial Review [2003] NI 43, [58].

(p 1055)   **In last complete paragraph, after 'implicit in the Act', insert–**

This is all the more so because, in the words of Sir John Dyson, '[t]he rules of natural justice are one of the most important pillars of the common law'.[10A]

(p 1055)   **In newly created footnote 10A insert–**

McNally v Secretary Of State For Education & Anor [2001] EWCA Civ 332, [39].

(p 1056)   **In footnote 10 at end insert–**

For an excellent summary of the law in this area, see *R (Niazi) v Secretary of State for Home Department* [2008] EWCA Civ 755.

(p 1057)   **In footnote 2 at end insert–**

See also *Odelola v Secretary of State for the Home Department* [2009] 1 WLR 1230, 1238, 1244, 1245.

(p 1057)   **In footnote 4 at end insert–**

and *R (Bancoult) v Secretary of State for Foreign and Commonwealth Affairs* [2009] 1 AC 453, 490–491.

(p 1062)   **In footnote 4 at end insert–**

As to when a court can reopen its decision, see, generally, *HKSAR v Tin's Label Factory Ltd* (2008) 11 HKCFAR 637.

(p 1064)   **In Example 329.10, after 'Immigration Appeals (Notices) Regulations 1984 reg 4(1)(a)', insert–**

s 329   (repealed)

(p 1067)   **In footnote 5 at end insert–**

s 330   ; *Poets Chase Freehold Co Ltd v Sinclair Gardens Investments (Kensington) Ltd* [2008] 1 WLR 768, 786–788.

(p 1068)   **In Example 330.9, delete 'Supreme Court Act 1981' and insert–**

Senior Courts Act 1981

(p 1069)   **At top of page, at end of quotation, before Code s 331, insert new paragraph as follows–**

Procedure Where equitable doctrines arise in a case, there may be a need for the case to be determined by a judge with specialist knowledge of those doctrines. In that event, the case will need to be adjourned to enable its determination by a specialist Chancery Circuit judge, a High Court judge of the Chancery Division or a Crown Court judge with the relevant experience and expertise.[1A]

(p 1069)   **In newly created footnote 1A insert–**

Serious Fraud Office v Lexi Holdings Plc [2009] QB 376, 405–406.

(p 1069)   **In footnote 2 at end insert–**

s 331   Contract law may so arise in a field based partly on contract and partly on statute: see, for example, *Buckland v Bournemouth University Higher Education Corp* [2010] EWCA Civ 121 (employment law). Further, the court may apply contract law in appropriate situations notwithstanding that, due to the interposition of statute, a true contract is not in question: *Warren v Random House Group Ltd* [2009] QB 600, at [17] (case under Defamation Act 1996 ss 2–4).

(p 1070)   **After sideheading 'Effect of Act on existing contracts', at end of sentence insert footnote indicator 1A.**

(p 1070)   **In newly created footnote 1A insert–**

This passage was approved in *Australasian Correctional Management Limited v Corrections Association of New Zealand (Inc)* [2002] 3 NZLR 250.

(p 1070)   **In footnote 5, at end, insert–**

As to the position at common law, without the input of the Gaming
Act 1710, see *Victor Chandler (International) Ltd v Zhou Chu Jian He*
(unreported, Hong Kong Court of Appeal, CACV 373 of 2007, 22 May
2008).

(p 1071)   **At the end of footnote 5, insert–**

Regarding construction contra proferentem see *K/S Victoria Street (A
Danish Partnership) v House of Fraser (Stores Management) Ltd & Ors*
[2011] EWCA Civ 904 at [68].

(p 1079)   **In footnote 5 at end insert–**

s 334   See also *Hin Lin Yee v HKSAR* [2010] 2 HKLRD 826. For the abolition
of the doctrine of *doli incapax*, and the criminal liability of persons who
have not attained the age of discretion (14), see *R v T* [2009] 1 AC 1310
and F A R Bennion, '*Mens rea and defendants below the age of
discretion*' [2009] *Criminal Law Review* 757–770,
www.francisbennion.com/2009/031.htm

(p 1080)   **In Example 334.4, after 'Consumer Protection Act 1987 s 20(1)',
insert–**

(repealed)

(p 1082)   **In footnote 8, at end, insert–**

See also *Coogan v News Group Newspapers Ltd* [2012] EWCA Civ 48
at [14].

(p 1083)   **After sideheading 'Position of the Crown', in sentence beginning
'This was made unnecessary', after 'Indictments Act 1915', delete,
where first occurring–**

and the

(p 1083)   **After sideheading 'Position of the Crown', in sentence beginning
'This was made unnecessary', after 'Criminal Procedure
Rules 2005', insert–**

(revoked in part)

(p 1083)   **In footnote 1, at end insert–**

Coogan v News Group Newspapers Ltd & Anor [2012] EWCA Civ 48
at [16]–[18].

(p 1083)   **In footnote 13 at end insert–**

As to autrefois acquit see *Coke-Wallis v Institute of Chartered Accountants in England and Wales* [2009] EWCA Civ 730.

(p 1084)   **At end of first passage, before sideheading 'Statement of offence' insert–**

Further, the principle does not apply where the first 'jeopardy' was vitiated by a procedural defect, such as a conviction inadvertently obtained on unsworn evidence.[3A] In any event, the principle has been modified by statute, so as to enable a person acquitted of an offence to be retried for the offence where there is 'new and compelling evidence'.[B]

(p 1084)   **In newly created footnote 3A insert–**

Green & Green Scaffolding Ltd v Staines Magistrates' Court [2008] EWHC 1443 (Admin), [10].

(p 1084)   **In newly created footnote 3B insert–**

Criminal Justice Act 2003 s 78. See further *R v A* [2009] 1 WLR 1947; *Re: Attorney-General's Reference (No 3 of 1999)* [2010] 1 AC 145. See also Code s 342.

(p 1086)   **In footnote 3 at end insert–**

s 335   *R v Athwal* [2009] 1 WLR 2430; *R v Horncastle* [2010] 2 WLR 47. Implied rules of evidence are taken to be imported in their latest form, unless the implication is to the contrary. For a fundamental change regarding the admissibility of infant evidence see *R v Barker* [2010] EWCA Crim 4, [33]–[52].

(p 1088)   **In footnote 3 at end insert–**

The wording of Example 335.6 has been judicially approved: *Iarnroid Eireann v Social Welfare Tribunal* [2007] IEHC 406.

(p 1088)   **In footnote 4 at end insert–**

This sentence has been applied by the Bokhary PJ and Lord Scott of Foscote NPJ, speaking for the Hong Kong Court of Final Appeal. They said 'if a statutory shortcut to the proof of essential matters is to be taken advantage of it is essential that the conditions of the statutory shortcut be strictly observed': *Tse Mui Chun v HKSAR* (2003) 6 HKCFAR 601, [53].

(p 1089)   **In Example 335.8, after 'Drug Trafficking Offences Act 1986', insert–**

(largely repealed)

(p 1090)   **At end of page insert–**

Fortunately, the view of Lord Hoffmann has since prevailed in the House of Lords,[10A] as it earlier had in the Hong Kong Court of Final Appeal.[10B]

(p 1090)   **In newly created footnote 10A insert–**

Re: B [2009] 1 AC 11. See also *Re: D* [2008] 1 WLR 1499.

(p 1090)   **In newly created footnote 10B insert–**

Solicitor 24/07 v Law Society of Hong Kong [2008] 2 HKLRD 576.

(p 1093)   **In footnote 3 at end insert–**

See the important judgment in *Director of Public Prosecutions v Wright* [2009] EWHC 105 (Admin), [2009] 3 All ER 726 (prosecution under Hunting Act 2004 s 1), particularly as to Art 6 of the European Convention on Human Rights and the distinction between the 'persuasive' and 'evidential' burdens on an accused.

(p 1094)   **In footnote 9 at end insert–**

As to quasi-estoppel, see *AAA v ASH* [2009] EWHC 636 (Fam), [2009] 4 All ER 641, [81].

(p 1097)   **In footnote 4 at end insert–**

See also *Ofulue v Bossert* [2009] 1 AC 990.

(p 1097)   **In Example 336.1, after 'Companies Act 1985 s 151', insert–**

s 336   (repealed)

(p 1098)   **In footnote 8, at end, insert–**

However, the statute will be held to extend to instruments governed by foreign law, thereby constituting a source of mandatory rules, where its terms, context or purpose indicate: see, for example, *Insight Vacations Pty Ltd v Young* (2011) 243 CLR 149 at [28]–[36].

(p 1100)   **In footnote 5, at end insert–**

See also *Neilson v Overseas Projects Corporation of Australia* (2005) 223 CLR 331.

(p 1105)   **After heading 'Comment on Code s 340', insert–**

s 340   This section of the Code has been judicially approved.[5A]

(p 1105)   **In newly created footnote 5A, insert–**

London Borough of Lewisham v Malcolm [2008] Ch 129 at [63]–[65]. The Court of Appeal added that 'a significant result of [an unlawful act attracting the maxim] is the court would not lend its assistance to it'. Further, 'an advocate should draw the attention of the court to the fact that the act relied on by a party is unlawful, if that is the case'.

(p 1116)   **In footnote 9 at end insert–**

s 342   In this context, 'the double jeopardy rule cannot be resuscitated under the guise of the interests of justice': *R v A* [2009] 1 WLR 1947, 1958. See further p 1084.

(p 1117)   **At end of sentence beginning 'A clumsy judicial translation', insert–**

The Supreme Court has arguably improved upon Brooke LJ's translation with 'too negligible for the law to be concerned with'.[2A]

However, Lord Phillips of the Supreme Court has emphasised 'I doubt whether it is ever possible to define, in quantitative terms, what for the purposes of the application of any principle of law, is *de minimis*'.[2B]

s 343   The importance of the principle was indicated by Lord Dyson of the Supreme Court, who recently remarked '[i]t goes without saying that the principle *de minimis non curat lex* (the law is not concerned with very small things) applies in the present context as in most others'.[2C]

(p 1117)   **In newly created footnote 2A, insert–**

Morge v Hampshire County Council [2011] 1 All ER 744 at [15].

(p 1117)   **In newly created footnote 2B, insert–**

Sienkiewicz v Greif (UK) Ltd [2011] 2 AC 229 at [108].

(p 1117)   **In newly created footnote 2C, insert–**

R (Alvi) v Secretary of State for Home Department [2012] UKSC 33 at [88].

(p 1117)   **After Example 343.2 insert–**

Example 343.2A The Court of Appeal had to decide whether a variant of poker was a 'game of chance' under the Gaming Act 1968 s 52(1). The variant involved both chance and skill. 'Game of chance' was defined by s 52(1) to include a game of chance and skill combined. The defendant argued that, in such a case, the element of chance had to predominate over that of skill. The Court rejected this argument. Referring to the *de minimis* principle, it said the element of chance should only be ignored 'where it is so insignificant as not to matter'.[6A]

(p 1117)   **In newly created footnote 6A insert–**

R v Kelly [2009] 1 WLR 701, 711.

(p 1118)   **At end of first sentence insert–**

It has even received recognition in the interpretation of a written constitution.[1A]

(p 1118)   **In newly created footnote 1A insert–**

Prem Singh v Director of Immigration [2003] 1 HKLRD 550, 575.

(p 1118)   **After Example 343.6, insert–**

However, the Court of Appeal has recently raised the possibility of whether the *de minimis* principle is distinct from the doctrine of substantial compliance. The latter may afford broader relief.

(p 1118)   **In newly created footnote 8, insert–**

National Union of Rail, Maritime & Transport Workers v Serco Ltd (t/a Serco Docklands) [2011] 3 All ER 913 at [78]–[87].

(p 1119)   **In footnote 4 at end insert–**

Note that the *de minimis* principle can be applied in a criminal case in favour of the prosecution: *Briere v Hailstone* [1969] Crim LR 36.

(p 1122)   **In footnote 2 at end insert–**

See also, with approval of Code s 343, *Farnell Electronic Components Pty Ltd v Collector of Customs* (1996) 72 FCR 125; *Roberts v Secretary of State for Social Security* [2001] EWCA Civ 910 at [8]–[15].

(p 1123)   **After 'See also Example 287.31', insert–**

However, as earlier indicated, the Court of Appeal has recently considered a distinction between the *de minimis* principle and the doctrine of substantial compliance. If that is so, departure from prescribed forms would also attract that doctrine, which may afford broader relief than the *de minimis* principle. There is no third alternative of a 'near miss principle'.

(p 1123)   **In newly created footnote 11, insert–**

National Union of Rail, Maritime & Transport Workers v Serco Ltd (t/a Serco Docklands) [2011] 3 All ER 913 at [78]–[87].

(p 1123)   **In newly created footnote 12, insert–**

Afzal v Secretary of State for Home Department [2012] EWHC 1487 at [44]–[53].

(p 1129)   **In Comment on Code s 346, at beginning, insert–**

s 346   This section of the Code has been judicially approved.[2A]

(p 1129)   **In newly created footnote 2A insert–**

R (Winchester College) v Hampshire CC [2009] 1 WLR 138, 152. See also the decision of the Alberta Court of Appeal in *Boardwalk Reit LLP*

v Edmonton (2008) 91 Alta LR (4th) 1, [75]. The Court added (at [76]):
'[c]ourts interpret statutes to relieve against more than total physical
impossibility. They demand of the citizen neither extreme ingenuity,
superhuman effort, nor massive unusual resources to comply with an
Act. All practical endeavours and a fair trial suffice'.

(p 1134)   **In footnote 9 at end insert–**

s 347   *R v S Ltd* [2009] EWCA Crim 85; [2009] 2 Cr App R 11.

(p 1139)   **In footnote 9, at end insert–**

s 348   See also *Malcolm v R* [2011] EWCA Crim 2069 at [110]–[111].

(p 1141)   **In footnote 9 at end, insert–**

s 349   See also *R v South Ribble Borough Council, Ex p Hamilton* [2000]
         EWCA Civ 518 and *Secretary of State for Communities and Local
         Government v Welwyn Hatfield Borough Council* [2011] UKSC 15.

(p 1142) **In Example 349.1, after 'Social Security Act 1975 s 24(1)', insert–**

         (repealed)

(p 1144)   **In Comment on Code s 350 at beginning insert–**

s 350   This section of the Code has been judicially approved.[1A]

(p 1144)   **In newly created footnote 1A insert–**

         See the decision of the Full Federal Court of Australia in *Re Sandvik
         Australia Pty Limited v Commonwealth of Australia* [1990] FCA 386,
         [12].

(p 1145)   **In footnote 1 at end insert–**

         R (Thomas) v Greenwich Magistrates' Court [2009] EWHC 1180
         (Admin); [2009] Crim LR 800 [18].

(p 1146) **After sideheading 'Agency principle' at end of paragraph, but
            before Example 351.1 insert footnote indicator 1A.**

(p 1146)   **In newly created footnote 1A insert–**

         This passage was approved in *Midlands Co-Operative Society Ltd v HM
         Revenue & Customs* [2008] EWCA Civ 305, [14].

(p 1149)   **At bottom of page, insert–**

s 352   Indeed, the vigilance principle has been taken so far as to mean that, as
         in the law of contract, a statutory requirement must, in the absence of an
         express time limit, by implication be performed within a reasonable
         time.[5A]

(p 1149)   **In newly created footnote 5A insert–**

See the decision of the Federal Court of Australia in *Boswell v Secretary, Department of Foreign Affairs and Trade* (1993) 46 FCR 434, 441. As to the law of contract, see, for example, *Behzadi v Shaftesbury Hotels* [1992] Ch 1, 12 and the decision of Lord Millett NPJ, for the Hong Kong Court of Final Appeal in *Lau Suk Ching Peggy v Ma Hing Lam* [2010] HKCFA 20, [40]–[43].

(p 1152)   **At bottom of page insert–**

Similarly, an Act may exclude liability in the event of 'voluntary assumption of risk'.[1A] The present view is that, where an Act employs a concept similar to the *volenti* principle, the words it uses 'must be given their ordinary meaning, and not be complicated by fine distinctions or by reference to the old common law doctrine'.[1B]

(p 1152)   **In newly created footnote 1A insert–**

See, for example, Animal Act 1971 s 5(2).

(p 1152)   **In newly created footnote 1B insert–**

Freeman v Higher Park Farm [2008] EWCA 1185, [48].

(p 1157)   **In Example 355.6, delete 'Perjury Act 1916' and insert–**

s 355   Perjury Act 1911.

(p 1160)   **After Example 355.13, insert new paragraph–**

On occasions, legislatures engage in cross-referencing between overlapping enactments. For example, in Australian federal statutes, where a provision enactment deals with a criminal matter, a note will direct the reader to related federal criminal legislation.[5A] However, the note is not part of the Act.[5B] In a 2003 case, the Ontario Court of Appeal had to decide whether a reference in one statutory provision to another statute was such a cross-reference or had some free-standing effect. It decided on the former, citing the Comment on Code s 355 and describing the provision as 'deliberate redundancy'.[5C] Had the Australian approach been taken, the question would not have arisen. In any event, the provision, being part of its Act, was better classified as a declaratory enactment.[5D]

(p 1160)   **In newly created footnote 5A insert–**

See, for example, Healthcare Identifiers Act 2010 s 15.

(p 1160)   **In newly created footnote 5B insert–**

Interpretation Act 1901 s 13(3).

(p 1160)   **In newly created footnote 5C insert–**

Guelph (City) v Wyndham Street Investments Inc (2003) 63 OR (2d) 481, [16].

(p 1160)   **In newly created footnote 5D insert–**

See further Code p 188.

(p 1160)   **After sideheading 'Different words to be given different meanings', at end of first sentence insert footnote indicator 10A.**

(p 1160)   **In newly created footnote 10A insert–**

This sentence has been judicially approved: *Omagh District Council, Re Judicial Review* [2007] NIQB 61, [50].

(p 1161)   **In footnote 1 at end insert–**

; *Re James* [2005] NIQB 38, [21]; *Davidson v M* [2009] CSIH 70, [15]. See also *Speciallaser Tech Inc v Specialloy Industries Ltd* [1999] 12 WWR 139, [12].

(p 1164)   **After sideheading 'Generalibus specialia derogant' at end of third sentence insert footnote indicator 2A.**

(p 1164)   **In newly created footnote 2A insert–**

See also *Henry Boot Construction (UK) Ltd v Malmaison Hotel Ltd* [2001] QB 388.

(p 1164)   **In footnote 5 at end insert–**

The passage from Pearce and preceding passages of the Code were applied in *Secretary for Justice v Tang Bun* [1999] 3 HKC 647, 652, 658. See also *Secretary for Justice v Lau Suk Han* [1998] 2 HKLRD 14, 22.

(p 1164)   **In footnote 9, at end insert–**

See also *Fun World Co Ltd v Municipal Council of Quatre Bornes* [2009] UKPC 8 at [59] and *Cusack v London Borough of Harrow* [2011] EWCA Civ 1514 at [19]–[21].

(p 1164)   **After sideheading 'Generalia specialibus non derogant', at end of quotation insert–**

The Court of Appeal has remarked that 'the Latin language puts the matter more pithily than English can'.[9A]

(p 1164)   **In newly created footnote 9A, insert–**

Gesner Investments Ltd v Bombardier Inc [2011] EWCA Civ 1118 at [42].

(p 1168)   **In Example 356.3, after 'Supreme Court Act 1981', insert–**

s 356   Senior Courts Act 1981

(p 1170)   **In Example 356.9, after 'Gaming Act 1968 s 34(3)(b)', insert–**

(repealed)

(p 1181)   **After heading Comment on Code s 363, delete first sentence and insert–**

s 363   This section of the Code, which has been judicially approved, is concerned with the first task of the interpreter, namely to arrive at the ordinary meaning of the word or phrase in question.

(p 1181)   **In the new footnote indicator 1, insert–**

See the opinion of Lord Brodie in *Imperial Tobacco Ltd v Lord Advocate* [2012] CSIH 9 at [175].

(p 1188) **In Example 363.13, after 'Policyholders Protection Act 1975 s 6(5)', insert–**

(repealed)

(p 1190)   **In footnote 11 at end insert–**

Compare *Majorstake Ltd v Curtis* [2008] 1 AC 787, 790–791, 804; *R (M) v Slough BC* [2008] 1 WLR 1808, 1825; *R (Aweys) v Birmingham CC* [2009] 1 WLR 1506.

(p 1190)   **At foot of page, insert–**

Example 363.21A The *National Assistance Act 1948* s 21(1)(a) empowers a local authority to 'make arrangements for providing residential accommodation for persons aged eighteen or over who … are in need of care of attention …'. Arden LJ (at [35]) cited a dictum that 'it would seem wrong to extend a duty owed to a person who satisfies a statutory requirement to a person who currently does not satisfy the requirement simply because he will or may do so in the future'. Later (at [40] she cited another dictum that 'where it was clear that a person was in the early stages of what would be likely to develop into much more serious illness, some flexibility was allowed provided that at all times there was indeed a need for care and attention'.

(p 1192)   **In footnote 5 at end insert–**

This passage was applied in *Blackpool Council Licensing Authority v Howitt* [2008] EWHC 3300 (Admin), [17]–[20]. See also *Pilling v Reynolds* [2008] EWHC 316 (QB), [2009] 1 All ER 163, [21] and *Fairfax v Ireton* [2009] 1 NZLR 540.

(p 1193)   **After first paragraph, including Example 363.28 insert new paragraph–**

Even so, a reference to a collective noun, such as a 'woodland', which includes things *in posse* as well as things *in esse* has been taken to include both.[2A]

(p 1193)   **In newly created footnote 2A insert–**

Palm Developments Ltd v Secretary of State for Communities and Local Government [2009] EWHC 220 (Admin), [42] (tree preservation order).

(p 1194)   **After Example 364.1 insert–**

s 364   *Example 364.1A* When considering the legal meaning of the definition of 'intellectual property' in s 72(5) of the Senior Courts Act 1981 Lord Neuberger MR said: '… the concept of "intellectual property" appears to have developed so as to render it unsafe to place much weight on the natural meaning of each of the two words, in order to decide whether a particular right is within its ambit'.[3A]

(p 1194)   **In newly created footnote 3A, insert–**

Coogan v News Group Newspapers Ltd & Anor [2012] EWCA Civ 48 at [37].

(p 1195)   **In footnote 1 at end insert–**

See further *Palm Developments Ltd v Secretary of State for Communities and Local Government* [2009] EWHC 220 (Admin), [26], where Cranston J said that such provisions 'avoid the need for unprofitable disputes'.

(p 1197)   **In footnote 2 at end insert–**

s 365   See further *Victims Compensation Fund Corp v Brown* (2003) 201 ALR 260, [34].

(p 1197)   **In paragraph beginning 'A case laid down the meaning', after 'Commons Registration Act 1965 s 22(1)(c)', insert–**

(repealed)

(p 1198)   **In footnote 6 at end insert–**

For evidential issues raised by the foregoing, see, for example, *Distribution Group v Commissioner of Taxation* (2000) 45 ATR 494, 500–502.

(p 1200)   **In footnote 4 at end insert–**

In *Schanka v Employment National (Administration) Ltd* (2000) 97 FCR 186, the Full Federal Court was 'not persuaded that *'duress'* in [the provision] is used in a context dealing with the same branch of the law as the cases in which courts have [generally] been concerned to apply it … Accordingly, we do not regard the expression as *'a free-standing legal term'* as that phrase is used in [Code, p 1199]'. So much may be accepted. However, care must always be taken not to confuse the presence of contrary intention with the outright absence of a free-standing legal term.

(p 1201)   **At top of page, insert–**

s 366   *Example 366.3A* Wilson LJ said 'The phrase "a child in need" … constitutes a term of art in [the Children Act 1989] which triggers duties thereunder, for the discharge of which a children's services authority is responsible. The phrase has no significance in relation to the duties under [the Housing Act 1996], for the discharge of which a housing authority is responsible.'[1A]

(p 1201)   **In newly created footnote 1A, insert–**

R (TG) v London Borough of Lambeth [2011] EWCA Civ 526 at [12].

(p 1210)   **In paragraph beginning 'If a slang term', after 'Children Act 1975', insert–**

s 369   (repealed)

(p 1215)   **At end of first full paragraph, insert–**

s 370   The Divisional Court accepted criticism of the expression 'saving life or limb' in Police and Criminal Evidence Act s 17(1)(e) as 'colourful [and] slightly outmoded' but explained that it 'indicates a serious matter — that … would involve some serious injury to an individual'.[2A]

(p 1215)   **In newly created footnote 2A insert–**

Syed v DPP [2010] 1 Cr App R 34, [11].

(p 1219)   **At top of page, after passage in inverted commas but before paragraph beginning 'Where an artificial meaning', insert–**

s 374   *Example 373.5A* Section 22(2)(a) of the Immigration Act 1971 (repealed) enabled rules of procedure to be made so as to enable 'the Tribunal, on an appeal from an adjudicator, to remit the appeal for determination by him in accordance with any directions of the Tribunal'. In context, 'appeal' was a homonym as the proceeding

before the adjudicator grounding the appeal to the Tribunal was
also called an appeal. Counsel argued that 'appeal' in s 22(2)(a)
had a consistent meaning, being 'appeal from an adjudicator', with
the result that the Tribunal could delegate the task of determining a
particular appeal to an adjudicator. The Court rejected the argument, effectively reading the second reference to appeal as 'the
appeal [that had been] to [the] adjudicator'. After referring to the
Comment on Code s 373, Scott Baker J (as he then was) said there
was 'no absolute rule that one word cannot have two different
meanings within the same section or subsection. True, it will only
rarely occur but the ultimate question is what did Parliament
intend'.[1A]

(p 1219)   **In newly created footnote 1A insert–**

R (Secretary of State for Home Department) v Immigration Tribunal
[2001] QB 1224, 1233. The judge also said (at 1227) that successor
legislation was 'not materially different' and '[f]or convenience ...
annexed to this judgment a table that shows the corresponding provisions
in the old and new law'.

(p 1227)   **In Example 378.3, after 'Section 6 of the Trade Descriptions
Act 1968', insert–**

s 378   (repealed)

(p 1227)   **In Example 378.6, after 'Trade Descriptions Act 1968 s 14(1)',
insert–**

(repealed)

(p 1228)   **In Example 378.9, delete 'Supreme Court Act 1981' and insert–**

Senior Courts Act 1981

(p 1242)   **In Comment on Code s 384, insert at beginning–**

s 384   This section of the Code has been judicially approved.[2A]

(p 1242)   **In newly created footnote 2A insert–**

See the decision of the Queensland Court of Appeal in *Pepper v
Attorney-General (No 2)* [2008] QCA 207, [32].

(p 1243)   **In Example 385.1, after 'Public Bodies Corrupt Practices
Act 1889', insert–**

s 385   (repealed)

(p 1243)   **In Example 385.1, after 'Prevention of Corruption Act 1916',
insert–**

(repealed)

(p 1244)   **In footnote 2 at end, insert–**

See also *Du Plessis v Fontgary Leisure Parks Ltd* [2012] EWCA Civ 409 at [37].

(p 1250)   **After Example 389.1 insert–**

s 389   *Example 389.1A* Section 11 of the Public Order Act 1986 required notice to be given of a proposal to hold a public procession, including the route of the procession, except where the procession was 'commonly or customarily held'. The issue arose: could a procession attract the exception without having a predetermined route? If not, the procession could not be held, as notice thereof could not properly be given. This implied prohibition would operate alongside an express prohibition elsewhere in the Act. The House of Lords applied the exception. Lord Rodger (Baroness Hale agreeing) said 'Where the Act contains a specific provision prohibiting certain processions, there is no room for implying into another provision a requirement which would have the effect of prohibiting a different type of procession'.[2A]

(p 1250)   **In newly created footnote 2A insert–**

Kay v Commissioner of Police [2008] 1 WLR 2723, 2735.

(p 1251)   **After sideheading 'Subsection (1)', at end of second sentence, insert–**

s 390   The Court of Appeal has stated that the maxim is 'equally simply explained by the ordinary proposition that when a legislative provision sets out who or what is within the meaning of an expression, it ordinarily means that no-one else or nothing else is'.[2A]

(p 1251)   **In newly created footnote 2A, insert–**

Wirral Metropolitan Borough Council v Salisbury Independent Living Ltd [2012] EWCA Civ 84 at [23].

(p 1255)   **In Comment on Code s 393 at beginning insert–**

s 393   This section of the Code has been judicially approved.[5A]

(p 1255)   **In newly created footnote 5A insert–**

See the decision of the Full Federal Court of Australia in *Eastman v Commissioner of Superannuation* (1987) 15 FCR 139, 148.

(p 1259)   **After 'Comment on Code s 396', insert–**

s 396   This section of the Code has been judicially considered.[2A]

(p 1259)   **In newly created footnote 2A, insert–**

Dunne v Donohoe [2001] IEHC 126 at [61].

(p 1261)   **In Example 396.12, delete 'Supreme Court Act 1981' and insert–**

Senior Courts Act 1981

(p 1263) **In Example 397.4, after 'Common Land (Rectification of Registers)**
Act 1989 s 1', insert–

s 397   (repealed)

(p 1268)   **In footnote 2 at end insert–**

R (Kaupthing Bank HF) v HM Treasury [2009] EWHC 2542, [37].

(p 1268)   **In footnote 2, at end insert–**

See also *Sugar v British Broadcasting Corporation & Anor* [2012] UKSC 4 at [49]–[52].

(p 1292)   **At top of page, after quotation, insert new paragraph–**

s 412   English judges have, on occasion, lamented the adoption of substantial effect where copyout would clearly do.[1A]

(p 1292)   **In newly created footnote 1A insert–**

Spencer-Franks v Kellogg Brown and Root Ltd and others [2008] UKHL 46, [2009] 1 All ER 269, [26]. For discussion of an error in transposing see *Marks & Spencer plc v Revenue and Customs Commissioners* [2009] UKHL 8, [8].

(p 1299)   **In footnote 2 at end insert–**

s 413   For a recent application of the Marleasing principle, see *R (on the application of Irving) v Secretary of State for Transport* [2008] EWHC 1200 (Admin.

(p 1309)   **At end of Comment on Code s 417, before Code s 418 insert–**

s 417   A claim for Francovich damages against the government for failing to implement Community law is a claim in tort to which the Limitation Act 1980 s 2 applies.[2A]

(p 1309)   **In newly created footnote 2A insert–**

Spencer v Secretary of State for Work and Pensions [2009] QB 358.

(p 1312)   **In footnote 2 at end insert–**

See further *AS (Somalia) v Entry Clearance Officer (Addis Ababa)* [2009] 1 WLR 1385, 1391–1392.

(p 1321)   **In Comment on Code s 420, at end of second paragraph insert–**

s 420   Nonetheless, the court may, on rare occasions, decline to follow a particular Strasbourg decision where the court has concerns as to whether the decision insufficiently appreciates or accommodates particular aspects of the domestic process.[3A]

(p 1321)   **In newly created footnote 3A insert–**

R v Horncastle [2010] 2 WLR 47, 97.

(p 1324)   **In footnote 3 at end insert–**

s 421   For a similar rule of interpretation relating to compatibility with a written constitution, see, for example, *HKSAR v Lam Kwong Wai* [2006] 3 HKLRD 808.

(p 1325)   **In footnote 4 at end insert–**

See further *Corporate Officer of the House of Commons v The Information Commissioner & Ors* [2008] EWHC 1084 (Admin), [2009] 3 All ER 403, [2] where the Divisional Court said 'It is a fundamental principle of our constitutional structures that Parliament should not normally be subject to judicial scrutiny or supervision. The House of Commons is answerable to its collective conscience, and in the ultimate analysis, to the electorate.'

(p 1325)   **In footnote 3 at end insert–**

More gratifying is the holding by the High Court of Justiciary, after referring to the discussion above, 'I consider that it is possible to come to a Convention compatible construction of [the provision at issue] without imposing such a degree of strain on the language as to require justification by reference to section 3 of the Human Rights Act': *M v Watson* [2009] HCJ 3, [26]–[27].

(p 1331)   **At end of fourth passage, after quotation ending 'instead to grant a declaration of incompatibility' insert, as a new paragraph–**

s 422   Fortunately, in a 2009 case, the House of Lords allowed an appeal against a decision of the Court of Appeal purporting to write words into the Standards Act 2000 s 82(4)(b) under the Human Rights Act 1998 s 3(1). The House substituted a declaration of incompatibility, with the House remarking 'it is not for us to attempt to rewrite the legislation'. To the extent this represents a shift away from s 3(1) and toward a declaration, it is welcome.[8A]

(p 1331)   **In newly created footnote 8A, insert–**

R (Wright) v Secretary of State for Health [2009] 1 AC 739, 748, 755.

(p 1335)   **In footnote 2 at end, insert–**

s 428   For an instance where a Minister indicated he was unable to make a
statement of compatibility as envisaged by Code s 426(1)(b) see *R
(Animal Defenders International) v Secretary of State for Culture, Media
and Sport* [2008] 1 AC 1312, 1340.

(p 1352) **Under sideheading 'Meaning of 'court' at end of paragraph insert–**

s 443   Nonetheless, in the case of a determinate sentence, the power of the
Home Secretary under s 35(1) to accept or reject a recommendation by
the Board to release prisoners on licence is not incompatible with
Art 5(4), as the foregoing does not give rise to a new issue affecting the
lawfulness of their detention.[5A]

(p 1352)   **In newly created footnote 5A insert–**

R (Black) v Secretary of State for Home Department [2009] 1 AC 949.

(p 1356)   **In footnote 2 delete text and insert–**

s 444   [2003] 2 AC 430, 445–447. See also *R (A) v Croydon LBC* [2009]
1 WLR 2557.

(p 1356)   **At bottom of page insert–**

It is uncontroversial that Art 6 'does not require a right of appeal, let
alone an appeal by way of rehearing'.[14A]

(p 1356)   **In newly created footnote 14A insert–**

R (Langley) v Preston Crown Court [2009] 1 WLR 1612, 1619.

(p 1360)   **Under sideheading 'Police powers', at end of sentence insert–**

s 446   It also applies to the retention and release by the police of criminal
records and related information.[11A]

(p 1360)   **In newly created footnote 11A insert–**

R (L) v Commissioner of Police [2010] 1 AC 410.

(p 1362)   **In footnote 7 at end insert–**

s 447   Thus, Art 9 'does not always guarantee the right to behave in the public
sphere in a way which is dictated by [religion]': *Ladele v London
Borough of Islington* [2009] EWCA Civ 1357; [2010] 1 WLR 955.

(p 1363)   **In footnote 1 at end insert–**

and *Ladele v London Borough of Islington* [2009] EWCA Civ 1357;
[2010] 1 WLR 955.

(p 1369)   **In footnote 1 at end insert–**

As to the scope of personal rights, see *Hanchett-Stamford v Attorney-General* [2009] Ch 173 (right of sole surviving member of unincorporated association to assets of association).

(p 1373)   **In footnote 8 at end insert–**

s 462   See also, *Corporate Officer of the House of Commons v The Information Commissioner & Ors* [2008] EWHC 1084 (Admin), [2009] 3 All ER 403, [43].

(p 1376)   **In footnote 5 at end insert–**

In relation to the words 'as it has effect for the time being in relation to the United Kingdom' see *R (On The Application of Bancoult) v Secretary of State For Foreign and Commonwealth Affairs* [2009] 1 AC 453.

Appendix C

Updated Text of Interpretation Act 1978

(p 1389)   **In section 16 annotations add underneath last annotation–**

See further: in relation to the application of sub-s (1) above, in so far as it relates to the annulment of any law under the St Helena, Ascension and Tristan da Cunha Constitution Order 2009, Sch 1, s 217(3): the St Helena, Ascension and Tristan da Cunha Constitution Order 2009, SI 2009/1751, Sch 1, s 217(3).

(p 1391)   **In section 20A:**

replace 'Community Instruments' in heading and 'Community Instrument' in body of section with 'EU instruments' and 'EU instrument' respectively.

(p 1395)   **In annotations insert–**

Amended by European Union (Amendment) Act 2008 s 3(3), Sch Pt 2.

(p 1395)   **Definitions–**

In definition 'Charity Commission', delete 'means the Charity Commission for England and Wales established by section 1A of the Charities Act 1993' and replace with [means the Charity Commission for England and Wales (see section 13 of the Charities Act 2011)].

(p 1396)   In definitions beginning 'The Communities', replace 'The Communities' with 'The EU' and 'the Community treaties' with 'the EU treaties'.

(p 1397)   In definition 'Comptroller and Auditor General' delete words after 'Auditor-General of Public Accounts' to end.

In definition '["The Immigration Acts"]' delete, 'section 64 of the Immigration, Asylum and Nationality Act' and replace with '[section 61 of the UK Borders Act 2007]'.

In between definitions 'Local land charges register' and 'London borough' insert–

["Local policing body" has the meaning given by section 101(1) of the Police Act 1996.]

(p 1398)   In definition 'London borough', replace '[or Part II of the Local Government Act 1992]' with '[, Part II of the Local Government Act 1992 or Part I of the Local Government and Public Involvement in Health Act 2007]'

In between definitions 'Person' and 'Police area', insert–

["Police and crime commissioner" means a police and crime commissioner established under section 1 of the Police Reform and Social Responsibility Act 2011.]

In definition beginning 'Police area' delete words, 'police authority'.

After definition of 'Police area', insert–

["Police authority", in relation to Scotland, has the meaning or effect described by sections 50 and 51(4) of the Police (Scotland) Act 1967.]

After definition of 'registered medical practitioner', insert–

(p 1400)   'Registered provider of social housing' and 'private registered provider of social housing' have the meanings given by section 80 of the Housing and Regeneration Act 2008 (and 'non-profit' and 'profit-making' in connection with a registered provider are to be read in accordance with section 115 of that Act).'

In annotation regarding definition 'Charity Commission' replace existing text with–

Definition 'Charity Commission' substituted by the Charities Act 2011, s 354(1), Sch 7, Pt 2, para 35.

Date in force: 14 March 2012: see the Charities Act 2011, s 355; for transitional provisions and savings see s 354(2), Sch 8, Pt 1 thereto.

In between annotations regarding definitions of 'Civil Partnership' and 'Committed for trial', insert–

Definition 'Comptroller and Auditor General' words omitted repealed by the Budget Responsibility and National Audit Act 2011, s 26(2), Sch 5, Pt 2, para 12.

Date in force: 1 April 2012: see SI 2011/2576, art 5.

In between annotations regarding definitions of 'Committed for trial' and 'The Corporation Tax Acts', insert–

'Definition beginning "The Communities" amended by European Union (Amendment) Act 2008 s 3(3) Sch Pt 2.'

(p 1401)   Date in force: 1 December 2009: see SI 2009/3143 art 2.

In annotation regarding definition ['The Immigration Acts'] insert at end of first sentence–

Definition amended by UK Borders Act 2007 s 61(4).

Date in force: 30 October 2007 (date of the Royal Assent of the UK Borders Act 2007) in the absence of any specific commencement provision.

In between annotations regarding definitions 'The Immigration Acts' and 'London borough' insert–

Definition "Local policing body" inserted by the Police Reform and Social Responsibility Act 2011, s 97(1), (2); for transitional provisions see s 98, Sch 15, Pts 3, 4 thereto.

Date in force: 16 January 2012: see SI 2011/3019, art 3, Sch 1, para (aaa).

In annotation regarding definition 'London borough', insert at end of first sentence–

, words '[, Part II of the Local Government Act 1992 or Part I of the Local Government and Public Involvement in Health Act 2007]' substituted by Local Government and Public Involvement in Health Act 2007, s 22, Sch 1, Pt 2, para 14"

Date in force: Local Government and Public Involvement in Health Act 2007: 1 November 2007: see SI 2007/3136, art 2(b).

Definition beginning 'Police and Crime Commissioner' inserted by the Police Reform and Social Responsibility Act 2011, s 97(1), (3); for transitional provisions see s 98, Sch 15, Pts 3, 4 thereto.

Date in force: to be appointed: see the Police Reform and Social Responsibility Act 2011, s 157(1).

Definition beginning 'Police area' remove reference to 'police authority' and add at the end, 'words omitted repealed by the Police Reform and Social Responsibility Act 2011, s 97(1), (4); for transitional provisions see s 98, Sch 15, Pts 3, 4 thereto'.

Date in force: 16 January 2012: see SI 2011/3019, art 3, Sch 1, para (aaa).

Definition beginning "Police authority" inserted by the Police Reform and Social Responsibility Act 2011, s 97(1), (5); for transitional provisions see s 98, Sch 15, Pts 3, 4 thereto.

(p 1402)   Date in force: 16 January 2012: see SI 2011/3019, art 3, Sch 1, para (aaa).

Definition beginning 'Registered provider of social housing' inserted by Housing and Regeneration Act 2008 s 277 Sch 9 para 5. Amended by SI 2010/844, art 6, Sch 2, para 1.

Date in force: 1 April 2010: see SI 2010/844 art 1(2), SI 2010/862, art 2.

Appendix F

Amended text of the Human Rights Act 1998

(p 1432)
In section 10

Remove from list of Subordinate Legislation references beginning 'Mental Health Act 1983' and 'Naval Discipline Act 1957'.

After reference beginning 'Marriage Act 1949' in list of Subordinate Legislation add, 'Asylum and Immigration (Treatment of Claimants, etc) Act 2004 (Remedial) Order 2011, SI 2011/1158 (made under sub-s (2)).' and 'Sexual Offences Act 2003 (Remedial) Order 2012, SI 2012/1883 (made under sub-s (2)).'

(p 1436)
In section 18

Add to list of Subordinate Legislation, 'Judicial Pensions (European Court of Human Rights) (Amendment) Order 2012, SI 2012/489.'

(p 1449)
In Schedule 2

Remove from list of Subordinate Legislation references beginning 'Mental Health Act 1983' and 'Naval Discipline Act 1957'.

After reference beginning 'Marriage Act 1949' in list of Subordinate Legislation add, 'Asylum and Immigration (Treatment of Claimants, etc) Act 2004 (Remedial) Order 2011, SI 2011/1158 (made under sub-s (2)).' and 'Sexual Offences Act 2003 (Remedial) Order 2012, SI 2012/1883 (made under sub-s (2)).'

(p 1451)
In Schedule 4

Add to list of Subordinate Legislation, 'Judicial Pensions (European Court of Human Rights) (Amendment) Order 2012, SI 2012/489.'

Index

Note An item not found in this Index may be included either in the list set out in Appendix E (pages 1419 to 1424) or in the Bibliography (pages 1475 to 1507).

Abbott CJ   1010, 1070
abbreviations   37, 1216
Abinger, Lord   869, 879
absolute liability – *see* **strict liability**
absurdity
  anomaly   521, 841–842, 917, 986–999,
           1021–1022, S93
  artificiality   969–971, 1003–1006
   and see **counter-mischief;**
     evasion of Act
  fragmentation of proceedings   S93
  futility   969–971, 999–1003
  illogicality   986–999
  impracticality   388n, 969–979
  inconvenience, avoidance of   382, 526,
        527, 870, 969–971,
        979–986
  literal construction and   459
  logical impossibility   973–974
  meaning of   969–971
  Pepper v Hart, rule in, and   616, 618–621
  presumption against   325–326, 527, 529,
        870, 969–971
  trivial acts – *see de minimus non*
    curat lex
  unreasonable dilemma   974
  – *and see* **counter-mischief;**
    evasion of Act
abuse of process – *see* **process**
academic point   143, 144, 175, 418, 780,
        1269
accidental fit – *see* **intention,**
  legislative
Ackner, Lord   177, 1270
acquis communautaire   1283, 1285
'acronymania'   737
act in law – *see* **judicial act**
act of God   1104–1105, 1176
Act of Parliament – *see* **Bill,**
  parliamentary; enactment;
  free-standing Act, doctrine of;
  heading; Parliament;

Act of Parliament – *contd*
  Parliament Roll; punctuation;
  section; statute; taxing Acts;
  treaty
  acting 'in execution of' an   95
  acting 'under' an   183
  administration of – *see* **enforcement**
    agencies
  adoptive – *see* **adoptive Act**
  'always speaking'   891
  amending   186
  amendment of – *see* **amendment to**
    Act
  amnesty, conferring   184, 189
  ancient – *see* **statutes**
  application of – *see* **application of**
    Act
  Appropriation   191
  assent to – *see* **Royal assent**
  atmosphere analogy   365
  attainder, of   189
  bad faith, whether vitiated by   234
  Bill for – *see* **Bill, parliamentary**
  chapter number of – *see* **chapter**
    number of Act
  citation in other Act   1391
  Clauses – *see* **Clauses Act**
  code of practice under – *see* **codes**
    of practice
  codifying – *see* **codification**
  commencement of – *see*
    commencement of Act or
    enactment
  components of – *see* **functional**
    construction
  consolidation – *see* **consolidation**
    Act
  constitution, incorporating   910
  constitutional   189, 305
  contravention of – *see* **disobeying**
    Act; statutory duty
  conveyancing   190

All references are to page numbers

Act of Parliament – *contd*
copyright in   183, 226–227
Crown, when bound by – *see*
   Crown
declaratory – *see* **declaratory**
   enactment
definition of   179–183
desuetude   15, 102, 277, 312–314, 572,
                                                         888
   – *and see* **Scotland**
disproprietory   846–847
duplication of application – *see*
   application of Act
editions, published official, of   230–232
enabling   241, 256
enactment procedure   213–216, 714–715
   – *and see* **enacting formula;**
      Royal assent
enforcement of – *see* **enforcement**
   agencies; legal policy;
   prosecution of offences
Estate   1072
evasion of – *see* **evasion of Act**
exemplification of   229
Expiring Laws Continuance Act –
   see **Expiring Laws**
   Continuance Acts
expiry of – *see* **temporary Act**
extent of – *see* **territorial extent of**
   Act
failure of   942
financial   190–191
   – *and see* **taxing Acts**
fixed-time   184, 187, 890, 909–911
floodlight analogy   192, 194, 196, 308,
                                             316, 325, 365
fraud, not vitiated by   233
general   183, 185–186
guidelines issued under   706
in pari materia – *see* **in pari**
   materia, Acts
Indemnity Act   184, 189, 909
integrity of   1028–1029
interpretation of – *see*
   interpretative criteria;
   interpretative factors;
   statutory interpretation
invalidity, grounds of   232–236
judicial notice of – *see* **judicial**
   notice
law reform   184, 187
   – *and see* **Law Commission;**
      Statute Law Revision Act
local – *see* **local Act**
long title of – *see* **long title**
mistake in – *see* **mistake**
model Act – *see* **adoptive Act**
modern statute – *see* **statutes**
naming of   735–739

Act of Parliament – *contd*
nature of   5, 191–194
non-homogeneous   1165
oblivion, of   184, 189
ongoing   184, 187, 890–910
overriding effect of   197–204, 304–305
'passing' of   744
permanent   183, 186
personal – *see* **personal Act**
personal application of – *see*
   application of Act
preparation of – *see* **Bill,**
   parliamentary
prerogative and – *see* **prerogative,**
   Royal
principal   183, 186, 607
private – *see* **private Act**
promulgation of – *see*
   promulgation of Act
public general   183–186
publication of – *see* **promulgation**
   of Act
purpose of – *see* **purposive**
   construction
references to   230–232
regulatory   829–830, 1006, 1066
remedial   207
renaming of   738–739
repeal of – *see* **repeal**
reprinting clause   228
residual powers in   256
retrospective – *see* **retrospectivity**
rewrite Act – *see* **tax law rewrite**
   Acts
Royal assent to – *see* **Royal assent**
rug analogy   198, S31
self-applying   183
short title of – *see* **short title**
specialty, as – *see* **specialty**
split   710
Statute Law Revision – *see* **Statute**
   Law Revision Act
suspensory   225
tax law rewrite – *see* **tax law**
   rewrite Act
temporal aspect of – *see* **time**
temporary – *see* **temporary Act**
territorial extent of – *see* **territorial**
   extent of Act
text of   213, 215–216, 225–230
three-fold consent, doctrine of   179–182,
                                       212–213, 223, 224,
                                       232–236, 407
transitional provisions of – *see*
   transitional provisions
treaty, implementing   190
types of   183–191
uniqueness of   204–206
validation   184, 189

Act of Parliament – *contd*
validity, challenge to 232–236
– *and see* **enactment; natural**
law
act of state
action founded on, jurisdiction S33
judicial notice of 823–824
nature of 238, 369
jurisdiction of courts 238
sovereign immunity – *see* **privileges**
and immunities
territory, relating to 329, 406
war 238, 369
– *and see* **Minister of the**
Crown
acta exteriora indicant interiora
secreta – *see* **intention,**
ascertainment of
acte clair 1306
action, cause of – *see* **cause of action**
actus curiae neminem gravabit 984
actus dei nemini facit injuriam – *see*
act of God
actus reus – *see* **criminal law**
adjudicating authorities
appellate jurisdiction, with 142–154
original jurisdiction, with 138–142
– *and see* **enforcement agencies**
administration of Act – *see*
enforcement agencies; statutory
power
Administrative Court 154, 155, 163
administrative law – *see*
decision-making rules; judicial
review; public law
Admiral, the 140, 141, 330, 351, 357, 368,
913
Admiralty – *see* **Admiral, the;**
jurisdiction
Adoptive Act 183, 186–187
– *and see* **Clauses Act**
adversarial system – *see* **court**
adviser, legal – *see* **advocate;**
solicitors; subject, the
Advisory Committee on Statute Law 231
advocate
adoption of text as part of argument 29,
34, 693
adviser, as 35, 42, 438
alternative arguments, presented by 433
checklist for 1383–1385
conduct of case, rights regarding 617–618,
692–693, 854, 1087
court technique 593–594, 1381–1382
court, interpretative function of, and 434–
435, 443
cross-examination by 777
duty of 435, 620, 623–627

advocate – *contd*
facts, preparation and presentation
of, by 426–427
failure to assist court S46
interpretative factors and 528, 575–576,
583, 955–956
interstitial articulation by 505, 534–537
lay 112–113, S18
legislative history, use of, and 617–618,
620, 623–627, 693
– *and see* **legislative history;**
***Pepper v Hart*, rule in**
Parliamentary Bar 184
parliamentary procedure, duty to
know 626–627
plausible 26
privilege regarding legal advice 244
role of 436–437, 443
specially appointed (SAA) 112, S17
– *and see* **Brandeis brief;**
central function of
practitioner; hairsplitting;
McKenzie friend;
pleading; skeleton
arguments; solicitors;
subject, the
affirmative resolution procedure –
see **delegated legislation**
Agag 485
age 200, 948n, 992
– *and see* **children**
agency 200, 1146–1149
– *and see* **employment; vicarious**
liability
aircraft, law prevailing on 386–387
airspace 334
Alderson, B 206
Aldous LJ 1185
aliens 366–367, 371, 383, 922
– *and see* **application of Act;**
foreign; European Convention
on Human Rights
Allan, T R S – *see* **Bibliography (pp**
1475 to 1507)
allegans suam turpitudinem non est
audiendus – *see* **illegality**
allegiance, duty of 379
Allen, Carleton Kemp 182, 203n, 241n,
392, 407n, 488, 865
– *and see* **Bibliography (pp 1475**
to 1507)
Allen, Layman – *see* **Bibliography**
(pp 1475 to 1507)
Allgemeines Landrecht 170
Alsatia 105
alter ego **doctrine** – *see* **Carltona**
principle
Alternative Dispute Resolution
(ADR) 102

All references are to page numbers

Alverstone, Lord 732
ambiguity
 contextual 445–446
 displacement of S82
 ejusdem generis principle and 1233–1234
 grammatical – *see* **ambiguity (grammatical)**
 noscitur a sociis principle and 1230
 resolving – *see* **interpretative criteria**
 semantic 445–446
 syntactic 445–446
 unrecognised 446–447
 vagueness and, contrasted 445–446
ambiguity (grammatical)
 general 447–448, S81
 interpretative factors, application of 444–447, 515, 521–523, 529–531, 551
 judgment or discretion, and 127–129, 444
 literal meaning, relation to 952–954
 nature of 443–444, 1190
 opposing constructions, and 257, 263, 429–438, 448–450, 972–973
 punctuation and 757–758
 relative 447–448
 syntactical or formal 557
  – *and see* **ambiguity; broad terms; differential readings; doubtful penalisation, principle against; legal meaning; *noscitur a sociis* principle; obscurity, semantic; politic uncertainty; repugnancy**
amendment to Act
 commencement of 288
 consequential 295–297
 consolidation Acts and 604–607
 construction of 288, 1166
 defective 413n
 delegated legislation, by 245, 293–295
 enactment procedure, mistake in 235–236
  – *and see* **mistake**
 extra-statutory concession – *see* **extra-statutory concession**
 implied 293, 295
 indirect express 145–146, 292–293, 295n, 301
 meaning 195, 214, 287–288
 Official Table 295
 power to propose, statutory 978–979
 printing corrections – *see* **printing corrections**
 reference to amended Act 298–199
 referential definitions and 572
 repeal and 288
  – *and see* **repeal**

amendment to Act – *contd*
 same session, in 287, 288, 1387
 substantive and temporal provisions 195–196
 textual 146, 288–292, 300
  – *and see* **punctuation**
 transfer of Minister's functions, on 85–86, 288–292
 transitional provisions – *see* **transitional provisions**
  – *and see* **free-standing Act, doctrine of; Henry VIII clause; repeal; retrospectivity**
amendment to delegated legislation 274–275, 1390
Amos, Maurice Sheldon – *see* **Bibliography (pp 1475 to 1507)**
analogy, statutory – *see* **statutory analogy**
ancillary powers, implied – *see* **implied ancillary powers**
ancillary rules of law
 express application of 1033, 1042
 implied application of 254, 1033–1042
 meaning 1033
 vacant provisions 1039
'and', use of 1192
Andrews, J – *see* **Bibliography (pp 1475 to 1507)**
Anisminic **principle** – *see* **decision-making rules**
anomaly – *see* **absurdity**
anonymity
 criminal cases, in 121
 drafting defect 567n
Anson, W – *see* **Bibliography (pp 1475 to 1507)**
anti-social behaviour order 94, 1356
anti-social behaviour order (*ASBO*) 1356
appeal
 academic point, on 144
 additional grounds of 56
 appellate courts 102, 116–118
 case stated, by 55, 146–147, 159
 consent order, against 1260–1261
 contempt of court and 148, 255
 county court, from 149
 county court, to 145
 Court of Appeal 113, 116, 139, 148–151, 392, 1396
 criminal 94, 149–151, 993
 Crown court, from 146–147, 149
 Crown court, to 146–147
 decision on appeal, against 149
 facts and 427
 'final' decision, against 109, 147, 414
 findings of fact, from S23
 fresh evidence on S25

All references are to page numbers

appeal – *contd*
High Court, from   147–148
High Court, to   146–147
Human Rights Act 1998 – *see*
    Human Rights Act 1998
interested person, by   S86
judicial and administrative
    discretion compared   144
'leapfrogging'   148, 151
leave to   106, 148–152
– *and see Scherer* **principle**
Lords, House of, to   151–152
magistrates, to   145
mistake of law, and   41
nature of   143, 392
point of law, meaning of   148
references to European Court and   1307
review and   102, 116–118, 1054n
right of   857–858
Supreme Court, to   S25
tribunals, from   147–148
   – *and see* **county court;**
      Divisional Court;
      evidence; jurisdiction;
      Lords, House of;
      magistrates; mandatory
      and directory
      requirements; mistake;
      notice; retrospectivity;
      time; tribunals
appearance *gratis*   58
Appellate Committee of House of
    Lords   152–153
application of Act
aliens, to   392
deemed location of omission   387–389
duplication of   393
extra-territorial   364
– *and see* **extra-territoriality**
foreign elements within the territory,
    and   364–371
'foreign' elements and   362–363
– *and see* **private international law**
matters both within and outside
    jurisdiction   381
non-resident Britons, to   378–384
non-resident foreigners, to   371–378
overseas property of resident
    foreigners   367
Parliament, to   1049
principles governing   193, 194–196, 327,
            360–364, 1098–1099,
            S100
resident foreigners, to   364–371
sovereign immunity – *see* **privileges**
    and immunities
   – *and see* **aliens;**
      exterritoriality;

application of Act – *contd*
  sovereign immunity – *contd*
   – *and see* **aliens; exterritoriality; –**
     contd
     extra-territoriality;
     uniform statutes
appropriate forum test   333
Arbab-Dehkordi, B   720
– *and see* **Bibliography (pp 1475**
    to 1507)
arbitration   54, 120, 270, 294, 447, 448,
          449, 478, 781, 782,
          800, 812, 974, 988,
          1087, 1193, 1260
archaisms   1181, 1213
Archbold, J F – *see* **Bibliography**
    (pp 1475 to 1507)
archival drafting – *see* **incorporation**
    by reference
Arden LJ   27, 200, 547, 1300n
Arizona, constitution of   171
arms, right to hold   S39
Arnold P   980
arson   374, 896, 991, 1124, 1125
artificial person
appearance by   112
company   87
creation of   239, 577, 903
included in 'person'   577
location, deemed, of   389–390
piercing the veil   389
powers of   239
rights of   103
   – *and see* **absurdity;**
      commercial enactments;
      Crown; local authority;
      public authority; *qui facit*
      *per alium facit per se***;**
      vicarious liability
artificiality – *see* **absurdity; artificial**
    person
ASBO – *see* **anti-social behaviour**
    order (ASBO)
Ashworth J   993
Ashworth, Andrew   94
– *and see* **Bibliography (pp 1475**
    to 1507)
'**asifism**'   146, 386, 759n
– *and see* **deeming**
Asquith of Bishopstone, Lord   910
assessments, drafting   S45
assessor   30, 394, 1355n
associated state, meaning of   339, 340, 345,
          1394, 1396
Astill J   90
Aston J   654
Atiyah, P S   418
– *and see* **Bibliography (pp 1475**
    to 1507)

All references are to page numbers

Atkin, Lord 29, 32, 42, 142, 418, 419, 467, 473, 563, 936, 956, 965, 1126
Atkinson, Lord 658, 813, 829
Attorney General
consent of 74
functions of 73–74, 97, 100, 435n, 623
guardian of public interest, as S14
prosecutions, role of in 96–98, 660, 1083
public interest immunity and 1095–1097
relator actions – *see* **relator action**
– *and see* **Crown Prosecution Service; Director of Public Prosecutions; Minister of the Crown; prosecution of offences; relator action**
Attorney General v Great Eastern Railway Co, rule in 256, 497
Attorney General v Lamplough, rule in x, 289–290
audi alteram partem **principle** 120, 1055–1056, 1061, 1111–1115, 1137, 1286
audience, rights of
layperson, grant to, S20
Auld LJ 506, 1040, 1196
Australia
amendments to Bill, interpretative use of, in 640
Australia Act 1986 338–339
Chief Magistrate, immunity from prosecution S19
common law presumption against retrospectivity S39
ejusdem generis principle, in 1236n
Hansard, use of, in 618, 673–677
hendiadys, use of, in 1197
independent Crown dominion, an 338–339
legislative history, use of, in 590, 592n, 611–612, 613n, 669n
mischief 929
Parts, division of Act into, in 749–750
'plant', meaning of, in 1215
punctuation, in 757
purpose clause, in 734
purposive construction in 944
self-defence, law of, in 556
taxing Acts, construction of S85, S91
autrefois acquit 374, 555, 810, 1083, 1084, S98–99
autrefois attaint 889
autrefois convict 810, 1083, 1084
avoidance – *see* **evasion of Act**
Avory J 715, 746, 748, 1084, 1085, 1454
Bacon, Francis 1102, 1226
– *and see* **Bibliography (pp 1475 to 1507)**
Bacon, Matthew – *see* **Bibliography (pp 1475 to 1507)**

Baggallay LJ 656
bailiff – *see* **enforcement agencies**
Baker, K 206n
Baker, (Sir George) P 661
Balcombe LJ 51, 55, 106, 294n, 937, 1307
Bankes LJ 1265
Bank of England 1394
Bank of Ireland 1395
bankruptcy 46, 371, 378n, 503, 772, 847, 947, 994, 1004, 1005, 1067, 1100
Barber **principle** 1279–1280
Barnes, Jeffrey W 6n, 124n, 431n, 547, 651n, 652n, 944 –
and see **Bibliography (pp 1475 to 1507)**
Barras **principle** 599–604, 694n, S60, S62
Barrington, Daines 7, 118, 477, 917, 1240
– *and see* **Bibliography (pp 1475 to 1507)**
Barwick CJ 640, 734
– *and see* **Bibliography (pp 1475 to 1507)**
baseline
meaning of 340–341
UK 340–341, 358
Bates, T St J N 475n, 723n
– *and see* **Bibliography (pp 1475 to 1507)**
Bayley J 1190
Beatson J 499n, 1291n, 1459
– *and see* **Bibliography (pp 1475 to 1507)**
Beaulac, Stéphane – *see* **Bibliography (pp 1475 to 1507)**
Beldam LJ 1305
Bell, John 8n, 135
– *and see* **Bibliography (pp 1475 to 1507)**
Bell, W E – *see* **Bibliography (pp 1475 to 1507)**
Bellamy, J G – *see* **Bibliography (pp 1475 to 1507)**
belt-and-braces phrase 1157n, 1189
benefit from own wrong – *see* ***nullus commodum capere potest de injuria sua propria***
benefit, statutory – *see* **statutory right**
Bennett **principle** 100
– *and see* **process**
Bennion, F A R – *see* **Bibliography (pp 1475 to 1507)**
Bennion's Gloss 828n
Bentham, Jeremy 24, 118, 397, 507, 527n, 564, 805, 922, 1173
– *and see* **Bibliography (pp 1475 to 1507)**
Berwick upon Tweed 42, 341–342

All references are to page numbers

Best CJ 1239
Better Regulation Commission 91
Better Regulation Task Force 91
Bevan, Aneurin 592
bias 1061
– *and see* **nemo debet esse judex in propria causa**
bilingual systems – *see* **legal meaning**
Bill of Rights [1689] 181, 236, 305, 836, 853, 1047, 1048, 1050
Bill, parliamentary
amendment to – *see* **amendment to Bill**
Civil List 191
commentary on 592
Consolidation Fund 191, 221
copyright in 183, 226–227
draft 180
enactment procedure – *see* **Act of Parliament**
endorsements on 214–215
enrolment of 227
explanatory material on, published by Government 641–644, 1454–1455
explanatory memorandum 641, 1454–1455
financial 191, 221
form of 180
hybrid 186, 1073
interpretation of enactment by reference to 180
judicial notice of – *see* **judicial notice**
legal status of 182, 205
money bill 223–224
notes on clauses 641–642
printing corrections – *see* **printing corrections**
private 184, 724, 733
– *and see* **Private Act**
private member's 621
promotion of S31
Royal Assent to – *see* **Royal assent**
'scope', doctrine of 728
sessional carry-over 180
statutory effect of 205
textual memorandum on – *see* **textual memorandum**
– *and see* **legislative history**
Bingham of Cornhill, Lord 101n, 125, 130, 131, 153, 202, 278, 369n, 415, 420, 550, 632, 688, 706, 783, 788, 806, 812, 823, 826, 837, 1006, 1090, 1200, 1201, 1311,

Bingham of Cornhill, Lord – *contd* 1312, 1314, 1324, 1327, 1348, 1360
– *and see* **Bibliography (pp 1475 to 1507)**
Birkenhead, Lord LC 640, 1128
Birks, Peter 12, 14
– *and see* **Bibliography (pp 1475 to 1507)**
Blackburn, Lord 335n, 497, 585, 614n, 677n, 775, 870, 899, 912, 1202
Blackburne J 244n, 494, 708
Blackett-Ord V-C 901
Blackstone, William 7, 30, 39, 40, 41, 46, 63, 64, 93, 96, 103, 139, 167, 182, 229, 238, 343, 344, 346, 347, 352, 356, 359, 365, 372, 408, 426, 458, 464, 471, 477, 478, 484, 491, 495, 513, 516, 559, 655, 668, 671, 760, 761, 773, 801, 802, 804, 806, 808, 838, 846, 875, 889, 895, 898, 920, 921, 924, 926, 948, 1002, 1009, 1072, 1083, 1125, 1133, 1135, 1137, 1172, 1175, 1176, 1198, 1246, 1247
– *and see* **Bibliography (pp 1475 to 1507)**
blasphemy and blasphemous libel S31
Blom-Cooper, Louis 1196n
– *and see* **Bibliography (pp 1475 to 1507)**
body corporate – *see* **artificial person**
Bokhary PJ S99
Bologna, law of 170
bona fides non patitur ut bis idem exigatur – *see* **double jeopardy**
Bond, M F – *see* **Bibliography (pp 1475 to 1507)**
Book, this
nature of ix, 12–14
philosophy of 1–5, 544–548
practitioner's bible ix
substance of 5
updating of x
– *and see* **Code, the**
Bouvier, John 751
– *and see* **Bibliography (pp 1475 to 1507)**
Bowen LJ 46, 423n, 427, 491, 681n, 979n, 1187, 1245

All references are to page numbers

Bowles, Gibson 191n, 205
box principle 907, 908–909
  – and see **updating construction;**
    words
Brabazon CJ 653
Bracewell J 87, 436n
Bracton 30, 801n
  – and see **Bibliography (pp 1475**
    to 1507)
Bradley, A W – *see* **Bibliography (pp**
  1475 to 1507)
Bramwell, B 870
Brandeis brief 595
Brandon, Lord 686n, 1029, 1131
Braun, A S4
Bray CJ 675
Brazil, P 652n
  – and see **Bibliography (pp 1475**
    to 1507)
breach of statutory duty, tort of
  class intended to benefit 76
  common law and 71
  damage intended to be covered 77–79,
    939
  difficulty of determining 69
  European Community law, under 71
  exclusive remedy, where 75
  general remedies for 67, 72
  Law Commissions' recommendation 70
  legislative intention and 68, 69, 70, 73–82
  mental element and 79
  misfeasance in public office and 72
  negligence and 68, 72, 82–84
  personal safety, high risk to, and 78–79,
    S11
  private law remedies for 67, 68, 70, 71,
    S9
  public law remedies for 67, 68
  relator actions and 73–74
  vicarious liability and 67, 72–73
  volenti non fit injuria and 1150–1151
  – and see **contempt of statute;**
    disobeying Act;
    magistrates; relator
    action; tort
Brett LJ 79
Bridge of Harwich, Lord 106, 403, 619,
    636, 1297
Brightman, Lord 117, 127, 321, 392, 800,
    850, 1024
'British Islands', meaning of 342, 1395
British overseas territory 1395
'British possession', meaning of 343, 1395
broad terms
  consistent interpretation of, required 803–
    804
  examples of 125, 146n, 419–421, 429,
    445, 1167–1170

broad terms *– contd*
  fact and degree, question of *– see*
    fact
  guidelines as to meaning of 129
  interpretation of 448, 803, 1167
  mobile in space 1170
  mobile in time 1169
  mobile in time and space 1170
  multiple 425, 1170
  narrowing by implication 1168–1169
  nature of 129
  processed 1169
  static 1169
Brodie, Lord S3, S46, S47, S61, S67, S106
Brooke LJ 107, 187, 605, 632, 642, 709,
    776, 782, 806, 822,
    831n, 856, 1075, 1117,
    1215, 1311, 1314,
    1318, 1319, 1367,
    S101
  –and see **Bibliography (pp 1475 to**
    1507)
Broom, Herbert 39n, 62, 63n, 408, 464,
    601n, 647, 864, 865,
    888, 889, 1129, 1250
  – and see **Bibliography (pp 1475**
    to 1507)
Brougham, Lord 184n, 228, 373, 398, 412,
    493, 576, 718, 719,
    1047, 1410, 1414,
    1418
Brown (Simon) LJ 332n, 402n, 414n, 576,
    580, 596n, 826, 838,
    924, 1135, 1136, 1238
Brown (Stephen) P 461, 681, 811, 1137,
    1294
Brown of Eaton-under-Heywood,
  Lord 950, 1367
Browne LJ 299, 796
Browne-Wilkinson, Lord 71, 72, 80, 81,
    83, 84, 126, 260n, 410,
    506, 563, 582, 617,
    620, 621, 622, 623,
    631, 632, 633, 634,
    635, 637, 646, 648,
    667, 669n, 670, 671,
    685, 695, 706, 707,
    788, 814, 828, 857,
    868, 971, 982, 1014,
    1020, 1050, 1053,
    1065, 1111, 1276n,
    1313
  – and see **Bibliography (pp 1475**
    to 1507)
Brownlie, I – *see* **Bibliography (pp**
  1475 to 1507)

All references are to page numbers

Brussels Convention on Jurisdiction and the Enforcement of Judgments in Civil and Commercial Matters 1354

Bryson J 673, 674n, 675
– *and see* **Bibliography (pp 1475 to 1507)**

Buckland, W W – *see* **Bibliography (pp 1475 to 1507)**

Buckley LJ 846, 996, 998, 1065, 1184, 1221

building regulations 1395

burden of proof
evidential burden 1091–1092, 1329
general 1091–1092
legal or persuasive burden 1091–1092, 1329
persuasive and evidential S100

Burn, R – *see* **Bibliography (pp 1475 to 1507)**

Burrow, James 757
– *and see* **Bibliography (pp 1475 to 1507)**

Burrows, J F – *see* **Bibliography (pp 1475 to 1507)**

burthysack 1136n

business
facilitating 55, 980–981, 1204
Moorcock The, doctrine of 1070
– *and see* **Law Merchant; restraint of trade**

Butler-Sloss P 118n, 787, 1008n, 1314, 1331, 1379

Buxton LJ 88, 435, 600, 811, 822, 855, 891, 909, S39

byelaws
breach of 78, 492–493, 1025
confirmation of 269–271
display of invalid, unlawfulness of 262
enforcement of 74
interpretation of 270, 1130
invalidity of 176n, 261–262
judicial review of 262
local authority, made by 269–271
ministerial control of 246, 269
nature of 269–271, 413
non-legislative 271
ultra vires 260–262
uncertainty, void for 270, 448
unreasonable, void if 269–270
– *and see* **delegated legislation;** *ultra vires,* **doctrine of**

Byles J 647, 654, 1017n, 1033, 1034, 1036, 1056

Cadogan v Morris **principle** 871

Cairns, Lord 34, 231, 308, 656, 736, 833, 1025, 1038, 1165

Calvert, H G – *see* **Bibliography (pp 1475 to 1507)**

Campbell, Lord 47, 108, 261n, 331, 332, 347, 988, 1007, 1187, 1212, 1239, 1245, 1252

Canada
aborigines' rights 1034–1035
acts in *paria materia* 1167
Canada Act 1982 338–339
delegated legislation in 247n
discrimination, legislation against 518
Hansard, use of, in 677–679, S67
human rights 518
legislative history, use of 651n
liberal construction requirement 519
multilingual jurisdiction 25
statements of compatibility with Charter of Rights and Freedoms 1335
Westminster Parliament and 338–339

canon law – *see* **ecclesiastical law**

canons of construction, linguistic
broad terms – *see* **broad terms**
construction as a whole – *see* **construction as a whole**
deductive reasoning, use of – *see* **logic, use of in interpretation**
nature of 1155
– *and see* **composite expressions; ordinary meaning; technical terms; words**

Cantley J 1161

capacity, legal – *see* **incompetents**

Cardozo J 849, 873, 874, 987

Cardus, Neville – *see* **Bibliography (pp 1475 to 1507)**

care plan review, drafting S45

Carltona **principle** 88–89, 273

Carnwath J 42n, 258n, 306, 681
– *and see* Bibliography (pp 1475 to 1507)

Carr, Cecil Thomas – *see* **Bibliography (pp 1475 to 1507)**

Carruthers J 669n

Carswell, Lord 45, 781

Carter, Ross – *see* **Bibliography (pp 1475 to 1507)**

Carus, Sjt 801

Casement, Roger 234n, 876n

castle, person's home is – *see* **domestic sanctuary, principle of**

casus male inclusus – *see* **rectifying construction**

casus omissus – *see* **rectifying construction**

causation 552–553, 953–954, 1162, 1269

cause of action 70, 77, 78, 81, 83, 84, 198, 422–423, 553, 627, 669, 711, 790, 809,

All references are to page numbers

cause of action – *contd*
811, 848, 951, 993,
1035n, 1105, 1106,
1107, 1108, 1116,
1141, 1379
accrual S45
– *and see* **legal proceedings;**
procedure, civil
caution, judicial review S14
central function of practitioner 438
central funds 1395
'Centrebinding' 923
certainty of law – *see* **predictability**
of law
certiorari **(quashing order)** – *see*
judicial review
cessante ratione legis cessat ipsa lex 888,
889
Chadwick LJ 772, 821, 827, 1281
Chalmers, Mackenzie 549, 718n, 1172
– *and see* **Bibliography (pp 1475**
to 1507)
chameleon word 1226, 1228
champerty 199, 777, 781, S77
Chancery Roll – *see* **Roll**
Chandos clause 720
Channel Islands 194, 343–344, 347
Channel Tunnel 346
chapter number of Act
interpretative use of 741–743
post-1962 practice 741–743
pre-1963 practice 741–743
type-face, significance of 185, 741–743
use of 185
Charity Commission 1395
Chaucer, Geoffrey 752
– *and see* **Bibliography (pp 1475**
to 1507)
children
abduction of 816, 1119
access to 1112
adoption of 51, 835–836, 894
application of enactment to 577–579
care of 543–544
care proceedings 883, 886, 957–958
court, role of, in respect of 105
custody of 780, 787–788
disciplining of 1317
education of 835
evidence by 461, 901, S99
guardian ad litem of 1137–1138
identity, restrictions on publication
of 130n, 867–868
immigration of 51, 809
legitimacy of 990
medical or psychiatric examination
of 1234–1235
need, in S108
open court principle and 120

children – *contd*
parents and 841, 1317
passports of 1045–1046
protection of 80, 461, 790, 845
welfare of 543–544, 841
– *and see* **evidence; foetus;**
incompetents; minor;
wardship
Chitty LJ 1250
– *and see* **Bibliography (pp 1475 to**
1507)
chose in action 953, 1035, 1072
Christianity 780–781, 842–843, 1259, S21
– *and see* **religion**
church court – *see* **ecclesiastical**
court
Church Commissioners 1395
Cicero 1126, 1203
– *and see* **Bibliography (pp 1475**
to 1507)
circulars, official – *see* **legislative**
history
citizen, the – *see* **doubtful**
penalisation, principle against;
legislation; subject, the
civil law and criminal law contrasted
– *see* **criminal law**
civil law, the – *see* **Roman law**
Clarke LJ 314, 839, 1269
clause – *see* **section**
Clauses Act 186, 187, 269, 758
– *and see* **adoptive Act**
Clauson J 1001
clausula derogatoria 405
clausula generalis non referta ad
expressa 1164
Cleasby, B 1217
Clerk of the Crown 217, 219
Clerk of the House of Commons 617
Clerk of the Parliaments
appointment of 226
Crown, as agent of 217, 227
enactment procedure, and 217, 745
settling text of Act by 225, 227–228, 745
cloning 906n, 907n
closure order (premises used for
drugs) 45, 360, 702
Clyde, Lord 904, 955, 967, S94
Cockburn CJ 565, 656, 751, 885, 1011,
1239
Cockburn, Lord 10
– *and see* **Bibliography (pp 1475**
to 1507)
Cocks, Ray – *see* **Bibliography (pp**
1475 to 1507)
Code for Crown Prosecutors 99
– *and see* **prosecution of offences**
Code, the
philosophy of 1, 10

All references are to page numbers

Code, the – *contd*
  summary of   14–18
  terms defined in, list of   1419–1424
    – *and see* **Book, this**
codes of practice   704, 706
codification
  custom and   608–609
  interpretation of codifying Act   608–609
  interstitial articulation and   509
  Lord Hershell's rule   608
  nature of   187, 201, 421, 608–609
  non-statutory law, effect on   1250
  prerogative and   608–609
    – *and see* **plain meaning rule;**
      practice; sub-rules
coffee bars, licensing of   185, 1016
Cohen LJ   1184, 1242
Cohen question, the   1184
Cohen, M D – *see* **Bibliography (pp**
  1475 to 1507)
Coke, Edward   26n, 30, 32, 41, 57, 62, 63,
                            68, 128, 134, 180, 203,
                            232, 304, 331, 337,
                            347, 356, 372, 393,
                            433, 471, 490, 654,
                            655, 668n, 697, 792,
                            801, 806, 814, 832,
                            888, 912, 945, 979,
                            982n, 1023, 1101,
                            1104, 1105, 1112,
                            1124, 1128, 1141,
                            1144, 1146, 1156,
                            1246, 1247, 1251,
                            1252
    – *and see* **Bibliography (pp 1475**
      to 1507)
Coleridge, Lord   72, 655, 656, 669, 1011,
                            1222
collective noun, reference to   S107
collective title
  interpretative use   764–765
  nature of   184, 603, 763, 764–765
  short title, descriptive words of,
    differing from   764–765
  updating, by implication   764–765
Collins (Lawrence) J   1264
Collins J   415, 1024, 1057
Collins MR   657, 1121
colonial legislature   1395
colony
  meaning of   345, 1395
  nature of   406
comity
  court and court, between   174, 332, S29,
                                          see Scotland
  international   328, 361, 367–368, 371–372,
                                   376, 818–819
  Parliament and courts, between   157, 233n,

comity – *contd*
  Parliament and courts, between – *contd*
                              445, 647–648, 695,
                                   776, 781, 965
    – *and see* **tacit legislation**
commencement of Act or enactment
  anticipatory delegated legislation   286–287
    – *and see* **delegated legislation**
  commencement provisions   277–287, 717
  court, adjourning, and   279
  different days for different
    provisions   283–286
  early rule on   280, 719
  European Community law and   279
  mandatory and directory
    requirements   285
  meaning of   277–279, 1395
  nature of   194, 325–326
  on date specified by order   281, 283–286
  on date specified in Act   280–283
  on event specified in Act   282
  on lapse of period specified in Act   282
  on passing of Act   280, 744
  parliamentary session, on
    commencement of   280, 719
  postponement of   280–281
  repeal before – *see* **repeal**
  retrospective – *see* **retrospectivity**
  textual amendment and   289–292
  time of   1387
    – *and see* **commencement**
      order; judicial review;
      political factors;
      retrospectivity;
      transitional provisions
commencement order   239, 253, 263, 278,
                            283–286, 287, 1052n
commercial enactments   332
comminution
  examples of   451–452, 522, 532, 755–756
  meaning   391
  selective – *see* **selective**
    comminution
Commissioners for Her Majesty's
  Revenue and Customs   190
committee reports – *see* **legislative**
  history
common law
  abolition of common law rules by
    Act   75, 198, 504, 1459–1460
  basis of   29, 917
  codification of – *see* **codification**
  criminal law concepts of   504, 1078
  custom and, compared   203
  declared by Act – *see* **declaratory**
    enactment
  developed by reference to Act   504, 695,
                                   816, 1314, 1459–1460

All references are to page numbers

common law – *contd*

enacting common law rule   201–202,
     1459–1460

English, overseas jurisdiction
   importing   S76

European Community directive and   1069

European Convention on Human
   Rights and   819–822, 1314

interpretative criteria as part of   513–514

justice of   1033

mischiefs, examples of   920

modified by Act   75, 197–204, 304, 501,
     812, 814, 1010–1011,
     1459–1460

nature of   347, 499n, 848, 926

precedent and   177

presumption as to statutory
   alteration of   504, 814–816, 829,
     1459–1460

revival of   309

rights under, statutory interference
   with   504, 848, 1459–1460

statute law, relation to   504, 589, 771,
     812–816, 848, 919,
     926, 1038, 1041,
     1199–1200, 1255,
     1459–1460

technicalities of – *see* **technicalities**

torture forbidden by   1348–1349
   – *and see* **implied ancillary
     rules; contempt of statute;
     contract; criminal law;
     custom; equity, rules of;
     negligence; nuisance; tort**

Commons, House of

delegated legislative power of   251

history of   719

journals of   234

judicial scrutiny, not subject to   S112

legislative procedure of   213–216

money, control over   251, 745, 1047–1049

orders of   251

resolutions of   186, 191, 205, 248–249,
     617, 666–673

time, expressions of, and   868–869
   – *and see* **Parliament**

commonsense construction rule

application of converse   555

examples of application of   55, 178, 387,
     882–883, 908, 1099n,
     1194, 1267, S87–88

failure to apply   554

greater includes less   555–557

implied repeal and   557

incommensurable elements and   556

lay interpretation, apposite to   558

nature of   178, 527, 551–558, 986, 1267

commonsense construction rule – *contd*

per incuriam decisions   554
   – *and see* **absurdity; ambiguity
     (grammatical)**

Commonwealth, the   333, 339–340, 348,
     406
   – *and see* **exclusionary rule, the**

communis error facit jus   913

Community law, definition of   1274
   – *and see* **European Community
     Law**

company – *see* **artificial person**

compatible construction rule – *see*
   Human Rights Act 1998

composite act or omission   327, 387, 388–
     389, 389

composite expressions   551, 557, 1181,
     1193–1197

composite restatement   402n, 453

Community law, definition of   1396

conceptualism   987

conditional fee agreement (CFA)   36, 781–
     782, 925, 1117

conditions – *see* **description,
   statutory; statutory duty;
   statutory power; statutory right**

confidence, law of   75, 119, 852
   – *and see* **good administration,
     duty of**

conflation of texts   292–293, 1166

conflict of laws – *see* **private
   international law**

consent – *see* **appeal; criminal law;
   Gillick test; order, court; *volenti
   non fit injuria***

consequential amendments – *see*
   amendment to Act

consequential construction

'adverse' consequences of   517, 871

'beneficent' consequences of   871, 874

consequences, weighing, and   871

European Community law, in   1284

examples of   388, 835n, 869–875

'floodgates' argument   872

mandatory and directory provisions,
   and   48–49

nature of   459, 869–875
   – *and see* **absurdity; evasion of
     Act; strict and liberal
     construction**

consolidation Act

Acts consolidating with
   amendments   604–607

Acts solely consolidating   604–607

amendments, with   S63

commencement of   281

difficulty in drafting   199

consolidation Act – *contd*
error in   880
– *and see* **rectifying**
      construction
inadequate, example of   809
interpretation of   604–607, 1161, 1166,
                                              1251–1252
Lord Herschell's rule   605, S63
nature of   189, 604–607
preliminary 'tidying up'   282
references to re-enacted provision   310–
                                              311
savings in – *see* **saving**
– *and see* **plain meaning rule**
conspiracy – *see* **criminal law**
constable – *see* **police**
Constitution for Europe   1276, 1315
constitutional enactment – *see* **Act of**
      Parliament; constitutional law
constitutional law
Act, constitutional   189–190
Act, unconstitutional   406
legal proceedings, rights as to   858
mandatory and directory
      requirements   49–50
Pepper v Hart, rule in, and   618
presumed application of rules of   1042–
                                              1050
– *and see* **Act of Parliament;**
      Crown; law; Minister of
      the Crown; Prime
      Minister
constitutional rights   190, 773, 1323
– *and see* **legality, principle of**
construction as a whole– *see*
      ***Attorney General v Lamplough*,**
      rule in; composite expressions;
      conflation of texts; European
      Convention on Human Rights;
      free-standing Act, doctrine of;
      functional construction; *in para*
      materia, **acts;** *noscitur a sociis*
      principle; repugnancy;
      transitional provisions; words
amendments to Act and   288
comminution and   402–403
conflicting statements in one
      instrument, and   1163
conflicting statements in separate
      instruments, and   1163
different words to be given different
      meanings   1160–1163
different words to be given same
      meaning   1161
equitable   S48
every word to be given meaning   1157–
                                              1160
– *and see* **tautology**
ex visceribus actus construction   1156

construction as a whole– *see* ***Attorney***
      ***General v Lamplough*, rule in;**
      composite expressions; conflation of
      texts; European Convention on
      Human Rights; free-standing Act,
      doctrine of; functional construction;
      in para materia, **acts;** *noscitur a sociis*
      principle; repugnancy; transitional
      provisions; words – *contd*
extra-territorial effect, Act given   S43
generous   S54
nature of   192, 465, 1155–1167
need for   89
overlap and   1160
provisos and   723–725
punctuation and   755same words to be given same meaning
Schedules and   721–723
specific and general provisions   1165
statutory requirement to disregard
      use of different words   1161
words with no meaning   1158–1159
– *and see* **meaningless terms**
construction as one – *see*
      incorporation by reference
construction in good faith – *see*
      illegality
construction summons   114, 847
construction, consequential – *see*
      consequential construction
construction, equitable   170, S48
– *and see* **equitable construction**
construction, linguistic – *see* **canons**
      of construction, linguistic
construction, rectifying – *see*
      rectifying construction
construction, rules of – *see* **rules of**
      construction
constructive meaning   1193
construe, meaning of   23–24
Community law, definition of – *see*
      European Community Law
consular officer   1396
consultation   247, 1057n, S34
contemporanea expositio   34, 702, 890, 912,
                                              914
contempt of court
appeal, right of   148
committal for   839
court, by   970
execution and   166
face of court, in   497–498, 754
fine for   975n
powers of court   140, 497–498, 754, 958,
                                              S22
prerogative orders and   165–166
prisoners and   255
reports of legal proceedings,
      restrictions on – *see* **open**
      court, the

All references are to page numbers

contempt of court – *contd*
right to bring proceedings   S14
strict liability rule   900
undertaking, breach of   116
contempt of statute   62, 63, 65, 66–67
context – *see* **construction as a**
whole; informed interpretation;
noscitur a sociis **principle**
continental shelf   335, 364
continuity, presumption of   913
contract
agency – *see* **agency**
application of law of   116, 1069–1071
breach of promise, action for   198
consent order   116, S18
contracting out   S8
court's jurisdiction, and   S8
existing, effect of Act on   1069
frustration of   1070
illegal – *see* **illegality**
ouster of jurisdiction by   S16
private Act as   1071
proper law of   1098
society's original   39
statute law, partially based on   S97
statutory modification of law of   200
– *and see* **arbitration; business;**
common law
contracting out – *see* **statutory right**
contradiction, principle of – *see*
logic, use of in interpretation
contravention of Act – *see*
disobeying Act
Convention on Jurisdiction and the
Enforcement of Judgments   1309–
1310
conviction   374
Cooke J   679
Cooke of Thorndon, Lord   777, 1155n,
1156, 1164, 1298n,
1312, 1331
Coté, Pierre André   1457–1458
copyout – *see* **transposition of**
European Community law
coroner   50, 250, 436, 501, 905–906, 975n,
1214–1215
corporation – *see* **artificial person;**
Crown; local authority; public
authority
Corporation Tax Acts   1396
correctness, presumption of   715, 1144–
1145
Corry, J A   677
– *and see* **Bibliography (pp 1475**
to 1507)
costs
burden of, duty to mitigate   112
capping   925–926
central funds, payment out of   894

costs – *contd*
conditional fee agreements   925
contributors to ('funders')   774n
follow the event, should   774
insurance against   508
non-party, payment by   499
order for   436, 499, 894
references to European Court and   1307
relator action, in   74
security for   1027
taxation of   117, 203n
trial, and legislative history   612, 624
– *and see* ***Pepper v Hart*, rule in;**
***Scherer* principle; solicitor**
Côté, Pierre-André – *see*
Bibliography (pp 1475 to 1507)
Cottenham, Lord   169, 723, 1137
counsel – *see* **advocate;**
Parliamentary Counsel
counter-intuitive readings   470, 1091n
counter-mischief   118–119, 620n, 890, 911–
912, 915, 942, 969,
1006, 1007–1008
county court   73, 102, 112, 113, 116, 117,
121, 141, 145–146,
149, 172, 229, 307,
478, 528, 792, 974,
996, 1007, 1184, 1226,
1253, 1254, 1396,
1406, 1415, 1437,
1438
court
access to   110
– *and see* **European Convention**
on Human Rights; justice;
open court
Administrative Court   138–139
Admiralty   140
– *and see* **jurisdiction**
adversarial system   426, 434–435, 1087
advocate and interpretative function
of   434–435, 443
Appeal, court of – *see* **appeal**
appellate   102
– *and see* **appeal**
cassation, of   158
Chivalry, high Court of   926
Commercial   140
Companies   138–139
County – *see* **county court**
criminal, presumption against civil
jurisdiction in   1049
Crown – *see* **Crown Court**
decisions of, statutory modification
of – *see* **processing of**
enactments, dynamic
definition of   103
delegation by   107, 1115

All references are to page numbers

court – *contd*

doubt, treatment of , by   867, 871
  – *and see* **doubt as to legal
    meaning**
ecclesiastical – *see* **ecclesiastical
  court**
European Court of Human Rights –
  see **European Court of
  Human Rights**
European Court of Justice – *see*
  European Court of Justice
evasion of Act by   1013
first instance, of   102, 1302–1303
function of   36, 103–104, 122
functus officio, when   1062
guidelines by   129
High – *see* **High Court**
illegality, duty to notice – *see*
  illegality
implied delegation of interpretation
  to, by Parliament   479
inferior   101, 116, 1038, 1226
inherent powers of – *see* **inherent
  judicial powers**
inquisitorial proceedings   436
inspection of Rolls by – *see* **Roll**
interpretative function of   27, 122–123,
                     479, 489
interstitial articulation by – *see*
  interstitial articulation
judgment, reopening of   114, S18, S97
jurisdiction of – *see* **jurisdiction**
leave of   62
legal meaning, duty to determine   24–25,
                            403
  – *and see* **non liquet** principle
legislator, as   479, 785, 803, 1137
magistrates – *see* **magistrates'
  court**
open – *see* **open court, the**
order of – *see* **order, court;
  inherent judicial powers**
overruling of precedents   172, 173, 177
Patents Court   140
private hearings – *see* **open court,
  the**
prize court   140, 148
procedure of – *see* **inherent
  judicial powers; procedure,
  civil; procedure, criminal**
proceedings to be conducted in
  public – *see* **open court, the**
reasons, duty to give   1062–1064
record, of   134, 139–140, 162
remedies – *see* **enforcement
  agencies**
reviewing   102, 116–118
rules of   49, 59, 246, 268, 807, 1398
  – *and see* **Civil Procedure Rules**

court – *contd*

Senior Courts   1398
small claims   54, 112
statute book, responsibility for   509
'statutory attorney', acting as   105
superior   101, 111–114, 139, 527–528
'Supreme court', definition of   1399
Technology and Construction Court   138–
                                 139
treaties, citation of, before   824
undertaking to   997–998, 1131
  – *and see* **advocate; appeal;
    comity; contempt of court;
    county court; criminal
    law; European Court of
    Justice; Crown Court;
    discretion; enforcement
    agencies; High Court;
    judges; judicial power of
    the state; judicial review;
    jurisdiction; legal policy;
    magistrates;
    non-justitiable matters;
    per incuriam decisions;
    practice; precedent,
    doctrine of; treaty;
    tribunals**
Court of Appeal – *see* **appeal**
Court of Judicature   1396
**Court of Justice of the European
  Communities (CJEC)** – *see*
  European Court of Justice
**Courts Service, Her majesty's
  (HMCS)**   121
Coventry Act   555
Cowen, D V – *see* **Bibliography (pp
  1475 to 1507)**
Cowley, David – *see* **Bibliography
  (pp 1475 to 1507)**
Cox, Archibald   651
Cozens-Hardy, Lord   383, 1065n
CPS – *see* **Crown Prosecution
  Service**
Craies, W F   7, 46n, 63, 228, 318n, 331,
                332, 333, 411n, 663,
                736, 1010, 1151, 1242,
                            1284n
  – *and see* **Bibliography (pp 1475
    to 1507)**
Craig, Paul – *see* **Bibliography (pp
  1475 to 1507)**
Cranston J   S107
Cranworth, Lord (Rolfe B)   373, 1158
Cretney, Stephen – *see* **Bibliography
  (pp 1475 to 1507)**
criminal conversation, abolition of   198
**criminal injuries compensation
  scheme**   251

All references are to page numbers

criminal law

accessories	1080
actus reus	416, 417
aiding and abetting	S62
civil law, distinguished from	69, 94, 1353
common law offences altered or	
replaced by statute	201
composite crime	388
concepts of	1078
consecutive sentences, totality	
principle	S52
consent and	1150
conspiracy	201
crime, definition of	63, 94
Crown, and	1083
defences	1085
direct action	201, 1135–1136
– and see **pressure groups**	
felony, abolition of term	64
fraud	202
hi-jacking	376
hybrid orders	94
implied application of	1077–1086
mens rea	41–42, 416, 417, 555, 1078–
	1080
– and see **strict liability**	
misdemeanour, abolition of term	64
nature of	92, 1354
new offences, creation of by courts	1085
nuisance	201–202
peace, Queen's *– see* **peace,**	
Queen's	
prosecutions *– see* **prosecution of**	
offences	
provocation	504, 578, S96
statutory alteration of	200
subliminal images, broadcasting of	65–66
terrorism	376, 1135
uniform application of	332
war crimes	189n, 238n
– and see **age, anti-social**	
behaviour orders	
(ASBOs), attorney	
General; contempt of	
statute; criminal	
procedure; doubtful	
penalisation, principle	
against; greater includes	
less; legal policy; *mala in*	
se; *mala prohibita*; **offence;**	
public international law;	
public mischief;	
retrospectivity; strict	
liability; suicide; Taafe	
defence; erritorial extent	
of Act	

criminal procedure

abuse of process *– see* **process**	
accused, naming of	121

criminal procedure *– contd*

appeals *– see* **appeal**	
arraignment	1013n
code	187–188
committal for trial	306, 318–319, 489,
	948, 949, 1395
Crown Court, in *– see* **Crown**	
Court	
de minimis principle and	1122–1123,
	S102
defences	91, 178, 274, 286, 1085
– and see **defences**	
duplicity rule	810, 1084–1085
evidence *– see* **evidence**	
exceptions rule *– see* **evidence**	
fitness to plead *– see* **incompetents**	
'indictable offence', definition of	1399
indictment	64, 160, 230, 295, 403, 811,
	1084, 1162, 1168
magistrates' court, in *– see*	
magistrates' court	
natural justice and	1081–1083
'offence triable either way',	
definition of	1399
oral hearing, right to	1352
preparatory hearing	114
retrospectivity and	807–808
Royal Commission 1981 on	99
self-incrimination	527, 1081–1083, 1355
sentencing	170, 803, 807, 1086,
	see appeal
'sent for trial', definition of	1398
silence, right of	59, 527, 1081–1083
'standard scale', definition of	1398
'statutory maximum', definition of	1399
'summary offence', definition of	1399
trial	1081
waiver of steps in	62
– and see **anonymity;**	
application of Act;	
criminal law; Crown	
Prosecution Service;	
double jeopardy;	
European Convention on	
Human Rights; judicial	
review; jurisdiction; jury;	
legal proceedings; open	
court, the; prosecution of	
offences; retrospectivity	
criteria, interpretative *– see*	
interpretative criteria	
Croke, George *– see* **Bibliography**	
(pp 1475 to 1507)	
Cross of Chelsea, Lord	995
Cross, Rupert	7, 12, 418n, 499, 517n, 587,
	592
– and see **Bibliography (pp 1475**	
to 1507)	
crossheading *– see* **heading**	

All references are to page numbers

'Crossman catalogue', the   681
Crown
  ambit of concept   207–208
  bound by Act, when   206–212, 239
  can do no wrong   206–212
  charter   239
  Commonwealth and – see
    Commonwealth, the
  courts, jurisdiction of, derived from   104
  criminal law and – see **criminal law**
  declaration by   250
  dispensing power of   300
  extra-statutory payments by   251
  financial initiative of   251
  franchise   165, 204, 209–210
  immunity, doctrine of   206–212
    – and see **Crown immunity,**
      doctrine of
  indivisibility of   96, 208, 406
  joinder of, in proceedings where
    declaration of incompatibility
    anticipated – see **Human**
    Rights Act 1998
  justice, and   103, 128–129
    – and see **judicial power of the**
      state
  letters patent of   217
  meaning   206–208
  orders of court and   209
  overseas territories, in   349–350
  parens patriae doctrine   814, 1044–1046,
      S96
    – and see **wardship**
  privilege – see **public interest**
    immunity
  proclamation by   250, 271, 548
  prosecutions, in name of   96
    – and see **prosecution of**
      offences
  provisions binding   S32
  regnal year   742–743
  suspending power of   300
  taking advantage of Act by   211–212
  time, does not run against   1083
  warrant of   783, 846, 1045
    – and see **act of state; Channel**
      Islands; Clerk of the
      Crown; Clerk of the
      Parliaments; delegated
      legislation; enacting
      formula; enforcement
      agencies; feudal tenures;
      forfeiture rule; Her
      Majesty's dominions; Her
      Majesty's independent
      dominions; Man, isle of;
      Minisfer of the Crown;
      Order in Council; Order
      of Council; peace,

Crown – *contd*
  warrant of – *contd*
    – *and see* **act of state; Channel**
      Islands; Clerk of the Crown;
      Clerk of the Parliaments;
      delegated legislation; enacting
      formula; enforcement agencies;
      feudal tenures; forfeiture rule;
      Her Majesty's dominions; Her
      Majesty's independent
      dominions; Man, isle of; Minisfer
      of the Crown; Order in Council;
      Order of Council; peace, – *contd*
      Queen's; precision
      drafting; prerogative,
      royal; Prime Minister;
      royal assent; saving;
      Sovereign, references to;
      taxing Acts; tort
Crown Court   140–141, 146–147, 149, 1396
  – *and see* **appeal**
Crown Estate Commissioners   1396
Crown immunity, doctrine of
  Crown taking benefit of an
    enactment, where not bound
    by it   211–212
  expressio unius principle and   210
  implied intention to bind Crown   208–209
  indirect application of   209
  nature of   206–212
  overseas territories and   212, S32
  private Acts and   212
  subjects, rights conferred on by
    prerogative, and   209–210
Crown Office – *see* **Administrative**
  Court
Crown Prosecution Service   95–100, 1013,
    1096–1097, S15
  – *and see* **prosecution of offences**
'culprit'   1216
Cumming-Bruce LJ   476, 1023
Curtis, Charles P   651
  – *and see* **Bibliography (pp 1475**
    to 1507)
custom   135, 152, 198, 203, 360n, 608, 1250
customary international law
  codifying   688–690
  nature of   S80
'Daily List' – *see* **Statutory**
  Instruments Issue List
damages   77, 627, 1030–1031
  – *and see* **Human Rights Act 1998;**
    judicial review; tort
Darling J   462
Davidson Review of implementation
  of European legislation (2006)   1295
Davis, G R C – *see* **Bibliography (pp**
  1475 to 1507)
Dawson J   676

All references are to page numbers

day, fractions of – *see* time
de bene esse – *see* evidence
De Burca, Grainne – *see*
    Bibliography (pp 1475 to 1507)
de facto office   241, 1356
de minimis non curat lex   1003, 1101, 1116,
                     1117, 1118, 1119,
                     1122, 1123, 1167,
                     1265, 1286, S101,
                     S102
De Tocqueville, Alexis   406
death   64, 72, 164, 847–848, 983, 988, 1183,
                1192–1193, 1258–
                1259
debt – *see* statutory right
decision-making rules
  Anisminic principle   110, 1050–1053, S16
  benefit from own wrong – *see*
      nullus commodum capere
      potest de injuria sua propria
  consultation   247, 1057n, S34
  decision endangering life   832
  delegation of powers   166, 324–325
  – *and see* **delegated legislation**
  due process, procedural   853, 1055–1059
  failure to decide   1064
  fairness – *see* **natural justice**
  'final' decision   109
  hearing both sides – *see audi*
      alteram partem **principle**
  implied application of   1050–1064
  intention, ascertainment of – *see*
      intention, ascertainment of
  judge in own cause – *see nemo*
      debet esse judex in propria
      causa
  legal policy, influence of – *see* **legal**
      policy
  legality and   1052–1053
  legitimate expectation   161,1056–1057,
                  1278–1279, S32
  natural justice – *see* **natural justice**
  policy decisions   1061
  procedural propriety   1055–1059
  – *and see* **irregularity,**
      procedural
  proportionality – *see*
      proportionality
  rationality and   1053–1055
  reasons for decision   1062–1064, 1254–
                   1255
  Wednesbury principle   125n, 144, 260,
                 1054–1055, 1312
  – *and see* **Carltona principle;**
      discretion; doubtful
      penalisation, principle
      against; judicial review;
      jurisdiction; Minister of

decision-making rules – *contd*
  Wednesbury principle – *contd*
  – *and see* **Carltona principle;**
      discretion; doubtful penalisation,
      principle against; judicial review;
      jurisdiction; Minister of – *contd*
      the Crown; *ultra vires*,
      doctrine ofdeclaration,
      judicial
  discretionary, whether   128
  grant of, statute affecting   75
  guidelines, as to   130, S20
  human rights incompatibility – *see*
      Human Rights Act 1998
  medical treatment, consent to   810n, 834,
                      1045
  nature of   102, 163
  offence, as to existence of   809–810
  ultra vires enactment   260
declaration, Royal   250
declaratory enactment   188, 293, 709, 718n,
                      923
  – *and see* **statutory exposition**
deductive reasoning – *see* **logic, use**
  of in interpretation
deeming   297, 389–390, 582–583, 949, 950–
           951, 1003–1005, 1072,
           1080, 1292
  – *and see* **absurdity; artificial**
      person; asifism; location,
      deemed
defences   58, 83–84, 286, 1108–1109
  – *and see* **pleading; procedure,**
      criminal
defendant, identity of   38
definite article   954, 1190
definition, statutory
  abandonment of, effect of   568–569
  Acts in *pari materia*, application to   708–
                    710, 1200
  ancillary documents, application to   566
  circular   568
  clarifying   561, 570–571
  common law meaning and   563–564
  compound   561
  comprehensive   561, 574–575
  contrary intention and   561, 570, 978
  delegated legislation and   265, 561–564,
                     575
  dictionary meaning and   562, S56
  different definitions of a term   465
  ejusdem generis principle and   1231–1245
  enlarging   561, 573–574, 1255–1256, S57
  exclusionary   561, 572–573
  failure to define, or define correctly   567,
                   1168, 1183
  failure to keep to, in drafting   566
  free-standing   561, 1000
  general   561, 569

All references are to page numbers

definition, statutory – *contd*
  in pari materia Acts   708–710
  inclusionary   1227
  Interpretation Act **1978**   561
    – *and see* **Interpretation**
      Act 1978
  judicial gloss on   575
  labelling   561, 571–572
  list of   575
  literal meaning of, and
    purpose-and-strained
    construction   959
  nature of   561–575, 1211
  non-free standing   1211
  noscitur a sociis principle, use in
    construction of   1227
  potency of term defined   183, 562–564,
    575
  purpose of   561
  referential   561, 572
  restricted   561
  simple   561, 562
  strained   S48
  substantive effect, having   565
  technical terms of – *see* **technical**
    terms
  unexpected meaning and   464–465

delay – *see vigilantibus non*
  dormientibus leges subveniunt

delegated legislation
  Act, amending   245
  Act, conflict with   244
  Act, does not override   244
  Act, modifying effect of   246
  affirmative resolution procedure   248
  amendment of – *see* **amendment to**
    delegated legislation
  annulment of   249
  anticipatory   243, 286–287
  'as if in Act'   244–245
  byelaws – *see* **byelaws**
  Code, application of   S35
  commencement of   273–274
  Community obligation,
    implementing   S35
  components of   716
  consult, duty to, on   247, 256
  contravention of   66
  declaration of incompatibility – *see*
    Human Rights Act1998
  delegate, types of   250–252
  disobeying – *see* **disobeying Act**
  drafting, quality of   264, 410, 413
  duty to exercise delegated powers   253–
    254, 285–286
  effect of   241–247
  enabling Act and   241, 243, 256, 598,
    706–708, 886
  – *and see* **Act of Parliament**

delegated legislation – *contd*
  enactments in   399–400
  executive instrument – *see*
    executive instrument
  exercise of power to make   243
  explanatory notes   265–266
  expressions in, have same meaning
    as in enabling Act   265
  general law, does not override   244
  implied ancillary powers to make   256
  incorporation by reference in   S76
  interpretation of   257–258, 263–266, 716,
    1388
  interpretation of Act, by reference to   242n
  intra vires interpretation to be
    preferred   257–258
  invalid provision, purported
    confirmation of   257
  issue by Stationery Office, effect of   274
  judicial notice of – *see* **judicial**
    notice
  judicial review of   247, 260
  laying before Parliament of   248
  legislative history, use of, in
    construction of   266, *295*
  – *and see* **legislative history**
  legislative intention of   269–270
  mandatory or directory   253
  nature of   237, 241–247
  negative resolution procedure   249, S34
  notice of   274
  orders   267–268
    – *and see* **order; Order in**
      Council; Order of
      Council; provisional
      order; special procedure
      order
  parliamentary control of   243, 248–249
  primary intention, rule of   262–263
    – *and see Padfield* **approach**
  quashing of – *see* **judicial review**
  ratification of, by Parliament   257
  reasons for   242
  regulations   268
  repeal and re-enactment of enabling
    provision, effect on   311
  retrospectivity and   324–325, S42
    – *and see* **retrospectivity**
  revocation of   275, 301
  rules – *see* **court; legal**
    proceedings; rules
  scrutiny, parliamentary, of   249, 264
  severance – *see* **severance**
  statute modified by   182, 325–326
  statutory instruments   241–247, 266–267
  sub-delegation   246, 272–273
  terminology of   246
  types of   266–272

All references are to page numbers

---

delegated legislation – *contd*
ultra vires – *see* **ultra vires**,
doctrine of
– *and see* **amendment to Act;
delegation of powers;
Henry VIII clause;
statutory power**
delegation of powers – *see Carltona*
**principle; court;
decision-making rules;
enforcement agencies; Minister
of the Crown**
democracy   2, 39, 474
Denman, Lord   109, 323n, 388, 654, 668,
736, 1199
Denning, Lord   33, 51, 55, 109n, 135, 165,
207, 208, 270, 434,
458, 465, 485, 500n,
507, 524, 593, 659,
662, 664, 668, 669n,
684, 685, 691, 692,
698n, 732, 739, 761,
775, 777, 784, 790,
793, 800, 803, 818,
839, 865, 903, 904,
936, 949, 966, 967,
975, 984, 1034, 1035,
1051, 1055, 1066,
1075, 1105, 1113,
1136, 1210, 1211,
1257, 1295
– *and see* **Bibliography (pp 1475
to 1507)**
description, statutory
construction in bonam partem – *see*
illegality
exceeded, where – *see* **greater**
includes less
mechanical etc apparatus   957, 1263, 1267
only partly met, where   1262–1270
– *and see* **evasion of Act;
severance**
desuetude – *see* **Act of Parliament;
Scotland**
**Developmental method of statutory
interpretation** – *see* **statutory
interpretation**
Devlin, Lord   97, 134, 150, 197, 379, 776,
780, 781, 790, 798,
813, 977, 986, 1015,
1196, 1233
– *and see* **the Bibliography (pp
1475 to 1507)**
devolution   6, 328, 1100, 1202, S3
Diamond, Aubrey L – *see*
Bibliography (pp 1475 to 1507)
Dias, R W M   23, 407n, 472, 795n
– *and see* **Bibliography (pp 1475
to 1507)**

Dicey, A V   406, 407, 843, 1044, 1192
– *and see* **Bibliography (pp 1475
to 1507)**
Dickerson, Reed   433, 446, 473
– *and see* **Bibliography (pp 1475
to 1507)**
dictionary, reference to – *see* **judicial
notice; reference, works of**
different words, construction of –
see **words**
differential readings
examples of   132–133, 618n, 623, 952,
1170
nature of   122, 130–133
– *and see* **impression, matters of**
Dilhorne, Viscount   448, 568, 649, 650, 663,
696n, 699, 700, 707,
809, 940, 945, 978,
998n, 1007, 1182,
1212, 1227, 1239
Dillon LJ   169, 508, 839, 1070, 1188, 1191,
1214
Dingwall, Gavin: – *see* **Bibliography
(pp 1475 to 1507)**
Diplock, Lord   35, 125, 627, 807, 1054
– *and see* **Bibliography (pp 1475
to 1507)**
direct action – *see* **criminal law**
direction   272
Director of Public Prosecutions   96
**Director of Revenue and Customs
Prosecutions**   96, 97
directory requirements – *see*
**mandatory and directory
requirements**
disciplinary committee   104
discovery   119, 526, 852
– *and see* **public interest immunity**
discretion
administrative   81, 89, 144, 820–821, 850
anomaly, avoidance of, by exercise
of   999
appeal from exercise of   142, 145
appellate court or body, exercise by
– *see* **appeal**
delegated legislation, as to making
of   253
discovery, as to ordering – *see*
evidence
'discretionary area of judgment',
so-called   1327
duty, as to enforcement of   45, 51
estoppel and   1094
European Convention on Human
Rights   1321
extra-statutory   51
fettering of   90, S12
guidelines, as to exercise of   130, 145,
1140

All references are to page numbers

discretion – *contd*

implied restriction of   820–821, 1130

interpretation, as factor in   80, 521, 533, 872–873, 999

judgment, distinguished from   80, 122, 123, 127–129, 619, S20

judicial   144, 313, 900

justly, to be exercised   798–799

nature of   55, 126–127, 253, 313, 396, 521, 949

party-political mischief and – *see* **mischief**

policy and operational contrasted   68, 81

prosecution of offences and   97

rationality and   1054–1055

reasons, duty to give   1062–1064

review of   117

– *and see* **common law; decision-making rules; judicial notice; judicial review; margin of appreciation;** *Padfield* **approach;** *Scherer* **principle; statutory power**

discrimination, legislation against

interpretation of   518–519, 600

race, on grounds of   726, 740, 873, 978–979, 1041

religion, on grounds of   842–843

sex, on grounds of   61, 740, 978–979, 1328

– *and see* **Canada; European Convention on Human Rights**

discrimination, legislation against sexual orientation, on grounds of   1328

disobeying Act

civil sanctions for – *see* **breach of statutory duty, tort of; tort**

consequence of disobedience unstated, where   45–46

criminal sanctions for   62–67

delegated legislation and   66

general   62–64, 68–69

impecuniosity as excuse for   126–127

– *and see* **public authority**

Law Commission, recommendation with respect to   66

persistent disobedience, treatment of   74

– *and see* **Act of Parliament; contempt of statute;** *de minimis non curat lex;* **evasion of Act;** *ignorantia juris neminem excusat;* **judicial review; law**

disorganised composition

consequences, interpretative, and   1249, 1250

examples of   329–330, 451–455, 536, 614–615, 970, 1159n

nature of   60, 409–413, 1250

provisos and   723–725

– *and see* **obscurity, semantic; precision drafting**

dispensing power – *see* **Crown**

distance, measurement of   581, 1388

diversity   133

Divisional Court

appeal from   147–148

appeal to   146–147

Court of Appeal as   158

departure from own decisions   175

divorce   787–788

Dixon, Sir Owen   S62

Dockray, M S – *see* **Bibliography (pp 1475 to 1507)**

document, service of – *see* **notice**

doli incapax, **abolition of doctrine of**   S98

domestic sanctuary, principle of   1007, 1124, 1125, 1126–1127

– *and see* **doubtful penalisation, principle against; European Convention on Human Rights**

dominant purpose test   1263

domus sua cuique est tutissimum refugium – *see* **domestic sanctuary, principle of**

Donaldson of Lymington, Lord   116, 174

Donoughmore Committee (1932)   271

Donovan, Lord   981, 1223

double detriment – *see* *bona fides non patitur ut bis idem exigatur*

double jeopardy   788, 1083, 1116, 1286, S99, S101

doubt as to legal meaning

causes of   325–326, 391, 515–516

must be 'real'   25–26, 176, 437, 515, 591–592, 624–625, 999

resolution of   391, 511, 591

– *and see* **doubtful penalisation, principle against**

term with different meanings   466–468

doubtful penalisation, principle against

citizenship rights, statutory interference with   858–859

deprivation or restriction of rights without compensation and   828–829, 849

family rights, interference with   840–842

– *and see* **domestic sanctuary, principle of**

All references are to page numbers

doubtful penalisation, principle against – *contd*
free assembly and association,
interference with 843–844
free speech, interference with 844–845
legal obligations, imposition of 853
legal process, statutory interference
with 853–858
– *and see* **legal policy**
life or health, interference with 780, 831–836
litigation, right of parties to
compromise, and 857
nature of 1–2, 517–518, 526, 527, 784, 825, 1062
physical restraint of the person 784, 836–840
– *and see* ***habeas corpus*;**
prisoners, rights of
privacy, statutory interference with 852
– *and see* **domestic sanctuary,**
principle of
property, interference with 829
– *and see* **taxing Acts**
public interest and 790
religious freedom, interference with 842–843
– *and see* **religion**
reputation or status, detriment to 851–852, 965
retrospectivity, presumption against,
and 317–319, 827
– *and see* **retrospectivity**
savings, interpretation of, and 726
status or reputation, statutory
interference with 851–852
voting rights, interference with – *see*
elections
drafter, legislative
amendments and 40, 640
commentary by, on Act drafted 712
intention of 475–477
interpretation, value of views of, in 33
mistakes by 415
role of 475–477
use of term 10n
– *and see* **Parliamentary**
Counsel
drafting error
commencement, as to 325–326
definition, as to 566
genus, depiction of 1234
law, mistake of – *see* **mistake**
legal doctrine flouted 875–877, 1148n
missed consequentials – *see*
amendment of Act
nature of 877
omission 924–925
presumption against 413–416

drafting error – *contd*
strained construction and 882, 1131
– *and see* **strained construction**
tautology – *see* **surplusage;**
tautology
transitional provisions, as to – *see*
transitional provisions
– *and see* **ambiguity**
(grammatical); deeming;
disorganised composition;
drafting technique;
homonyms; mandatory
and directory
requirements; obscurity,
semantic; rectifying
construction
drafting, legislative
Acts in pari materia, of – *see* ***in***
***pari materia*, Acts**
archival – *see* **incorporation by**
reference
competence presumed 413–416, 1217
complexity of 135
compression of language – *see*
ellipsis
computer, by 232
criticism of 409–416, 452–455, 614–615, 700–701, 804–805, 840, 1250
delegated legislation, of 410, 413
encompassing the unforeseen 481
ex abundanti cautela 1258
government control of 412
judges, by 464
numbers, expressing 1216
plain language – *see* **plain language**
movement
precision drafting – *see* **precision**
drafting
private bills, of 410
reform of – *see* **statute law**
'shorthand' in 447
style of 413–416, 866, 892
words used correctly in,
presumption that 1186
– *and see* **drafter, legislative;**
drafting error; drafting
technique; meaningless
terms; Parliamentary
Counsel Office; user of
legislation
drafting technique – *see* **amendment**
to Act; asifism; belt-and-braces
phase; broad terms;
codification; comminution;
consolidation Act; copyout;
disorganised composition;
drafting error; drafting,
legislative; enactment;

All references are to page numbers

drafting technique – *contd*
  examples; functional
  construction; heading;
  implication; incorporation by
  reference; Jamaica Schedule;
  Keeling Schedule; order, court;
  plain language movement;
  precision drafting; purpose
  clause; saving; Schedule;
  section; weightless drafting
  accidental fit   482–483
  amendment, method of   146
   – *and see* **amendment to Act**
  commencement provisions – *see*
    commencement of Act
  common sense, reliance on – *see*
    **commonsense construction
    rule**
  'elegant variation'   1160
  European Union   1461–1473
  'general principle' approach   487–488
  'individual', use of word   577
  lay persons, when intended to read
    text   35–36
  overlapping technique – *see*
    belt-and-braces phrase
  shorthand, drafter's   447
  sweeping-up provisions   1014
  transitional provisions   325
 – *and see* **transitional provisions**
Drake J   989
Driedger, E A   8, 23, 473, 546, 587, 899, 1233
 – *and see* **Bibliography (pp 1475
  to 1507)**
drunkenness, intentional or reckless   S45
Du Parcq, Lord   69, 70, 436, 437, 1102n
due process   851, 853, 1055
 – *and see* **decision-making rules;
  legal proceedings; process**
Dunn LJ   669, 1185
Duomatic **principle**   60
**duplication of statutory remedies,
  powers etc**   393
Durack, P   740
duress   1046, 1105, 1134–1135, 1136, S108
duty – *see* **court; good
  administration, duty of;
  legislation; moral duty;
  statutory duty**
Dwarris, F   7, 463, 1250n
 – *and see* **Bibliography (pp 1475
  to 1507)**
Dworkin, Gerald – *see* **Bibliography
  (pp 1475 to 1507)**
Dworkin, Ronald   14, 132, 514, 523n, 770, 771, 772, 778, 782
 – *and see* **Bibliography (pp 1475
  to 1507)**

Dyson J   602, S96, S101
Eady J   1329
Eardley-Wilmot, J E – *see*
  Bibliography (pp 1475 to 1507)
Earl Warren CJ   858
ecclesiastical court   117, 154, 163
 – *and see* ecclesiastical law
ecclesiastical law   154, 157, 197–198, 775, 1041
 – *and see* ecclesiastical court
Dunn LJ   669, 1185
EC Treaty (Treaty of Rome) defined   1274
Edelman, Justice   S48, S49
Edmund-Davies, Lord   170n, 412n, 525, 599n, 872, 1126
education, convention right to – *see*
  **European Convention on
  Human Rights**
Edwards, J L G   74n
 – *and see* **Bibliography (pp 1475
  to 1507)**
Edwards, Susan   133n
 – *and see* **Bibliography (pp 1475
  to 1507)**
EEA agreement   1396
EEA state   1396
Eire   354
ejusdem generis principle
  description of   1231–1234
  examples of   671n, 1229, 1231–1245
  exclusion, express, of   1242–1243
  exclusion, implied, of   1244–1245
  general words followed by narrower
    term   1242–1243
  genus   1234–1237
  nature of   1231–1245
  single term   1237–1239
  terms followed by wider residuary
    words   1239–1241
  terms surrounding wider word   1241–1242
Eldon, Lord   435, 478, 1011
elections   54, 68n, 859, 957, 1046–1047
elegant variation   1160, 1161
Eliot, T S   967
Ellenborough, Lord   229, 736n, 832
Ellesmere, Lord   33, 170n, 412n, 599n
ellipsis   x, 450, 488, 491, 493, 1176, 1231, S50
Elwyn-Jones, Lord   284
emails   905n
embracery   199
emergency powers   250
employment   1146–1147
 – *and see* **agency; vicarious
  liability**
Employment Appeal Tribunal   104, 147
employment tribunal
  contracting out of agreement, void   S8
enabling Act – *see* **Act of Parliament**

All references are to page numbers

enacting formula   216n, 224, 225, 226, 713, 718, 719, 741, 744–745

enacting history – *see* **legislative history**

enactment
citation of   1391
classification of   396–401
common law rule, replacement of, by   609
constitutional   49
curtailing legislative power, purporting to   405
declaration of incompatibility and – *see* **incompatibility, declaration of, under Human Rights Act 1998**
effectiveness of, challenge to   404–409
international law, contrary to   409
interpretative   27
meaning of   396–401
mischief of – *see* **mischief**
multi-lingual   24
modifying a judicial decision   401
natural law, contrary to   407–408
nature of   396–401, 718
operation of, dual aspect to   393
opposing constructions of – *see* **opposing constructions**
purpose of – *see* **purposive construction**
substantive and procedural contrasted   400
– *and see* **limitation of actions**
territorial extent of – *see* **territorial extent of Act**
validity of, challenge to   404–409
unit of inquiry, as   391, 394–396
– *and see* **comminution; delegated legislation; legal thrust of enactment; legislation**

enforcement agencies
adjudicating with appellate jurisdiction   142–154
adjudicating with original jurisdiction   138–142
administrative and executive   85–92, 166–167, 479, 702–706, 974–977, 1058, 1145
amendment, legislative, statutory duty to propose   978–979
authorising   92–93
bailiffs   166–167
charging orders   166
delegation by   167
enforcement procedures, scope of   97
'enforcement', meaning of   28n
entrapment and   95

enforcement agencies – *contd*
failure by   87
interpreters as   27–28
investigating   93–95
judicial review of discretion exercised by   90
legislative power of – *see* **court**
local authorities as   88
membership, types of   104
procedure to be used by   28
processing of enactments, dynamic, by   167–178
prosecuting   95–96
– *and see* **prosecution of offences**
remedies available to   114–118
sheriff's officers   166
supervisory   93–95
transfer and distribution of legislative functions   86
types of   27–28
– *and see* **court; correctness, presumption of; discretion; enforcement notice; evasion of Act; legislative history; police; processing of enactments, dynamic; statutory power; tax avoidance; taxing Acts; trespass**

enforcement notice   51, 56, 88–91, 270, 789

enforcement procedure   28, 97

enforcement procedures   28, 138

England   346, 1396
– *and see* **Berwlck upon Tweed; Monmouthshire**

Engle, George – *see* **Bibliography (pp 1475 to 1507)**

entrapment   95

equitable construction   169, 170, 441, 463–465, 587, 1065–1066, 1137, S48

equity of a statute – *see* **equitable construction**

equity, rules of
Acts framed with view to   1068
equitable construction contrasted   1065–1066
follow the law   500
implied application of   61, 1064–1069
law fused with   198n, 761
need for specialist application   1067
nobile officium – *see* **nobile officium**
regulatory statutes and   1066

All references are to page numbers

equity, rules of – *contd*
remedies for infringement of Act　61, 74,
　1067
– *and see* **confidentiality;**
　estoppel; injunction;
　laches
specialist knowledge of　S97
Erle CJ　1112
– *and see* **Bibliography (pp 1475**
　to 1507)
error – *see* **drafting error; mistake**
Ert, Gibb van – *see* **Bibliography**
　(pp 1475 to 1507)
Esher, Viscount (Brett LJ)　75, 79, 722
Eskridge, William N Jr　7, 893n, 1458,
　1459, 1460
– *and see* **Bibliography (pp 1475**
　to 1507)
estoppel
cause of action　1116
discretion and　1094
equitable　1067
executive　92, 616, 633–640
general　106, 1067
in pais　1094
issue　788–789
per rem judicatam (res judicata)　106, 788–
　789
quasi　S100
EU Treaty (Maastricht Treaty),
　defined　1274
eugma　525n
European Charter of Fundamental
　Rights　1315
European Commission of Human
　Rights　1320
European Community – *see*
　European Union
European Community law
acte clair　1306
agreements, pre-EC Treaty　1275–1276
arrest warrant　1286–1287, S14
Barber principle and　1279–1280
Community instrument, reference to　1391
composition of　1274
delegated legislation implementing
　obligation of　S35
direct effect of　1287–1290
directives　1288–1289
double jeopardy, presumption
　against, in　1286
drafting technique　1284n
effectiveness of, principle of　1277
Francovich damages, claim for　S111
human rights and　1276, 1285
ignorance of　43
incompatibility of UK law with　1293–
　1300

European Community law – *contd*
interpretation of　8, 465, 1283–1287,
　1299–1300
legal certainty, principle of, in　1277–1279
legitimate expectation, principle of,
　in　1278–1279
member states laws　1275, 1309
natural justice, concepts of, in　1285–1286
principles of　1275–1276
proof of　1283
proportionality, principle of, in　1280–1282
– *and see* **proportionality**
public policy, in　785
purposive construction in　966–968
– *and see* **purposive**
　construction
regulations, direct effect of, in　1289
retrospectivity, presumption against
　in　1279–1280
solidarity, principle of, in　1277
status of　1273, 1282, 1293–1300
strict construction in　1286
subsidiarity, principle of, in　1282
transposition of – *see* **transposition**
　of European Community law
Treaty provisions, direct effect of,
　in　1287–1290
UK law, effect of, on　1293–1300
– *and see* **Developmental**
　method of statutory
　interpretation; foreign;
　judicial notice;
　predictability of law
European Convention on Human
　Rights
Art 1 (respect for human rights)　1318
Art 2 (right to life)　xi, 836, 1319, 1347,
　1348, 1441–1442
Art 3 (torture)　836, 1348, 1443
– *and see* ***Soering*** **principle**
Art 4 (slavery and forced labour)　840,
　1350, 1443
Art 5 (liberty and security)　840, 858,
　1350, 1442–1443
Art 6 (fair trial)　121, 845, 858, 1062n,
　1316, 1353, 1444,
　S100
Art 7 (no punishment without law)　318–
　319, 322, 1445
Art 8 (private and family life)　120, 842,
　852, 1314, 1445
Art 9 (thought, conscience and
　religion)　843, 1445, S113
Art 10 (expression)　845, 852, 1434, 1445
Art 11 (assembly and association)　844,
　1434, 1446
Art 12 (marriage)　842, 1316, 1446
Art 13 (right to an effective remedy)　1318
Art 14 (discrimination)　1446

European Convention on Human Rights –
contd
Art 15 (derogation)   1377
Art 16 (political activity of aliens)   1318,
    1347, 1367, 1446
Art 17 (abuse of rights)   1318, 1446
Art 18 (restrictions on rights)   1318, 1447
changing standards   1317
derogation from   1433–1436
description of   819–822
European Community law, in – *see*
    European Community Law
expulsion from state of which a
    citizen   859
extent of   1321
First Protocol, Art 1 (protection of
    property)   851, 1357, 1447
First Protocol, Art 2 (education)   842, 1447
First Protocol, Art 3 (free elections)   859,
    1447
government policy principle   1355
illegality and   1320
'incorporation' into English law   1311,
    1319
inquests   1348
interpretation of   1321, 1322
judgment and discretion   128
legal policy on, pre-1998 Act   1038
legal proceedings under – *see*
    Human Rights Act 1998
legal status of – *see* **Human Rights
    Act 1998**
origins of   1319
'overridden by parties' agreement or
    waiver   62, 1315, 1320, 1353
proportionality   1312
reservation to   1434–1435, 1449–1450
statutory interpretation and – *see*
    **delegated legislation; Human
    Rights Act 1998; intention,
    legislative; statutes; strained
    construction; reading down**
uniform interpretation   1321
waiver of rights under   62
who is bound by   1319
who is protected by   1319
    – *and see* **doubtful penalisation,
    principle against; human
    rights; Human Rights
    Act 1998; margin of
    appreciation; public
    international law**
European Court of Human Rights   1316
European Court of Justice
advocates-general of   1301
court declining to follow judgment   S112
Court of First Instance of   1302–1303
'creative jurisprudence' of   1284–1285,
    1301–1302

European Court of Justice – *contd*
interpretation by   1283–1287
judges of   1301
jurisdiction of   1302–1303
nature of   1274, 1300–1302
precedent and   177
remedies available from   1308–1309
strict construction by   1286, 1310
Treaty rulings   612–613, 1309–1310
weighing and balancing
    interpretative factors, by   1280n,
    1285–1286
European Union
composition of   6
law of – *see* **European Community
    law**
legislation of, drafting guidelines as
    to   1461–1473
European Union, enlargement of   1315
Evans LJ   850, 993, 1005
Evans, Jim   652n
    – *and see* **Bibliography (pp 1475
    to 1507)**
Evans-Lombe J   470, 1298
evasion of Act
adjournment of hearing, by   279, 1013
avoidance, distinguished from   1014–1017
court, by   1013
deferring liability, by   1024–1025
express provision against   1010–1011
fraud on an Act   1010–1014, S94
indirect   1023–1024
injunction, use of, to prevent   1025–1026
integrity of Act and   1028–1029
legal proceedings, hindering – *see*
    legal proceedings
presumption against   1009–1014
repetitious acts, by   1025–1026
tax avoidance – *see* **tax avoidance**
    – *and see* **Ramsay** principle
Eve J   59
Eveleigh LJ   460, 492, 993, 1254
Everett, C W – *see* **Bibliography (pp
    1475 to 1507)**
Evershed, Lord   43, 606n, 961, 994, 1004,
    1184
    – *and see* **Bibliography (pp 1475
    to 1507)**
every word to be given meaning –
    see **construction as a whole**
evidence
Act, of   184, 228, 233, 234–235
    – *and see* **judicial notice**
admissibility of   125, 525, 1026, 1223–
    1224
affidavit   158, 806
burden of proof – *see* **burden of
    proof**

evidence – *contd*
certifying of facts by Minister – *see*
    Minister of the Crown
child, of   461, 901, S99
compellable   813, 857
cross-examination   777
Crown privilege – *see* **public**
    interest immunity
de bene esse, admission   596, 693
depositions   52
discovery   525
– *and see* **discovery**
DNA   1361
estoppel – *see* **estoppel**
European Community instrument,
    admissibility as   1283
exceptions rule   1090–1094
expert   1088, 1223–1224
– *and see* **judicial notice**
fresh   150, 1088
hearsay   1086n
implied application of rules of   1086–1097,
     S99
judge, by   103, 428
Official Journal of the European
    Communities, admissibility as   1283
parliamentary proceedings, of   181, 234–
     235
parole evidence rule   647
personal Act, of   185
preamble or recital, statement in   731–733,
     735
presumption of fact in lieu of   1086, 1145
privilege   59–60
publication of   121
public interest immunity – *see*
    public interest immunity
Queen's   99
report, statement in   1148
rules of, implied importation of   1086–
     1097
silence, right to – *see* **procedure,**
    criminal
standard of proof – *see* **standard of**
    proof
statutory instrument, of   274
technical terms, of   1205–1206, 1223–1224
torture, of   1349
without prejudice rule   1097
witnesses   29, 813, 857, 1106
words, of meaning of   1223–1224
– *and see* **advocate;**
    enforcement agencies;
    European Community
    law; fact; judicial notice;
    jury; retrospectivity;
    technical terms
Ewing, K D – *see* **Bibliography (pp**
    1475 to 1507)

ex abundanti cautela   211, 565, 725, 1014,
     1165, 1250, 1258
ex post facto **law** – *see* **retrospectivity**
ex visceribus actus **construction** – *see*
    construction as a whole
examples
added by amendment   740
delegated legislation, in   741
primary legislation, in   739–741
reliance on   739–741
value of   17
– *and see* **technical terms**
exception – *see* **Act of Parliament;**
    evidence; proviso
exclusionary rule, the
chronological development of   652–666
Commonwealth, in   673–682
– *and see* **Australia; Canada;**
    Ghana; New Zealand
consolidation Acts and   606
control of its procedure by court
    and   680–682
parole evidence rule and   647
reasons for   625, 645–652
relaxation of – *see* ***Pepper v Hart*,**
    rule in
statement of rule   644
– *and see* **amendment to Bill;**
    Bill, parliamentary;
    comity
execution   166
executive – *see* **executive power;**
    separation of powers, doctrine
    of
executive agencies – *see* **enforcement**
    agencies
executive estoppel – *see* **estoppel**
executive instrument   43, 270, 272, 324
– *and see* **enforcement notice;**
    ignorantia juris neminem
    excusat; **order**
executive power, abuse of
abuse of   87
Paliamentary powers, separation   S8
exercise of judgment
application of enactment, in relation
    to   124–126
breach of statutory duty, in relation
    to   67–68, 80–82
discretion, confused with   127–129
fact and degree, questions of – *see*
    fact
guidelines as to   129–130
nature of   124–127, 629–630, 1167–1168,
     1170
reopening of judgment   114, S18, S97

All references are to page numbers

---

exercise of judgment – *contd*
review of 117
– *and see* **broad terms;**
differential readings;
discretion
existence 1192–1193
Expiring Laws Continuance Acts 186
explanatory material on Bill,
interpretative use of 641–644, 1456
explanatory memorandum – *see* **Bill,**
parliamentary
explanatory notes – *see* **delegated**
legislation
expressio unius **principle**
Crown immunity and 210
definitions and 988
designation words and 1252–1254
examples of 65, 337, 1250–1259
exception, categories of, and 1256–1257
extending words and 1255–1256
judicial notice and – *see* **judicial**
notice
nature of 76, 1250–1259, S10
savings and – *see* **saving**
specific procedures and 1254–1255
expressum facit cessare tacitum 89, 490,
525, 1225, 1249, 1250,
1251
– *and see* **expressio unius principle**
extent – *see* **territorial extent of Act**
exterritoriality 369–370
extradition 100, 136, 188, 209, 361n, 374,
876, 898, 945, 1000,
1286–1287, 1350,
1444, S84
extra-statutory concession 15, 191, 277,
299–300, 635, 703,
1021
extra-statutory discretion 51
extra-statutory payment 251
extra-statutory payments, crown, by 251
extra-territoriality 363, 370, 371–378, 374,
376, 378, 382
extrinsic material – *see* **legislative**
history
ex turpi causa non oritur actio – *see*
illegality
fact
ascertainment of 587
evidence of – *see* **evidence**
fact and degree, questions of 428–429,
1262–1270
factual outline, the – *see* **factual**
outline, the
generalising 424–426
ignorance of – *see* **ignorance**
judicial notice of – *see* **judicial**
notice
matrix of 587, 591

fact – *contd*
mistake of – *see* **mistake**
presentation of 426–427
proof of 427
– *and see* **evidence**
relevant and irrelevant 391, 423–428
unforeseen 482–483
– *and see* **fact and law; factual**
outline, the
fact and law 122, 393, 1221–1222
– *and see* **fact; factual outline, the**
factors, interpretative – *see*
interpretative factors
factual outline, the
function of 391, 416–421
judicial use of 416–421
mistake of fact and – *see* **mistake**
nature of 391, 416–421
relevance S45
statutory 416–421, 425–426
– *and see* **fact**
Fagan, J – *see* **Bibliography (pp**
1475 to 1507)
fairness – *see* **legal policy; natural**
justice
Falconer of Thoroton, Lord 3
– *and see* **Bibliography (pp 1475**
to 1507)
family law
'clean break' principle 787–788
family rights, interference with – *see*
doubtful penalisation, principle
against; European Convention
on Human Rights
Farwell LJ 650, 657, 699n, 1198, 1257
fasciculus – *see* **format of Act**
Ferguson, William – *see*
Bibliography (pp 1475 to 1507)
feudal tenures 359
fiction – *see* **absurdity; artificial**
person; asifism; deeming
Field J 843, 970
figures – *see* **numbers**
finance – *see* **Bill, parliamentary;**
Commons, House of; Crown;
disobeying Act; jurisdiction;
money; taxing Acts
Financial Memorandum 641
Financial Services Authority 157
financial year 1396
Finch CJ 407
Finlay, Judge John 923
Finlay, Lord 976
Fitzgibbon LJ 657
Fleta 652
– *and see* **Bibliography (pp 1475**
to 1507)
foetus 105, 500, 509, 577–578, 600, 834n,
957–958, 1370

All references are to page numbers

footnotes – *see* **format of Act**

Forbes J   42, 294, 526, 528, 811, 830

foreign

  aspects regarding application of Act
    – *see* **application of Act**

  context, english word used in – *see*
    words

  conviction   1084

  courts   1100

  jurists – *see* **jurists**

  law   393–394, 1100
    – *and see* **European Community**
      law; judicial notice

  matters   976, 1212–1213, 1215–1216

  money – *see* **money**

  nationals   988

  passport   1045–1046

foreseeability   80

forfeiture rule   1142

formalities – *see* **technicalities**

format of Act   719–720, 749–750

forms   52, 54, 1123

Fortescue J   1112

Fortescue, John – *see* **Bibliography**
    (pp 1475 to 1507)

'**forthwith**', meaning of   558

Foskett J   S42

Fowler, H W – *see* **Bibliography (pp**
    1475 to 1507)

Fox LJ   78n, 320, 951, 1030, 1074

Frankfurter J   666
    – *and see* **Bibliography (pp 1475**
      to 1507)

Fraser of Tullybelton, Lord   521, 740, 829,
          985, 997, 1114, 1150,
          1189

fraud – *see* **evasion of Act; illegality**

freedom – *see* **doubtful penalisation,**
    principle against; legal policy;
    speech, freedom of

free-standing Act, doctrine of   289, 293,
          384n, 1165, 1166

free-standing term   346, 352, 1039, 1200,
          1211

French J   S79

Friedmann, W   773
    – *and see* **Bibliography (pp 1475**
      to 1507)

Fry LJ   1211

functional construction

  amendable descriptive components
    of Act   713–714, 727–741

  delegated legislation and   265

  operative components of Act   713–714,
          718–726

  rule   466, 713–717

functional construction – *contd*

  unamendable descriptive
    components of Act   713–714, 741–
          758

    – *and see* **Act of Parliament;**
      chapter number; enacting
      formula; examples; format
      of Act; heading;
      incorporation by
      reference; long title;
      preamble; proviso;
      punctuation; purpose
      clause; purview; recital;
      repugnancy; saving;
      Schedule; section; short
      title; sidenote

functus officio   1062, 1305

fungible property   1067

futility – *see* **absurdity**

G v G, principle in   144

Gaffney approach   175–177

game of chance   S101

Gane, C P – *see* **Bibliography (pp**
    1475 to 1507)

garbled text – *see* **rectifying**
    construction

Gardiner, Lord – *see* **Bibliography**
    (pp 1475 to 1507)

Gaveston, Piers   832

Geddes, R S   8

gender   579, 909, 1046–1047, 1047, 1202,
          1212, 1327, 1328,
          1332, 1387–1388,
          1410

general notice   271, 273

generalia specialia derogant   1164

generalia specialibus non derogant   304,
          306, 307, 1164

Geny, Francois – *see* **Bibliography**
    (pp 1475 to 1507)

Ghana   170, 349, 680

Ghosh, I J   588n, 607n
    – *and see* **Bibliography (pp 1475**
      to 1507)

Gibbs CJ   300n

Gibraltar   330

Gibson (Peter) LJ   80, 448n, 603, 809, 971,
          1183

Gibson, J – *see* **Bibliography (pp**
    1475 to 1507)

Gifford, D J – *see* **Bibliography (pp**
    1475 to 1507)

Gillick test   1150n

Gladstone, W E   314

Glanvill   30

Gleeson, Hon Murray   S3

Glidewell LJ   750, 868, 1013n, 1054, 1118,
          1188

All references are to page numbers

Global method of statutory
    interpretation – *see* statutory
    interpretation
gloss, judicial – *see* judicial gloss
Gloster J   897, 1167
Goddard, Lord CJ   11, 32, 332n, 488, 1121,
                                         1187
Goff of Chieveley, Lord   103n, 707, 821,
                                      899–900
Goffmann, Erving – *see*
    Bibliography (pp 1475 to 1507)
'golden rule'   12–13, 514, 545, 870
good administration, duty of   91
Goodall, Judge Anthony Charles   1213
Goodall, Kay   ix, 1n, 634n, 826n, 1381
    – *and see* Bibliography (pp 1475
    to 1507)
Goode, Roy   32
    – *and see* Bibliography (pp 1475
    to 1507)
Goodhart, A L   660
    – *and see* Bibliography (pp 1475
    to 1507)
Gordon, Richard – *see* Bibliography
    (pp 1475 to 1507)
Goudie, James – *see* Bibliography
    (pp 1475 to 1507)
Gough, W J – *see* Bibliography (pp
    1475 to 1507)
Goulding J   586, 1208
government   475, 514, 962–963, 1061
    – *and see* Crown; enforcement
    agencies; government
    departments; Minister of the
    Crown; Prime Minister
government department
    Act, in charge of   610
    enforcement agency, as   85–86
    guidelines issued by   90, 702–706, S71
    official statements by   703, S70
government 'in right of the'   348–350
government policy principle   858n, 1355
Governor-General   1396
Gowers, Ernest   557, 1189, 1219
    – *and see* Bibliography (pp 1475
    to 1507)
Graham J   1182
Graham, R N   1457–1459
    – *and see* Bibliography (pp 1475
    to 1507)
grammatical meaning   11, 15, 24, 25, 103,
                        123, 441, 443–444,
                        446, 447, 451, 453,
                        454, 455, 456, 466,
                        490, 523, 529, 531,

grammatical meaning – *contd*
                        533, 548, 586, 754,
                        864, 878, 952, 966,
                                         1177
    – *and see* ambiguity
    (grammatical); legal
    meaning; ordinary meaning;
    plain meaning rule
Gray, J C – *see* Bibliography (pp
    1475 to 1507)
'Great Britain', meaning of   346–348
greater includes less   39, 555–557
Greenberg, Daniel   7n, 191n, 411n, 1284n
    – *and see* Bibliography (pp 1475
    to 1507)
Greene, Lord   89, 407, 1018, 1053, 1199
Greenwood, Christopher – *see*
    Bibliography (pp 1475 to 1507)
Greschner, D   518
    – *and see* Bibliography (pp 1475
    to 1507)
Grey, T – *see* Bibliography (pp 1475
    to 1507)
Griffith, J A G – *see* Bibliography
    (pp 1475 to 1507)
Griffiths, Lord   89, 125, 129n, 508, 601,
                        627, 630, 636, 665,
                        670, 1002, 1013, 1185
Grove J   412, 413, 477, 657, 970, 1015,
                                         1132
guardian ad litem   1103, 1137, 1140
Guide to Legislative Procedures   181, 616,
                                643n, 706n
guidelines, statutory   129, 704
    – *and see* broad terms; court;
    discretion; government
    departments; legislative
    history
guides to legislative intention – *see*
    interpretative criteria
Gulmann, Adv Gen   **1286n**
Gummow, Justice W M C   1459–1460
    – *and see* Bibliography (pp 1475
    to 1507)
Gunasekara, Gehan N – *see*
    Bibliography (pp 1475 to 1507)
Gurney, B   879
Gutteridge, H C   29
habeas corpus   136, 166, 197, 343, 564, 837,
                        838, 839, 994, 995,
                                   1002, S84
Hadley, E A   63n
    – *and see* Bibliography (pp 1475
    to 1507)
Hailsham of St Marylebone, Lord   177,
                        322, 786, 803, 1210
    – *and see* Bibliography (pp 1475
    to 1507)
Hailsham, Viscount   961, 1208

All references are to page numbers

hairsplitting 26, 866
Haldane, Viscount 646, 658, 867, 1048, 1058
Hale, Baroness S66
Hale CJ 809, 843n
Hale J 543
Hale, Matthew – *see* Bibliography (pp 1475 to 1507)
Halkerston, Peter – *see* Bibliography (pp 1475 to 1507)
Halsbury, Earl of 33, 57, 118, 379, 418, 419, 471, 477, 478, 614n, 645, 656, 657, 694n, 696, 986, 1194
Halsbury's Laws of England 549, 699, 702–703
Hanbury, H G – *see* Bibliography (pp 1475 to 1507)
Hannen P 361n, 1098
Hansard – *see* legislative history
Hanworth, Lord 1217, 1263
Hardcastle, H – *see* Bibliography (pp 1475 to 1507)
Hardcastle, R S59
hardship – *see* duress
Hardwicke, Lord 331
Hargrave, Francis – *see* Bibliography (pp 1475 to 1507)
Harman J 169, 715n, 736n, 745, 754, 842, 901n, 962, 1214
Harman LJ 415, 755, 888, 994, 1121
Harries, Jill – *see* Bibliography (pp 1475 to 1507)
Harris, D J – *see* Bibliography (pp 1475 to 1507)
Harris, J W – *see* Bibliography (pp 1475 to 1507)
Harrison, Nicolas – *see* Bibliography (pp 1475 to 1507)
Harrison, W Graham – *see* Bibliography (pp 1475 to 1507)
Hart, H L A 171n, 507n, 514, 515n, 893
– *and see* Bibliography (pp 1475 to 1507)
Hartley, T C 1302n
– *and see* Bibliography (pp 1475 to 1507)
hate incident 94
Hatherley, Lord 655, 902n, 903
Hatsell, J – *see* Bibliography (pp 1475 to 1507)
Hatton, Christopher 7
– *and see* Bibliography (pp 1475 to 1507)
Havery, Judge Richard 1346
Hawkins, W 63n
– *and see* Bibliography (pp 1475 to 1507)

heading
alteration of 215–216
– *and see* printing corrections
delegated legislation, in 716
interpretation by reference to 715, 745–746, 1454–1456
nature of 745–746
– *and see* functional construction rule
health, danger to – *see* doubtful penalisation, principle against; legal policy
hear both sides – *see* audi alterum partem principle
Heathcote-Amory, David – *see* Bibliography (pp 1475 to 1507)
Hebrides, the 356
hendiadys 1197
Hengham CJ 33
Henry LJ 118, 127, 143, 246, 626, 745n, 1000n, 1140, 1218
Henry VIII clause 245–246, 294n
Heptarchy, the 353
Her Majesty's Courts and Tribunals Service S19
Her Majesty's dominions 327, 348–350
Her Majesty's independent dominions 327, 350
Her Majesty's Revenue and Customs 1396
Her Majesty's Stationery Office – *see* HMSO
Herman, Shael 800, 965n
– *and see* Bibliography (pp 1475 to 1507)
Herschell, Lord 75, 605, 608, 609, 889n, 1163, S63
Heuston, R F V – *see* Bibliography (pp 1475 to 1507)
Hewart, Lord 196, 465, 763, 1138, 1139
Heydon J S20
Heydon's Case, resolution in 471, 1009–1010, 1034
High Court 102, 111–114, 138–140, S62
– *and see* court
high seas
jurisdiction over 356
meaning of 350–351, 385–387
hijacking 376, 1211
Hilbery J 491
Himsworth, C S3
Hine, R L 752n
– *and see* Bibliography (pp 1475 to 1507)
Hirst LJ 1079
history, legislative – *see* legislative history

All references are to page numbers

HMSO 226–227
– *and see* **Queen's Printer;**
Stationery Office Limited,
The
Hobbes, Thomas 182, 894
– *and see* **Bibliography (pp 1475**
to 1507)
Hobhouse of Woodborough, Lord 199,
494, 681n
Hodgson J 854n, 927, 1011, 1157
Hodson, Lord 993
Hoffmann, Lord 12n, 82, 86n, 117, 127,
442, 499n, 562, 576,
590, 602, 632, 633,
639, 646, 704, 732,
770, 799, 822, 900,
904, 949, 957, 1081,
1090, 1147, 1159,
1170, 1195, 1223n,
1288, 1291, 1324,
1326, S57, S99
Hogan, B – *see* **Bibliography (pp**
1475 to 1507)
Holmes J 36, 132, 394n, 801, 830, 986,
1156
– *and see* **Bibliography (pp 1475**
to 1507)
Holroyd J 749
Holt CJ 913
Home Office 87
home, sanctity of – *see* **domestic**
sanctuary, principle of
homonym 1217–1219
– *and see* **words**
Hong Kong 25, S112
intermediate appellate court,
reversal of decision S73
Honoré, T 805n
– *and see* **Bibliography (pp 1475**
to 1507)
Hooper J 1140
Hope of Craighead, Lord 45, 148, 192,
265, 347, 515, 637,
638, 671, 805n, 876,
1033, 1139, 1316,
1318, 1335, 1345, S31
Horabin, I S – *see* **Bibliography (pp**
1475 to 1507)
house – *see* **domestic sanctuary,**
principle of
Howard J 991
– *and see* **Bibliography (pp 1475**
to 1507)
Hudon, Edward G – *see*
Bibliography (pp 1475 to 1507)
human body
damage to S59
rights in S59

human rights 2, 518–519, 790, 1050, 1276
– *and see* **doubtful penalisation,**
principle against; European
Community law; European
Convention on Human
Rights; Human Rights
Act 1998
Human Rights Act 1998
amendment of 1320
commencement 1311
common law and 822
compatibility, ministers' statements
of 1334, 1439, S112–113
compatible construction rule under 2, 509,
885–886, 1322, 1426–
1427
Convention jurisprudence, duty to
take account of 1321
'Convention rights', meaning of 1317,
1425–1426
damages under 1346
declaration of incompatibility – *see*
incompatibility, declaration
of, under Human Rights Act
199
drafting of 1312, 1322
effect on legislation 6, 1312, 1322
general ix
incompatibility, declaration of – *see*
incompatibility, declaration
of, under Human Rights
Act 1998
incompatible acts and omissions of
public authorities 1338
interpretation of 1313, 1439–1440
other legislation, words not written
into S112
public authority, liability of 1338, 1428–
1432
remedial orders to rectify
incompatibility 1335, 1433, 1448–
1449
Scotland, procedures in, under – *see*
Scotland
text of 1425–1451
treatment of in this book 1312, 1315
Hume, David (Baron Hume) 10, 1136n
– *and see* **Bibliography (pp 1475**
to 1507)
Hunt, Brian – *see* **Bibliography (pp**
1475 to 1507)
Hunt, Murray 1
– *and see* **Bibliography (pp 1475**
to 1507)
Hutchison LJ 1034
Hutton, Lord 417, 509, 552, 609, 615, 743n
Hutton, Noël 738, 753
– *and see* **Bibliography (pp 1475**
to 1507)

All references are to page numbers

hypothetical point – *see* deeming;
　　legal proceedings
id certum est quod certum reddi
　　potest　　982
ignorance
　　adviser, of　　42
　　– *and see* **advocate**
　　English law of, by foreigner　　42
　　fact, of　　40, 59
　　law, of　　40–44, S5
　　– *and* see *ignorantia juris*
　　　　neminem excusat; mistake
ignorantia eorum quae quis scire
　　tenetur non excusat　　41
ignorantia juris neminem excusat　　**40, 41**
　　– *and see* **legislation; limitation of**
　　　　actions; mistake; mistake of
　　　　law
ignorantia facti excusat　　41
Ilbert, Courtenay　　33
　　– *and see* **Bibliography (pp 1475**
　　　　to 1507)
illegality
　　allegans suam turpitudinem non est
　　　　audiendus　　1105–1111
　　contracts or covenants and　　61, 1069–1070,
　　　　　　　　1107
　　court's duty to notice　　1110
　　defences, effect on　　1108–1109
　　domicile, and　　1111
　　European Community law and　　1111
　　European Convention on Human
　　　　Rights and　　1320
　　fraud　　201, 793, S77
　　impracticability and　　977–978
　　in bonam partem (in good faith)
　　　　construction　　792–795
　　locus poenitentiae and　　1111
　　reliance on　　1105–1111, S100
　　residence, and　　1111
　　scope of　　1105–1111
　　severance　　61, 1110
　　third party rights and　　1108–1109
　　– *and see* **decision-making**
　　　　rules; evasion of Act; legal
　　　　policy; *nullus commodum*
　　　　capere potest de injuria sua
　　　　propria; **severance; tax**
　　　　avoidance
immigration
　　appeal　　S108–109
　　permission to marry in United
　　　　Kingdom　　S53
immigration Appeals Tribunal　　142
Immigration Acts, The　　1396
immorality　　501, 976
　　– *and see* **legal policy; moral duty**
immunities – *see* **privileges and**
　　immunities

impecuniosity　　78–79, 126–127
implication
　　ancillary powers, of　　497–498
　　broad terms – *see* **broad terms**
　　courts, implied powers of – *see*
　　　　inherent judicial powers
　　Crown immunity, as to　　210
　　– *and see* **Crown immunity,**
　　　　doctrine of
　　definitions and　　569
　　delegated legislation and – *see*
　　　　delegated legislation
　　description only partly met, where –
　　　　see **description, statutory**
　　duties, as to　　37
　　European Convention on Human
　　　　Rights　　1319
　　– *and see* **European Convention**
　　　　on Human Rights
　　express words exclude　　1249–1250
　　– *and see* *expressio unius*
　　　　principle
　　'if any', of　　1269–1270
　　imprecise language and　　496
　　legitimacy of　　491–499
　　limitation on express words, of　　498–499
　　literal construction and　　463
　　logic, in – *see* **logic, use of in**
　　　　intepretation
　　mandatory and directory
　　　　requirements, as to – *see*
　　　　mandatory and directory
　　　　requirements
　　maxims, application of – *see*
　　　　maxims, legal
　　nature of　　487–490
　　'necessary'　　210, 493–494
　　oblique reference, by　　1259–1262
　　'obvious'　　495
　　persons lacking capacity, exclusion
　　　　of – *see* **incompetents**
　　powers, and – *see* **statutory power**
　　'proper'　　113, 495–496
　　related law, affecting　　499–501
　　right, implied extinguishment of　　499
　　rules of law, implied application of
　　　　– *see* **implied ancillary rules**
　　statutory description, partially met,
　　　　and　　1262–1270
　　use of　　50, 373
　　– *and see* **amendment to Act;**
　　　　application of Act;
　　　　ejusdem generis **principle;**
　　　　expressio unius **principle;**
　　　　expressum facit cessare
　　　　tacitum; **processing of**
　　　　enactments, dynamic;
　　　　statutory power;
　　　　territorial extent of Act

All references are to page numbers

---

implied ancillary maxims – *see* maxims, legal
implied ancillary powers 497–498, S51
implied ancillary rules – *see* ancillary rules of law
impossibility 404–405, 973–974, 1129–1133, S102–103
– *and see impotentia excusat legem*
impotence – *see impotentia excusat legem*
impotentia excusat legem 1128
impracticability – *see* absurdity
impression, matters of 130, 586, 1030
– *and see* differential readings
in bonam partem construction – *see* illegality
in pari materia, Acts 6, 184, 189, 588, 603, 604, 605, 708, 709, 710, 738, 759, 764, 765, 795, 889, 919, 951, 954, 1165, 1167, 1200
– *and see* collective title; construction as one; incorporation by reference; legal regimes; legislative history
in personam, proceedings – *see* legal proceedings
in rem, proceedings – *see* legal proceedings
inarticulate major premise – *see* judge
incapacity – *see* incompetents
incompatibility, declaration of, under Human Rights Act 1998
Crown, joinder of, in proceedings 1333, 1427–1428
delegated legislation, in respect of 1333, 1428
primary legislation, in respect of 1330, 1428
rectifying of legislation 1335, 1433
– *and see* Human Rights Act 1998
Income Tax Acts 1396
incompatibility, declaration of, under Human Rights Act 1998
effect of 1333
primary legislation, in respect of 1331
incompetents
bodily interference with 834
court, role of, in respect of 105
criminal enactments, application to 193, 1042, 1077–1078
housing of 125, 1012–1013
limitation period for 988
open court principle and 120
'person', reference to 578

incompetents – *contd*
property of, interference with 847
– *and see* children; death; discrimination, legislation against; foetus; *impotentia excusat legem*; mental disability; procedure, criminal
inconsistency – *see* repugnancy
inconvenience – *see* absurdity
incorporation by reference
archival drafting 140, 151, 161, 162, 199, 209n, 759–761, S76
construction as one 759, 762–764
general 758
nature of 758–765, S76
– *and see* Clauses Act; collective title; common law; functional construction; High Court; *in pari materia*, acts; Keeling Schedule; practice
indemnity Act – *see* Act of Parliament
India 247n, 333n, 343n, 693–694
'individual', meaning of 577, 1275
inducing words – *see* Schedule
infants – *see* children
information
power to publish 90
required to be true 37
information technology, implications of 377
informed interpretation
ambiguity and 587
common law and 589
consolidation Acts and 604–607
– *and see* consolidation Act
context 588–590, 919
contextual material, submitted to court de bene esse 596
doubt and 25, 26
explanatory material on Bill and 641–644
facts and 587
Law Commission's views on 590–591
legal knowledge required 593, 716, 804–805
need for 122
predictability of law and 590–591
prolonging proceedings and 590–591
rule 585–588
treaties and 682–691
– *and see* legislative history
inherent judicial powers
alteration of unperfected judgment 112, S18
alteration of perfected judgment S18
codification of 203

All references are to page numbers

inherent judicial powers – *contd*
effectiveness of court orders,
    ensuring   113, 787, 1002–1003
jurisdiction, statutory   51, 203
nature of   111–114, 123, 1045
procedure, as to   102, 111–114, 596, 598,
    644, 680–682, 691–
    692
    – *and see* **jurisdiction**
injunction
Crown immunity – *see* **Crown
    immunity, doctrine of**
form of   115
mandatory and directory
    requirements   56
    – *and see* **mandatory and
    directory requirements**
power to grant   73, 114–116, 128, 163,
    811, 1025–1026, 1067
types of   114–116
    – *and see* **equity, rules of;
    judicial review**
injustice – *see* **justice**
inner London borough   1397
intellectual property, legal meaning   S107
intention, ascertainment of   1104
intention, legislative
accidental fit to unforeseen
    circumstances   482–483
contrary intention, apparent   978
convenient phantom, as   S49
delegated legislation, as to – *see*
    delegated legislation
determination by judiciary   123, 337, 367,
    377
drafter and   475–477
duplex approach to   477–479
enforcement powers, statutory, and   88
European Community law, effect
    on   1299–1300
express   S56
fictitious, whether   472–474, 477–481
'freezing' of   170
function of the concept   472
guides to – *see* **interpretative
    criteria**
Human Rights Act 1998, effect of,
    and – *see* **Human Rights
    Act 1998**
implied – *see* **implication**
incomplete   481
mandatory and directory
    requirements, in – *see*
    **mandatory and directory
    requirements**
motive, distinguished from   484–486
non-existent, where   366, 480–481
paramount criterion, as   18, 86, 438, 469–
    472

intention, legislative – *contd*
preamble as guide to   731–733
purpose or object, distinguished
    from   483–784
repeal and – *see* **repeal**
retrospectivity and   317, S41
    – *and see* **retrospectivity**
sections, organisation of, as guide to   720–
    721
tacit legislation and – *see* **tacit
    legislation**
textual amendment and   289–292
    – *and see* **legal policy;
    legislative history;
    predictability of law;
    processing of enactments,
    dynamic**
total invalidity   S6
interest   1256, 1259
interest reipublicae ut sit finis litium
    – *see* **protracted legal
    proceedings, interest of state to
    avoid**
interim relief   1297, 1353
'internal waters', meaning of   334, 341, 351
**International Convention for the
    Protection of Performers,
    producers of Phonograms, and
    Broadcasting
Organisations (1961)**   70
**International Covenant on Civil and
    Political Rights (1966)**   322n, 683,
    1354
international law – *see* **private
    international law; public
    international law**
international organisations – *see*
    privileges and immunities
interpret, meaning of   23–24
Interpretation Act 1978
contrary intention and   575, 583
definitions in   576–583, 1200, 1387, 1394–
    1403
    – *and see* **definitions, statutory**
free-standing terms and   1199–1200
general   575–583, S11
other legislation, supplementing and
    not overriding   S58
'person', definition of   1399
    – *and see* **artificial person**
post, service by – *see* **service**
provisions to which applicable   576, 1404–
    1405
purpose of   S58
subordinate legislation, construction
    of   1388
text of   1387–1408
time, treatment of   1388
white paper on   1409–1417

All references are to page numbers

---

interpretation, rules of – *see* rules

interpretation, statutory – *see* statutory interpretation

interpretative conventions – *see* presumptions of construction

interpretative criteria
checklist of 1383–1385
common law, part of 513–514
excluded by implication 1262
legal policy, changes in, and 537–539
nature of 24, 511–515
operation of 512–513
statutory 514
types of 514–515
– *and see* **interpretative factors; legal policy; statutory interpretation**

interpretative factors
'bundles' of 524
change in weight of 537–539
consistent result from, effect of 521–523
grammatical ambiguity – *see* **ambiguity (grammatical)**
nature of 511–515, 519–523
number of, in a case 525–526
positive and negative 520–521
priority between 526–527
same interpretative criterion, drawn from 525
semantic obscurity – *see* **obscurity, semantic**
strained construction – *see* **strained construction**
weighing and balancing of 523–528, 852, 866–867, 873, 905–906
weight indicated by enactment, where 528–529
– *and see* **interpretative criteria; strict and liberal construction**

interpretative presumptions – *see* presumptions of construction

interpretative principles – *see* legal policy; doubtful penalisation, principle against

interpreter of enactment
types of 26–36
– *and see* **Judges**

interstitial articulation
advantages of 509
effect of 171
examples of 171, 490, 507–508, 530, 534–537, 1005, S52
meaning of 504, 1176–1177
– *and see* **advocate; codification; judicial gloss; sub-rules**

investigating agencies – *see* enforcement agencies

Ireland
'British Islands', as part of 342
general 796
name of 354
treated as 'home' country, on occasion 355
United Kingdom, as part of 354
– *and see* **Eire; Irish Free State; Northern Ireland**

Irish Free State 342, 354

irregularity, procedural 50, 51, 1111
– *and see* **decision-making rules**

Irvine of Lairg, Lord 955n, 1051, 1052, 1331
– *and see* **Bibliography (pp 1475 to 1507)**

Jackson (Robert H) J 626
– *and see* **Bibliography (pp 1475 to 1507)**

Jackson, Bernard S **217**

Jacob J 622

Jacobs (F G) Adv Gen 1281n

Jamaica Schedule 196–197

James LJ 1005

James V-C 784, 1133n

Jamieson, N J 472
– *and see* **Bibliography (pp 1475 to 1507)**

jargon – *see* legal terms; technical terms

Jauncey of Tullichettle, Lord 81, 209, 902

Jekyll MR 785

Jenkins LJ 1259

Jenkins, David – *see* **Bibliography (pp 1475 to 1507)**

Jessel MR 484, 783, 866

John, Rowena – *see* **Bibliography (pp 1475 to 1507)**

joint tenants 579, 1207

Jones, Timothy H – *see* **Bibliography (pp 1475 to 1507)**

Jowitt, Earl 465
– *and see* **Bibliography (pp 1475 to 1507)**

Joyce J 772

judge
antagonism to legislation, former 814–816
appointment of 2–5
bias by – *see* **nemo debet esse judex in propria causa**
checklist of interpretive criteria 1383
comprehension of meaning of enactment, difficulty of 451–453
de facto 1356
dicta, inadequate 10, 11

judge – *contd*
drafting, inadequate, response to   409–413
    – *and see* **disorganised composition**
early legislation, as drafter of   652–653
ellipsis, recognition of   493
    – *and see* **ellipsis**
function of   393–394, 548
inarticulate major premise underlying decisions   132
independence of   152–153
interpretative factors, reluctant acknowledgement of   527–528, 544–547
interpreter of legislation, as   102, 108, 122–133, 588–589, 697–701
interstitial articulation by   506–507, 548
law, knowledge of, presumed   42, 133, 1221–1223
legislative language, knowledge of presumed   1221–1223
legislator, as   11, 168–170, 785–786
    – *and see* **court**
lis, concerned to decide   29, 392, 430
misbehaviour by   118–119
mistake of law by   135, 728–729
    – *and see* **mistake**
Parliament, respect for   963–965
    – *and see* **comity**
philologist, as   1221
precision drafting, recognition of   411
pre-trial powers of   984
private knowledge of   428
prosecutors, criticism of   99
puisne   140
recusal by   394, 1139
statutory interpretation, function exclusive to   699
    – *and see* **statutory interpretation**
text writers, views on – *see* **jurists**
uniform terminology for interpretation, and   589–590
well-informed, need to be   137–138, 591, 593, 641, 691
witness, as   103
    – *and see* **assessor; court; death; delegated legislation; differential readings; discretion; drafting, legislative; evidence; judicial notice; judicial power of the state; legal policy; legislative history; magistrates; political factors**
Judge, Lord LCJ   S20

judge in own cause – *see nemo debet esse judex in propria causa*
Judge, Igor (President)   170
judgment
exercise of – *see* **exercise of judgment**
form of   62, 117
reopening of   114, S18, S97
secret   118
summary   26
    – *and see* – **appeal**
judicial act   1120
    – *and see* **act in law**
Judicial Appointments Board   2–5
judicial assistant   394, 595
Judicial Committee of the Privy Council   154, 333, S27
    – *and see* **Privy Council**
judicial gloss   480–481, 491, 506, 548
    – *and see* **interstitial articulation**
judicial notice
Act, of   136, 184, 196, 233, 1387
Al Qaeda, fats about   S21
Bill, of   43, 196
common law, of   136
custom, of   136
delegated legislation, of   135
dictionary, reference to   1222–1223
discretion as to taking   134
doctrine of   133–138
European Community law, of   136, 1283
European Court of Justice, decisions of   135, 613
expertise, non-legal, of   138
fact, of   28–29, 136–138, 428
judge's private knowledge   428
law, of   28–29, 133–136, 599–600
legislative history, of   610
local authorities, financial situation of   S21
meaning of words, of   1202, 1221–1223
personal Act, not judicially noticed
    – *and* – *see* **personal Act**
public international law, of   823, S21
publication, alternative mans of   S21
scope of   134
social transformation in attitudes, of   S21
technical terms, of   1202
treaty, of   823
    – *and see* **Act of State; evidence**
judicial power of the state   9, 101, 103, 104, 152, 392, 434
    – *and see* **Crown**
judicial review
agencies subject to   90, 91
    – *and see* **enforcement agencies**
alternative remedies, need to pursue   159–161
Anisminic clause   109–110, S16

All references are to page numbers

judicial review – *contd*
anticipatory	111
application for	155
breach of statutory duty, for	67, 71
byelaws, of	270
categories of case	161
certiorari – *see* **quashing order (*certiorari*)**	
challenges in other proceedings	164
commencement order, of failure to make	284–286
Court of Appeal and	158
Crown immunity – *see* **Crown immunity, doctrine of**	
damages	163–164
decisions of enforcement agencies	90, 91
declaration	163
– *and see* **declaration**	
delegated legislation, of	166, 247, 253, 260
discretion, as to exercise of	1054–1055, 1059
evidence in	158
good administration, duty of	91
habeas corpus and	166, 838–839
– *and see* ***habeas corpus***	
Hansard, citing	670–671
High Court decision, of	108
injunction, grant of	163
– *and see* **injunction**	
last resort, remedy of	154
leave for	155, 163
locus standi	158–159, 539, 776–777
mandatory order (mandamus)	56, 110, 154, 161–162
national security and	104
nature of	90–91, 95, 154–166, 1051
Ostler clause	109
prerogative instrument, of	240
prerogative order	111, 162–163
principles governing – *see* **decision-making rules**	
private Act, and	156
prohibiting order (prohibition)	117, 154, 162–163
prosecutions	100
public law remedy – *see* **public law**	
quashing order (*certiorari*)	109, 110, 162
quo warranto	154, 165–166
relief, discretion to grant or refuse	S13
religion and	157
remedies available for	161–166
severance	258–259
– *and see* **severance**	
standing	158, 539, 776–777
supervisory rather than appellate	158
Supreme Court and	158
time factors	159, 872

judicial review – *contd*
university disputes	110
– *and see* **appeal;** *Carltona* **principle; contempt of court; contempt of statute; doubtful penalisation, principle against; enforcement notice; jurisdiction; prisoners, rights of; reference, works of**	

Judicial Studies Board | 130
Junius, Letters of | 800n
jurisdiction
absence of	50, 116
Admiralty	330, 357, 368, 913
agreement, whether conferrable by	105–106, 143
appellate – *see* **appeal**	
civil and criminal contrasted	1049, 1354
contracting out	62
court, of, interference with contractual right	S9
court's determination as to its	111–114
criminal – *see* **procedure, criminal**	
doubt as to	50, 105–106
duplication of	811
European Convention on Human Rights and	1318
excess of	50–51, 107
failure to exercise	106–107, 112
implied	105–106, 559
inherent – *see* **inherent judicial powers**	
mandatory and directory requirements	50–51
– *and see* **mandatory and directory requirements**	
nature of	104–107, 559
non-court, of	105–106
ouster clause	S16, S17
ouster of	108–111
resource implications	107
states, disputes between	106–109
submission to	105, 375
– *and see* **appropriate forum test; Brussels Convention on Jurisdiction and the Enforcement of Judgments in Civil and Commercial Matters; commencement of Act; court; decision-making rules; estoppel; exterritoriality; magistrates;** *Scherer* **principle; territorial extent of Act; territorial waters**	

All references are to page numbers

---

jurists
  authority of, early   30–31
  cited by judges   31–32
  deceased, need to be?   32–33
  errors in textbooks   31, 32
  foreign   34
  interpreters as   28–34
  judges and barristers as authorities   28, 32
  living, authority of   32–33
  opinions of   712
jury
  commonsense construction rule, and   558
  function of   393–394
  grand   489
  interpretation by   558
  judge's instructions to   781
  mistake of law by   118
  public authority, not   1379
  public interest and   791–792
  question left to   52
  trial by   554, 781, 854, 926, 992, 1083,
                                       1356, S85
  – *and see* **procedure, criminal**
justice
  access to   255, 854
  law should serve   795–799
  natural – *see* **natural justice**
  should be done   142–144, 1138
  should be seen to be done   1138–1139
  – *and see* **European Convention
      on Human Rights, Human
      Rights Act 1998; open
  court, the**
  – *and see* **court;
      decision-making rules;
      legal policy; legal
      proceedings; Parliament;
      retrospectivity**
  injustice, toleration of   S78
Justinian   30, 170, 817
– *and see* **Bibliography (pp 1475 to
    1507)**
Kafka, Franz   252
Kay LJ   242, 815
Keeling Schedule   643
  – *and see* **incorporation by
      reference**
Keenan, D J – *see* **Bibliography (pp
    1475 to 1507)**
Keene LJ   1372
Keir, D L – *see* **Bibliography (pp
    1475 to 1507)**
Keith of Avonholm, Lord   421, 955
Keith of Kinkel, Lord   51n, 127
Kelly CB   30
Kennedy LJ   1358
Kenny, C S   926n
  – *and see* **Bibliography (pp 1475
      to 1507)**

Kent, Harold   412, 589
  – *and see* **Bibliography (pp 1475
      to 1507)**
Kenyon CJ   653
Kerr LJ   977, 1011
Kersell, J E – *see* **Bibliography (pp
    1475 to 1507)**
Kersley, R H – *see* **Bibliography (pp
    1475 to 1507)**
Khan, A N – *see* **Bibliography (pp
    1475 to 1507)**
Kiefel J   S78
Kilgour, D G   654n, 666n, 681
  – *and see* **Bibliography (pp 1475
      to 1507)**
Kilner Brown J   1027
Kindersley V-C   1223
Kipling, Rudyard   883n
  – *and see* **Bibliography (pp 1475
      to 1507)**
Kirby M   S77
Kirby P   675, 676
  – *and see* **Bibliography (pp 1475
      to 1507)**
Knox J   493, 568, 950
Labouchère, H   482
Lacey, Nicola – *see* **Bibliography (pp
    1475 to 1507)**
laches   1067
lacuna – *see* **rectifying construction**
land
  definition of   581, 1398
  meaning of   1030, 1258
  occupier's liability   1073
  rights over   846–849, 1030
  – *and see* **leasehold
      enfranchisement;
      property; trespass**
Landon, P A – *see* **Bibliography (pp
    1475 to 1507)**
Lands Clauses Acts   1397
Lands Tribunal   106, 142, 146
Landsdowne, Lord   225n
Lane, Lord   135, 554, 730, 787, 805, 835,
                       845, 962, 990, 1003,
                      1030, 1142, 1256,
                                     1269
Langdale, Lord   434, 699
Langton, Stephen   412
Lanham, David – *see* **Bibliography
    (pp 1475 to 1507)**
Latey J   152
Latham J   1253
Latin, use of   1101–1103, 1117, 1203, S101,
                                      S105
law
  anticipated change of   695
  casual change of   782, 812–816

All references are to page numbers

law – *contd*
  certainty, need for – *see*
    predictability of law
  church – *see* **ecclesiastical law**
  churning – *see* **law-churning**
  consistency in, need for – *see* **legal policy**
  corpus juris (body of law)   197
  ecclesiastical – *see* **ecclesiastical law**
  equality before   330–331
  expertise, is an   129
  foreign – *see* **foreign**
  ignorance of – *see* ***ignorantia juris neminem excusat***
  integrity of, need to preserve   782, 993–995
  international – *see* **private international law; public international law**
  judicial disregard of   313–314
  judicial notice of – *see* **judicial notice**
  liberty removed not granted by   782–783, 821–822, 844–845, 846
  nature of   6, 36–37, 40, 191–194, 197–198, 206–207, 363, 395
  point of   148
  predictability of – *see* **predictability of law**
  protection by   372–373
  public – *see* **public law**
  reports – *see* **precedent, doctrine of**
  rule of   140n, 193, 1135
  soft   706
  – *and see* **Act of Parliament; common law; delegated legislation; equity; European Community law; fact and law; implied ancillary rules; justice; law-churning; Law Commission; law merchant; legal policy; legal proceedings; legislation; Lords, house of; maxims, legal; mistake; natural law; statute law**
law-churning   135n, 928
Law Commission
  breach of statutory duty, views on   70
  changing social values and interpretation, views on   904
  components of Act, interpretation by reference to, views on   715–726
  consolidation Acts and   606
  contempt of statute, views on   66

Law Commission – *contd*
  delegated legislation, interpretation of, views on   716
  disobeying Act, views on   66
  history of   32n
  legislative history, views on   612, 650, 692
  'mischief', views on   922–923
  reports of, reference to   32, 614–615, 661
  – *see* **legislative history**
  statutory interpretation, views on   519, 590–591, 592
  territorial waters, views on   334, 335n
  users of legislation, views on   804
Law Commission: – *see* **codification**
law management – *see* **central function of practitioner**
law merchant   136, 609n, 1070
Law Officers – *see* **Attorney General**
law reports
  neutral citation   856–857
  precedent and   854–855
  – *and see* **precedent, doctrine of**
  procedures regarding   119
  restrictions on   120
  – *and see* **open court, the**
Law Society, supervisory function of   92
Lawrence J   841
Laws LJ   53, 90, 95, 97, 101, 390, 708, 757
  – *and see* **Bibliography (pp 1475 to 1507)**
Lawson, F H – *see* **Bibliography (pp 1475 to 1507)**
Lawton LJ   173, 550, 586, 662, 949, 1085, 1148, 1157, 1207
Le Sueur, A P   836n
  – *and see* **Bibliography (pp 1475 to 1507)**
Learned Hand J   588
leasehold enfranchisement   848, 1023n
Lee J   676
legal adviser – *see* **advocate**
legal aid   457, 704, 911, 925, 975, 1023
legal certainty – *see* **predictability of law**
legal concepts   1040
legal meaning
  bilingual systems   25
  deductive reasoning, use of – *see* **logic, use of in interpretation**
  doubt as to – *see* **differential readings; doubt as to legal meaning**
  endorsement   S4
  grammatical meaning and, contrasted   441–443
  intellectual property   S107
  interpreter's duty to arrive at   24–25, 592, 699
  legislative history and   24

All references are to page numbers

legal meaning – *contd*
multilingual systems   25
nature of   24–26, 123, 175–177, 394, 430,
     441–443, 592, 1197
paradoxical   1192
partial meaning point   x
time point   x
wide and narrow construction – *see*
     strict and liberal
     construction
     – *and see* **opposing**
     constructions; plain
     meaning rule; processing
     of enactments, dynamic
legal policy
adopted by reference to Acts   765, 769,
     775–776, 781–782,
     816
arbitration, regarding   812
avoidance of duplication   1116
categories of   779–782
cause of action, as to   422
changes in   499, 537–539, 776–777, 785–
     786
common law and   771, 775
conflicts within   779, 790–792
   – *and see* **interpretative factors**
constituent elements of   773–778
court required to observe   1100
court, citizen's access to   108, 112
disputes, settlement of   807
duplication of offences, avoidance
     of   810
duplication of remedies, avoidance
     of   810
equality before the law   330–331, 782, 853
European Convention on Human
     Rights, and – *see* **European**
     Convention on Human
     Rights
evasion of Act – *see* **evasion of Act**
fairness, principle of   374, 770, 795–799
finality   582, 787–788
freedom, restraints on   784–785, 836–840,
     965
imported by Acts   1038
impracticability, need to avoid   977
inconvenience – *see* **absurdity**
international law – *see* **private**
     international law; public
     international law
international relations   817–824
interpretative criteria and   537–539
jury, constitutional right as   854
jury, exclusion of trial by   854
law should be certain and
     predictable   799–807
law should be consistent   782, 808–812
law should be effective   1277

legal policy – *contd*
law should be just   177, 795–799
   – *and see* **justice**
law should be knowable   194
law should not be changed casually   812–
     816
   – *and see* **law**
law should serve the public interest   211–
     212, 319–320, 786–
     795, 1046
legal principles and   765, 769–786
legal proceedings – *see* **legal**
     proceedings
legal process, rights of   854
liberty of the person, safeguarding
     of   52, 836–840
   – *and see* **doubtful penalisation,**
     principle against; *habeas*
     corpus; **prisoners, rights of**
life and health, preservation of   537–539,
     780, 831–836, 1134,
     1257
   – *and see* **doubtful penalisation,**
     principle agains
morality and   773–778, 780
   – *and see* **immorality; moral**
     duty
municipal law should conform to
     international law   817–824
   – *and see* **public international**
     law
nature of   168, 765, 769–786
overlapping legal regimes,
     minimisation of   809–810
penalisation, doubtful – *see*
     doubtful penalisation,
     principle against
preserving the peace – *see* **peace,**
     Queen's
property rights, and   42, 52–53, 58, 537–
     539, 785, 828–829,
     846–851, S7
public and private interests, conflict
     between, and   790–792
public policy, and   62, 765, 769, 772
reasonableness, and   770
rights removed not conferred – *see*
     law
security of the state, regarding   104, 379,
     779, 1046, 1135
statutory interpretation and   778
tax avoidance schemes and   1019
   – *and see* **tax avoidance**
waiver of statutory right   62
   – *and see* **application of Act;**
     costs; counter-mischief;
     court; European
     Convention on Human
     Rights; European

All references are to page numbers

legal policy – *contd*
  waiver of statutory right – *contd*
   – *and see* **application of Act; costs;**
    counter-mischief; court;
    European Convention on Human
    Rights; European – *contd*
    Community law;
    extra-erritoriality; human
    rights; illegality; implied
    ancillary rules; intention,
    legislative; jurisdiction;
    justice; law; maxims,
    legal; legislative steer;
    natural law; open court,
    the; predictability of law;
    principles of construction;
    religion; retrospectivity
legal proceedings
  academic or hypothetical point 143, 164,
    1306
  adjournment of 113, 279, 997
  anomalies regarding 997
  avoidance of protracted 787–788
  change of law, effect on 320
  civil and criminal distinguished 93–94
  conduct, right to 854–855
  costs – *see* **costs**
  defences – *see* **defences;**
    procedure, criminal
  defendant, absence of 1081
  delay, minimizing 320, 590–591, 983–985
  due process – *see* **process**
  evidence in – *see* **evidence**
  facilitate, need to 320, 975–977, 1026–
    1027
  forum non conveniens, doctrine of 374
  in personam 687–688, 1065
  in rem 687–688, 997, 1027, 1065
  inconvenience to 983–985
  jury, trial by – *see* **jury**
  lengthening of, need to avoid 590–591,
    983–985, 984
   – *and see* **protracted legal**
    proceedings, avoiding
  letter before action 1002
  litigant in person 113
  open court, principle of – *see* **open**
    court, the
  parties, duties of 509
  pleading – *see* **pleading**
  pointless 320, 1001–1002
   – *and see* **protracted legal**
    proceedings, avoiding
  publicity of – *see* **open court, the**
  reporting, restrictions on – *see* **open**
    court, the
  rules of court – *see* **court**
  satellite litigation, – *see* protracted
    legal proceedings, avoiding

legal proceedings – *contd*
  seat of justice, access to – *see*
    justice
  service of process – *see* **service**
  technicality, need to minimize – *see*
    technicalities
   – *and see* **advocate; court;**
    doubtful penalisation,
    principle against; equity;
    justice; legal aid; legal
    policy; limitation of
    actions; predictability of
    law; procedure, civil;
    procedure, criminal
legal scholars – *see* **jurists**
legal terms
  contextual interpretation of 1200
  conveyancing 190
  creation, judicial, of 1213
  free-standing 28, 1199–1200
  interpretation of 1199–1203
   – *and see* **technical terms**
  multi-jurisdictional enactments, in 1202–
    1203
  status, as to 1201–1202
  terms of art 1200–1201
  uncertain meaning of 1202
legal thrust of enactment 15, 391, 392,
    396, 416, 417, 419,
    421–423, 425, 428,
    433, 516, 941, 1174,
    1175, 1267
  – *and see* **comminution;**
    enactment; factual outline,
    the; precision drafting;
    selective comminution
legality, principle of (constitutional
  rights) 2, 190, 773, 822–823, 843–844,
    1048n, 1324, S81, S82
Leggatt LJ 1013n
legislation – *see* **Act of Parliament;**
  delegated legislation; intention,
  legislative; legal regimes;
  legislator; statute; statute law;
  tacit legislation
  ancient 695
  duty to obey – see **disobeying Act;**
    ignorantia juris neminem
    excusat
  extra-territorial – *see*
    extra-territoriality
  modifying a judicial decision 401
  promotion of S63
  understanding of 40–44, 801, 1184–1185
   – *and see* **user of legislation**
legislation by reference – *see*
  incorporation by reference
Legislative and Regulatory Reform
  Act 2006 91

All references are to page numbers

---

legislative drafting – *see* **drafting, legislative**

legislative history
amendment to Bill and   640–641
basic rule   610–612
commentaries on Act   712
committee reports   614–616, 694, 696–697, 711–712, 924, 936–937
consolidation Acts and   604–607
costs and   612, 624
delegated legislation and   266, 598
enacting history   588–590, 609–702
guidelines   704, S71
Hansard   616–640, 1245, 1332
   – *and see* **exclusionary rule, the;** *Pepper v Hart*, **rule in**
inherent power of court to consider   123, 692
inspection of, by court   691–692
legislative intention, as guide to   697–698
literal meaning and   700–701
mischief, to ascertain   696–697
nature of   598, 610–612
official statements on meaning of Act   702–706, S70
parliamentary history – *see* **exclusionary rule, the;** *Pepper v Hart*, **rule in**
persuasive nature of   698–701
post-enacting history   588–590, 702–712
pre-enacting history   588–590, 599–604, 1208–1209
private judicial use of   691
specific reference to in enactment   612–614
treaty – *see* **treaty**
weight given to   610, 612, 892–893
white papers and   643, 692n
   – *and see* **amendment to Bill; Bill, parliamentary; comity;** *contemporanea expositio*; **informed interpretation; judicial notice; Law Commission; legal meaning; predictability of law; tax avoidance; taxing Acts**

legislative intention – *see* **intention, legislative**

legislative sentence   398
   – *and see* **drafting, legislative; enactment**

legislative steer   782

legislator
early – *see* **statute**
executive as – *see* **Minister of the Crown**

legislator – *contd*
intention of – *see* **intention, legislative**
interpreter, as   26–27
judge as – *see* **court**
mistake by – *see* **mistake**
nature of   26–27
purpose of – *see* **purposive construction**
   – *and see* **Parliament**

legitimate expectation – *see* **decision-making rules**

LEGOL   473n, 1174

Leigh, Ian – *see* **Bibliography (pp 1475 to 1507)**

Leng, Roger – *see* **Bibliography (pp 1475 to 1507)**

Lenz, Adv Gen   1284n

Lester of Herne Hill, Lord – *see* **Bibliography (pp 1475 to 1507)**

Leung, Matthew – *see* **Bibliography (pp 1475 to 1507)**

Lewis, B N – *see* **Bibliography (pp 1475 to 1507)**

Lewis, G – *see* **Bibliography (pp 1475 to 1507)**

Lewison J   S21

lex non cogit ad impossibilia – *see* **impossibility**

liabilities, statutory transfer of   827

liberal construction – *see* **strict and liberal construction**

liberty of the person – *see* **legal policy; doubtful penalisation, principle against**

liberty removed not granted   782–783, 821–822, 844–845, 859

licensing – *see* **enforcement agencies; local authority**

Lightman J   32, 128, 508, 704, 891, 1156, 1241, 1379, 1455

limitation of actions
anomalies   988, 993
Crown and – *see* **Crown**
equity, and   500
exterritoriality, and   370
historical   996
ignorance of law, and   44
judicial treatment of   130
pleading of – *see* **pleading**
procedural and substantive rules, distinction between   392, 948–949
reasons for   800–801, 932, 996
rectification and   173
retrospectivity and   321
specialties and   39
   – *and see* **specialty**
statutory right and   601

All references are to page numbers

Lincoln (Anthony) J   500
Lindley MR   371, 697, 1236
Lindsay J   46, 452
linguistic canons – *see* **canons of
    construction, linguistic**
literal construction
    anomaly and   997–998
    arguments for and against   42, 461–463,
           803, 864–869, 1002–
             1003
    context and   840
    enacting history and   700–701
    integrity of Act, preserving, and   1029
    Law Commission's criticism of   461–462
    legal certainty and   803
    maxims and   1101
    nature of   432, 455–456, 458–461, 533
    ouster clauses, watering down of   108
    public interest and   791
    – *and see* **canons of
        construction, linguistic;
        factual outline; 'literal
        rule'; predictability of law**
'literal rule'   12, 13, 457, 458, 459, 460,
           545, 547–459, 653,
           864–869, 1177, 1178,
             1179
    – *and see* **literal construction**
litigation – *see* **doubtful penalisation,
    principle against; legal
    proceedings**
Littledale J   412, 994
Littleton (Thomas) J   26n, 30, 1186
Llewellyn, Karl   815
    – *and see* **Bibliography (pp 1475
        to 1507)**
Lloyd J   31, 311, 681, 810
Lloyd of Berwick, Lord   153, 601
local Act   92, 123, 183, 185, 203, 245, 743,
           793, 1229, 1242,
           1247 – *see* **private Act**
local authority
    administration of enactment by   87, 97,
           366, 1002
    audit of   76
    charges, power to make   88, 1048
    councillors etc 934, 953, 1001, 1139–1140
    delay by   1149, S103
    European Convention on Human
        Rights and   1319
    legal proceedings by   74, 815
    licensing by   92
    local Acts, and – *see* **local Act**
    Local Commissioner for
        Administration   1140
    local planning authority   87
    meetings of   54
    officer of   1107
    'person aggrieved', as   173

local authority – *contd*
    policy decision by   83
    powers of   87–88, 400, 497–498, 1047–
             1048, S51
    residential accommodation,
        provision of   S106
    taxation by   1047–1048
    territory of   351
    – *and see* **adoptive Act;
        byelaws; enforcement
        agencies; provisional
        order; public authority**
local government
    change to structure of   S59–60
local land charges register   1397
location, deemed   327, 387, 389–390
Lock, G F – *see* **Bibliography (pp
    1475 to 1507)**
Locke, John   39, 773, 800, 801
    – *and see* **Bibliography (pp 1475
        to 1507)**
logic, use of in interpretation
    ambiguous middle term   1175–1177
    conceptualism – *see* **conceptualism**
    contradiction, principle of   1177–1179
    deductive reasoning   1171–1179
    hypothetical syllogism   1174–1175
    implication   1173
    inarticulate major premise – *see*
        judge
    inductive and deductive reasoning   1172–
             1173
    interpretation, use in   126, 986–987
    syllogism   1172–1175
    symbolic   1174
    – *and see* **LEGOL**
London borough   1397
London, Greater   6n, 292
long title
    drafting deficiencies, remedying, by
        reference to   730
    ejusdem generis principle and   1234
    extent of Act and   336–337
    function of   727–731
    interpretative use of   379, 701, 727–731,
           1098, 1099
    mischief, identifying, by   935, 941
    mistakes in   730–731
    parliamentary procedure and   717, 728
    purpose, legislative, and   960–961
Lopes LJ   1251
Lord Chancellor   3, 140, 217, 219, 222,
           231, 1045, 1397
Lord Chancellor's Department   229n
Lords, House of
    abolition of, proposals for   405
    Appellate Committee, of   151–153
    appellate functions of   148–153
    commune forum, as   333, S42

All references are to page numbers

Lords, House of – *contd*
law, duty to oversee 151–152
legislative procedure 213–216
 – *and see* **Act of Parliament**
legislature, as part of 40, 475
precedent and 168, 174–175
 – *and see* **precedent, doctrine of**
resolutions of 248–249
revising chamber as x
 – *and see* **Act of Parliament;**
    Lord Chancellor;
    Northern Ireland;
    Parliament; precedent,
    doctrine of; Scotland
Loreburn, Lord 412, 787
Lowry, Lord 163n 203, 524, 566, 620, 753,
    958, 1042, 1053, 1054,
    1065
Lücke, Horst Klaus 8n, 546
 – *and see* **Bibliography (pp 1475**
    to 1507)
Lush J 724
Lushington, Dr 372, 558, 874, 1007, 1182
Lusky Louis 893n
 – *and see* **Bibliography (pp**
    1507)
Luxmoore LJ 659
Lyndhurst, Lord 30
Lynskey J 907
MacCormick, D N 8n, 131, 430, 437, 538n,
    770, 808, 1178
 – *and see* **Bibliography (pp 1475**
    to 1507)
MacDermott, Lord 442, 1220
Mackay of Clashfern, Lord 617, 624
Mackinnon LJ 452
 – *and see* **Bibliography (pp 1475**
    to 1507)
Macmillan, Lord 79, 377, 414n, 956, 1198
Macnaghten, Lord 331, 545, 784, 796, 804,
    1223
Macpherson J 210
magistrates' court
appeals from 145
appeals to 145
commonsense construction rule, and 558
definition of 1397
jurisdiction, civil 75, 92, 141, 1259
jurisdiction, criminal 141, 315, 998n
lay magistrates 92, 141, 558
procedure before 279, 884, 997, 1060,
    1202
supervisory functions of 92
warrant 811, 1075
 – and *see* **contempt of court;**
    court; death; evidence;
    inherent judicial powers;
    legal proceedings;
    procedure, criminal

Magna Carta 180, 189n, 412, 836, 837n,
    847, 853, 912, 916,
    1014, 1351
Maine, Henry J S 817, 895
 – *and see* **Bibliography (pp 1475**
    to 1507)
maintenance 199, 777–778, S77
Maitland, F W 11, 104n, 204, 234n, 894n,
    1165
 – *and see* **Bibliography (pp 1475**
    to 1507)
mala in se 39, 1049
mala prohibita 39, 1049
 – *and see* **strict liability**
maladministration 135n, 681, 1140
 – *and see* **enforcement agencies**
malice 80, 93, 417, 895, 1092
Mallory, J R – *see* **Bibliography (pp**
    1475 to 1507)
Man, Isle of 342, 346, 347, 351–352, 484
Mance LJ 1289, S32, S43
Mancini J 1301
 – *and see* **Bibliography (pp 1475**
    to 1507)
mandatory and directory
    requirements 23, 40, 44–57, 63, 65,
        66, 110, 114, 118, 248,
        253, 256, 285, 397,
        400, 460, 569n, 956,
        1055n, 1132, 1133n,
        1469, 1471
mandatory order (mandamus) – *see*
    injunction; judicial review
Mann LJ 109, 110, 120, 413, 435, 614, 736,
    779, 905, 1095, 1168
Mann, F A 690n
 – *and see* **Bibliography (pp 1475**
    to 1507)
Mansfield, Lord 365, 463, 604, 708, 780,
    800, 845, 1011, 1108
Marcello, D A 477n
 – *and see* **Bibliography (pp 1475**
    to 1507)
Marcellus 1209
margin of appreciation 1281, 1282, 1314,
    1318, 1326, 1327,
    1361, 1369
marginal note – *see* **sidenote to**
    section
Mark, R 922n
 – *and see* **Bibliography (pp 1475**
    to 1507)
market 1037
Markesinis, Basil – *see* **Bibliography**
    (pp 1475 to 1507)
Markson, H E 805
 – *and see* **Bibliography (pp 1475**
    to 1507)

All references are to page numbers

Marleasing principle   1298–1299, 1323,
                                            S111
Marmor, A   13
marriage   911, 1099, 1132, 1215–1216
Martin, Andrew – *see* Bibliography
    (pp 1475 to 1507)
Martin, B   1187, 1221
masculine and feminine – *see* gender
Mason CJ   360n, 651, 676
    – *and see* Bibliography (pp 1475
      to 1507)
massage parlours, licensing of   92, 185
Maugham, Viscount   956
Maule J   1212
    maxims, legal   1103
    nature of   1101–1103
Maxwell, D – *see* Bibliography (pp
    1475 to 1507)
Maxwell, Peter   7
    – *and see* Bibliography (pp 1475
      to 1507)
May LJ   43, 142, 603, 942, 1102
May, Thomas Erskine – *see*
    Bibliography (pp 1475 to 1507)
McCardie J   1235, 1237, 1243, 1244
McCowan LJ   602, 1013
McCullough J   433, 1006
McGlynn, C   133
    – *and see* Bibliography (pp 1475
      to 1507)
McKenzie friend   112, S17, S18, S20
McLeod, Ian   13n, 122n, 132, 637, 638n,
                                  1092n, 1223n
    – *and see* Bibliography (pp 1475
      to 1507)
McNair, A D – *see* Bibliography (pp
    1475 to 1507)
McNeill LJ   1227
McWhirter, Norris   65
meaning – *see* archaisms; composite
    expressions; grammatical
    meaning; homonyms; judicial
    notice; legal meaning; legal
    terms; meaningless terms;
    noscitur a sociis principle;
    ordinary meaning; technical
    terms; updating construction;
    words
meaningless terms   453–455, 1219, 1220–
                                            1221
Measure, interpretation of   1391
mechanical etc apparatus – *see*
    description, statutory
medical treatment   833–834, 921–922
Megarry V-C   32, 234, 246n, 753, 754, 783,
                        950, 1002, 1028, 1189,
                                  1246, 1257
    – *and see* Bibliography (pp 1475
      to 1507)

Megaw LJ   802
Mellinkoff, D   171n, 185n, 751, 757
    – *and see* Bibliography (pp 1475
      to 1507)
Mellish LJ   61, 1065
Mellone, S H   1174
    – *and see* Bibliography (pp 1475
      to 1507)
mens rea – *see* criminal law
mental disability   52, 77, 125, 867, 884, 887
    – *and see* incompetents
Miers, D R   7, 549
    – *and see* Bibliography (pp 1475
      to 1507)
Mill, J S   1224
Millett, Lord   446, 494, 633, 710, 809, 969,
                              1124, 1323, S104
Milmo J   555
Milner, JB – *see* Bibliography (pp
    1475 to 1507)
Milton, John   952
    – *and see* Bibliography (pp 1475
      to 1507)
Minister of the Crown
    administration of enactment by   85–86
      – *and see* enforcement agencies
    certifying of facts by   824
    delegation by   88–89, 273
      – *and see* decision-making rules
    delegation to   241, 251–252
      – *and see* delegated legislation
    knowledge, imputation of   87, 88–89
    policy decision by   82
    powers under Legislative and
      Regulatory Reform Act 2006   91
    remedies against   207–208
    submissions to court by   86
    transfer of functions of   85–86
      – *and see* Attorney General;
        Carltona principle;
        Crown; discretion;
        enforcement agencies;
        government; legislative
        history; legislator;
        Lord Chancellor; Ministry
        of Justice; prerogative,
        Royal; Prime Minister;
        Secretary of State
Ministry of Justice   252
minor – *see* age; children; wardship
mischief
    ambit of   77–78, 929
    ascertaining the   621, 696–697, 931–933
    casus male inclusus and   887–889
    changes in   895–897
    changes in law, and   897
    common law mischiefs, examples of   920
    counter-mischief – *see*
      counter-mischief

All references are to page numbers

mischief – *contd*
drafting error, as 924–925
enactment, of 929–933
Heydon's Case, resolution in 697, 918–922
identifying 929, 933, 935–937
in pari materia Acts and 708–710
interpretation by reference to 883, 937–939, 1000–1001, 1245
legal 916–917, 923–926
lesser includes greater 557
meaning of 916–918
multiple ordinary meanings and 1188
objections to the term 922–923
party-political 927–929, 940–941
phasing out of 934
preamble as guide to 731–933
presumptions as to 80, 915
remedy for 78–79, 933–734, 940–942
social 78–79, 772, 901–904, 916, 922–923
statutory 923–926
treaty, giving domestic legislative effect to, and 935
unknown 936–937
 – *and see* **'mischief rule'**;
  Pepper v Hart, **rule in**;
  purposive construction;
  updating construction
'mischief rule' 12–13, 545, 943
misdemeanour, statutory 63, 64, 199, 922
 – *and see* **contempt of statute**
misdescription 1024
misfeasance in public office – *see*
  public office
misrepresentation 43, 446, 622, 793
 – *and see* **tort**
mistake
Act, in 228
defence, as 41–42
drafting in 415
enactment procedure in 232–236
fact, as to 41, 421, 883
law, as to – *see* **mistake of law**; *per incuriam* **decisions**
mitigation as 40
rectifying mistake of law – *see*
  rectifying construction
statutory interpretation, in 293n, 303–304, 1156
 – *and see communis error facit jus*; **drafting error;
  judges; jurisdiction;
  mistake of law; precedent,
  doctrine of; printing
  corrections; rectifying
  construction; Royal
  assent; slip rule**
mistake of law
Acts, in 228

mistake of law – *contd*
compensation for 41
drafter, by 27, 1270
fact, when mistake as to constitutes
  mistake of law 421
general 41–42
guidelines, in 129
ignorantia juris neminem excusat –
  see ignorantia juris neminem excusat
judge, by 108, 135
Parliament, by 604, 694–695, 709–710
slip rule 110, S18
 – *and see* **mistake;** *Padfield*
  approach; *per incuriam*
  **decisions; rectifying
  construction**
modus et conventio vincunt legem 57
Mogridge, C – *see* **Bibliography (pp
  1475 to 1507)**
Moncrieff, Lord 337
money
bill – *see* **money Bill**
foreign 378
public 84–85, 126, 190–191, 1130
references to 245, 378, 909
resource implications relative to
  decision making 107, 126–127
 – *and see* **Bill, parliamentary;
  Commons, house of;
  Crown; debt, statutory;
  Parliament; Parliament
  Acts 1911 and 1949; Royal
  assent; tax avoidance;
  taxing Acts**
money Bill 191n, 223, 224, 251n, 567
Monmouthshire 352–353
'month', definition of 1397
Moorcock, the, doctrine of – *see*
  business
moot point 143
moral duty 39, 407–408, 780–781, 939
 – *and see* **immorality; legal policy**
More, Thomas 35
 – *and see* **Bibliography (pp 1475
  to 1507)**
Morgan J S44
Morgan, Jonathan – *see*
  Bibliography (pp 1475 to 1507)
Morle, André – *see* **Bibliography (pp
  1475 to 1507)**
Morris of Borth-y-Gest, Lord 178, 233, 475, 732, 873, 1056
Morris, Geoffrey ix
Morris, J H C – *see* **Bibliography
  (pp 1475 to 1507)**
Morritt V-C 775, 1372, 1379
Morton of Henryton, Lord 573, 709n, 791n
Moses L J 634, 635, 693, 799

All references are to page numbers

Moses LJ – *see* Bibliography (pp
    1475 to 1507)
Moulton, Lord   658
multilingual systems – *see* legal
    meaning
Mummery LJ   105n, 128, 135n, 431, 615,
    797, 848, 1105, 1139,
    1142n, 1314, S28, S56
Munday, Roderick   579n, 638, 643n, 857n,
    1103
    – *and see* Bibliography (pp 1475
    to 1507)
Munro, C R – *see* Bibliography (pp
    1475 to 1507)
Murphy, Jim   91
Murphy, W I – *see* Bibliography (pp
    1475 to 1507)
Murray, D F – *see* Bibliography (pp
    1475 to 1507)
Mustill, Lord   113, 125, 143, 322, 681, 778,
    869, 1058, 1059, 1143
name, company   37
National Debt Commissioners   1397
natural justice
    contrary legislative intention and   1060–
    1062
    criminal law and   1081
    European Community law, in – *see*
    European Community law
    fairness   211–212, 374, 430–431, 460,
    797–798, 977, 1055–
    1059, 1111–1115,
    1352, 1353, 1355,
    1357
    legitimate expectation and   1056–1057
    mandatory and directory
    requirements – *see* **mandatory**
    and directory requirements
    nature of   148, 1058
    reasons, duty to give   1062–1064
    representations, opportunity to
    make   1058–1059
    requirements of   316
    transparency   1059
    – *and see* ***audi alteram partem***;
    decision-making rules;
    justice; nemo debet esse
    judex in propria causa;
    notice; retrospectivity
natural law   233, 407–408, 773, 1137, 1141
ne exeat regno – *see* prerogative,
    Royal
necessitas non habet legem – *see*
    necessity
necessity – – *see* duress;
    impossibility; *impotentia*
    excusat legem
negative resolution procedure – *see*
    delegated legislation

negligence
    breach of statutory duty   71, 82–84
    contributory   114
    European Convention on Human
    Rights and   1349
    not impliedly authorised by statute   68
    nuisance and   1076
    tort of   419, 537–538, 579, 775, 833–834
    vicarious liability for   1074
    – *and see* natural justice;
    nuisance; tort
Neill LJ   50n, 201, 563, 1086
Neill of Bladen, Lord – *see*
    Bibliography (pp 1475 to 1507)
nemo debet bis vexari – *see* B
nemo debet esse judex in propria
    causa   1056, 1136
neologism   1181, 1211, 1213
Neuberger of Abbotsbury, Lord   190, 524,
    595, 695, 747n, 1311,
    1339, S26, S27, S65,
    S107
New Zealand
    extra-territorial legislation and   327
    Hansard, use of, in   679–680, S67
    international legislation, common
    approach to, and   333
    Law Commission   679
    liberal construction requirement, in   519
    Maori land   1206
    national law, reading as consistent
    with international law   S80
    Statute of Westminster and   339
    tax avoidance and   1018n
    Westminster Parliament and   327, 338,
    348n
Newey, Judge John   815
Newman, Cardinal   26
Nicholl MR   718
Nicholls of Birkenhead, Lord   75, 95n, 144,
    192, 333n, 470, 494,
    506, 592, 875, 946n,
    1059, 1089, 1200,
    1264, 1312, 1317,
    1322, 1325, 1326,
    1332, 1339, 1340,
    1362, 1366
nobile officium   877, 878
Nolan, Lord   130, 446, 775, 844, 1139
non liquet principle   24, 448, 453
    – *and see* meaningless terms
non obstante, device of   238
non-existence – *see* existence
non-justitiable matters   107, 360, 364
Norman, Ken – *see* Bibliography (pp
    1475 to 1507)
Normand, Lord   430, 589n
North J   1001

All references are to page numbers

Northern Ireland

application of legislation 1393

extent of Act to 336–338

– *and see* **territorial extent of Act**

Northern Ireland Court of Criminal Appeal 322

'Northern Ireland legislation', definition of 1397

Northern Ireland Statutory Publications Office 232n

territory of 354, 355

terrorism and 820

noscitur a sociis **principle** 525, 1225–1231, 1234, 1259, 1262

– *and see ejusdem generis* **principle; rank principle**

notes on clauses 641–642, 642, 643, 663, 699

notice, statutory

appeal, of 56

construction of 55

fax, by 1149

form of 54

fraudulent 793

internet, by 1149

invalid 871

mandatory or directory, whether 50, 54, 55

need for 59, 422, 957, 1113, 1255, 1261

quit, to 1072

service of 38, 55n, 570, 582–583, 1113, 1149

waiver of 59–60, 1068–1069

withdrawal of 55, 1068–1089

– *and see audi alteram partem* **principle; enforcement notice; general notice**

Nottingham, Lord 653

Nourse LJ 172, 793, 971, 1113, 1159, 1192, 1227

Nugee, E 1158

nuisance

byelaws for suppression of 269

common 1201

history of 1075–1076

ingredients of 1075–1076

power to take proceedings for 815

statutory 163, 1002

varieties of 1075–1076

whether authorised by statute 68, 82–83, 200–201, 1075–1076

whether committed where statutory power exercised 498, 1075–1076

– *and see* **negligence; tort**

nullus commodum capere potest de injuria sua propria 1141

number 579–581, 1387–1388

– *and see* **fractions; singular and plural**

O'Boyle, M – *see* **Bibliography (pp 1475 to 1507)**

objective test

duress 1134–1135

justice, and 123

provocation and 504, 578, S96

statutory duty, as to 65–66, 68, 80

obscurity, semantic

'corrected version' 451–455, 551, 954

interpretative factors and 531–532, 954

nature of 451–455, 954

remedying 451–455, 531–532

– *and see* **disorganised composition; plain meaning rule; rectifying construction**

Odgers, Charles 7, 647n, 902n, 1233

– *and see* **Bibliography (pp 1475 to 1507)**

offence

duplicated 583, 810, 1391

extra-territoriality and 374

– *and see* **extra-territoriality**

ingredients of 202

location of 374

meaning 1119

prosecution of – *see* **prosecution of offences**

– *and see* **contempt of court; contempt of statute; criminal law; criminal procedure**

office – *see* **public office**

Office of Fair Trading 87, 92

Office of Public Sector Information (OPSI) 227

Official Journal of the European Communities 1283

Official Solicitor, the 799

officer of Revenue and Customs 1398

oil rig, law prevailing on 386

Oliver of Aylmerton, Lord 670, 986n, 1455

Ombudsman

general 80, S11

Parliamentary 157n

Pensions 106, 142

omission of words – *see* **rectifying construction**

omission to act 327, 387–389, 895, 1193

omne majus continet in se minus – *see* **greater includes less**

omnia praesumuntur rite et solemniter esse acta – *see* **correctness, presumption of**

onus of proof – *see* **burden of proof**

open court, principle of the

hearings in camera 119–120

open court, principle of the – *contd*
nature of 103, 118, 1115, 1357
reporting restrictions and 119–120, 306,
528, 845, 867–868,
936
– *and see* **anonymity**
transparency S29
opposing constructions
ambiguity and 448–450
– *and see* **ambiguity
(grammatical)**
examples of 467, 841, 998, 1007–1008
form of 429–438
inquisitorial proceedings, in 436
significance of 123, 429–438, 695, 871,
1176
– *and see* **interpretative factors**
Order in Council 85, 194, 237–240, 250,
266, 286, 344
Order of Council 251
order, search for 1, 6
order, administrative or legislative 89,
267–268, 278, 1051
– *and see* **commencement order;
costs; court; delegated
legislation; enforcement
agencies; executive
instrument; Order in
Council; Order of Council;
provisional order;
revocation, power of; special
procedure order;** *ultra vires*,
doctrine of
order, court
consent 116, S18
inherent powers of court regarding 112,
1002–1003
invalid, duty to obey until set aside 102,
115–116
jurisdiction, made without 50
– *and see* **jurisdiction**
quashing of 116, 787
statutory power to make 104
ultra vires 91
ordinance 271, 272, 359, 802, 1228
ordnance map 1398
ordinary meaning
constructive meaning and 1193
educated usage, in 1184–1185
foreign context, ordinary English
meaning presumed 1193
multiple ordinary meanings 1186–1188
nature of 443–444, 1181–1193
no ordinary meaning 1188
non-legal expertise, used to
determine 1183
officially laid down 1183
prima facie to be given 177–178, 870

ordinary meaning – *contd*
substance rather than form
presumed, in 1191–1192
technical meaning and 1198–1199, 1206–
1209
– *and see* **plain meaning rule;
technical terms; uniform
statutes**
ordination of women 293n
Orkneys, the 347, 356
Ormrod LJ 810, 904, 929, 964, 984, 1007,
1200
Ostler clause – *see* **judicial review**
Otton LJ 331n
ouster clause – *see* **jurisdiction**
outer London borough 1397
overlapping meaning 1160, 1189, 1194–
1195, 1197
– *and see* **belt-and-braces phrase;
words**
overruling 172–177
– *and see* **precedent, doctrine of**
pacta privata juri publico derogare
non possunt 60, 61
Padfield **approach** 53, 89, 90, 260, S12
– *and see* **delegated legislation;
discretion**
Page, Alan C 7
– *and see* **Bibliography (pp 1475
to 1507)**
pairs of words – *see* **words**
Pakistan x
palm tree justice 471, 513, 551
Pannick, David 594, 595
– *and see* **Bibliography (pp 1475
to 1507)**
paragraphing – *see* **format of Act**
pardon
Bill for 213
power to grant 238n
parens patriae **doctrine** – *see* **Crown**
Park J 523
Parke, B 514, 653, 875, 879, 1105, 1182
Parker CB 847n
Parker LJ 835, 998, 1158, 1159
Parker, Graham 7
– *and see* **Bibliography (pp 1475
to 1507)**
Parker, Lord 404, 824, 865, 908, 938, 953,
992, 1026, 1145, 1186,
1222, 1244, 1267
Parliament – *see* **Act of Parliament;
Bill, parliamentary; Clerk of
the Parliaments; delegated
legislation; evidence; intention,
legislative; legislative history;
legislator; Lords, House of;
mistake; Parliament Acts 1911
and 1949; printing corrections;**

All references are to page numbers

Parliament – *contd*
Royal assent; tacit legislation; territorial extent of Act
absurd result, does not intend 969–971, S92
body purporting to assume function of 180
does nothing in vain 1000, 1157
ellipsis, recognition of 493–494 *see* **ellipsis**
government as emanation of 475
journals of 181, 234–235
judges and 1325
judicial function of 152
jurisdiction of – *see* **territorial extent of Act**
justly, presumed to act 795–799, 963–965, 1104
– *and see* **justice**
law and custom of 743
law, knowledge of, presumed to have 547
legality, principle of 822–823, S81, S82
legislative intention 471
members of 40
mistake as to existing law, by 709–710
'Muslim Parliament', so-called 180n
ouster clause and parliamentary sovereignty S16
powers of, curbs on 405
powers of and powers of executive S15
powers of, and powers of executive S15
primary law making role S37
privilege of 182, 666–673, 1049
– *and see* **contempt of Parliament**
procedure of, control over 181, 714–715
proceedings in 644–645
– *and see* **exclusionary rule, the; Pepper v Hart, rule in**
prorogation of 222
public expenditure, authority for 1047–1049
Roll – *see* **Parliament Roll**
session 719
sovereignty of 197, 233, 236, 316, 406–407, 409
style of 354
taxing powers of 1047–1049
– *and see* **Commons, House of; tax avoidance; taxing Acts**
Parliament Acts 1911 and 1949
Acts that have been passed under 225, 246
money Bills and 224–225
other Bills, and 224–225
remodelling of legislative procedure by 242
validity of 235
Parliament Roll 227, 234, 751–752, 757

Parliamentary agent 184
Parliamentary Bar 184
Parliamentary Counsel 40, 66, 250, 264, 476, 738
Parliamentary Counsel Office 415, 476, 724
Parliamentary election 1398
Parliamentary proceedings, privileged 182, 666–673, 678n
– *and see* **contempt of Parliament; Parliament**
Parmoor, Lord 55, 239
Parris, H W – *see* **Bibliography (pp 1475 to 1507)**
Parts, division of Act into 749–750
– *and see* **Australia; format of Act**
patents 333, 411, 548, 570, S67–8
Patten J S23
Patterson J 669
Patteson J 994n, 1129
PAYE income 1398
PAYE regulations 1398
peace, Queen's 93, 96, 791–792, S13
Pearce, D C 8
– *and see* **Bibliography (pp 1475 to 1507)**
Pearce, Lord 131, 1036
Pearson, Lord 403
penal Act – *see* **doubtful penalisation, principle against; retrospectivity; uniform statutes**
Pennycuik J 983
Penzance, Lord 47, 723, 1215
Pepper v Hart, **facts and law in** 627–632
Pepper v Hart, **rule in**
advocate, duty of 623–627
clarity of sponsor's statement, need for 616
constitutional law and 618
control of its procedure by court and 680–682
costs and 624
criminal statutes, application to 633
de bene esse admission 596
earlier decision, overruling 616, 627
enactments to which applicable 618–621
facts and law in *Pepper v Hart,* 444
inadmissibility of ministerial statement on Act, under 705
judicial application of 620–621
judicial practice prior to 654–666
– *and see* **exclusionary rule, the**
legislative history, and 616–640
mischief aimed at by enactment 621
objections to 672
– *and see* **exclusionary rule, the**
parliamentary materials 616, 617, S64–66, S69

All references are to page numbers

***Pepper v Hart*, rule in** – *contd*
  penal statutes, application to   633
  promoter's statements   616, 622–623
  relaxation of   S65–66
  resolution of House of Commons
    and   617
  sponsor's statements   616, 622–623
  statement of rule   616
  when applicable   616, 617–618
  – *and see* **amendment to Bill;**
    contempt of Parliament
perfection, alteration of order before
  or after   112, S18
***per incuriam* decision**
  commonsense construction rule,
    failure to apply, and   554
  departure from   173–174, 504n
  examples of   106, 173–174, 583n, 730,
      1329
  nature of   173–174, 554
  – *and see* **comity**
'person'   576–579, 1399
  substance form or part of   576
  – *and see* **Interpretation Act 1978**
personal Act   136, 183, 184, 185, 743, 1163,
      1374, 1440
  – *and see* **private Act**
perverting the course of justice   S47
Phillimore LJ   715, 748, 1224, 1454, 1455
Phillimore, Robert   818
  – *and see* **Bibliography (pp 1475**
    to 1507)
Phillips of Worth Matravers MR,
  Lord   32, 508, 817, 1103, 1145, 1194,
      1278, 1319, S80, S81,
      S101
Phillips, G G – *see* **Bibliography (pp**
  1475 to 1507)
Pigot's case, rule in   236
Pill LJ   137n, 183, 294n, 360, 415, 974n,
      1113
Pitt, William (Lord Chatham)   1124
place   388, 1267–1268
  – *and see* **application of Act;**
    location, deemed; omission to
    act
plain English – *see* **plain language**
  movement
plain language movement   36
plain meaning rule
  codifying Acts and   609
  – *and see* **codification**
  consolidation Acts and   605
  – *and see* **consolidation Act**
  meaning of   548–551
  where meaning not 'plain'   551
  – *and see* **interpretative**
    criteria; interpretative
    factors

pleading
  demurrer   426
  implied application of rules of   114
  matters required to be pleaded   58, 393
  punctuation in   752
Plowden, E   206
Plowman J   517
Plucknett, T F T   7, 8, 513, 652, 653n, 972n,
      1010
  – *and see* **Bibliography (pp 1475**
    to 1507)
plural – *see* **singular and plural**
police
  acting in execution of duty   1126–1127
  'acting in execution of' an Act   95
  area   1398
  arrest powers   152
  authority   1398
  chief constables, duties of   98
  constable, office of   93, 199, 425, 1075,
      1263
  criminal records and related
    information, retention and
    release of   S113
  discipline   1095, 1268
  duty to enforce law   98, 844, 934, 974
  – *and see* **legal policy;**
    prosecution of offences
  entry, powers of   199, 201
  investigation by   93, 783, 837, 1117, 1358
  obstruction of   1133
  prosecution and – *see* **Crown**
    Prosecution Service;
    prosecution of offences
  stop and search   1360
  – *and see* ***de minimis non curat***
    ***lex*; evidence; good**
    administration, duty of
politic uncertainty   52, 684, 1323
political factors
  commencement of Act, affecting   283–284
  drafting style, affected by   763
  enactment, behind   484, S50
  evasion of Act, in relation to   1015–1016
  exercise of statutory power, behind   1268–
      1269
  party ideology   922, 1219
  politic uncertainty – *see* **politic**
    uncertainty
  purpose clause   734
  – *and see* **purpose clause**
  Sunday observance   895
  unnecessary legislation, behind   916n,
      927–928
  – *and see* **mischief**
Pollock CB   78, 516, 655, 1187, 1221
Pollock MR   58

All references are to page numbers

Pollock, Frederick 32
– *and see* **Bibliography (pp 1475 to 1507)**
polygamy 929, 1098
Pope, Alexander 131
– *and see* **Bibliography (pp 1475 to 1507)**
Popplewell J 305, 527, 644, 668n, 669, S39
Porter, Lord 435, 729, 941, 1229
– *and see* **Bibliography (pp 1475 to 1507)**
post, service by – *see* **service**
Potter LJ 1161
Potter, Platt – *see* **Bibliography (pp 1475 to 1507)**
Potts J 131
Powell J 653
power – *see* **executive power, abuse of; statutory power**
practice
archival drafting and 199, 759–761, S76
changes in 34
codification of 608
contemporanea expositio – *see* ***contemporanea expositio***
directions 112n
interpretation, effect on 51, 321
origin of 34
preservation of 199, 913
Royal assent, concerning – *see* **Royal assent**
saving for – *see* **saving**
– *and see* **statutory power**
practitioner, central function of – *see* **central function of practitioner**
Prashar, Lady (Usha) 3
– *and see* **Bibliography (pp 1475 to 1507)**
Pratt CJ 846
preamble
interpretative use of 356, 731–733, 961, 1099
mischief, determining, by 935
nature of 339, 731–733
private Acts, in 731–733
purpose, legislative, and 356, 961
repeal of 731–733
statutory instrument 254
use of 731–733
– *and see* **evidence; private Act; purpose clause; recital**
precedent, doctrine of
common law and 177
Court of Appeal and 174, S29
erroneous decisions and 503–504
European Court of Justice and 177
factual outline, the – *see* **factual outline, the**
irreconcilable decisions S30

precedent, doctrine of – *contd*
law reports, and 854–855
Lords, House of, and 168, 174–175, 504
nature of 168–178, 427, 502–504, 514, 808–809
obiter dictum 168, S28
obsolete precedent 172
over-generalising facts 424
overruling – *see* **overruling**
Pepper v Hart, rule in, implications for 627
per incuriam decision – *see* ***per incuriam* decisions**
previous transactions, effect on 175–176
ratio decidendi 168, S28
reasons, failure to give 169
– *and see* **reasons, duty to give**
references to European Court of Justice and 1305–1306
– *and see* **interstitial articulation; legal thrust of enactment; processing of enactments, dynamic; sub-rules**
precision drafting
comminution and 401–404
implied repeal, presumption against, and 305
nature of 409–413, 709, 1234
provisos and 723–725
punctuation and 752
sanctions for breach of Act, statement of 75
selective comminution and 402–403
predictability of law
declaration of incompatibility, and – *see* **Human Rights Act 1998**
European Community law principle of 801–803, 1277–1278
– *and see* **European Community law**
European Convention on Human Rights and 1322
knowability – *see* **promulgation of Act**
literal construction and 869
principle of 590–591, 799–807
sentencing and 803–804
– *and see* **differential readings; legal policy; legislative history; retrospectivity**
preposition 755, 756, 1189
prerogative instrument
interpretation of 240, 818
nature of 237–240, S33

All references are to page numbers

prerogative instrument – *contd*
  territorial extent of   343–344
  – and see **Act of State; Order in**
    Council; Order of
    Council; prerogative,
    Royal
prerogative order – *see* **judicial**
  review
prerogative, Royal
  Channel Islands and – *see* **Channel**
    Islands
  chartered corporation – *see*
    artificial person
  choosing Minister to administer an
    Act   85–86
  comity of nations, and – *see* **comity**
  curbing of   548
  habeas corpus, and – *see* **habeas**
    corpus
  judicial review and   238, 240
  nature of   237–240
  ne exeat regno, writ of   1125
  orders etc under – *see* **habeas**
    corpus; judicial review;
    Order in Council; Order of
    Council; prerogative
    instruments
  parens patriae, doctrine of – *see*
    wardship
  Royal charter – *see* **Royal charter**
  statutory curtailment of   204, 239
  territorial waters, as to – *see*
    territorial waters
  territory of the state, as to   334, 356
  third power   238
  – and see **act of state; Crown**
prescription   203, 1037
pressure groups   975, 1135–1136
  – and see **criminal law**
presumptions of construction
  absurdity, against – *see* **absurdity**
  consequences of a construction,
    consideration of – *see*
    consequential construction
  evasion, against – *see* **evasion of**
    Act; tax avoidance
  implications and – *see* **implication**
  literal construction, favouring – *see*
    literal construction
  maxims, favouring application of –
    see **maxims, legal**
  mischief, as to – *see* **mischief;**
    'mischief rule'
  nature of   863
  'no-scheme' rule   442
  Parliament knows existing law, that   547
  Pointe Gourde rule   442
  purposive construction, favouring –
    see **purposive construction**

presumptions of construction – *contd*
  rectification of error, favouring –
    see **rectifying construction**
  remedy for mischief, favouring –
    see **mischief; 'mischief rule'**
  rules of law, favouring application
    of – *see* **implied ancillary**
    rules
  text as primary guide, favouring –
    see **literal construction**
  updating construction, favouring –
    see **updating construction**
  – and see **correctness,**
    presumption of;
    interpretative criteria;
    ultra vires, **doctrine of**
Prime Minister   85
  – and see **government; Minister of**
    the Crown
principle of legality – *see* **legality,**
  principle of
principles of construction   514, 543–544
  – and see **interpretative criteria;**
    legal policy
Pringle, Karen – *see* **Bibliography**
  (pp 1475 to 1507)
printing correction   216, 224, 225, 226, 715,
        716, 727, 741, 753,
        1455
prison rules – *see* **prisoners, rights of**
prisoners, rights of
  citizenship rights   858–859
  clear authority needed to imprison   837
  courts, access to   854
  hunger strikes   833
  legitimate expectation of   1057
  licence, release on   868, S113
  Parole Board   1061
  Prison Rules   255, 1005–1006, 1050
  remission, loss of   1005–1006
  – and see **contempt of court;**
    European Convention on
    Human Rights; *habeas*
    corpus
privacy – *see* **domestic sanctuary,**
  principle of; doubtful
  penalisation, principle against;
  European Convention on
  Human Rights
private Act
  construction of   1072
  contract law and – *see* **contract**
  Crown immunity and – *see* **Crown**
    immunity, doctrine of
  desuetude and   313
  drafting of   410, 910–911
  interpretation of   910–911
  judicial notice of – *see* **judicial**
    notice

All references are to page numbers

---

private Act – *contd*
  judicial review and – *see* **judicial**
    review
  local Act – *see* **local Act**
  nature of   183–191
  personal Act – *see* **personal Act**
  procedure   184–185
  promoter of   184
  property law and   1072
  publication of   184
  recital in, as evidence   735
  savings in   1163, 1165
    – *and see* **savings**
  validity of   233
    – *and see* **Act of Parliament;**
      special procedure order
private international law
  application of Act   367
  contract and, interpretative
    implications   1097–1100
  legislative intention and   1097–1100
  presumption, general, enactment
    imports   1097–1100
  statutory regulation of   1097–1100
  taxing acts and application of   381
    – *and see* **extra-territoriality**
private prosecutions – *see*
  prosecution of offences
privileges and immunities
  diplomatic   368–369
  general   360, 367–368
  international organisations   369–370
  professional privilege   436, S79
  prosecution, from, Chief Magistrate
    enjoring   S19
  public interest immunity – *see*
    public interest immunity
  removal of   244
  sovereign immunity 368–369, 1034–1035,
          S61
    – *and see* **act of state;**
      application of Act
  state immunity 368–369, 1034–1035
    – *and see* **act of state;**
      application of Act
  visiting forces   370
  waiver of   370–371
    – *and see* **contempt of**
      Parliament; exception;
      exterritoriality; judges;
      Parliament
Privy Council
  full name of   250
  Judicial Committee of   154, 504, S27
  legislative powers of   250
    – *and see* **Order in Council;**
      Order of Council
probate action   436

procedural due process – *see*
  decision-making rules
procedure, civil 51, 58, 320–322, 42–4232,
      807, 984, 1030–1031,
      1084
  – *and see* **decision-making rules;**
    inherent judicial powers;
    irregularity, procedural;
    legal proceedings; pleading;
    retrospectivity
procedure, criminal – *see* **criminal**
  procedure
procedure, statutory
  mandatory and directory   50–51
    – *and see* **mandatory and**
      directory requirements
  waiver of   58
proceedings, legal – *see* **legal**
  proceedings
process
  abuse of   53, 100, 161, 163, 787–788,
      1357
  due   853
    – *and see* **decision-making rules**
  immunity from – *see*
    exterritoriality; privileges
    and immunities; sovereign
    immunity
  service of   167, 1191–1192
    – *and see* **irregularity,**
      procedural
processing of enactments, dynamic
  broad terms – *see* **broad terms**
  courts, by   392, 479, 893
    – *and see* **interstitial**
      articulation
  enforcement agencies, by   167–178, 893
  factual outline, the – *see* **factual**
    outline
  implication, finding and declaring –
    see **implication**
  judicial recogntion   S49
  nature of   392–393, 502–504
  processed terms, use of – *see*
    Barras **principle**
  reversal by legislation 319, 344, 401, 499,
      815, 842, 895, 932,
      941, 1110
  sub-rules – *see* **sub-rules**
  tacit parliamentary approval of – *see*
    tacit legislation
  updating meaning of Act by – *see*
    updating construction
    – *and see* **judicial gloss; legal**
      thrust of an enactment;
      precedent, doctrine of;
      technical terms
processing of enactments, static   502
proclamation – *see* **Crown**

All references are to page numbers

---

professional misconduct   1055, 1088
prohibition (prohibiting order) – *see*
　　judicial review
promulgation of Act
　　entry on Rolls – *see* **Roll**
　　late   230n
　　legal certainty and   801
　　methods of   228–229
　　promulgation list   229
　　publication by Stationery Office 184, 228
　　revised editions   230–231
　　settling of text   225–230
　　validity, effect on   228–230
　　– *and see* **Act of Parliament**
proof – *see* **burden of proof;**
　　standard of proof
property
　　alienability of   847
　　law of, implied application of   1072
　　nature of   58
　　private Acts and property law   1072–1073
　　rights of, safeguarding – *see* **legal**
　　　　policy
　　waiver of statutory rights to   57
　　– *and see* **land**
proportionality
　　European Community law, in   1054–1055,
　　　　　　　　　　　　　　　　1280–1282
　　UK law, in   1054–1055, 1312
　　– *and see* **decision-making**
　　　　rules; European
　　　　Community law;
　　　　European Convention on
　　　　Human Rights
prosecution of offences
　　body corporate, by   99
　　charge, choice of   99
　　Code for Crown Prosecutors   99
　　commencement of prosecution   101
　　Crown, in name of   96
　　discretion and   97
　　facilitating   1026–1027
　　history of   96, 1083
　　immunity from, offered   99
　　overzealous   100
　　policy regarding   98–100, 202, 682–683
　　private prosecutions   96, 100–101, 927,
　　　　　　　　　　　　　　　　　S14, S15
　　prosecutive power of the state 96, 98, 99
　　stale offences   99
　　time limits   99, 202, 1013, 1086
　　– *and see* **Attorney General;**
　　　　criminal procedure;
　　　　Crown; Crown
　　　　Prosecution Service;
　　　　Director of Public
　　　　Prosecutions; Director of
　　　　Revenue and Customs
　　　　Prosecutions; enforcement

prosecution of offences – *contd*
　　time limits – *contd*
　　　　– *and see* **Attorney General; criminal**
　　　　　　procedure; Crown; Crown
　　　　　　Prosecution Service; Director of
　　　　　　Public Prosecutions; Director of
　　　　　　Revenue and Customs
　　　　　　Prosecutions; enforcement –
　　　　　　contd
　　　　　　agencies; judicial review;
　　　　　　nolle prosequi; **offence;**
　　　　　　peace, Queen's; police;
　　　　　　process
protracted legal proceedings,
　　avoiding   582, 787–788
　　– *and see* **estoppel**
provisional order   185n, 224, 245, 268
proviso
　　burden of proof and   723–725
　　disorganised composition and   723–725
　　drafting errors in   1148n
　　interpretation of   723–725
　　nature of   399, 723–725
　　precision drafting and   723–725
　　saving compared   723–725
　　– *and see* **evidence; private Act**
public authority – *see* **artificial**
　　person; discretion; local
　　authority
　　acts and omissions of, incompatible
　　　　with Human Rights Act 1998
　　　　– *see* **Human Rights**
　　　　Act 1998
　　claim against   163
　　– *and see* Human Rights
　　　　Act 1998
　　Crown   206–212
　　– *and see* **Crown**
　　decisions by, rules governing taking
　　　　of   1050–1064, 1268
　　fairly, must act   211
　　financial considerations – *see*
　　　　disobeying Act
　　Human Rights Act 1998 and
　　　　decisions of – *see* **Human**
　　　　Rights Act 1998
　　neglect of duty by   38
　　negligence by   84
　　pressure groups, and   1135–1136
　　property of   828–829
　　'public body', whether   898, 1243
　　public law, and – *see* **public law**
　　statutory duty, mode of discharge by   37,
　　　　　　　　　　　　　　　　50–51, 211
　　　　– *and see* **statutory duty**
Public Bill Office   745
public document   1222
public document, construction of 1222

All references are to page numbers

public good construction – *see*
statutory interpretation

public interest – *see* **legal policy;**
public interest immunity

public interest immunity   259, 525, 538,
786, 791, 1094–1097,
1268

public international law
application of Act and   378–384
crimes under   376, 1000
disputes between states   107
domestic incorporation of, by
judicial decision   817
extra-territoriality recognised by   378–384
judicial notice of,   S21
national law conforms to,
presumption that   362–363, 370,
817–824
nature of   817–824
piracy jure gentium   376, 1000
territorial waters and   356–358
– *and see* **adoption; comity;**
extra-territoriality; high
seas; treaty

public law
civil law, remedy arising in   S9
nature of   68–71, 82, 155, 789, 1050–1051
private law compared with   155–157
public and private interests, conflict
between, and   790–792
remedies   S9
rise of   68–70
– *and see* **breach of statutory**
duty, tort of;
decision-making rules;
judicial review

public mischief   1007, 1085

public nuisance – *see* **nuisance**

public office
appointment to, presumed valid   1145
meaning of   166
misfeasance in   72
usurpation of   166

public order – *see* **peace, Queen's**

public park   185

public policy
comity of nations and – *see* **comity**
conflicting considerations   790–792
contracting out, and – *see* **statutory**
right
estoppel and   788–789
European Union, in – *see* **European**
Union
legal professional privilege and   788–789
nature of   499n, 501, 772, 785–788, 1151
protracted legal proceedings,
avoidance of   787–788

public policy – *contd*
retrospectivity and – *see*
retrospectivity
– *and see* **illegality, legal policy;**
nullus commodum capere
potest de injuria sua
propria; **privileges and**
immunities; restraint of
trade

public procession   185, 1232, S110

publication of Act – *see*
promulgation of Act

Pufendorf, S von   170, 445, 456, 459, 1182,
1203
– *and see* **Bibliography (pp 1475**
to 1507)

Pugh, Idwal   86
– *and see* **Bibliography (pp 1475**
to 1507)

punctuation
alteration of   215–216
comma   738, 876
delegated legislation, interpretation
of, by reference to   716
error in   751–758, 878, 1219n
interpretation by reference to   714, 716,
751–758, 1249
legislation, in   185, 751–758
private Acts, in   185
public Acts, in   185n
semi-colon   S75
textual amendment and   292
use of, in legislation,
misapprehension over   751–758
– *and see* **precision drafting;**
updating construction

Purchas LJ   899, 1050

purpose clause
drafters' dislike of   734–735
European Community law, in   1286–1287
nature of   734–735, 959–963
rare in UK legislation   734–735
use in interpretation   734–735, 959–963
– *and see* **preamble; recital**

purposive construction
alteration of purpose and   951
deeming provisions and   949–751
European Community law and UK
law, compared   966–968, 1284
examples of   381, 687
government policy and   962–963
identifying purpose   800, 946
judicial acceptance of purpose   960–962
literal construction contrasted   945
multiple ordinary meanings and   1187
nature of   944–951
natural meaning   S90
non-purposive-and-literal
construction   951–952, 954–955

purposive construction – *contd*
  operative provisions and   959
  presumption in favour of   943–944
  provision mandating   S53
  purposive-and-literal construction   944–945, 951–955
  purposive-and-strained construction   944, 955–959
  retrospectivity and   319
  statutory statement of purpose – *see* **purpose clause**
  taxing Acts – *see* **taxing Acts**
  treaties   687, 689–690, 961
  unknown or doubtful purpose   963
  – *and see* **teleological interpretation**
purview – *see* **enacting formula**
quashing order (*certiorari*) – *see* **judicial review**
Queen's peace – *see* **peace, Queen's**
Queen's printer   226–227, 231, 266, 267, 274, 879, 1283
Quekett, A S – *see* **Bibliography (pp 1475 to 1507)**
qui facit per alium facit per se – *see* **agency**
quilibet potest renuntiare juri pro se introducto   57, 371, 375
quo warranto – *see* **judicial review**
Radcliffe, Lord   602, 606, 869–870, 914
  – *and see* **Bibliography (pp 1475 to 1507)**
Radin, Max   473, 480
  – *and see* **Bibliography (pp 1475 to 1507)**
Radzinowicz, L – *see* **Bibliography (pp 1475 to 1507)**
Ramsay **principle**   538, 1018–1023
Ramsey, Lynn E   1291n
  – *and see* **Bibliography (pp 1475 to 1507)**
rank principle   988, 1225, 1226, 1234, 1240, 1245–1247
rating   548
rating of property   548, 798, 799, 804, 914, 950, 954, 1115, 1205
ratio decidendi – *see* **factual outline, the; precedent, doctrine of**
Rawlings, R W – *see* **Bibliography (pp 1475 to 1507)**
reader of legislation – *see* **user of legislation**
'reading down'   1324
  – *and see* **strained construction**
Reading, Marquis of   867
'real doubt'   S4
real and personal – *see* **legal proceedings**

reasonableness   38, 43, 132–133, 269–270, 424–425, 770, 791–792, 956n
reasons, duty to give – *see* **B**
recital   253, 254, 267, 727, 731, 733, 735, 847, 850, 959, 960, 1471, 1472
  – *and see* **preamble; purpose clause**
recklessness, test for   420–421
record   647
  – *and see* **court**
rectifying construction
  casus male inclusus   887–889
    – *and see* **broad terms**
  casus omissus   169–170, 811, 885–887, 1329
  conflicting texts   889
  examples of   325, 574
  garbled text   878–881
  meaning, error of   881–885
  nature of   875–889, S86
  punctuation error – *see* **punctuation**
  subordinate legislation, of   887
    – *and see* **incompatibility, declaration of, under Human Rights Act 1998; meaning; mistake; nobile officium; obscurity, semantic; repugnancy; slip rule**
recusal   394, 1139
reddendo singula singulis **principle**   1247–1249
redundancy – *see* **surplusage**
reference, works of   134, 1222, 1224
  – *and see* **dictionary reference to; judicial notice**
referential legislation – *see* **incorporation by reference**
reform – *see* **Law Commission; statute law; Statute Law Revision Act**
Reform Act 1832   244–245
Refugee Convention   S68
registered medical practitioner   1398
registered midwife   1398
registered nurse   1398
Regnal year – *see* **Crown**
regularity, presumption of – *see* **correctness, presumption of**
Reid, Lord   169, 411, 433, 457, 502, 520, 538, 549, 644, 650, 660, 661, 694, 696, 699n, 714, 716, 746, 747, 753, 790, 797, 816, 851n, 872, 873, 940, 966, 972, 973, 981, 1001, 1037, 1049,

Reid, Lord – *contd*
  1052, 1079, 1094n, 1096, 1112, 1131, 1166, 1220, 1222, 1223, 1454
relator action 73, 74, S10
religion 780–781, 842–843
  – *and see* **Christianity;**
    discrimination, legislation
    against; doubtful
    penalisation, principle
    against; European
    Convention on Human
    Rights; Jews; moral duty
rent, meaning S89
Renton report 487, 643n, 735n, 739, 1166n
repeal
  advance, in 302
  amendment and 288
  commencement of Act, before 282–283
  delegated legislation and – *see*
    delegated legislation
  'double' repeal, practice of 302–304
  effect of 197, 301–302
  express 293, 300–301
  implied 300–301, 304–305, 991, S38, S39
  in same session 300, 302
  nature of 194, 300–302
  proviso, and 723–725
  re-enactment, and 310–312, 1391
  reference to repealed enactment 310–311
  referential definitions, and 572
  repeal of 1390
  repealed enactment considered as
    legislative history 604
  – *and see* **legislative history**
  'revoke', use of term 301
  savings on – *see* **saving**
  Schedule – *see* **Schedule**
  successor provisions S38, S109
  transitional provisions, and – *see*
    transitional provisions
  twice over 302–304
  – and see *Attorney General v*
    Lamplough, **rule in;**
    generalia specialibus non
    derogant; **generalibus**
    specialia derogant;
    strained construction
  types of S38
repugnancy
  of different Acts 889
  strained construction, requiring 466, 741
  – *and see* **strained construction**
  within same Act 465–466, 559, 1163
  – *and see* **construction as a**
    whole; duplication of
    statutory remedies, powers
    etc; *genenalia specialibus*

repugnancy – *contd*
  within same Act – *contd*
    – *and see* **construction as a whole;**
      duplication of statutory remedies,
      powers etc; *genenalia specialibus*
      – *contd*
    non derogant; generalibus
    specialia derogant; logic,
    use of in interpretation;
    rectifying construction
reputation, detriment to – *see*
    doubtful penalisation, principle
    against
res ipsa loquitur 1077, 1103
res judicata – *see* **estoppel**
res magis valeat quam pereat rule 558, 559, 849
restitution 1074, 1107
restitutio in integrum 1074
retrospectivity
  amending enactment, of 320
  common law presumption against S39
  declaratory enactment, of 187
  delegated legislation S42
  doubt, causes of 325–326
  European Community law,
    presumption against in 1279–1280
  events over a period 322–324
  evidential provisions 322
  nature of 315–320
  penalty, increase of 322
  pending actions, and 320
  presumption against 177, 315–320, 323, 807–808, 1279–1280
  procedural provisions, and 320–322
  public interest and – *see* **legal**
    policy
  – *and see* **delegated legislation;**
    European Convention on
    Human Rights; legal
    proceedings; taxing Acts
Revenue and Customs Prosecutions,
    director of 97
Revenue and Customs,
    commissioners for 96, 352n
review – *see* **appeal; judicial review**
revocation, power of 90
  partial S50
Ribeiro PJ S73
Richardson J 611
Richardson, H G – *see* **Bibliography**
    (pp 1475 to 1507)
right, implied extinguishment of 499
right, statutory – *see* **statutory right**
rights, human – *see* **human rights**
Rix LJ 848
Robertson, E (Lord Lochee) – *see*
    Bibliography (pp 1475 to 1507)
Robertson, Lord 1047

All references are to page numbers

Robinson, R G F   562n
 – *and see* **Bibliography (pp 1475**
   to 1507)
Robson, Glenna – *see* **Bibliography**
   (pp 1475 to 1507)
Roch LJ   136, 574, 1057, 1300
Rockall, Isle of   355, 356
Rodger of Earlsferry, Lord   497, 550, 1010,
                         1166, 1339, S11, S32,
                                        S110
Roll
 Chancery   227, 234
 inspection of   228, 234
 nature of   227
 Parliament – *see* **Parliament Roll**
 Statute   1010–1011
Roman law   6, 12, 13, 21, 28–30, 41, 197,
                       347, 463, 876–877,
                       1106, 1116, 1291,
                                        1298
Romer LJ   108, 871, 1233
Romilly MR   757, 769
Rose LJ   104n, 170, 326, 547, 555, 621, 700,
                         729n, 818, 928
Roskill, Lord   69, 76n, 161n, 304, 305, 411,
                       532, 533, 539, 602,
                       620, 761n, 777, 812,
                       816, 899, 985, 1160,
                               1195, 1252
Ross, David   591
Ross, Ursula – *see* **Bibliography (pp**
   1475 to 1507)
Rougier J   1089
Rousseau, J J   39
Rowe, Henry   476
 – *and see* **Bibliography (pp 1475**
   to 1507)
Rowlatt J   488, 496n, 849
Roxburgh J   588
Royal assent
 absence or illness of Monarch,
   during   222
 commission, by   220–222
 communication of, to Parliament   220–222
 date of   226
 demise of Crown and   223
 error as to   235
 formula   185, 221
 in person   220–222
 letters patent signifying   217–218
 money Bill   224
 notification, by   220–222
 Parliament Acts 1911 and 1949   224–225
 procedure, two-stage   216–217, 714
 refusal of   218
 regency, during   223
 signification of   217–220

Royal assent – *contd*
 text of Act and   226
   – *and see* **chapter number;**
     Clerk of the Parliaments;
     Parliament Acts 1911 and
     1949
Royal charter   239
Royal Commission on Criminal
   Procedure 1981   99
Royal prerogative – *see* **prerogative,**
   Royal
Rozenberg, Joshua – *see*
   Bibliography (pp 1475 to 1507)
Ruggle, George   752
rule of law – *see* **law**
rules
 delegated legislation, type of   268
 interpretation of   413
rules of construction
 basic rule   544–548
 common law   543–544
 common sense, use of – *see*
     commonsense construction
     rule
 contrary intention   547
 functional construction rule – *see*
     functional construction
 informed interpretation rule – *see*
     informed interpretation
 nature of   543–544
 plain meaning rule – *see* **plain**
     meaning rule
 pluralistic   547
 principles of construction and,
   contrasted   543–544
 regard to nature of an enactment   548
 rule where meaning not 'plain'   551
 statutory   129, 543–544
   – *and see* **interpretative**
     criteria; *res magis valeat*
     quam pereat **rule**
rules of court – *see* **court**
Russell of Killowen, Lord   965, 997, 1144
Rutherforth, Thomas – *see*
   Bibliography (pp 1475 to 1507)
Sachs LJ   1208
Safire, William – *see* **Bibliography**
   (pp 1475 to 1507)
Saint German, Christopher – *see*
   Bibliography (pp 1475 to 1507)
Sainty, J C – *see* **Bibliography (pp**
   1475 to 1507)
Sales J   S66
Salmon, Lord   131, 790, 1007n, 1095
salus populi suprema lex   773, 1046
same words, construction of – *see*
   words; homonyms

All references are to page numbers

Sampford, Charles   6n
  – and see **Bibliography (pp 1475**
    to 1507)
sanctions for contravention *– see*
  contempt of statute; disobeying
  Act; offence; statutory duty;
  tort
Sanders, Andrew *– see* **Bibliography**
  (pp 1475 to 1507)
Sankey, Lord   659, 678n, 910
Sardinia Sulcis, **The, rule in**   172
Savill LJ   586, 1265
saving
  commencement of substituted
      provisions and   310
  common law and   309
  Crown. for   207
  general   725–726, 1389–1390
  interpretation of   725–726, 1163, 1165
  nature of   725–726
  practice, for   220
  private and personal Acts, in   1163
  proviso and, compared   725
  repeal of enactment, effect on   188, 303,
       307–310
  revocation of delegated legislation,
      on   308
  special   308
  – and see **privileges and**
    immunities; proviso
Sayles, G *– see* **Bibliography (pp**
  1475 to 1507)
Scalia J   651n
Scarman, Lord   35n, 246, 366n, 403, 467,
     492, 523, 534, 538,
     558, 588, 639, 649,
     651, 663, 686, 716,
     773, 774, 792, 823,
     834, 841, 843, 845,
     925, 933, 962, 965,
     1038, 1057, 1087,
     1119, 1127, 1156,
     1228, 1244, 1255
Schedule
  byelaws, to   269
  format of   721–723
  forms in   1123
  inducing words of   721–723
  interpretation of   721–723
  notes to   721–723
  repeal   302–304, 721–723
  statutory instruments and   295
  use of   721–723
  – and see **functional**
    construction; Jamaica
    Schedule; Keeling
    Schedule
scheme   271

Scherer **principle**   148–149, 461n
  – and see **also jurisdiction**
Schiemann LJ   176, 875, 950, 1121
Scilly, Isles of   346, 347
Scotland
  Act, extending to, presumption of   336–
       338
  desuetude of Acts in   313n
  English law, treatment in   1038, 1202–
       1203
  devolution and   6
  Human Rights Act 1998 procedures
    in *– see* **Human Rights**
    Act 1998
  law of   331–332, 347, 387, 984, 1038,
       1125, 1136n
  nobile officium *– see nobile*
    officium
  pleading in   434n
  presumption of uniform application
    of enactment in   331–332
  pre-Union law, act altering   333
  private prosecution in   927
  punctuation, treatment of, in   753–754
  sheriff principal   1398
  territory of   355–356
  Union with Scotland Act 1706   236, 250n,
       333, 347
  – and see **devolution; Lords,**
    house of; Scottish
    Parliament; technical
    terms; territorial extent of
    Act
Scott LJ   902, 1238, S32
Scott Baker J   621, 1167, S109
Scott of Foscote, Lord   117n, 127n, 360n,
     363, 366n, 562, 1108,
     S73, S99
Scott v Scott, rule in *– see* **open**
  court, principle of the
Scott, C P   1184
Scottish Parliament   242, 1392, 1396
  – and see **Scotland**
Scrivener, Anthony   1102
  – and see **Bibliography (pp 1475**
    to 1507)
Scrutton LJ   134, 137, 453, 519, 714, 738,
     848, 962, 1029, 1071,
     1110
  – and see **Bibliography (pp 1475**
    to 1507)
seabed   334, 335
  – and see **territorial waters**
seas, beyond the   1214
'seas, beyond the'   1214
Secretary of State   86, 252, 1398
  – and see **Minister of the Crown**
section
  enacting formula and   718, 719–721

All references are to page numbers

section – *contd*
  name – *see* **section name (sidenote,**
      heading or title)
  organisation of, as guide to
      legislative intention   719–721
  paragraphs in   719–721
  sidenote to – *see* **section name**
      (sidenote, heading or title)
  statement of purpose of   719–721
  subsections   719–721
    – *and see* **functional**
          construction
section name (sidenote, heading or
    title)
  alteration of   715, 747–749
  delegated legislation, interpretation
      of, by reference to   716
  formerly sidenote   747–749
  interpretation by reference to   715, 747–
                                749, 1014, 1454–1458
  nature of   747–749
    – *and see* **functional**
          construction
security of state – *see* **legal policy**
Sedgwick, T   464
Sedley LJ   10n, 82, 125n, 156, 470, 551,
                            600, 698, 699, 784,
                            828n, 1033, 1159,
                            1060n, 1316, 1292n,
                                            S44
    – *and see* **Bibliography (pp 1475**
          to 1507)
Selborne, Earl of   **306**
Selden, John   **229**
    – *and see* **Bibliography (pp 1475**
          to 1507)
selective comminution
  examples of   367, 403, 416, 432, 532,
                            534–537, 701, 882,
                                            1126
  implied words   x
  meaning of   401–404
    – *and see* **comminution**
self help   35
self-incrimination – *see* **procedure,**
    criminal
Sellers LJ   74, 848
semantic obscurity – *see* **obscurity,**
    semantic
Senior Courts – *see* **court**
Sentencing Guidelines Council   704
separation of powers, doctrine of 104, 121,
                                1326, 1354
Serious Fraud Office   94
Serious Organised Crime Agency   S42
service
  notice, of – *see* **notice**
  post, by   570, 582–583, 1388
  process, of – *see* **process**

service – *contd*
  waiver of procedural rules of   58
severance
  contract, in   61
  delegated legislation, in   254–255, 258–
                                            259
  illegality and   1110
  where matter only partly within
      statutory description   1270
sewerage undertaker   1398
sex discrimination – *see*
    discrimination, legislation
    against
sex shops, licensing of   92, 185, 187
sexual offences prevention order   393n
sexual orientation   914, 1328
    – *and see* **transsexuality**
Shadwell V-C   335n
Shakespeare, William – *see*
    Bibliography (pp 1475 to 1507)
Sharma, Sujata – *see* **Bibliography**
    (pp 1475 to 1507)
'shall'   46n
Shaw LJ   496, 554, 984, S92
Shaw of Dunfermline, Lord   746n, 753,
                                            1103
Shaw, Terence – *see* **Bibliography**
    (pp 1475 to 1507)
Shawcross and Beaumont – *see*
    Bibliography (pp 1475 to 1507)
Shearman J   983
Shee, Sjt   137
Sheen J   665, 906, 988
Sheldon J   318
Shepherd, Nigel – *see* **Bibliography**
    (pp 1475 to 1507)
sheriff   166, 167, 229, 878, 904, 1195, 1399,
                                1437, 1438
sheriff's officer – *see* **enforcement**
    agencies
Shetlands, the   347, 356
ship, law prevailing on   385–386
short title
  informal   736
  interpretation by reference to   714–715,
                                738, 935
  mischief, determining, by   935
  misleading   353
  nature of   735–739
  punctuation in   738
  wording of   735–739
    – *and see* **collective title;**
          functional construction;
          Royal assent
sidenote to section – *see* **section**
    name (sidenote, heading or
    title)
signature   219, 223, 236, 388, 603, 905n,
                                992, 1040

All references are to page numbers

Silber J   100, 305, 582
silence, right of – *see* procedure,
    criminal
Simon Brown LJ – *see* Brown
    (Simon) LJ
Simon of Glaisdale, Lord   372, 476, 478,
                                587, 645, 660, 662,
                                669, 696, 700n, 726,
                                731, 961, 976, 986,
                                1118, 1173, 1198,
                                                1220
Simon, Viscount   588, 870, 898, 1018, 1038,
                                                1235
Simonds, Viscount   51, 108, 379, 452, 458,
                                588, 668, 669, 819,
                                                1144
Singer J   781, 841, 847n
singular and plural   579–581, 1387–1388
    – *and see* number
skeleton argument   593–596 , 855n
Slade LJ   290, 630, 731, 748, 776, 948
slang   1181, 1209–1213
slavery   365, 372, 382, 840, 1124, 1350,
                                                1443
slip rule   110, 146, 839, S18
Slynn of Hadley, Lord   260n, 904
Smith (Peter) J   1313
Smith, A T H – *see* Bibliography (pp
    1475 to 1507)
Smith, J C   420, 517, 1080
Smith, John – *see* Bibliography (pp
    1475 to 1507)
Smith, K J M   1036
    – *and see* Bibliography (pp 1475
    to 1507)
social attitude, change in   S21
social security appeal tribunal   142
social security appeal tribunals   142
Soering principle   1349
solicitor
    acting as   774n
    agent, as   363, 1148–1149
    body corporate as   577
    duty of   48
    foreign   363
    negligence of   788n
    practising certificate   92, 794
    professional indemnity insurance   1067
    – *and see* advocate; central
        function of practitioner;
        costs; legal proceedings;
        subject, the
Somervell of Harrow, Lord   589n
sovereign immunity – *see* privileges
    and immunities
special procedure order   268
specialty   39, 647, 1237n
    – *and see* limitation of actions

speech, freedom of
    broadcasting and   820
    conditional nature of   197
    defamation and   821
    press censorship   312
    – *and see* discrimination,
        legislation against;
        doubtful penalisation,
        principle against;
        European Convention on
        Human Rights
Spencer, J R   284n, 404, 451, 920
    – *and see* Bibliography (pp 1475
    to 1507)
Spiliada principle   333n
St Germain, C   653
Stair, Viscount   877, 1008
    – *and see* Bibliography (pp 1475
    to 1507)
Stamp LJ   1227
standard of performance   48
standard of proof
    civil   1088–1091
    common law applies where Act
        silent   1088–1091
    criminal   830, 977, 985–986, 1088–1091
    enactment detrimental to rights, and   830
    interlocutory proceedings, in   1088–1091
    unusual   1088–1091
    – *and see* burden of proof;
        evidence
Stanley Burnton J   138, 335, 544, 972
stare decisis – *see* precedent,
    doctrine of; processing of
    enactments, dynamic; sub-rules
state
    act of – *see* act of state
    emanation of – *see* European
        Community law
    immunity – *see* privileges and
        immunities
    judicial power of – *see* judicial
        power of the state
    security of – *see* legal policy
    – *and see* Crown; legal policy
Stationery Office Limited, The   226, 666
    – *and see* HMSO
statute book
    defects in   923–926
    drafting of   409–413, 804–806
    free-standing Act, doctrine of   1165
    modern growth of   815
    nature of   483
    publication of   230–232
    'statute book of the session'   742
    Statute Law Database   232
    tacit legislation   996
    'tidying' of   188, 509, 897

All references are to page numbers

statute book – *contd*
  undermining of, by recourse to
    Hansard   652, 657
    unified system   309
statute law
  nature of   5, 182
  reform of   12
Statute Law Committee   231
Statute Law Revision Act   188, 725–726
Statute Law Society   1166n
statutes
  ancient   184, 189, 232
  deficiencies of   9–10
  glossing of   33, 170
    – *and see* **judicial gloss**
  early   182, 652–653, 719, 916–918, 1216
  legal meaning of, duty to determine   24–
      25, 403
  'modern'   184, 189, 232
  nature of   182–183
  obsolete, repeal of   509
  overlapping enactments   S104
  prerogative and   239, S33
  primacy of   201
  statute book – *see* **statute book**
  Statutes in Force   231
  Statutes of the Realm   226
  Statutes Revised   231
  subordinate legislation modifying   182
  uniform – *see* **uniform statutes**
    – *and see* **Act of Parliament;**
      Human Rights Act 1998;
      judicial gloss; user of
      legislation
Statutes in Force – *see* **Statutes**
Statutes of the Realm – *see* **Statutes**
Statutes Revised – *see* **Statutes**
statutory analogy   499–501
  – *and see* **implication**
statutory benefit – *see* **statutory**
  right
statutory debt – *see* **debt, statutory**
statutory declaration   980, 1399
statutory definitions – *see*
  definitions, statutory
statutory description – *see*
  description, statutory
statutory discretion – *see* **discretion**
statutory duty
  absolute   37, 59
  act of God and   1104–1105
  after performance of, matters arising   56
  ambit of   37, 591, 1130
  amendment, legislative, to propose   978–
      979
  breach of, civil sanctions for – *see*
    breach of statutory duty, tort
    of; tort; *volenti non fit injuria*
  breach of, consent, and   1150–1151

statutory duty – *contd*
  breach of, criminal sanctions for –
    see **contempt of statute;**
    criminal law
  breach of, technical   56
  common law duty, corresponding,
    and   75
  compliance, mode of   37–38
  continuity of   1388–1389
  contracting out of, when not
    permitted   60–62
  contracting out of, when permitted   57–60
  discretion, must not be reduced to   126
  doubtful – *see* **doubtful**
    penalisation, principle
    against
  duplication of duties or remedies   810,
      1000
  duty *sub modo*   37, 57, 59, 60
  enforcement of   57, S10
  'gateway' duty   810
  hardship, as defence for
    non-performance of   39
  impecuniosity, defence of   126–127
  implied   49
  manner of performance required   37–38,
      49
  necessity, as defence for
    non-performance of   39
  over-performance of   39
  performance from time to time   581–582
  prohibitory and mandatory   63, 65
  resource implications – *see* **money**
  tort, application of, to   1073
  types of   37
  volenti principle – *see* ***volenti non***
    fit injuria
    – *and see* **discretion; disobeying**
      Act; judicial review;
      mandatory and directory
      requirements; moral duty;
      reasonableness; statutory
      power; statutory right
statutory exposition   122, 188n, 293
  – *and see* **declaratory enactment**
statutory inspectorates   93
statutory instrument – *see* **delegated**
  legislation
Statutory Instruments Issue List
  ('Daily list')   267, 274
statutory interpretation
  affordability, relevance of   107
  basic rule   ix, 2, 13, 176, 544–548
  changed view of legal meaning   151
  consequential provisions   295–297
  construction summons   114
  corpus juris, within   193
  court, exclusive function of – *see*
    Judge

All references are to page numbers

---

statutory interpretation – *contd*
delegated legislation, by reference
    to   242n, 706–708, 710
delegated legislation, of   257–258, 263–
                266, 716
  – *and see* delegated legislation
Developmental method of (EU)   1283–
              1287, 1323
doubtful penalisation, leaning
    against possibility of   S83
dynamic   1457
equitable construction – *see*
    equitable construction
Global method of (common law
    system)   5, 9, 13
Hansard, use of – *see* **exclusionary**
    rule, the; *Pepper v Hart,* **rule**
    in
history of   8, 11
importance of   6–9, 13–14, 151
in pari materia Acts, use of, in   708–710
intuition, use of   470
judicial rulings on   114, 151
lay person, by   1222–1223
legal policy and   778
legality, principle of   822–823, S81, S82
long title and   727–731
method of   191–192
    – *and see* **interpretative**
        criteria; interpretative
        factors
mistake in – *see* **judges; mistake of**
    law
NESSSI Method   1
old Acts, drafting style in, and   866
Originalism   1457
over-subtlety in, to be avoided   806–807,
        866
paragraphing and   720, 749
pejorative connotation of   170–171
perverse   461
pluralism of   13
private property, expropriation of   S83
prolonging proceedings where
    arising   S61
public good construction   319
public interest   791–792
'reading down'   1324
reform of   12
Schedule, notes to, and   721–723
semi-colon, significance of   S75
statute, nature of, and   191–192
statutory regulation of   171
sub-rules and – *see* **sub-rules**
taxpayers, inconvenience to   981–982
teological – *see* **teological**
    interpretation
treaties, use of   682–691
two-stage approach to   591–592

statutory interpretation – *contd*
uniform terminology for   589–590
viscera, use of   470
  – *and see* **amendment to Bill;**
    Bill, parliamentary;
    canons of construction,
    linguistic; Book, this;
    Code, the;
    counter-intuitive readings;
    definitions, statutory;
    'golden rule';
    hairsplitting;
    Interpretation Act 1978;
    interpreter of enactment;
    Law Commission;
    legislative history; literal
    construction; 'literal rule';
    'mischief rule'; opposing
    constructions; prerogative
    instrument; presumptions
    of construction; principles
    of construction; purposive
    construction; rules of
    construction; strained
    construction; uniform
    statutes; Vienna
    Convention on Law of
    Treaties

statutory mischief – *see* **mischief**
statutory misdemeanour – *see*
    contempt of statute
statutory power
administration of   91
ancillary powers – *see* ***Attorney***
    General v Great Eastern
    Railway, **rule in; implication;**
    local authority
anticipatory exercise of   1389
concurrent   499
conditional   257, 868
    – *and see* **description, statutory**
consult, duty to – *see*
    decision-making rules;
    delegated legislation
continuity of   1388–1389
discretionary or elective terms, in   S13
duplication – *see* **duplication of**
    statutory powers, remedies
    etc
duty to exercise   51, 253
exercise of, from time to time   581–582
functions distinguished   S51
implied narrowing of   152, 492–493, 498–
        499
invalid exercise of   165–166
nuisance and – *see* **nuisance**
practice and   34
quo warranto – *see* **judicial review**
reversal of exercise of   90

All references are to page numbers

---

statutory power – *contd*

search, to	496
tort law, application of, to	1073

– *and see* **discretion;
implication; local
authority; mandatory and
directory requirements;
statutory right;** *ultra vires*,
doctrine of; *vigilantibus
non dormientibus leges
subveniunt*

statutory procedure – *see* **procedure,
statutory**

Statutory Publications Office (SPO)	231

statutory right

conditional	53–54

– *and see* **description, statutory**

contracting out of	60–62
death, survival on	847–848
debt	72

duplication – *see* **duplication of
statutory powers, remedies
etc**

limitation period – *see* **limitation of
actions**

other rights, effect on	52

specialty, as – *see* **specialty**

waiver of, when not permitted	60–62, 1096–1097
waiver of, when permitted	57–60, 1096–1097

– *and see* **illegality; statutory
power**

statutory rules and orders	266
Staughton LJ	70, 318, 436, 820, 827, 853, 992n, 1141, 1191, 1248n

Stein, Alex – *see* **Bibliography (pp
1475 to 1507)**

Stephen, J F – *see* **Bibliography (pp
1475 to 1507)**

Stephenson LJ	507, 816, 954
Sterndale, Lord	722
Stewart, Gordon	747n

– *and see* **Bibliography (pp 1475
to 1507)**

Steyn, Lord	128, 153, 176, 538, 547, 551, 583, 601, 622, 632, 633, 637, 638, 642, 682n, 782, 803, 868, 943, 945, 967, 970, 1010, 1013n, 1055, 1323, 1324, 1331, 1340, 1361, 1455, 1456, S16, S61, S64
Stockdale, John Joseph	205
Stocker J	1077

Stone, R T H – *see* **Bibliography (pp
1475 to 1507)**

Stone, Samuel – *see* **Bibliography
(pp 1475 to 1507)**

Strachey J	694

strained construction

absurdity and	970, 972–973
ambiguity and	872

– *and see* **ambiguity
(grammatical)**

compatible construction rule – *see*
Human Rights Act 1998

consequential construction	872

contradiction, principle of – *see*
logic, use of in interpretation

declaration of incompatibility – *see*
Human Rights Act 1998

deeming provision and	951–955
dicta opposing	457–459
examples of	148, 367, 459–461, 493, 515–516, 798, 882, 883–885, 938, 956, 958, 974–975, 983, 989–990, 1021, 1131, 1218, 1329
inconvenience, avoidance of, and	979
judicial acceptance of	169, 872, 966, 972–975, 1029
judicial reluctance to admit using	457–458
nature of	169, 456–458, 490, 515–516, 1324
public interest and	791
reasons justifying	212, 458–463, 480, 482, 490, 523, 529, 533–537, 700, 791, 972–973, 1020, 1116, 1177, 1179, 1218, 1299–1300
universal repealer, the	459–460
when inapt	319

– *and see* **absurdity;
consequential
construction; drafting
error; equitable
construction; purposive
construction; repugnancy**

Street, A G – *see* **Bibliography (pp
1475 to 1507)**

strict and liberal construction

consequences, regard to	516–519, 874–875
counter-mischief and	1007–1008
duty to obey legislation	37–40
factual error and liberal construction	883
interpreter, and	34–36

legal adviser and – *see* **advocate**

liberal construction, nature of	516–519
savings	726
strict construction, nature of	516, 848–849, 1007–1008
terminology of	519

All references are to page numbers

---

strict and liberal construction – *contd*
updating, where need for – *see*
  updating construction
wide and narrow meaning   431, 516–519
– *and see* **doubtful penalisation,**
  principle against;
  ignorantia juris neminem
  excusat; **informed**
  interpretation; legislation,
  – *and see* **doubtful**
  penalisation, principle
  against; equitable
  construction; precision
  drafting

strict liability   43, 79, 176, 899, 900, 1026,
1079, 1104, 1146,
1148
– *and see* **mala prohibita; vicarious**
  liability

Stuart-Smith LJ   72, 587, 615, 619, 620,
1201, 1261

sub-delegation – *see* **delegated**
  legislation

subject, the
duty to obey legislation   36–40
interpreter   34–44
legal adviser and – *see* **advocate**
– *and see* **doubtful penalisation,**
  principle against;
  ignorantia juris neminem
  excusat; **informed**
  interpretation; legislation

subjective test
differential readings   130–133, 952
judgment and   127, 133
justice, and   123
legislative intent   968
movement towards   538
– *and see* **objective test**

subordinate legislation – *see*
  delegated legislation;
  Interpretation Act 1978;
  prerogative, Royal

sub-rules   167, 171–172, 177–178, 417, 418,
437, 438, 479, 502,
503, 606, 608, 629,
710, 792
– *and see* **interstitial articulation;**
  processing of enactments,
  dynamic; statutory
  interpretation

subsection   720
subsidiarity   1273, 1282, 1471, 1472
suffragan bishop, appointment of   314
sui generis, **persons who are not** –
  see **incompetents**
suicide   297, 501, 775, 1036, 1089
assisted, Code for Prosecutors   S14

Sullivan, A M   427n
– *and see* **Bibliography (pp 1475**
  to 1507)
Sullivan, Ruth   714n
– *and see* **Bibliography (pp 1475**
  to 1507)
Summers, Robert S   7
– *and see* **Bibliography (pp 1475**
  to 1507)
summons – *see* **process**
Sumner, Lord   313, 776, 780, 996
Supreme Court   139, 739, S15
appeal to   S25
court, as   S15
criticism of creation of   S26
House of Lords decisions, binding
  nature of   S30
Judicial Committee of the Privy
  Council, members of   S27
members   S26
Privy Council followed in
  preference to   S52
Supplementary Panel   S26
– *and see* **court**
Supreme Court of the United
  Kingdom   152–153, 739
surplusage   305, 315, 461, 539, 1041, 1157–
1160, 1233
– *and see* **construction as a whole;**
  tautology
suspending power – *see* **Crown**
Sutherland, J A   482n
– *and see* **Bibliography (pp 1475**
  to 1507)
Swinfen-Eady LJ   537
Sykes, C S – *see* **Bibliography (pp**
  1475 to 1507)
Taafe defence   42
tacit legislation   171, 711, 894–895, 996
limits of   711
– *and see* **comity; intention,**
  legislative
tacking   224
tailpiece   27
Tapper, C F H – *see* **Bibliography**
  (pp 1475 to 1507)
tautology   146, 147, 1157–1160
– *and see* **overlapping meaning;**
  surplusage
tax avoidance
advance clearance and   1022
anti-avoidance enactments   819, 850–851,
931, 1017–1023, S94
Franco scheme   432n, 705
general   1017–1023
Inland Revenue rulings on   705
Ramsay principle – *see* **Ramsay**
  principle
right of   S94

All references are to page numbers

---

tax avoidance – *contd*
tax mitigation and, contrasted   1017–1018,
1021–1022
Westminster principle – *see*
Westminster **principle**
– *and see* **evasion of Act; taxing**
Acts
tax law rewrite Acts   191, S31
taxing Acts
Australia, construction in   S85, S91
Crown and   300
definitions and   567
double taxation   850
drafting of   898, 964, 1166, 1199
enforcement of   97, 99
extra-territoriality and   363–364, 381
implication in   298–299, 814, 974–975
interpretation of   332, 705–706, 829–830,
937, 965–966, 974–
975, 1261, S85
nature of   190–191, 850–851
provisional collection of taxes   190–191,
251
retrospectivity and   323
'Tax Acts, The', definition of   1399
tax law rewrite Act – *see* **tax law**
rewrite Act
taxpayers, inconvenience to, and   981–982
uniformity of application of   332
– *and see* **Act of Parliament;**
Bill, parliamentary;
domestic sanctuary,
principle of; doubtful
penalisation, principle
against; enacting formula;
evasion of Act;
extra-statutory concession;
extra-territoriality;
illegality; money;
Parliament; privileges and
immunities;
retrospectivity; tax
avoidance; uniform
statutes
Taylor of Gosforth, Lord   244, 320, 928
technical contravention   S7
technical terms
Act's extent, and   331–332
context in which used   1204, 1205, 1206,
1209
conveyancing   190
different technical meanings   1197–1199
evidence of meaning   1223–1224
examples of meaning   739–741
free-standing   1039
interpretation of   331–332, 11971209
legal terms – *see* **legal terms**
multiple meanings of term   1198–1199
non-legal terms   1203–1206

technical terms – *contd*
ordinary and technical meaning   1206–
1209
ordinary language, use of   1203–1204
term with both ordinary and
technical meaning   1206–1209
– *and see* **box principle;**
foreign; technicalities
technicalities   35, 51, 56, 332, 400, 416, 839,
920, 921, 938, 980
– *and see* **irregularity, procedural;**
pleading; technical terms
technology, developments in – *see*
updating construction
teleological interpretation   546, 1284
– *and see* **European Community**
Law; purposive construction;
statutory interpretation
Templeman, Lord   206, 476, 478, 508, 643,
665, 703, 832, 839,
967, 975, 990, 1020,
1024, 1166, 1188,
1190, 1298n
temporal operation of Act – *see* **time**
temporary Act   183, 186, 311–312, 312,
926, 1412
tenancy
exclusion of protection, void   S8
tenancy in common   1040
tense   892, 1190–1191, 1464
– *and see* **time**
Tenterden, Lord   653, 879, 1182
Terence   802, 965
terminology, legal   61
terms, meaning of (list)   1420
territorial extent of Act
application of Act, contrasted   328
– *and see* **application of Act**
basic rule   327–329
change of territory   329
composition of Act's territory   334–335
extent to Her Majesty's dominions   329–
330, 338–340
– *and see* **Australia; Canada;**
Her Majesty's dominions;
Her Majesty's
independent dominions;
Man, Isle of, new Zealand
'extent', meaning of, in   329–330
implied   328
implied ancillary rules and   1037
legal policy and   1038
non-residents – *see* **application of**
Act
principles governing   194–196, 327–340,
1098–1099, S100
Scotland   363

All references are to page numbers

territorial extent of Act – *contd*
uniform meaning throughout extent 330–334
  – *and see* **uniform statutes**
United Kingdom, presumption
    extent limited to 328, 335–338
  – *and see* **extra-territoriality**
territorial waters
Home Secretary's certificate 358
meaning of 334, 356–358
  – *and see* **baseline; high seas;**
    Northern Ireland
territory, surrender of 238n, 406
terrorism – *see* **criminal law**
text writers, opinions of – *see* **jurists**
text, legislative 5
textual amendment – *see*
  amendment to Act
textual memorandum xi, 643
Thankerton, Lord 105, 785, 786, 850, 1061
Thompson J 693n
Thomson LJ-C 495
Thornton, G C 242n, 314n
  – *and see* **Bibliography (pp 1475**
    to 1507)
Thorpe CJ 229
Thorpe LJ 999
three-fold consent, doctrine of – *see*
  Act of Parliament
Thring, Lord 7, 410, 411, 412, 415, 718,
    732, 734, 747, 749,
    891, 892, 1249
  – *and see* **Bibliography (pp 1475**
    to 1507)
time
anomalies as to 989
commonsense construction rule and 868–869
corresponding date rule 1040
Crown, does not run against 1083
day 196, 273, 278–279, 1119–1121
de minimis principle – *see* **de**
  minimis non curat lex
exclusive day rule 1119–1121
expressions of 868–869
Greenwich Mean Time 581
inclusive day rule 1119–1121
limits 113, 202, 1198–1199
  – *and see* **prosecution of**
    offences
'month', definition of 581
period 431, 1119–1121
summer time 581
temporal operation of Act 196
tense 581, 1190–1191
zones 196
  – *and see* **Act of Parliament;**
    age; *audi alteram partem*
    principle; commencement

time – *contd*
  zones – *contd*
    – *and see* **Act of Parliament; age;** *audi*
      alteram partem **principle;**
      commencement – *contd*
      of Act; Crown; death;
      delegated legislation;
      evasion of Act;
      Interpretation Act 1978;
      judicial review; limitation
      of actions; notice;
      procedure, criminal;
      retrospectivity;
      transitional provisions
tip-off 425–426
title – *see* **collective title; long title;**
  short title
Tomlins, T E – *see* **Bibliography (pp**
  1475 to 1507)
Toohey J 651, 676
tort
class benefiting from breach S11
common employment, doctrine of 198
contravention of enactment as – *see*
  breach of statutory duty, tort
  of
Crown and 387
damages for 176, 1256
detinue, abolition of 198
implied application of law of 1073–1077
private prosecutor, action against S15
statutory 67–85
statutory authorisation of
  commission of 68, 75, 84, 1074–1075
statutory modification of law of 169, 198, 889
  – *and see* **confidentiality;**
    extra-territoriality;
    interest;
    misrepresentation;
    negligence; *nuisance; res*
    ipsa loquitur; restitutio in
    integrum; **strict liability;**
    territorial waters;
    trespass; vicarious lability;
    volenti non fit injuria
Tosswill, T M S – *see* **Bibliography**
  (pp 1475 to 1507)
Toulson J 244, 315
trade – *see* **business; restraint of**
  trade
transitional provisions 15, 194, 256, 277,
    288, 289, 291, 312,
    314–315, 315, 323,
    325, 326, 717, 886,
    934, 940, 1070, 1112,
    1320, 1336, 1403,

All references are to page numbers

transitional provisions – *contd*
    1431, 1438, 1441,
    1448, 1473 –
  and see **retrospectivity**
transparency, open court principle   S19
transposition of European
    Community law
  copyout technique and   1291, S111
  failure of   1292
  methods of   1290–1293
  residual national law and   1292
  UK transposing enactment,
    interpretation of   1291–1292
transsexuality   909n, 1142n, 1327
travaux préparatoires – *see* **legislative**
  history; treaty
'Treasury, The', definition of   1399
treaty
  citation of   824
  common law, effect accorded by   S79
  direct enactment of   683
  drafting of   684
  enactment, giving effect to   518–519
  foreign language text of,
    interpretation of enactments
    and   686
  implementation of   190, 518–519, 682–
    691, 818–819, 961
  interpretation of   518–519, 682–691.S16
  interpretation of enactment, use in   107,
    682–691
  judicial notice of – *see* **judicial**
    notice
  non-justiciable in municipal court or
    tribunal   107, 364
  reference to   518–519, 961
  scheduled to Act   684–685
  status of   682–691, 818–819
  travaux préparatoires   686–687
  uniform statutes – *see* **uniform**
    statutes
  – *and see* **European Court of**
    Justice; European
    Convention on Human
    Rights; exterritoriality;
    extraterritoriality; foreign;
    legislative history;
    privileges and immunities;
    public international law;
    purposive construction;
    ultra vires, **doctrine of;**
    Vienna Convention on
    Law of Treaties
trespass
  carelessness and   83–84
  hunting and   426
  implied application of law of   1075
  nature of   1126–1127
  theft and   484

trespass – *contd*
  'tolerated trespass'   1075n
tribunal
  appeal from   147
  delegation   S15
  employment   118, 788
  expert   117
  general   141–142
  jurisdiction of   104
  reasons, duty to give   1062–1063
  – *and see* **appeal; court;**
    decision-making rules;
    Employment Appeal
    Tribunal; enforcement
    agencies; land;
    non-justitiable matters
trivia, treatment by law of – *see* **de**
  minimis non curat lex
Trollope, Anthony   123
  – *and see* **Bibliography (pp 1475**
    to 1507)
'trustee of land', definition of   1399
'trust of land', definition of   1399
truth impliedly required   38
Tuckey LJ   555
Tudor Evans J   775, 1230
Turnbull, John H – *see* **Bibliography**
  (pp 1475 to 1507)
Turner LJ   471, 614n, 1223
Twining, W   549
  – *and see* **Bibliography (pp 1475**
    to 1507)
typographical error – *see* **rectifying**
  construction
ubi jus ibi remedium   68
ultra vires, **doctrine of**
  'as if enacted in this Act'   257
  byelaws, and   260–262
  confirmation and   257
  delegated legislation, and   254–262, 832
  disapply, attempts to   258
  examples of *ultra vires* provisions   259–
    260
  nature of   254–262, 1051
  orders   91
  retrospectivity   324
  severance – *see* **severance**
  taxation, and   259
  validity, presumption of   257–258
  – *and see* **ambiguity;**
    decision-making rules;
    implication; jurisdiction
unborn – *see* **foetus**
undertaking – *see* **court**
Unger, R M   124
  – *and see* **Bibliography (pp 1475**
    to 1507)
Ungoed-Thomas J   233
uniform construction   690–691

All references are to page numbers

uniform statutes 333, 824
unincorporated association 576
  criminal liability 576, S59
  sole remaining member, rights of S114
United Kingdom
  meaning of 358, 1399
  nationals of, defined 380
  nature of 6
United Nations Commission on
  International Trade Law
  (UNCITRAL) 187
United States
  constitution of 316
  legislation and common law,
    relationship of, in 815
  legislative history, experience of use
    of, in 626, 651, 678n
Universal Declaration of Human
  Rights 852
universal repealer, the – *see* strained
  construction
university disputes 110
unjust enrichment, doctrine of 1072
unlawful act not impliedly
  authorised by statute 1126–1127
  – *and see* negligence; nuisance
unnecessary enactment 1003
updating construction
  definition of 890
  employment, as to 900
  European Community law 1299
  expressio unius principle and 1259
  impossibility, supervening 1130
  judicial approach, changes in 899–900
  law, changes in 897, 1041
  limit of 890, 914
  medical science, advances in 907
  mischief, on change of 895–897, 901–904
  Parliament's approach, changes in 900
  presumption favouring 889–914
  punctuation and 757
  responses to Code s 288 1457–1460
  social conditions, on change of 897, 901–904, 906
  technology, on development in 905–906
  words, change of meaning of, and 907–909
  – *and see* legislative history
Upjohn, Lord 660, 693n, 716
user of legislation 403, 804–806
  – *and see* legislation; subject, the
Uthwatt, Lord 937
vacant provision 606, 1039
Valéry, Paul 1458n
  – *and see* Bibliography (pp 1475
  to 1507)
validation Act – *see* Act of
  Parliament

van Ert, Gib – *see* Bibliography (pp
  1475 to 1507)
Van Gerven Adv-Gen 1274n, 1278, 1284n
Vancise, J A 518
Vaughan-Williams J 464
Veale J 1008
vehicle registration mark 1035
vexatious litigation S85
vicarious liability 67, 72, 73, 1041, 1074, 1077, 1146–1147
  – *and see* agency; employment
Vienna Convention on Consular
  Relations 369
Vienna Convention on Diplomatic
  Relations 1253
Vienna Convention on Law of
  Treaties
  codifying customary international
    law 688–690
  entry into force of 688
  rules of interpretation laid down by 618, 688–690
  – *and see* treaty
vigilantibus non dormientibus leges
  subveniunt 1149
Vinelott J 35, 138, 630, 748
Vinogradoff, Paul – *see* Bibliography
  (pp 1475 to 1507)
visitor (academic) 110
Vogenauer, Stefan 8, 546, 633n
  – *and see* Bibliography (pp 1475
  to 1507)
volenti non fit injuria 1101, 1150, 1151, S104
voting rights – *see* elections
Wade, H W R – *see* Bibliography
  (pp 1475 to 1507)
Waite LJ 832
waiver – *see* notice; privileges and
  immunities; statutory right
Wales 6n, 25, 346, 347, 359, 725, 731, 735, 744, 1246, 1392, 1399
Walker of Gestingthorpe, Lord 135, 509, 548, 1156, S4, S31
Walker, D M – *see* Bibliography (pp
  1475 to 1507)
Wall LJ 704, 774, 1062, 1183
Waller LJ 314, 721, 797, 1188, 1367
Walpole, Horace 214
Walton J 56, 1227
war – *see* act of state
Warbrick, C – *see* Bibliography (pp
  1475 to 1507)
Ward LJ 128, 142, 681n, 1102
Ward, Chris – *see* Bibliography (pp
  1475 to 1507)
wardship 203n, 436, 811, 814, 845, 917, 984, 1044–1046, 1255
  – *and see* Crown

All references are to page numbers

Warner J   495, 525, 1209
warrant   45, 141, 152, 165, 193, 199, 218,
                          238n, 271, 333, 460,
                          497, 534, 535, 783,
                          811, 838, 846, 876,
                          934, 1045, 1075, 1082,
                          1144, 1264, 1286,
                                          1441
  – and see Crown; magistrates
Warrington of Clyffe, Lord   864
Warsaw Convention 1929   32
Waterhouse J   297
waters – see high seas; internal
    waters; territorial waters
Watkins LJ   131, 160, 482, 615, 759, 836,
                                    964, 1002
Watson, Lord   75, 494, 605n, 913
Webster J   833, 834, 1076
Wedderburn, Lord   664
Wednesbury principle – see
    decision-making rules
weightless drafting   1196–1197
  – and see drafting technique
Wensleydale, Lord (Parke B) 514, 653, 870
West, W A – see Bibliography (pp
    1475 to 1507)
Westbury, Lord   654
Westminster principle   538, 1018
  – and see tax avoidance
Whately, R   124
  – and see Bibliography (pp 1475
    to 1507)
Wheare, K C – see Bibliography (pp
    1475 to 1507)
white paper – see legislative history
Widgery, Lord   553, 558, 645, 661, 685,
                          813, 993, 1002, 1003,
                          1012, 1141, 1235
Wilberforce, Lord   31, 47, 101, 110, 137,
                          190n, 305, 366, 387,
                          388, 431, 513, 526,
                          587, 605, 613, 637,
                          645, 685, 686, 687,
                          690, 699, 721, 797,
                          849, 850, 897, 902,
                          932, 944, 964, 966,
                          992, 1019, 1051, 1066,
                          1076, 1077, 1092,
                          1194, 1207, 1208,
                          1222, 1265, 1341
Wilde J   404
Willes J   233, 408, 493, 494, 646, 653, 654,
                          658, 727, 749, 751,
                                          859
Williams, Glanville   43, 517, 525, 805, 830,
                          888n, 938n, 1229
  – and see Bibliography (pp 1475
    to 1507)

Williams, Jane M – see Bibliography
    (pp 1475 to 1507)
Williams, L Norman – see
    Bibliography (pp 1475 to 1507)
Willis J   866n
Willis, J W   545
  – and see Bibliography (pp 1475
    to 1507)
Wills J   1251
Wilson J   676, S108
Wilson, Alida – see Bibliography (pp
    1475 to 1507)
Winckel, Anne – see Bibliography
    (pp 1475 to 1507)
Winn J   1243
Winterton, J – see Bibliography (pp
    1475 to 1507)
Wisdom, A J T D – see Bibliography
    (pp 1475 to 1507)
without prejudice rule – see evidence
women – see discrimination,
    legislation against; ordination
    of women
Wood J   307, 935
Woolf, Lord   26, 44, 45, 96, 97, 105n, 137,
                          155, 156, 157, 163n,
                          173, 174n, 261n, 429,
                          526, 571, 595, 855,
                          891, 984, 1051, 1055,
                          1087, 1091, 1095,
                          1103, 1134, 1135,
                          1139, 1151, 1214,
                          1312, 1313, 1314,
                          1328, 1331, 1334,
                          1342, 1346, 1365,
                          1366, 1378
  – and see Bibliography (pp 1475
    to 1507)
words
  'box principle' and   907–909
  commonly confused   1189
  different words given different
      meanings   1160–1163
  different words given same meaning   411,
                                        1161
  'elephant words'   1183
  every word to be given meaning   1157–
                                        1160
  foreign context, application in 1215–1216,
                                  1229–1230
  meaning, change in   907–909
  modifiers   1194
  nature of   445
  neutral, determining meaning of   1227–
                                        1228
  no meaning, with   1158–1159
  numbers, drafted in   1216
  order of   1190

All references are to page numbers

words – *contd*
 ordinary meaning of – *see* **ordinary
  meaning**
 overlapping meaning of 1160
 pairs of 1195–1197
 purpose of 11
 same words given different
  meanings 1212, 1217
 same words given same meaning 1160,
 1217
 surplus – *see* **surplusage**
 tautologous – *see* **tautology**
 wrong place in Act 881n
 – *and see* **archaisms; broad terms;
  chameleon word; construction
  as a whole; doubt as to legal
  meaning; evidence;
  grammatical meaning;
  homonyms; legal meaning;
  meaningless terms; neologisms;
  ordinary meaning; pairs of
  words; singular and plural;
  slang; strained construction;
  technical terms; updating
  construction**

Wrenbury, Lord 659

Wright, Lord 32, 659, 696n, 698, 786, 816,
 1235

writing 59, 137, 905, 1399

wrong, profit from – see **nullus
 commodum capere potest de
 injuria sua propria**

Zander, Michael 27n, 180n, 203n, 217,
 244n, 278n, 355n,
 360n, 411n, 504, 608,
 803, 855n, 875n
 – *and see* **Bibliography (pp 1475
  to 1507)**

zeugma 525